WELFARE
REFORM

International Social Security Series

In cooperation with the
International Social Security Association (ISSA)
Neil Gilbert, Series Editor

WELFARE REFORM

A Comparative Assessment of the French and U.S. Experiences

Neil Gilbert
Antoine Parent
editors

International Social Security Series
Volume 10

Routledge
Taylor & Francis Group

LONDON AND NEW YORK

The International Social Security Association (ISSA) was founded in 1927. It is a nonprofit international organization bringing together institutions and administrative bodies from countries all over the world dealing with all forms of compulsory social protection. The objective of the ISSA is to cooperate at the international level, in the promotion and development of social security throughout the world, primarily by improving techniques and administration in order to advance people's social and economic conditions on the basis of social justice.

The responsibility for opinions expressed in signed articles, studies, and other contributions rests solely with their authors, and publication does not constitute an endorsement by the International Social Security Association of the opinions expressed by them.

First published 2004 by Transaction Publishers

Published 2017 by Routledge
2 Park Square, Milton Park, Abingdon, Oxon OX14 4RN
711 Third Avenue, New York, NY 10017, USA

Routledge is an imprint of the Taylor & Francis Group, an informa business

Library of Congress Catalog Number: 2003054124

Library of Congress Cataloging-in-Publication Data

Welfare reform : a comparative assessment of the French and U.S. experiences   / Neil Gilbert and Antoine Parent, editors.
        p. cm.—(International social security series ; v. 10)
    Includes bibliographical references and index.
    ISBN 0-7658-0802-1 (pbk. : alk. paper)
        1. Public welfare—France.   2. Public welfare—United States.
    3. France—Social policy—1995-   4. United States—Social policy—
    1993-   I. Gilbert, Neil, 1940-   II. Parent, Antoine.   III. Series.

HV268.W44   2003
361.6'8'0944—dc21

                                                                        2003054124

    ISBN 13: 978-0-7658-0802-8 (pbk)

Contents

expectation to be wrong. ADC did not wither away—it blossomed. From 1940 to 1960, 1 to 3 million recipients received welfare benefits annually (Department of Health, Education and Welfare, 1974). After 1960, the number of welfare recipients among families with dependent children climbed significantly, reaching a high of 14.2 million people in 1994; since the mid-1990s, however, the number of families in the national caseload has declined by over 50 percent.

A number of factors contributed to the rising welfare caseload between 1960 and the mid-1990s, including the mounting rates of divorce and out-of-wedlock births. Between 1940 and 1960, unmarried women gave birth at a low and fairly stable rate, rising from 3.8 percent to 5.3 percent of all births (U.S. Bureau of the Census, 1981). From 1960 to 1996, however, the rate of births to unmarried women increased six-fold, climbing from 5.3 to 32.4 percent of all births (U.S. Bureau of the Census, 1998)—teenagers accounted for about one-third of all births to unmarried women. And at the same time, the ratio of divorces to marriages doubled from about 25 percent to 50 percent. The huge increases in divorce and out-of-wedlock births to teenage mothers, which started in the 1960s, changed the composition of welfare recipients and swelled the public assistance rolls.

During the same period that the welfare rolls were growing, society experienced an unprecedented shift of women's labor from the household to the market economy. Between 1960 and 1997, the labor force participation rate of married women with children under the age of six multiplied from 18.3 percent to 63.6 percent.[2] This normative shift in the role of motherhood not only placed great strains on working-and-middle class women with young children, but also dulled public sympathy for programs that paid women to stay at home and care for their children. These demographic and normative developments gave impetus to the move from income maintenance to work-oriented provisions. But workfare as we know it in the United States, did not arrive overnight—it was an extended journey marked by a series of increasingly rigorous reforms crafted over a period of more than three decades. These reforms included: the 1962 "Service" Amendments, the 1967 Work Incentive program (WIN), the Family Support Act of 1988, and the 1996 program of Temporary Assistance for Needy Families (TANF).

Rehabilitative Services

The Social Security Amendments of 1962 are often referred to as the "Service" Amendments because they provided significant federal funding for social services to accompany the financial assistance that was delivered to public welfare recipients in the AFDC program. The aim of these services was to rehabilitate welfare recipients through intensive social casework that sought to change their behavior in ways that would help them become economically independent. The implicit view here was that poverty stemmed from individual deficiencies that could be alleviated through the social casework process. This was different from the view of welfare recipients that prevailed up through the 1950s, when they were considered "victims of external circumstances such as unemployment, disability, or death of the family breadwinner," who "needed to be relieved—not treated or changed" (McEntire and Haworth, 1967).

Although the 1962 Amendments also provided for other forms of service such as homemakers and foster-home care, the essential feature was the provision of social casework. While this was not specified in the law, Derthick (1975) notes, "welfare professionals in the Bureau of Family Services knew more or less what they meant by 'services.' Fundamentally and at a minimum, it meant casework by a trained social worker."

There is an intangible quality about casework service, which has led skeptics to observe that social casework "is anything done for, with, or about the client by the social worker. If a social worker discusses a child's progress in school with an AFDC mother, a check is made under 'services related to education....' When the discussion turns to the absent father and possible reconciliation, a check is made under 'maintaining family and improving family functioning'" (President's Commission on Income Maintenance, 1970). Others have characterized these services as "little more than a relatively infrequent, pleasant chat" (Handler and Hollingsworth, 1971). Indeed, in practice it was not uncommon for social workers to see their clients less than once a month for thirty minutes (Handler and Hollingsworth, 1969).

Whether social casework at its professional best could resolve problems of economic deprivation, which is highly doubtful, is another matter. While the 1962 Service Amendments sought to provide high-level professional casework services, the results were seriously limited by the dearth of trained social workers available for these jobs and turnover difficulties in departments of public assistance (Steiner, 1971). In 1966, the national turnover rate for public assistance agencies was 22.8 percent—almost double the national turnover rate of all professionals in civil service positions on federal, state, and local levels at that time (Kermish and Kushin, 1969).[3] The huge turnover rates, large caseloads, the demands of eligibility certification (while trying to establish a casework relationship), and the omnipresent bureaucratic regulations of public assistance made it very difficult to implement and test the professional casework service orientation. Whatever its benefits, social casework as practiced under the 1962 Amendments was not a cure for poverty—a point dramatically underlined by the addition of almost one million recipients to the public assistance rolls between 1962 and 1966. It is interesting to note that this 33 percent increase in the national welfare caseload occurred over almost the same period that the unemployment rate (1960-1965) had declined from 5.5 percent to 4.5 percent.

From "Soft" to "Hard" Services

The failure to reduce economic dependency combined with social casework's intangible quality made these services a prime target of congressional dissatisfaction, which was expressed in the 1967 Social Security Act Amendments. Prior to the 1967 Amendments, federal grants for services went mainly to pay the salaries of social caseworkers (Rein, 1975). As these Amendments wended their way through Congress, "the old slogans—service instead of support, rehabilitation instead of relief—were abandoned and work and work incentives became the new thing in the continuing search for relief from relief costs" (Steiner, 1971). Policymakers formed a distinction between "soft" talking services—such as advice and counseling—and more tangible and wide-ranging "hard" services, such as day-care, drug treatment, and work training, which soon became emphasized (Derthick, 1975).

It should be noted that the "soft" casework services were not entirely soft, since the caseworkers were also responsible for determining their clients' continuing eligibility for welfare grants.

The 1967 reforms not only downplayed the clinical aspects of social casework but administratively divorced casework functions from those of eligibility/income-maintenance responsibilities.[4] The separation of income maintenance from casework/counseling functions was predicated on the assumption that services would be improved because the social worker-client relationship would no longer be tinged by the coercive undertones emanating from the worker's discretionary authority over the client's budget. Clients, presumably, would be free to accept or reject services as needed, and caseworkers, released from the task of administering grants, would have more time to engage in a voluntary service enterprise. Although this was a plausible line of reasoning, there was virtually no empirical evidence on either the strength of caseworkers' coercive powers or their effects on relationships with clients. It was also plausible, as Handler and Hollingsworth (1969) suggest, that the coercion argument was exaggerated and in the absence of routine home visits welfare clients would be reluctant to seek help in relation to personal matters from an unknown official. This line of reasoning was supported by research findings, which showed that AFDC recipients made higher demands for services and expressed greater satisfaction when service and income maintenance were combined (Piliavin and Gross, 1977).

To solidify the shift from a "soft" rehabilitative service orientation to a "hard" work-oriented-service approach, the 1967 Amendments established the Work Incentive (WIN) Program. (The program was dubbed WIN, because the precise acronym for the Work Incentive Program—WIP—had an unseemly sound to it.) WIN emphasized employment training services and day care, as well as providing a financial incentive for welfare recipients to seek work (the first $30 of monthly earnings plus one-third of the remainder were exempted from determination of eligibility for public assistance).

The results of WIN were not greatly encouraging. Of the 167,000 people who enrolled in WIN through March 1970, more than one-third dropped out of the program and, all told, only 25,000 got jobs. The clients who moved on to work were those best prepared for jobs. A high percentage of them probably would have found employment sooner or later without the assistance from WIN—which is to say, WIN's winners were "creamed" from the pool of applicants. In light of the program's "conspicuously unspectacular performance," one study concludes that "the wisdom of expanding WIN is questionable, and the theoretical arguments for such a move are even more dubious" (Levitan and Taggart, 1971: 53). Another analysis of the WIN experience suggests that the program's shortcomings endured to the end. In 1982, only 3 percent of the AFDC clients registered for the WIN program in New York State were placed in a job; an additional 5 percent found employment through their own efforts. In a distinct echo of the earlier findings, the 1982 study observed, "those who eventually are served generally represent the easiest to employ—those most likely to get jobs without the help of special services" (Sunger, 1984).

Although WIN did not require mothers to take work training or jobs, this program marked the first significant bend on the path from welfare services to workfare. WIN rested on at least three assumptions: (a) that jobs were available for anyone who really wanted to work (recall that unemployment had declined from 5.5 to 4.5 percent between 1960 and 1965); (b) that lack of skills and adverse attitudes toward work could be rectified through work-training and supportive services, reinforced by financial incentives; and (c) that welfare recipients would voluntarily respond to these opportunities (Gilbert, 1995).

From Voluntary to Mandatory Participation

In 1981, a series of state-initiated workfare demonstration programs were launched. The research on these variants of WIN showed somewhat more encouraging results than the earlier studies—although a substantial proportion (from 40 to 80 percent) of participants still remained unemployed after six to fifteen months (Gueron, 1987). The more positive results of these later studies, particularly a large-scale eight-state six-year evaluation of WIN demonstration programs by the Manpower Demonstration Research Corporation, made an important contribution to the development of the Family Support Act of 1988, according to Erica Baum (1991), one of FSA's architects.

In 1988, WIN was replaced by the workfare provisions of the Family Support Act (FSA), which differed from WIN in several respects. The most important difference, perhaps, was the mandatory directive for the participation of welfare mothers. Under the Family Support Act, federal regulations required AFDC recipients with children over three years of age to participate in the Jobs Opportunities and Basic Skills (JOBS) programs operated by each state and then to seek employment. States had discretion to go even further and lower the age of exemption to mothers with one-year-old children. The FSA imposed no time limits on how long one may receive welfare, but those who do not participate in the work training and job search efforts could have their AFDC grants reduced or eliminated. In addition to requiring participation in work training programs, the Family Support Act offered AFDC recipients incentives to take paid employment by extending childcare services and Medicaid health coverage for twelve months after a family was no longer eligible to receive public assistance grants due to increased income from employment. Along with the incentives the FSA imposed a range of behavioral requirements. Teenage mothers with children under three were required to complete their high school education or to acquire a high school equivalency diploma; single mothers applying for AFDC were obliged to help establish paternity for purposes of holding absent fathers accountable for child-support payments; unwed teenage mothers had to live with a parent or other adult relatives or reside in a foster home or some other adult-supervised living arrangement.

To some extent, mandatory participation in workfare programs, educational demands, social controls, and requirements for the establishment of paternity imposed by the Family Support Act of 1988 reflected a changing philosophy of social protection. The new philosophy emphasized the civic duties and social obligations that accompany welfare entitlements more than the right to income maintenance (Mead, 1986; Gilbert, 1995). The list of behavioral requirements delivered a forceful message to welfare recipients to shape up. Heretofore, public assistance agencies had occasionally paid lip service to this message, but now the welfare bureaucrats had become seriously devoted to implementing the work-oriented legislative mandate. The old mold of entitlement to welfare-as-income-maintenance was broken. States followed with a rush of work-oriented demonstrations and reforms, which culminated in the passage of the Personal Responsibility and Work Opportunity Reconciliation Act (PRWORA) of 1996.

Ending Welfare as We Knew It

The Personal Responsibility and Work Opportunity Reconciliation Act of 1996 eliminated the AFDC program, replacing it with the Temporary Assistance for Needy Families (TANF) program—which achieved President Clinton's campaign promise to "end welfare as we know it," if not exactly along the lines he might have envisioned.

Under TANF, states receive a fixed level of federal funding to provide income support to poor families with children. The total federal allocation to all states—starting out at $15.3 billion a year, plus a $2 billion contingency fund--was based on the amount states spent on AFDC in 1994 (Guyer, Mann, and Super, 1996). As it turned out, this sum was considerably more than adequate to cover the costs of welfare caseloads into at least 2001, since these caseloads had already declined by almost 48 percent between 1993 and 1999. Still, by substituting the TANF block grant for the open-ended funding arrangement under AFDC, Congress effectively eliminated the federally guaranteed entitlement to public assistance that was granted sixty-one years earlier by the Social Security Act.

In addition to rescinding the federal entitlement to welfare by capping the level of federal funding for public assistance to needy families, TANF introduced several sweeping changes in the fundamental character of public assistance, among the most important of which involve the devolution of responsibility to states. The federal block grant is available for states to use "in any manner reasonably calculated," which advances the general goals of the legislation. Thus, the states have considerable discretion on how to allocate federal funds to provide, for example, cash aid, emergency assistance, child care, job training, education, and job subsidies. States have wide latitude in designing incentives and sanctions to motivate welfare recipients; in California, for example, benefits are linked to school attendance, and in Michigan, absent fathers who do not make required child support payments lose their driver's license and other professional licenses.

Under TANF, states also have the authority to limit assistance to particular categories of poor families (such as new residents), to impose "family caps" on their aid formula-denying mothers additional benefits if they have children while on welfare, and to structure service delivery pretty much as they choose. The movement toward privatization of service delivery, which started with the 1967 welfare reforms, has gained increased momentum under TANF. Many states have begun to privatize their job (Gilbert and Terrell, 2002).

Although TANF grants substantial authority to the states to structure welfare programs, allocate funds, and assess results according to their own designs, the program remains framed by a number of stringent federal rules. Indeed, TANF imposes a rather significant array of "personal responsibility" rules on the states, prohibiting assistance for varying categories of the most "undeserving" poor (teen moms living in their own homes and mothers who are uncooperative in establishing paternity). Federal rules also obligate states to meet strict timetables with respect to employment, and demand increased state attention to education and training programs addressing out-of-wedlock pregnancies and statutory rape. According to the federal mandate, welfare recipients must be engaged in some kind of work-related activity to continue to receive benefits under TANF after their first two years of support. However, the rules do not specify exactly how the work requirements must be satisfied. It is not clear, for example, whether self-employment, work for family members, volunteer or other unpaid work will count as a job (Smolensky, Evenhouse, and Reilly, 1997)

Arguably, the most severe federal regulation involves the 60-month limit on federal assistance. Beyond the initial two-year limit on assistance for recipients who are unemployed, the 60-month limit bars states from providing cash benefits to families for more than a total of five years during their lifetime. Under this regulation states may exempt up to 20 percent of TANF recipients from the five-year limit due to family hardship. One of the critical challenges facing state policymakers is defining the nature and severity of "family hardship" that should qualify for exemption of the five-year limit. Already advocates for needy groups, such as victims of AIDS/HIV and other chronic disabilities, battered women, and grandparents providing kinship foster care, are mobilizing to protect their constituencies (Swarms, 1997). The allowance for a 20 percent exemption from the five-year limit, however, may still leave a significant number of families vulnerable to the loss of aid. Analyses of the length of time on welfare indicate that 37 percent (single spell analysis) to 49 percent (multiple spell analysis) of persons beginning a welfare spell will remain on the rolls for five years or more (U.S. House of Representatives, 1994). As the most able recipients enter the labor market and caseloads are reduced to families with the greatest social and educational deficits, the basic challenge of welfare reform—moving long-term recipients from welfare to work—will emerge.

This brief foray into the reform of public assistance in the United States illustrates how the purpose and scope of this program was transformed, responding, in part, to changes in family life—rising divorce rates and out-of-wedlock births—and a normative shift in the employment expectations of mothers with young children. The course of change was punctuated by four distinct phases, as illustrated in table 3.1. First, counseling services to rehabilitate welfare recipients were injected into a program originally designed to provide income maintenance. Next, the emphasis switched to more utilitarian services, such as day care for children, and work-related incentives along with

Table 3.1
From Welfare to Workfare: The Path of Reform

Statutes	Legislative Emphasis	Client Requirement	Professional Role
1935 ADC	Income maintenance deserving widows	Care for their children	Sending the money
1962 "Service" Amendments	Rehabilitative services casework/counseling	Receive services	Clinical/therapeutic service
1967 WIN Program	"Hard" services work training/incentives	Voluntary participation in work training	Coordination/case management of work training activity
1988 FSA	Work training and job search incentives	Mandatory participation in training	Case management/ monitoring participation in training
1996 TANF	Employment/time-limited benefits with incentives, sanctions, & waivers	Mandatory training and work	Case management/ Monitoring employment, time limits. Assessing waivers & sanctions

opportunities for voluntary participation in work training programs. Then voluntary work training and job search activities became mandatory. Finally, incentives for engaging in work-related activities were joined with sanctions for those who failed to cooperate, going to work within two years became mandatory, and the duration of benefits was capped by a 60-month lifetime limit. As the objective of moving welfare recipients into paid employment became increasingly well focused and widely accepted, new policies introduced more forceful incentives and social controls, which were strictly implemented by line-workers in the public assistance bureaucracies.

Initial Effects and Implications

As the current phase of welfare reform under TANF comes to the end of its first five years it is a fitting time to take stock of the preliminary results of the U.S. experience and ask: How well does workfare work? Does the U.S. experience have any implications for France? As already noted, the exacting work-oriented welfare reforms that began as demonstration projects in the early 1990s and concluded with the establishment of TANF were accompanied by a remarkable and unprecedented decline in the welfare caseload, which plunged by more than 50 percent from the historic high of 5.1 million families in March 1994. The 1990s were a booming period when the unemployment rate fell to a 30-year low of 4.3 percent. Precisely how much of the caseload reduction was due to the pressures of reform and how much to the draw of employment opportunities is hard to untangle.[5] In assessing the outcomes of the U.S. experience, Gary Burtless (chap. 1) sheds some light on how economic growth impacts the U.S. welfare participation rate and Christel Gilles, Christain Loisy, and Antoine Parent (chaps. 9 and 10) examine how caseloads and poverty are influenced by economic growth in France and the United States.

Examining the broad consequences of welfare reform, Alan Weil (chap. 6) highlights ten major findings from a multi-year large-scale evaluation— Assessing the New Federalism project (ANF). Among these findings, Weil reports on how current policies may influence family structure and the effects of welfare reform on the well-being of children and various subgroups within the welfare client population.

Although many recipients who left the welfare rolls in the United States went to work full-time, a surprising number of mothers seemed to be leaving welfare without taking regular jobs. Those who left the rolls without working often received public support from other sources, including Social Security, Supplemental Security Income, and Food Stamps; in Alabama the $329 food stamp allotment for a family of three in 1999 was almost twice as high as the welfare benefit. They also drew significant support from preexisting co-residency arrangements. Analyzing the scope and importance of these arrangements, Douglas Besharov (chap. 11) suggests that to fully assess the economic and emotional well-being of single-mother families that have left welfare we must take cognizance of the fundamental role of co-residency.

Finally, in talking about the U.S. experiences with welfare reform, we occasionally lose sight of the fact that these experiences often vary by state, particularly since the legislation grants states a high degree of latitude in implementing the general guidelines for workfare. Jordan Matsudaira and Sheldon Danziger (chap. 7) spotlight this issue by analyzing state-specific impacts of welfare reform policies on welfare utilization, employment, personal earnings, and family income of single mothers.

Does the U.S. journey from welfare to workfare have any implications for France? With the advent of the Revenu Minimum Insertion (RMI) program, France has introduced a means-tested work-oriented benefit that moves in the same direction as the welfare reforms in the United States. However, as Michel Dolle (chap. 4) indicates, the integration contract which RMI claimants are required to sign within three months does not entail a compulsory requirement for a job search. Moreover, despite the legislative requirement, the majority of claimants fail to sign an integration contract. In implementing the RMI, it appears that officials and welfare bureaucracies at the local level have not strictly applied the national guidelines.

One might draw a parallel here to the U.S. experience up to the mid-1990s when line-workers in local public assistance agencies were less than forceful in implementing the work-oriented provisions of the Work Incentive Program and the Family Assistance Program. By the mid-1990s, in the United States the emerging emphasis on civic duties and social obligations and the increasing labor force participation of married women signified a normative shift, which diluted public support for programs that paid women who stayed at home caring for children. Local officials and line-workers in public assistance bureaucracies were not immune to this normative shift reflected in the 1996 TANF legislation.

There is some indication that a similar decline in public support for income maintenance benefits in the absence of firm work requirements may also be underway in France. An annual poll of French attitudes and living conditions by the National Family Allowance Fund agency shows that over the last decade expressions of a positive view of RMI as a program that gives people a boost that helps them pull through difficult periods, declined from about 70 percent to 45 percent of respondents. At the same time, an expression of the negative view of this program as creating a risk of encouraging people not to work rose from approximately 30 percent to 55 percent of respondents (Observatoire National de la Pauvreté et de L'Exclusion Sociale, 2001). If this trend in public opinion continues, social policies in France may advance further down the road from income maintenance to workfare.

Notes

1. This was not the only group covered under the Social Security Act of 1935. Initially, three categories of needy people were eligible for public assistance. In addition to dependent children in poor families, these categories included the poor elderly and the blind. In 1950, a fourth category, the permanently and totally disabled, was added. Although public assistance covers these additional categories of welfare recipients, the focus of analysis in this chapter centers upon the evolution of ADC, which is the largest and most controversial program.

2 . Overall, 71.1 percent of married women with children under17 years of age were in the labor force in 1997. U.S. Bureau of the Census, *Statistical Abstract of the United States, 1998* (Washington, DC: Government Printing Office, 1998).

3 . A study of turnover in public assistance agencies in New York City during 1964 indicates that 30 percent of the workers resigned within nine months of their appointment (Lawrence Podell, 1967).

4 . In 1977, this administrative separation at the local level was reinforced at the federal level by placing income-maintenance programs under the Social Security Administration and joining social service and human development programs under the Office of Human Development Services.

5. One estimate suggests that between 1993 and 1996 the falling unemployment rate accounted for almost 50 percent of the caseload reduction (Danziger, Moffitt, and Pavetti, 1998). Studies in the later years conclude that in 1996 to 1999 only about 10 to 20 percent of the decline could be attributed to the strong economy (Besharov and Germanis, 2000).

References

Baum, E. (1991). "When Witch Doctors Agree: The Family Support Act and Social Science Research." *Journal of Policy Analysis and Management* 10:4 (Fall): 603-615.

Besharov, D. & Germanis, P. (2000). "Welfare Reform—Four Years Later." *The Public Interest* 140 (Summer): 17-35.

Danziger, S., Moffitt, R., & Pavetti, L. A. (1998). *Is Welfare Reform Working? The Impact of Economic Growth and Policy Changes: A Congressional Briefing*. Washington, DC: Consortium of Social Science Associations.

Department of Health, Education and Welfare. (1974). *Social Security Bulletin*. Washington, DC: Government Printing Office.

Department of Health and Human Services. (1996). *Indicators of Welfare Dependence and Well-Being: Interim Report to Congress*. Washington, DC: Department of Health and Human Services.

Derthick, M. (1975). *Uncontrollable Spending for Social Service Grants*. Washington, DC: Brookings Institution.

Gilbert, N. (1995). *Welfare Justice: Restoring Social Equity*. New Haven, CT: Yale University Press.

Gilbert, N., & Terrell, P. (2002). *Dimensions of Social Welfare Policy*. Boston: Allyn and Bacon.

Gueron, J. (1987). "Reforming Welfare with Work." *Public Welfare* (Fall): 13-25.

Guyer, J., Mann, C., & Super, D. (1996). *The Timeline for Implementing the New Welfare Reform Law*. Washington, DC: Center on Budget and Policy Priorities.

Handler, J., & Hollingsworth, J. (1971). *The Deserving Poor: A Study of Welfare Administration*. Chicago: Markham Publishing.

Handler, J., & Hollingsworth, J. (1969). "The Administration of Social Services and the Structure of Dependency: The Views of AFDC Recipients." *Social Service Review* 43:4 (December): 412.

Kermish, I., & Kushin, F. (1969). "Why High Turnover? Social Work Staff Losses in a County Welfare Department." *Public Welfare* (April): 138.

Leiby, J. (1978). *History of Social Welfare and Social Work in the United States.* New York: Columbia University Press.

Levitan, S., & Taggart III, R. (1971). *Social Experimentation and Manpower Policy: The Rhetoric and the Reality.* Baltimore, MD: Johns Hopkins University Press.

McEntire, D., & Haworth, J. (1967). "Two Functions of Public Welfare: Income Maintenance and Social Services." *Social Work* 12:1 (January): 24-25.

Mead, L. (1986). *Beyond Entitlement: The Social Obligations of Citizenship.* New York: Free Press.

Observatiore National de la Pauvreté National et de L'Exclusion Sociale. (2001). *2000 Report.* Paris: La Documentation Francaise.

Piliavin, I., & Gross, A. (1977). "The Effects of Separation of Services and Income Maintenance on AFDC Recipients." *Social Service Review* 51 (September): 389-406.

President's Commission on Income Maintenance. (1970). *Background Papers.* Washington, DC: Government Printing Office.

Rein, M. (1975). "Social Services as a Work Strategy." *Social Service Review* 49 (December): 519.

Steiner, G. (1971). *The State of Welfare.* Washington, DC: Brookings Institution.

Sunger, M. B. (1984). "Generating Employment for AFDC Mothers." *Social Service Review* 58:1 (March): 32.

Smolensky, E., Evenhouse, E., & Reilly, S. (1997). *Welfare Reform: A Primer in 12 Questions.* San Francisco: Public Policy Institute of California.

Swarms, R. (1997). "Welfare Family Advocates, Once Allies Become Rivals." *New York Times,* 27 March, A1.

U.S. Bureau of the Census. (1998). *Statistical Abstract of the United States.* Washington, DC: Government Printing Office.

U.S. Bureau of the Census. (1981). *Statistical Abstract of the United States: 1981.* Washington, DC: Government Printing Office.

U.S. House of Representatives. (1994). *Overview of Entitlement Programs: 1994 Green Book.* Washington, DC: Government

4

Income Support Policy in France

Michel Dollé

Assessing the French and the U.S. welfare policy experiences may be done from various points of view, such as the fight against poverty, the reduction of income inequalities, or the transition from welfare to work. The differences between the French and the U.S. structure of income impact all these aspects. In the first part of this analysis, a rough sketch of the French income structure and of the role of social transfers is drawn. Next, the different means-tested benefits will be briefly described. Then, the income support policies are examined in a normative perspective. The last part of the chapter deals with the relationship between income support policies and employment, in the context of the present labor market situation in France.

The Context of Income on France

Assessing the French and U.S. experiences of welfare policies—in particular how they combat poverty, reduce income inequalities, or help the transition from welfare to work—requires taking into account the gap between earnings and income, which is greater in France than in the United States. The difference is threefold: first, a larger social and fiscal wedge (defined as the difference between the labor cost and net earnings); second, a larger set of social transfers, whether they are means-tested or not; and third, more accessibility to public and/or social services like public education or healthcare.

A Large Social and Fiscal Wedge

- *Social contributions.* Employers and employees pay compulsory social contributions. The rates of the various contributions depend on the gross wage level. At the mean level of full-time job wages, the employees' social contribution is 13.2 percent and the employers' contribution rate is about 39 percent of the gross wage (if the firm has an agreement between the employer and the employees on a 35-hour-weekly working time due to a basic allowance reducing the employers' contribution). The rate is 41.5 percent if there is no agreement (see table 4.1).

Table 4.1
Employers' and Employees' Social Contributions*
(in % of the average gross wage of a full-time worker)

| | | January 2001 | |
| | | Employers' | Employers' |
Type	Total	Contributions	Contributions
Health insurance	13.55	12.8	0.75
Pension	25.95	15.5	10.45
Unemployment	5.80	3.8	2.0
Familial allowances	5.4	5.4	
Housing	0.85	0.85	
Training	2.1	2.1	
Industrial accident	1.0	1.0	
Total	54.65	41.45	13.2

*The table does not take into account the reduction of the employers' contribution for the firm working on 35 hours/week working time.

Source: Barème social périodique, January 2001 Liaisons sociales

Both employees' and employers' rates of contribution are slowly decreasing when the gross wage grows above the mean level.[1] In fact, when the social transfer system was created after World War II, it was organized mainly as an insurance: if risk is not linked with income (e.g., health insurance), then the higher the wage, the lower the contribution rate. The system progressed to a general coverage of every resident and turned toward the purpose of redistribution. The contributions eventually became proportional to the wage. Moreover, financing pensions (or unemployment insurance), which are rather proportional to wages and have a growing importance in the total of social transfers, tend toward the same result.

By contrast, in the bottom of the wage distribution since 1993, the employers' contribution rate on low wages has become progressive, in order to fight against unemployment among low-qualified workers. At the minimum wage level, the employers' contribution rate today is equal to 15.5 percent and the employees' contribution rate remains at 13.2 percent. In France, then, the social wedge[2] is much larger than in the United States; it is also rapidly growing between the minimum and the median wage level.

Income tax. Two kinds of income tax are levied in France:

- A set of two taxes (CSG and CRDS) applied to all earnings, pension and capital income.[3] The CSG taxation was introduced in 1991 to replace in part the employees' contribution for pensions and (progressively) almost all the employees' contribution to health insurance. The CRDS taxation was introduced in 1996 to reduce the debt of the social security system (taken as a whole). The rate of CSG/CRDS taxes differs for earnings (7.6 percent), capital income (8 percent), and pensions (4.3 percent). In principle, the tax rate on unemployment benefits is 4.3 percent, but for unemployed people who earned less than a threshold set at around the median wage, the rate is, in fact, 0.5 percent.
- The *progressive income tax* is based on family income. There is no standard child deduction, but the tax paid depends on the size of the family: the tax scale is applied to the family income divided by the fiscal size of the family (1 for a single person, 2 for a couple, each child represents an additional 0.5). If the family income divided by the fiscal size is less than 4055€ (tax due in 2000 affecting income of 1999) the tax rate is zero. About one-third of households do not pay any income tax beyond the CSG/CRDS (*Contribution Sociale Généralisée/Contribution au Remboursement de la Dette Sociale*).
- Another tax depends upon the household income (and the family size): the housing tax, collected by local authorities. The relative burden of this housing tax, in fact, decreases with the household income.

The Employment premium. During the year 2000, the French government made the decision to reduce the progressive income tax rates. This reduction obviously does not redistribute any money to households who do not pay the income tax. It was decided to reduce the rate of the social taxation CSG on wages down to zero at the SMIC (the French minimum wage, see below) level, and increased the taxation rate to the normal rate of 7.5 percent at the 1.4 SMIC level. This reform was judged unconstitutional,[4] and the government changed the instrument slightly and created an Employment Premium, whose economic characteristics are rather similar. The premium is calculated separately for each wage in a family, but under a ceiling depending on the family size.[5] Initially, it was planned that the premium was to be implemented by a third during the 2001, 2002 and 2003 fiscal years. In fact, for the year 2001, two-thirds of the final premium was paid, rather than just one-third; the increase was decided upon to protect against the risk of a depressed household consumption after the September 11 crisis. The employment premium will, in fact, reduce to about 1.0 the CSG/CRDS rate on the hourly minimum wage. The premium decreases by 13 percent with the rise of the wage and is cancelled out at 1.4 SMIC.

Social Transfers

In France, more than in many other European countries, social transfers represent a large part of the family income. Some of them are means-tested (or decrease with the level of earnings and capital income), but there are also universal family allowances.

Housing benefit. The housing benefit is an allocation for anyone renting accommodations or, in some cases, having to pay off debt for the purchase. The aid varies with the rent, the family size, its earnings or capital income and the location (see table 4.1). For a full-time employee earning the minimum wage during the year 2000 and living in Paris or its suburbs, the housing benefit represents 5 to 30 percent of the gross wage (7 to 43 percent of the net wage) depending on the family size.

Child benefits. As seen above, for families paying income tax, the "family size system" works like a child benefit increasing with income under a rather high ceiling. In addition, there are different *child benefits*:

- A universal family allowance—*allocations familiales*—for families with at least two children under the age of 20: the amount depends on the number of children. This allowance is not means-tested.

Two other child benefits are means-tested:

- The first one is paid from the third month of pregnancy to the third year of childhood "Allowance for young children" (*allocation pour jeune enfant APJE*).
- The second is paid for families with three or more children (*complément familial*).

Child care benefits. Besides nursery schools (see below) and public day-nurseries, there are two child care benefits. The first benefits families who employ at home someone to take care of their children: "Domestic Care Allowance" (*allocation pour la garde d'enfant à domicile AGED*). The other reduces the cost of specialized employees taking care of children in their home: Aid for families employing agreed nursery-assistant (*aide aux familles pour l'emploi d'assistantes maternelles agrées AFEAMA*). A part of child care expenses may also be deducted from the income tax.

Another type of child care benefit is an allowance given when the parent is directly responsible for the child's care; it is given to employees who stop working for that purpose (they must have at least two children in the family)—*allocation parentale d'éducation APE*.

Some Examples of the Income Structure

Table 4.2 shows the transition from earnings to net income in 2000. We assume here that people live in Paris and that children are between 3 and 20

Table 4.2
Monthly Earnings and Income in €

Year 2000		Social and Fiscal Wedge			Social Transfers			
	Earnings	Employees' Contribution	Csg-Crds	Income Tax and Local Taxes	Housing Benefit	Child Benefits	Net Income	Net Income per Consumption Unit
living alone								
Minimum wage	1083	145	82	30	61	0	886	886
1,7*(Minimum wage)	1840	247	140	163	0	0	1291	1291
lone parent 1 child								
Minimum wage	1083	145	82	8	206	74	1127	867
1,7*(Minimum wage)	1840	247	140	64	31	74	1495	1150
couple no children								
Minimum wage	1083	145	82	8	127	0	974	650
1,7*(Minimum wage)	1840	247	140	64	0	0	1390	927
couple 2 children								
Minimum wage	1083	145	82	0	276	105	1236	589
1,7*(Minimum wage)	1840	247	140	20	110	105	1649	785
couple 3 children								
Minimum wage	1083	145	82	0	352	375	1582	659
1,7*(Minimum wage)	1840	247	140	8	199	375	2021	842

* As the table uses fiscal year 2000 legislation, it does not take into account some changes in housing taxation and housing benefits nor the employment premium. As the child care benefits are not used by every family, they are not taken into account here. Source: French Treasury, Department of economic studies (Direction de la Prévision) Model Pâris. See Lamotte (2000) www.cerc.gouv.fr/meetings/colloquemai2000/maiLAMOTTE.doc

years old. Two levels of earnings are considered in this example, corresponding to a full-time job at the minimum wage and approximately to a full-time job at the median wage.

Both Housing and Child benefits play an important role in explaining the gap between net earnings and income. So when assessing the problem of the transition of means-tested recipients to employment and earnings, it is important to take into account the calculation rules for these allocations.

Access to Public and Social Services

Some of the differences between France and the United States are introduced by access to public services[6] (such as education) or social insurance (health insurance).

Education in France is provided mainly by public institutions (or largely funded by state and the local authorities). This begins with nursery school: one-fourth of two-year-old children and almost all three-year-olds are taken care of free of charge in public nursery schools. Most of the students go to public colleges or universities and the registration fees are by comparison, no lower than the U.S. public or private ones.

Health insurance is compulsory for every worker. An employee, as well as his family, having worked 60 hours during a month is insured for one year. Health insurance also covers retired people and those receiving unemployment benefits. Health insurance covers most of the expenses in this field. Health care amounts to about 12 percent of household consumption[7] and less than a quarter of health expenses are paid by the households. For this last part, most French households have a complementary private health insurance to which employers contribute, in some cases. The health insurance system also provides replacement income for employees who have to stop working because of sickness (or replacement income for pregnant and mothers of infants up to 16 weeks).

Until the beginning of 2000, regular residents, who were out of work and were not insured through a member of their family, could enter the Universal Health Insurance System (CMU) on a personal contribution basis. For some families getting means-tested benefits (like RMI, see below), local administrations took into consideration the personal contribution. In fact, many people (about 700,000) were not insured until the creation in January 2000 of the "Universal Health Coverage" (*couverture maladie universelle*—CMU), the purpose of which is to make access to medical care easier and to give low-income people complementary insurance. The CMU is therefore an in-kind and means-tested benefit we should also take into account in our assessment.[8]

Unemployment Benefits

There are two different unemployment benefits: unemployment insurance and a means-tested unemployment benefit.

The *unemployment insurance benefit* today is called Allowance for a Return to Work (*allocation de retour à l'emploi* ARE). The unemployment insurance system, managed by employers and the unions through the UNEDIC, was reformed in July 2001 in a more active way. The allocation is proportional to the wage (under a threshold) received before unemployment. The replacement rate and the time limit depend on the work history from the previous job. People have to seek a job, and they must accept any convenient employment offer (but this is far from being as strict a constraint as it is, for example, in the UK or in other European countries such as the Netherlands or Germany). Under the new system, the public employment service [National Employment Agency (ANPE)] is going to develop a set of different personalized services to help job seekers.

The amount of the benefit depends on a "daily reference wage" calculated over the year prior to the job contract break-up, up to a 9100€ per month ceiling in 2001. The daily allocation amounts to 57.4 of the daily reference

Table 4.3
Time Limit of the Unemployment Insurance Benefit (ARE)

Employment duration	Time limit of the benefit
4 months during the 18 preceding months	4 months
6 months during the 12 preceding months	7 months
8 months during the 12 preceding months; less than 50 years old	15 months
8 months during the 12 preceding months; 50 years old or more	21 months
14 months during the 24 preceding months; less than 50 years old	30 months
14 months during the 24 preceding months; 50 years old or more	45 months
27 months during the 36 preceding months; 50- 54 years old	45 months
27 months during the 36 preceding months; 55 years old or more	60 months

Source: Barème social périodique, January 2001 Liaisons socials.

gross wage. As employee contributions are lower for unemployed than employed people and the CSG-CRDS rate on the benefit is also lower for most of the unemployed people, the effective replacement rate is higher.

The *means-tested unemployment benefit*, called the Specific Solidarity Allowance (*allocation de solidarité spécifique* ASS), is allotted to long-term unemployed persons who are no longer eligible for insurance benefits. To be eligible for the ASS, people must have worked at least 5 of the 10 years prior to unemployment. People aged 55 years to 57.5 years, having worked 20 years or more receive a Supplementary Solidarity Allowance, as do people older than 57.5 years, having worked 10 years or more. The income threshold is presented in table 4.4.

People who have worked more than 40 years, are younger than 60, and who receive the *solidarity allowance* (or RMI) may receive a Specific Waiting Allowance (*allocation spécifique d'attente* ASA).

Unemployed people who are at least 57.5 years, or who are at least 55 and have worked more than 40 years, may receive unemployment benefits (ARE or ASS) without seeking a job (they are called *dispensés de recherche d'emploi* DRE). People who receive unemployment benefits (ARE or ASS) are allowed to work part time ("reduced activity"). Their benefit is then partly reduced, depending on the part-time job wage (the marginal taxation rate is about 0.6 for those receiving the ARE benefit). Another advantage of working in the "reduced activity" system is to postpone the time limit applied to the insurance benefit ARE.

In 2000, 2.8 million people were unemployed, following the ILO definition of unemployment, while 3.8 million were recorded in the National Employment Agency[9] (350,000 were DRE [*Dispensés de Recherge d' Emploi*], 1.7 million received the ARE insurance benefit and 0.4 million the means-tested benefit ASS.

Unemployed people who obtain neither the insurance benefit (ARE) nor means-tested unemployment benefits (ASS) are mostly young people, entering the labor market. Most of them do not have enough work history to be eligible for the insurance benefit.

Minimum Wage

In France as well as in the United States and/or in several other developed countries, *the main income support instrument is the minimum wage.*

The first French national minimum wage, the SMIG, was created as an inter-industry guaranteed minimum wage by a law passed in 1950 (SERC, 1999); this law tends to organize the general framework of industrial partnership between employers and unions. The decree says the SMIG "must be considered as a *social minimum* owed to every wage earner who brings his work to a firm." To prepare this decree, the government asked a commission of employers and trade-unions[10] to evaluate the minimum budget needed by a worker living alone in Paris.[11] The SMIG was then indexed based on the consumer price index. The gap between the SMIG and the mean wage grew rapidly until 1968 and the general strike following the students' demonstrations of that year. In 1970, the SMIG was replaced by the SMIC, a "minimum wage for growth." The main change is that the purpose of this instrument is to fight against wage inequality. The new index-linking rules mention that the SMIC must grow every year, at least as half of the mean workers' hourly wage. In addition, the law indicates that, "the annual raises are intended to eliminate any durable distortion between the growth of the SMIC and the evolution of economic development and earnings."

The minimum wage in France is more or less in line with article 3 of the 1970 ILO convention (n°131):

> The elements to be taken into consideration in determining the level of minimum wages shall, so far as possible and appropriate in relation to national practice and conditions, include: (a) the needs of workers and their families, *taking into account the general level of wages* in the country, *the cost of living*, social security benefits, and the *relative living standards of other social groups*; (b) economic factors, including the requirements of economic development, levels of productivity and the desirability of attaining and maintaining a high level of employment.

The first French minimum wage, the SMIG, was more in line with an absolute definition of needs, whereas the SMIC is based on a relative one. This is similar to the differences between the measurement of poverty with an absolute definition (as in the U.S.) or with a relative one as in Europe.

In fact, until 1983 the SMIC grew faster than the average wage and contributed to reducing the wage dispersion in the bottom D5/D1 for full-time jobs. After 1983, it grew approximately in line with the mean or median wage.

The U.S. minimum wage, created under the Fair Labor Standard Act, follows similar purposes. See FLSA section 2 (a) and (b):

Box 4.1
French Minimum Wage

Value on 01/01/2002
Gross minimum wage   (full time on 35 hours per week basis)
Since a monthly guarantee of earnings has been created for employees paid at the Seismic level when the legal work week was reduced from 39 hours to 35 hours, the following calculation is made on the hypothesis that the firm works on a 35-hour per week basis with an agreement between the employer and the employee, and so gets the highest reduction of employers' contribution.

With a monthly gross earning guarantee of 1,095€ the gross wage is 8.21€ per hour with an **hourly labor** cost of 9.47€ .

The net monthly earning for a full-time job is 948€ when the calculated net of the employees' contribution and 864 net of employees' contribution and income social taxation (CSG-CRDS).

The role of the SMIC in the labor market regulation

In 1997, the ratio of the minimum labor cost to the median labor cost was roughly 0.5 in France and 0.4 in the United States (or in United Kingdom,[12] Canada, or Belgium), –0.45 in Netherlands—according to data from the OECD and our own calculations (see SERC, 1999).

In July 2000, 13.6 percent of the employees (about 2 million) of the private sector are "SMIC-paid"; their wages are therefore automatically raised with the SMIC. In other sectors they were 0.6 million. (The number of SMIC earners is still unknown for July 2001, but will probably be greater due to the work week reduction.)

The SMIC earners are often young employees, women, and work in small or very small businesses.

Finally, an employee whose wage is tied to the SMIC may earn more: some premiums (overtime, seniority, casual contracts) are not taken in account in the SMIC. For example, in 1994, about 40 percent of the employees who were automatically raised with the SMIC earned 10 percent more than the value of the minimum wage.

(a) The Congress hereby finds that the existence, in industries engaged in commerce or in the production of goods for commerce, of labor conditions detrimental to the maintenance of the minimum standard of living necessary for health, efficiency, and general well-being of workers (1).... (b) It is hereby declared to be the policy of this Act,...to correct and as rapidly as practicable to eliminate the conditions above referred to in such industries without substantially curtailing employment or earning power.

According to the FLSA, the level of the U.S. national minimum wage is determined by a vote of Congress and there are no formal rules determining either the level or its evolution. But section 4(d) (1) of the FLSA makes some references, quite similar to the formal rules of indexing the French SMIC:

The Secretary shall submit annually in January a report to the Congress covering his activities for the preceding year and including such information, data, and recommendations for further legislation in connection with the matters covered by this Act as he may find advisable. *Such report shall contain an evaluation and appraisal by the Secretary of the minimum wages* and overtime coverage established by this Act, together with his recommendations to the Congress. In making such evaluation and appraisal, *the Secretary shall take into consideration any changes* which may have occurred *in the cost of living and in productivity and the level of wages in manufacturing*, the ability of employers to absorb wage increases, and such other factors as he may deem pertinent."

Poverty and the Poverty Threshold

Unlike the United States, there is no official poverty threshold used as a basis for determining the eligibility for some benefits. Rather, statisticians use a relative concept of poverty. French statisticians use a poverty line defined as half the median disposable income per equivalent adult[13] (the statistical unit being households). The European statistical office (Eurostat) uses 60 percent of the median computed for individuals, but also 50 percent or 40 percent. Thus, the number of people below the poverty line is, as is well known, rather disputable.

Capital income is greatly underestimated in the surveys. Some statistics exclude the capital income from the household income for the determination of the poverty line. This does lower the effective median income, but the consequences on the poverty rate are doubtful: some retired people—for example, self-employed retired—may have little earning or pension and be counted as poor though they have, in fact, a much greater income.

The French poverty rate (computed for households) as estimated by the Insee survey and the Inland Revenue Office, was about 7 percent in 1997. Using the European Community Household Panel, the poverty rate (computed for individuals) was about 16 percent in 1996 using a 60 percent threshold (about 9 million people) and 9 percent (5.3 million) using a 50 percent threshold.[14] In the 40 to 60 percent bracket there are about 7 million people. The poverty rate is lower in France than in most of the European countries[15] (except Denmark, Luxembourg, Austria, and the Netherlands). In 2000, the poverty line, estimated using the French definition, was around 580€ net disposable monthly income for an individual (and 870€ for a couple).

In France, the poverty rate decreased during the 1970s and 1980s and has been more or less stable since. The fall of the poverty rate was due mainly to improvements for retired households. Recent retirees often receive higher pensions due to longer work and pension insurance; and, more often than before, many recent retirees are couples, both of whom worked, and therefore receive pensions.

Poverty is growing slightly among the working-age population. This is due both to the growing income of the retired which raises the median income— and the poverty line with it—and to the growing unemployment or underemployment. This evolution emphasizes the necessity of income support for the working poor.

The Means-Tested Benefits

Means-tested benefits, called *social minima* in France, have been set up to allow specific people to reach a minimum income.[16] Four of these benefits deal with people out of the labor market because of age or disability: Minimum Pension (MV, created in 1941), Disability Minimum (MI, 1930), Disabled Adult Allowance (AAH, 1975), and Widowhood Benefit (1980). The four other benefits can be claimed by people depending on age and capability of work: Lone Parent Benefit (API, 1976), Benefit for First-Job Seeker (AI, 1979), Solidarity Allowance (ASS, 1984), and the last benefit, the RMI "Minimum Income for Integration," which was created in 1988. The main characteristics of these eight benefits are summed up in table 4.4.

Most of the means-tested benefits were created as extensions of the social insurance mechanism. At first, this was for people who did not work enough to get a sufficient pension or disability insurance, and then progressed to include people not eligible for social insurance (for example, people who have never worked).

The rules determining the amount of the benefit, the income eligibility threshold, and the various income are often derived from the rules of each different social insurance. Consequently, they differ from one another and this may create some discrepancies in the income of people who receive one or another benefit.

To compare the French and the U.S. welfare systems, it is necessary to take into account at least three means-tested benefits in the French model: the unemployment means-tested ASS, the single parent API, and the RMI. For example, the main welfare allowance in the United States is TANF (Temporary Assistance for Needy Families), which targets families with children (and mostly

Table 4.4
Means-Tested Benefits in France

Type	Name	Jan-02 Monthly benefit Individuals €	Jan-02 Income threshold €	Time limit	2000 Recipients (thousands) Metropolitan France	2000 Beneficiaries[1] (thousands) Metropolitan France
Aged 65 and more	Minimum vieillesse (MV) Minimum pension	569[2]	583[2]	None	700	930
Disability	Minimum invalidité (MI) Minimum pension	569		None	99	149
Disability	Allocation adulte handicapé (AAH) Disabled Adult Allowance	569	558[3]	None	689	1075
Widowhood aged <55	Allocation veuvage Widowhood Allowance	503	629	3 years	19	29
Lone parent	Allocation de parent isolé (API) Lone Parent Benefit	513[4]	513[4]	One year after getting a lone parent or until the youngest child is 3 years old.	157	426
Long-term unemployment	Allocation de solidarité spécifique (ASS) Solidarity allowance	406	935[5]	None but the case is examined every 6 months	430	1033
Job seeker	Allocation d'insertion (AI) First-Job Seeker benefit (special conditions for example people leaving prison)	282	846[6]	One year	32	48
General	Revenu minimum d'insertion (RMI) Minimum Income for Integration	406[5]	406[5]	None	965	1892

1) Beneficiaries: recipients, spouses, and children.
2) 1021 € for a couple; ceiling 1021 Euro.
3) The resources are those of the preceding year; the threshold is then the precedent amount of the benefit. The income threshold for a couple is 1116 Euro.
4) Amount for a pregnant woman. Add 171 per child.
5) 1470 € for a couple (the family allowance is not taken into account in the resources).
6) 1412 € for a couple.
7) 730 € for two persons (couple or lone parent with a child), 851 € for three, 852 € for four; add 162 € for each other child.
Data for Metropolitan France. In the DOM (French overseas departments) there are 271,000 recipients and 498,000 beneficiaries.
Source: French Minister for employment and social affairs, DREES (Department for research and statistics on social affairs).

single-mother families). In France, at the end of 1999, among the 1,120,000 RMI recipients (in Metropolitan France and Overseas Department), 641,000 were living alone, 48,000 were couples without children, 180,000 were couples with children, and 250,000 were single-parent families (half of which had only one child). For a comparison with the United States, we must add 250,000 single-parent families, the recipients of the API (157,000), and about 40,000 recipients of the ASS. Thus, the single-parent families represent only about 29 percent of all the recipients of these three means-tested benefits.

On December 31, 2000, about 24 percent of RMI recipients were less than 30 years old (few of them were less 25) and 17 percent were between 30 and 34. This proportion declined with age, due partly to the reduction of unemployment with age and/or a better unemployment benefit coverage. For the ASS recipients, the age structure reveals an older population, as opposed to the young population of API beneficiaries.

Table 4.5
Age Structure of the Recipients (distribution as a %
of total income support recipients by age groups)

	RMI	ASS	API	Total
Less than 20		0	10	1
From 20 to 24	4	2	27	5
From 25 to 29	27	4	25	20
From 30 to 34	18	11	18	16
From 35 to 39	13	14	11	13
From 40 to 44	12	15	5	12
From 45 to 49	11	17	3	12
From 50 to 54	8	18	1	10
From 55 to 59	5	19		8

Source: French Ministry for employment and social affairs, DREES (Department for research and statistics on social affairs) Demailly, Algava, and Gilles 2001.

The Architecture of the RMI

Since the RMI is the most recent means-tested benefit created in France, and the latest safety-net, it is useful to examine it more precisely. French legislators insist on the RMI law based on the principle and purposes of this benefit. The first article is as follows:

"Everyone who, due to his age, his physical or mental condition, or due to the economic or employment situation, is unable to work, has the right to obtain from the society a decent means of living. The social and professional integration of people in difficulty is a national duty. To that end, a Minimum Income for Integration is created." The second article specifies the counterpart for the claimant: "Everyone living in France whose income is lower than…, who is 25 years of age or more and who takes on a commitment to participate in any activity, once defined with him, which appears necessary to his social or professional integration, has the right to…receive the RMI."

Three comments can be made:

1. The beginning of the first article of the law refers explicitly to the French Constitution (1946 Preamble). This is similar to the 1961 German law creating a minimum income (HLU) referring to the German Constitution or with the Dutch 1965 (ABW) law. There is a fundamental right for *everyone* to obtain a decent standard of living, with the main purpose of helping the person become socially or professionally integrated.
2. French Members of Parliament were very reluctant to bind the RMI benefit to a job-seeking constraint. The RMI was initially designed mainly for people suffering from social exclusion and often far from able to find a job; therefore it was not a "third degree" of unemployment benefit.[17] So in the "contract for integration" that the claimant has to sign within three months, there is no compulsory requirement about job research. Moreover, most of the RMI recipients do not actually sign any contract. Here the French law differs from the Dutch, German, or British ones that stipulate that minimum income support beneficiaries have to seek a job, in the same way as those receiving unemployment insurance benefits, unless they have young children or are disabled.
3. However, the income support policy written in the RMI law is closer to a "Welfare to Work" paradigm than to a "Universal Income" policy. Eligibility for a minimum income is said to be dependent on the inability to find a job and the purpose of the benefit is to help the recipient to find the means for social and professional integration. This is in line with another principle of the French Constitution (1946 Preamble): "*Everyone has the duty to work* and the right to find a job."

RMI and Work

The RMI program bases eligibility on family income, with the formula used to calculate the level of the allowance similar to the one employed to define eligibility (the earning disregard differs; see below). The level of income is estimated on a quarterly basis (the level of income reached in the preceding quarter determines the allowance for the following quarter). Some resources are not disregarded: pensions, unemployment benefits, disability benefits, capital income, and most of the child benefits. Housing benefits are taken into account for a lump sum depending on the family size; the difference between the effective house benefit and this disregard adds to the family income.

Others, such as the Allowance for Young Child (APJE) or the Allowance for School Attendance, are not taken into account.

When people claim the benefit, earnings are not disregarded. But, when a recipient moves to work, earnings disregards apply: earnings are entirely disregarded until the first quarterly revision plus the following quarter, and at only 50 percent the following three quarters. At the end of year 2000, about

14 percent of RMI recipients in Metropolitan France benefited from the earnings disregards mechanism.

The French Transfer system is, in fact, much more complicated than the sketch drawn above. Housing benefits use three different instruments. Among child benefits, only three have been briefly presented but there are many more (such as a single-parent general benefit which is not means-tested, a means-tested allowance for children attending school, and an income tax deduction for families with children attending school or university). Because of such complexity, the situation of people out of work receiving means-tested benefits can diverge highly from the situation of working people. Moreover, this incongruity is reinforced by the great variety of in-kind benefits that local authorities also provide to recipients—such as free access to public transportation—depending on specific eligibility rules that vary according to geographic location.

In order to assess the French income support policy, it is thus useful to return to some normative considerations with regard to the coherence of the welfare system, in particular, in light of the labor market.

Income Support Policies: A Normative View

The government (or in some countries, the Parliament) determines the minimum wage and the level of the *social minima* (the means-tested benefits). What can be said about these implicit or explicit choices?

What Should Be the Value of the Minimum Wage?

As we have seen before, the ILO conventions as well as the French or the U.S. laws consider that the minimum wage must be determined by taking into account a normative view of the needs of workers and their families (in France as in the 131 ILO conventions an objective of limiting income inequalities is added) and the economic situation.

Considering the minimum wage as a social minimum, a question should be answered: What size family should a (full-time) job, paid at the minimum wage, decently support?

Decency is a rather confusing notion. Though the law does not give a strict definition, we may try to compare the level of income emanating from a full-time job at minimum wage with the poverty threshold and examine which family size it lifts out of poverty.

Minimum wage and poverty. In France, regardless of family size, the income reached by a family with a full-time worker paid at the SMIC level is above the poverty line because of housing and child benefits, which are rather substantial for people earning around the minimum wage (see table 4.2).

In the United States, the situation is relatively different. The 1999 report[18] to Congress required by section 4(d)(1) of the FLSA underlines that:

for individuals (those not supporting families), the minimum wage has consistently exceeded the poverty level. On the other hand, for an individual trying to support a family, the minimum wage has lost some of its ability to generate a standard of living above the poverty line. In 1968, a full time worker earning the minimum wage was able to support a family of four at slightly below the poverty threshold.... In 1997, it again just exceeded the poverty threshold for a two persons family.

The problem would likely be even greater if the United States used a relative poverty definition similar to the one used in France or elsewhere in Europe.

Family and labor market participation. Another problem is the "standard" model of labor market participation. Considering the rise of women in the workforce, the predominant model of couples is no longer the single breadwinner but one in which both people work, or at least with the wife working part-time.

Table 4.6
Labor Market Participation Rate in %, According to
the Employment Characteristics of the Couple

	%				
	1985	1986	1991	1997	2001
Two in Jobs	**55,0**	**55,9**	**59,9**	**60,2**	**65,4**
Two full-time jobs	41,1	41,2	44,2	39,3	42,9
Two jobs of which at least one part-time job	13,8	14,7	15,8	20,9	22,5
Of which one involuntary part-time job			2,5	5,1	4,6
One in job, the other unemployed or inactive	**40,6**	**39,5**	**35,6**	**34,1**	**30,0**
One full-time job, the other unemployed	7,1	7,6	7,3	9,2	7,1
One in full-time job the other inactive	32,0	30,3	26,7	22,2	20,5
Two unemployed or inactive	**4,4**	**4,7**	**4,4**	**5,7**	**4,6**
Total	100	100	100	100	100

Couples with spouses aged 17 to 59, where neither is retired.
Source: French Labor Force Survey, CERC calculations CERC, 2002.

From that perspective what can we say about the minimum wage? A full-time worker, living alone and paid at the SMIC level, is far above the poverty line (net income is around 886€ per month, poverty line 580€ in the example of table 4.1). The income of a single breadwinner couple is slightly above the poverty line; if the labor participation's model is two full-time workers or even one spouse working full time and the other member part time, the family income is far above the poverty line. These results will be reinforced once the Employment Premium is applied. In France, as stated before, the poverty line is not an official threshold, but begins to be considered a reference for some public policies (for example, the Universal Health Coverage, CMU). In fact, the political or social target to combat poverty is now more a question of the level of the means-tested benefit (see table 4.7). Changing the level in the minimum wage (SMIC) refers more either to the aim of controlling earning inequalities or to economic considerations. The change in the SMIC may be more dependant of either an objective of controlling earnings inequalities or economic considerations (especially its incidence on employment for the lowest qualified manpower).

Some considerations about the working time. These results have been calculated under the assumption that there is at least one person in the family working full time. But full time is quite conventional or is determined by the law as it is in France: the law defines both a ceiling for weekly hours (for health reasons) and legal working hours (based on which employers have to pay overtime premium). When the legal working time changed from 39 hours a week to 35 at the beginning of year 2000, the government made the decision to keep unaffected the monthly minimum earnings. This decision is consistent with the definition of the minimum wage as a social minimum since *"the needs of workers and their families"* are not reduced in due proportion to working hours. But this full wage compensation[19] raises the labor cost and may have a negative impact on low-qualified employment. To avoid this negative effect, it was necessary to reduce employers' contributions so that the labor cost did not rise too much. However, the problem has not been fully resolved since the "guarantee of monthly earnings" must be suppressed by July 2005 (through a rise of the SMIC), without having yet defined the way to achieve this.

Why Does the Level of Means Tested Benefits Differ?

As can be seen in table 4.4, there are, roughly speaking, two different levels for means-tested benefits[20]: an individual gets 569€ when he is unable to work and only 406€ if he is of an age and capacity to work. The differences remain for the net disposable income, calculated for various family sizes and locations. How to justify such a difference? If the purpose of the benefit is to cover the needs of the recipient ("rights to obtain from the society a decent means of living"), then you cannot justly claim that the needs of people between 25 years and 64 years are less than those of people older than 65. A second approach is to consider judicial theories. In the discussion about the reduction of inequalities, some argue that society has to correct the consequences of handicaps for which the person is not responsible, but it does not have to correct the consequences of private choice on work or leisure. From this perspective, French society would consider the unemployed partly responsible for their situation. Another illustration of that is the supplementary benefits for long-term unemployed people who are older than 55 and, as such, have little chance to be employed. The third, and probably the dominant explanation, is that French society sees compatibility between the constitutional principles: (a) *"Everyone has the duty to work,"* and (b) *"Everyone who...is unable to work has rights to obtain from the society a decent means of leaving,"* implying that *"work must pay,"* and that a transition from welfare to work must produce a rise in income. "Work must pay" not only for economic reasons (theories about the need of financial incentives to enter the labor market), but also for reasons of social justice.

Minimum Wage and Means-Tested Benefits

- *SMIC and Minimum Pension*
  The minimum wage (net of employees' contributions and CSG-CRDS) amounts to 864€; the minimum pension for an individual is 569€ and for a couple 1021€ (housing benefits may be received in both cases so the gap remains when considering the net income). This tends to confirm that the implicit model of labor participation, in France, is no longer the single breadwinner, but rather dual-income couples.
- *SMIC and RMI*
  The RMI allowance for an individual is about 40 percent of the minimum full-time wage (net of employees' contribution and social taxation), and the ratio for net income is about 67 percent (see table 4.4). For a couple, the ratios are 57 percent and 81 percent, respectively. The gap between the minimum wage and the RMI is rather important, whichever labor market participation model (single or double breadwinner)

Table 4.7
Comparison of Net Disposable Income for RMI
Recipients and People Working on Part-Time or Full-Time
Jobs Paid at the Minimum Wage Level

Year 2000	earnings	Social and Fiscal wedge			Social transfers			net income	net income per consumption unit
		employees contributions	Csg-Crds	Income tax and local taxes	RMI	Housing benefit	Child benefits		
living alone RMI	0	0	0	0	342	255	0	598	598
0.5*SMIC	541	73	41	1	0	188	0	614	614
1*SMIC	1083	145	82	30	0	61	0	886	886
lone parent RMI	0	0	0	0	417	350	74	840	646
1 child 0.5	541	73	41	0	0	308	74	809	623
1	1083	145	82	8	0	206	74	1127	867
Couple RMI	0	0	0	0	490	304	0	794	530
no child 0.5	541	73	41	0	63	304	0	794	530
1	1083	145	82	8	0	127	0	974	650
Couple RMI	0	0	0	0	597	406	105	1108	527
2 children 0.5	541	73	41	0	169	406	105	1108	527
1	1083	145	82	0	0	276	105	1236	589
Couple RMI	0	0	0	0	482	463	375	1320	550
3 children 0.5	541	73	41	0	54	599	375	1320	550
1	1083	145	82	0	0	352	375	1582	659

Source: French Treasury, Department of economic studies (Direction de la Prévision) Model Pâris.

is used as a reference. This is consistent with a hierarchy of principles that "work must pay." This condition is also explicit in the German means-tested benefit HLU, but not in Dutch law. In the Netherlands, the ABW allowance for a couple is strictly equal to the minimum wage (75 percent for an individual living alone); so "work may not pay" for a couple, but the recipient, as for every unemployment benefit recipient, must seek a job.

In France, work does pay, when considering a full-time job. But some problems arise when considering the situation of part-time jobs, and these grow in importance with the size of the family.

Income Support and Employment

Do the means-tested, and more generally, the income support policies impede employment, especially for low-skilled people? This has been the subject of much public debate over the past few years in France.

The main way to support income is to help people find a job and to obtain sufficient earnings. As seen above, poverty is mainly due to unemployment or underemployment and not to the level of the minimum wage.

Minimum Wage and Income Support

- The SMIC is an instrument to limit the inequality in hourly wages. It is not a sufficient device anymore to fight against poverty emanating from underemployment. Moreover, there is a debate about the relationship between the level of the French minimum wage and unemployment:

  People who believe that high unemployment among low skilled workers is partly due to the high labor cost advocate avoiding any increase in the cost of low skilled labor relative to the average cost of labor. Any increase in the level of net wages without raising labor costs calls for the introduction of higher progressiveness of the social and tax wedge. The decision to keep unchanged the monthly amount of the SMIC while the legal working time changes from 39 to 35 hours raises the minimum labor cost (in absolute value as in relative value to the mean or median labor cost) in spite of a reduction of employers' contributions. And this problem may be reinforced until 2005 by mechanical consequences of the 35 hours law.[21] Of course, for those who think that there is no negative relation between the SMIC labor cost and the level of low-skilled worker employment, all of this is irrelevant.

- This question is more controversial in other countries: clearly, the effect of the minimum wage on employment depends on its level. In the United States, a vast amount of research[22] concurs on a negative correlation between the rise of the minimum wage on the level of employment.[23] And for the United Kingdom, the lack of any minimum wage leads to a negative effect on both earnings inequality and economic performance.[24] The new national minimum wage, introduced in

April 2000, was a real income support for millions of people, and it seems that there were no negative consequences on employment.

- Even if one neglects the consequences of an increase of the SMIC upon employment, the minimum wage has a rather low effect on redistribution, since employees receiving the minimum wage belong to households whose total income is distributed on a rather large part of the income scale. These results have been well documented, in the case of the United States, in studies that compare the distributive effects of a rise in the federal minimum wage or the EITC rate.[25] The same results appear in France: when increasing the SMIC level, the main positive effects on household incomes affect the second to fifth decile of the income distribution and are less important for poor households, since they are often out of work.

The Employment Premium

As seen before, the employment premium affects largely the individual net earning, so its effect on the redistribution of household income is similar to a rise in the level of the SMIC (without the potential negative effect on low-skilled employment), and not with the effect of a rise in the EITC which depends on the family earning as can be seen in figure 4.1.

Figure 4.1
Redistribution Through a Rise Respectively in the SMIC and in the Employment Premium

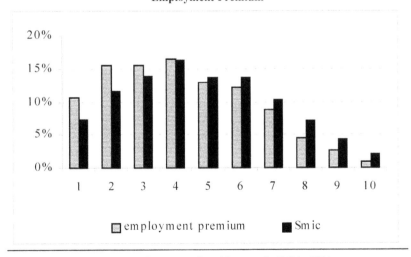

Source: CERC "Access to employment and social protection" Feb. 2001.
This chart represents the distribution of the employment premium budget through deciles of income per consumption unit and the distribution of a rise of the SMIC level, assuming that it has no effect on employment.

Income Support and Underemployment

If the main source of poverty among working households is the fact that they do not find enough hours of work during the year (due to part-time jobs or short-term contracts) then a benefit which is proportional to the amount of earnings (like the French employment premium or the U.S. EITC) cannot be an efficient solution to the problem.

Part-time jobs or short-term contracts have developed en masse in France over the past ten years, due to the employment crisis, as well as to structural factors like the growth of the service sector. What kind of policies may reduce their impact on poverty?

- First these types of jobs are not always necessary. Firms may have the same level of flexibility to respond partly to fluctuations in demand by organizing internally to allow greater flexibility. This may be the role of firm agreements. Some firms, for instance, change their organization in this way through firm agreements implementing the reduction of the work week to 35 hours.
- Second, these types of jobs must not be encouraged through, for example, subsidies. (In the early 1990s part-time jobs where subsidized through the reduction of social employers' contributions; the reduction has since been suppressed.
- A third policy target is to help people entering such precarious jobs to use them as a step to better jobs. This may also be the role of industry-wide agreement as, for example, a national agreement between Dutch Employers and Unions attempts to do by giving priority to a firm hiring people on full-time or permanent contracts over employees on part-time and short-term contracts. Another way is to develop on-the-job training for people on precarious contracts.
- For people working part time and/or having a short-term contract paid at the minimum wage, the net disposable income is often the same (and in some cases lower) as the income they could have without working and being recipients of, say, the RMI. In these kinds of jobs "work does not pay." And for many other jobs work pays little or not enough.

This is a serious political issue. Should the social transfer system be shaped so that every job pays (i.e., so that the implicit marginal tax on labor would always be less than 100 percent and perhaps less than a threshold like 80 percent)? Or is it good that the welfare system allows people to refuse "bad jobs"?

- To "make work pay" needs first to take care of the rules of many allowances or benefits, when they depend on family incomes. In France, most of the means-tested allowances (housing benefits, some child benefits) are calculated by considering earnings (and capital income)

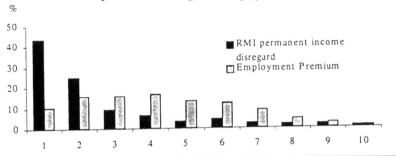

Figure 4.2
Redistribution Through Permanent Earnings Disregard Applied to RMI
Recipients and Through the Employment Premium

Source: CERC "Access to employment and social protection" Feb. 2001.
This fSWigure is similar to figure 4.1: distribution of the budget of the two instruments
between the deciles of income per consumption unit.
The two instruments are calibrated to have the same cost.

Figure 4.3
Constraint with the Employment Premium
and the RMI Permanent Earnings Disregard

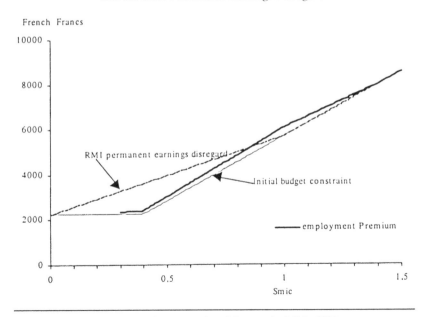

Source: CERC "Access to employment and social protection" Feb. 2001.

as income but not social transfers. When moving to work, earnings reduce the means-tested benefits (i.e., the RMI allowance) as well as the housing benefit.[26] Similar imbalances may occur when access to specific in-kind benefit (such as free public transportation) depends on conditions such as receiving the "RMI" or being registered as unemployed are not conditional on total income. Since 1998, the government has reduced the main problems in that field (housing benefit, housing taxation).

- In France, the general child allowance (*allocation familiale*) applies to the second (or more) child only. For that reason there is a peculiar problem with families (couples or single parents) moving to work since the "RMI" benefit takes into account each child of the family. So the level of earnings at which "work begins to pay" is relatively high in families with children. However, it remains that, since there is a means-tested benefit for people out of work, some jobs cannot pay if there is no earnings disregard, or if the earnings disregard is temporary. The only way to make work pay is to have a permanent income disregard in a benefit, like the RMI, that will decrease with the level of earnings. This type of instrument would have greater redistributive effects (see figure 4.2) and greater financial incentives for a transition from welfare to work (see figure 4.3).

This proposition was made in the beginning of 1999 by Godino but had not been accepted by the government during the debate on income support, which ended with the creation of the "Employment Premium." One of the reasons was that this type of instrument could increase the risk of developing "bad jobs."

Conclusion

In conclusion, after this description of the French situation, it seems difficult to improve the various income support policies using direct instruments; a rise in the minimum wage (relative to the median wage) may increase the risk of unemployment for low-skill workers, and compensating for this risk by reducing the employers' social contribution is now difficult as it will lead to financing the pensions or the unemployment benefits through taxes on people paid at the SMIC level.[27] Such a reform would change the nature of the French pension system. Reinforcing the redistribution through social transfers dependent upon household income may lead to a political problem with the French middle classes. The best way, then, to support income is probably to enhance employment through macroeconomic or structural policies, such as reducing inequalities in education and qualifications.

Notes

1. The rates of the social contribution are given for gross wage's brackets which are defined as multiple of a threshold called "*plafond de sécurité sociale.*" The monthly threshold amounted to 2280€ in 2001.

2. Defined as employers and employees social contributions in percentage of the labor cost.
3. In fact, some financial investments are not taxed.
4. The Constitutional Court judged that the CSG was an Income Tax and, due to this, must take into account the size of the family. If the CSG is perceived with a flat rate, this family condition is satisfied, but if the rate is growing with the earnings, it must take into account the earnings of the whole family.
5. For a full description of this instrument, see "Access to Employment and Social Protection," first report of the CERC, February 2001.
6. The matter is not the public utilities (electricity, telecommunication, etc.) since the prices paid by household are largely market ones.
7. French national accounts 2000.
8. In the transition from welfare to work, the differences regarding health insurance between France and the United States are the following: In France, people leaving a mean-tested benefit such as the RMI to work keep health insurance and may only have a problem paying for a private complementary insurance; in the United States, people leaving TANF to work may lose Medicaid (at least for oneself and sometimes for the children) without getting health insurance through the firm where he or she works.
9. People, registered in the ANPE who are working in reduced activity, are not unemployed following the ILO definition. This is one of the various reasons for the discrepancy between the data.
10. Unions and management did not agree on a budget and the government decided by itself the level of the minimum wage.
11. The needs of a family with children were not taken into account explicitly, but a part of these supplementary needs were covered by family allowance; for example, there was a special means-tested allowance for a family where the wife did not work (*allocation de salaire unique*), which does not exist yet.
12. Data for 1999, when a minimum wage was introduced in the United Kingdom.
13. The equivalent scale used in France is 1 for the first adult, 0.5 for the others—including children aged 14 or older, 0.3 for children aged less than 14.
14. The difference between the Insee's measure (7 percent) and the Eurostat's measure is mainly due to the fact that the households at the bottom of the income distribution are more often of greater size, and partly due to the difference of surveys used.
15. The rank differs according to the poverty line that is chosen.
16. These benefits differ, in their general purpose, from housing or child benefits even when they are means-tested.
17. Unemployment growth in the beginning of the 1990s, and the hardening of the unemployment insurance benefit in 1992 rapidly changed the characteristics of the population of recipients: many of them are now close to the labor market.
18. Probably the last report issued by the DOL wage and hour division?
19. The "35-hours" law introduced, for people paid at the SMIC and working in firms on a 35 hours/week time, a "guarantee of the monthly earnings " equal to the amount of the hourly SMIC, at the moment of the working-time reduction, multiplied by 39.
20. Once taken apart the first job-seeking allowance, which is now reduced to very peculiar situations and has few recipients, and the lone parent allowance, which depends on the situation of the recipient (pregnancy and/or young children).
21. The law also provides that by July 2005 the SMIC will be increased so as to cancel out the monthly guarantee. The gradual change over to the 35-hour week will induce a mechanical upward revision of the SMIC, while remaining within the minimum revision limits (indexing in accordance with purchasing power for half of the evolution of hourly paid workers).

22. See, for example, D. Card and A. B. Krueger, "Minimum Wages and Employment: A Case Study of the Fast Food Industry in New Jersey and Pennsylvania," *American Economic Review* 84, 4 (1984).
23. But there are also other people who reach the opposite conclusion.
24. See, for example, the first report of the Low Pay Commission, *The National Minimum Wage* (London, 1998).
25. See, for example, R. V. Burkhauser, K. A. Couch, and A. J. Glenn (1995), "Public Policies for the Working Poor: The Earned Income Tax Credit versus Minimum Wage Legislation," *Discussion paper,* No. 1074, Institute for Research on Poverty, Madison, Wisconcsin.
26. The reduction of the housing benefit was postponed until people left the RMI, but at this level of earning the disposable income was reduced (the marginal rate of taxation was higher than 100 percent).
27. This may be chosen, for example, in Denmark, where a large part of the pensions is financed with income tax.

References

Barème Social Périodique. (2001). Liaisons sociales ed. Paris. January.

Burkhauser, R. V., Couch, K. A., & Glenn, A. J. (1995). "Public Policies for the Working Poor: the Earned Income Tax Credit versus Minimum Wage Legislation." *Discussion paper,* n° 1074, Institute for Research in Poverty.

Card, D., & Krueger, A. B. (1984). "Minimum Wages and Employment: A Case Study of the Fast Food Industry in New Jersey and Pennsylvania." *American Economic Review* 84, 4.

CERC. (2001). "Access to Employment and Social Protection" (*Accès à l'emploi et protection sociale*). Paris: La Documentation Française.

http://www.cerc.gouv.fr/rapports/report1cerc.pdf

CERC. (2002). "The Long Road to the Euro: Growth, Employment and Income 1985-2000" (*La longue route vers l'Euro*). Paris: La Documentation Française.

http://www.cerc.gouv.fr/rapports/report2cerc.doc

SERC. (1999). "Le SMIC, salaire minimum de croissance." Paris: La Documentation Française.

www.cerc.gouv.fr/rapports/rapports.html

Demailly, D., Algava, E., & Gilles, C. (2001). "The Recipients of Mean Tested Benefits in 2000" (*Les allocataires de minima sociaux en 2000*). Paris: DREES.

http://www.sante.gouv.fr/drees/etude-resultat/er-pdf/er148.pdf

Lamotte, H., Guimbert, S., & Lefebvre, E. (2000). "The Consistency of the French Income Support Mechanisms" (*Quelle cohérence dans les dispositifs français de soutien aux bas revenus?*). Paper presented at the seminar "Working Poor in France," Evry. May.

http://www.cerc.gouv.fr/meetings/colloquemai2000/wpmai2000.html

Law Pay Commission. (1998). First Report, "The National Minimum Wage." London. June.

5

Workfare and *Insertion*: How the U.S. and French Models of Social Assistance Have Been Transformed

Sylvie Morel

Introduction

The nature of social assistance, that is, policies aimed at relieving the effects of poverty,[1] has changed over the last decades: state support to the able-bodied poor no longer depends solely on a lack of income or resources, but comes now with a new set of behavioral requirements for the poor. This usually means coupling cash benefits with a process of employment integration. Thus, we may say that the "relation of assistance" has been transformed into a relation of "reciprocal obligations." The United States and France present two contrasting, and even opposing types of reciprocal approaches in social assistance: the U.S. approach can be described as workfare, while the French approach is *insertion* (Morel, 2000). From many different points of view, the two approaches constitute two fundamentally different ways of dealing with poverty: *assistance customs*, concepts of poverty, citizenship and solidarity, and actual practices in the field.

Since we first defined the models of workfare and *insertion* in the mid-1990s, important reforms in social assistance have been adopted in both countries. The American welfare system changed dramatically in August 1996 when the Personal Responsibility and Work Opportunity Reconciliation Act (PRWORA) replaced the Aid to Families with Dependent Children (AFDC) program[2] and the related Job Opportunities and Basic Skills (JOBS) program with Temporary Assistance for Needy Families (TANF). On its side, France put in place in July 1998 an ambitious set of policies primarily aimed at combating exclusion (*Loi d'orientation sur la lutte contre les exclusions*, LOLE); this law was in continuity with the *Revenu Minimum d'Insertion* (RMI) (minimum income *insertion*) program created ten years earlier.[3] Along with these profound changes in the social assistance system, both countries transformed other related public policies in order to increase welfare recipient employment, expanding support services for employment integration as well as financial incentives.

With all these major changes, the models of workfare and *insertion* are confronted with new national conditions. Thus, the time has come to reconsider these models by examining the extent to which they have undergone transformation. This is the subject of our chapter. Firstly, to provide a background for our discussion, the models of workfare and *insertion* will be briefly outlined. Secondly, we will review some of the key changes occurring since the mid-1990s in the United States and France, as it concerns the reciprocity relation between the able-bodied poor and the state. Thirdly, a brief synthesis of these transformations will be presented in order to examine the validity of the two reference models. However, one fact should not be overlooked at any point: reciprocity in social assistance, especially in its American version of "welfare," is an openly gendered issue as long as female family heads with children are the families most directly affected by workfare. Thus, from the American perspective, the welfare recipients that have to be "reformed" are poor women. This reality graphically raises a set of specific issues: the juggling of family and employment responsibilities, occupational segregation in the labor market with poor quality jobs, domestic violence against women, and so on. We will also touch briefly upon these issues throughout this chapter.

Workfare and "*Insertion*": Two Distinctive Models of Reciprocity

The "reciprocal obligations" approach in social assistance is related to specific policies in the United States and in France: the notion of workfare refers predominantly to AFDC-TANF, while the notion of *insertion*, which concerns a wide range of policies, is established in the framework of the RMI.[4] To facilitate the understanding of the following, we must point out that our analysis of workfare and *insertion* is supported by a more fundamental theoretical vision that targets a renewal of economic theory. We are working to replace "standard economic theory" by another analytical framework put forward by the heterodox economists who founded the United States institutionalist movement in the early twentieth century, in particular John R. Commons (1934). The institutionalist approach based on the work of Commons takes a completely different direction than orthodox economic theory in both methods and concepts. The reality of conflict in the distribution of wealth is a focus of the analysis. The approach is evolutionary, trans-disciplinary and ethical. Instead of examining, as do orthodox economists, the action of disembodied, isolated "economic agents," the institutionalist analyst deals with *people* as *"citizen-individuals"*; in other words, the economic subject is considered an *individual* connected with various networks of social relations, and as a *citizen* endowed with *rights and duties*. Now, the researcher can consider an evaluation of the *economic status* instituted in social terms for individuals. The focus put on *rights and duties, customs*, and on the institutional interaction between social assistance, employment, and the family in our study of workfare and *insertion* stems directly from this theoretical standpoint.

It is possible to make a schematic representation of the main characteristics of the two opposing reciprocal approaches (see table 5.1). A broad review of the two countries obviously entails certain shortcuts or omissions. Nonetheless, we feel that the exercise of pointing out the striking features and key oppositions of the two reciprocal models is valuable for the purpose of comparative analysis. Firstly, it is important to outline the specific ways, as can be noted in table 5.1, in which social assistance is structured in the United States and in France (1.1). The U.S. system is highly decentralized and category-based. In contrast, the French social assistance system is centralized and partially unified. The starting point for building a social assistance model based on reciprocity is a characterization of the new social subject about to enter into a relationship of reciprocal obligations with the state (1.2). To identify the representations made of this "subject-citizen," we must examine the concepts and discourse that serve to construct the image of the poor within a given society. Thus, the "welfare-recipient-citizen" of the workfare system is characterized as "dependent," whereas the target subject of the *insertion* system is "excluded." Since workfare and *insertion* are based on opposing concepts of poverty, they also have diverging objectives (1.3). Workfare is mainly intended to fight dependency, *insertion* to fight exclusion. The *formula* of rights and duties (1.4) that typifies each of the two reciprocal approaches illustrates the social relation existing between the poor and the state. Essentially, the question is to discover which party is assigned primary responsibility for obligations in the new reciprocal relationship. Workfare and *insertion* are based on opposing concepts of citizenship and social ties: the image of the poor "dependent" mother derives from the logic of the *contrepartie*, whereas the image of the "excluded" derives from a logic based on social indebtedness. Assistance customs (1.5) are the *unorganized rules* that prevail within the institution. The rules, which direct the customary behavior of individuals, date back many years, and the ancient forms of the current rules can be traced back to the history of each country concerned, revealing the strength of culturally specific representations of poverty. From this point of view, once again, workfare and *insertion* display many differences. Workfare is a direct consequence of the *custom of deservingness,* whereas *insertion* is an extension of the *custom of solidarity.* In other words, the difference between workfare and *insertion* is based on the endurance of the characteristics of the assistance-related customs of the countries concerned, revealing a remarkable degree of continuity. The workfare/*insertion* opposition does not simply reflect, then, a temporary divergence between national experiences, a chance occurrence, but distinctive modes of *social control* in each of the two countries.

The concepts of reciprocity in the workfare and *insertion* approaches also differ in terms of the related obligations (1.6). Workfare is designed according to a category-based logic, while *insertion* follows a universalist logic. In both France and the United States, the new obligations of social assistance are connected to a range of activities whose nature illustrates two different concepts of the social integration of assistance recipients (1.7). Workfare proposes a model of professional integration, whereas *insertion* combines both the social and the professional dimensions. Workfare therefore offers a more restricted definition of what is meant by the integration of the poor into society. The workfare and *insertion* models also differ in that they derive from different dynamic interactions between assistance, employment, and the family (1.8). In the workfare model, family has precedence over employment in terms of the evolution of social assistance, whereas the opposite holds true for the *insertion* model. As well, workfare and *insertion* activities are often integrated into differing regulatory frameworks (1.9). In an *insertion* based-system, beneficiaries often become wage earners, whereas in a workfare system, they generally remain "recipients." Finally, in both countries, we have observed institutional dynamics of regression (1.10). Once again, these are moving in opposite directions. In the United States, employment regulation determines assistance regulation and has led to a gradual erosion of social assistance, whereas in France today the assistance regulation influences employment regulation, with a similar effect.

Table 5.1:
Different Types of Reciprocal Logic in Social Assistance—United States/France
(mid-1990s)

1.1 The structure of the social assistance system: decentralized/category-based or centralized/unified. The U.S. system is highly decentralized (mainly designed and managed by individual states) and category-based (eligibility is defined on the basis of specific characteristics—marital status, age, etc.—in addition to the income and resource test). Single-parent families have, historically, made up the major group of recipients of the U.S. social assistance system, both in terms of number and through their "visibility" in debates on how to reform the system. In France, on the other hand, the main part of the social assistance system (the RMI on its transfer side and the system of social minima) is centralized. It is also partially unified: the RMI in not category-based, but it is superimposed on the preexistent system of social minima. However, with regard to the insertion activity aspect, the French system is more decentralized.

1.2. Representation of the social assistance "subject-citizen": "dependent" or "excluded." The analysis of the *rules* instituting the "welfare recipient-citizen" has highlighted the existence of two opposite images of the "subjects" of the "relation of assistance" in the United States and France. Clearly, while the *insertion* recipient is considered to be "excluded," the workfare recipient is seen as "dependent." The dependency theme is central to the conception of workfare and assistance in the United States The dominant idea emerging from American debates about workfare is one in which poverty is seen as an individual problem and the interaction of the poor with social assistance is regarded as having a negative effect on recipients' behavior. The workfare recipient is identified as an individual who is "trapped" in the vicious circle of social assistance, unable to escape from his or her situation of dependency and find a normal position of individual autonomy in society. The dependency thesis thus socially constructs the recipient as a person who has been "deresponsibilized" and who must be given the *duty* to correct this internal dysfunction. In contrast, welfare recipients who are viewed as "excluded," are not "culprits" but "victims" of society's disorganized *rules*. Social deviancy is not mainly attributed to the poor but to society as a whole. RMI recipients remind society of its dysfunction, especially in the field of employment, family, and social protection. Consequently, rules that redefine the social contract between the state and the poor are, in the case of *insertion*, based on an appeal for a concerted effort to help those who are excluded. This is clearly laid out in the RMI Law, which declares *insertion* a "national imperative." With the theme of "exclusion," which is the corollary and antithesis of *insertion*, themes of "precariousness" and "exposure" appear. The phenomenon of "new poverty" is seen to reflect this set of social problems. The problem of exclusion, which stems from the idea of solidarity, thus concerns society as a whole because the latter is identified as being both responsible for the problem, and also the place where it can be resolved.

1.3 The main objective: fighting dependency or fighting exclusion. The main objective of workfare is to fight dependency, and also to preserve the work ethic. Because of this, workfare seeks to reinforce the incentive to work and to make assistance consistent with U.S. values. The question of equity is also very much present in the workfare approach. Imposing work in exchange for assistance is presented as a way to place recipients and working American mothers on an equal footing, since the latter have to work to earn a wage. A reduction in the cost of social assistance is also an important objective of workfare policies. In the workfare system, the rights of the poor are balanced against the rights of taxpayers. The *insertion* approach is completely different. The main objective of *insertion* is to fight against "exclusion," seen as a "social fracture" that must be healed. The objective of the RMI program is "to ensure participation in the life of the community in the name of recognition of the right to citizenship" (Paugam, 1991). Whereas the term "exclusion" is nonexistent in the United States welfare debate, it underlies the actions of all the French partners in the new RMI program. The question of "exclusion," in France, concerns not only the "fringes" of society, but constitutes an issue affecting the whole of society, since it is responsible for failing to integrate the poor. Because of this, the focus is on the responsibility of the community towards those who are "excluded." This is a long way from the individualistic conception of the fight against poverty exemplified in the workfare approach. In the "*insertion*" system, the "excluded" are compared to the "included," in other words wage earners with jobs, and the emphasis is placed on the *rights* to which not everyone has access, rather than on the *duty* of wage earners to work. Another point to bear in mind is that the fight against exclusion in France does not target a reduction in social assistance costs.

1.4 The *formula of rights and duties*: **the individual duty of the poor versus the collective duty of society.** Workfare represents the imposition of a new *duty*, where before there was only a *right* (AFDC benefits and the duty of domestic work). It is designed to reflect a relationship of *"contrepartie"*: a *right* (social assistance) carries with it a *duty* (work or other forms of activity) for the recipient. Workfare therefore emphasizes the individual *duty* of the poor recipient to make a contribution to society by individually demonstrating the kind of deserving behavior that will make him or her a citizen. *Insertion*, on the other hand, institutes a *right* for the beneficiary, that corresponds to a collective *duty*, mainly assumed by the state, to insert the excluded beneficiary into a community that he or she is already, and unconditionally, a member. Moreover, in the case of the RMI, the structure involves a double *right*, combining the *right* to an allowance (the minimum income) and the *right* to *insertion*, within a dynamic in which *insertion* "finalizes" the allowance (Lafore, 1992). In other words, *insertion* is not based on the logic of the *contrepartie*, but rather on the notion of social debt. *Insertion*, far from being the condition for benefiting from the allowance, "becomes an objective and not a condition" (CNE-RMI, 1992: 112).

1.5 Assistance *customs*: **the** *custom of deservingness* **and the** *custom of solidarity*. In the United Sates, the custom of deservingness derives historically from the fact that U.S. assistance policies have been based on the British custom of Poor Laws. This custom has the distinctive feature of emphasizing the selection of the poor on the basis of merit; the split between deserving and non-deserving poor, or the definition of rules to distinguish among the poor on the basis of their "ability to work" for the establishment of separate treatment, is a dominant characteristic of the social assistance program. The U.S. custom of deservingness has a second characteristic, that of having been, historically speaking, openly directed towards a control of the work patterns of women within the family. This characteristic derives from the category-based nature of the social assistance system, within which single-mother heads of family have always been the largest group. The custom of deservingness by gender is reflected in the United States by the adoption of rules such as the "suitable home" rule, which is applied as part of the assistance program for needy mothers. As in the case for the *rules* defining employability, this *working rule* of the custom of deservingness controlled a *duty* involving, not paid work, but household work, illustrating the gender dimension in the mechanisms set up to regulate the *contrepartie* for work in society. Differentiation of the poor, and different treatment according to employability, are also a constant in assistance policies in France. However, in France, a major break occurred in the wake of the French Revolution, setting out the principles for the "republican pact." Assistance was redesigned to reflect the imperative notions of citizenship, making the integration of individuals into the body of society a major political issue. In short, whereas the "custom of deservingness" dominated the evolution of assistance in the United States, in France the notion of solidarity was added, going on to become the main foundation for the organization of "public assistance." The principle of solidarity gave French assistance *custom* its characteristic flavor. During the nineteenth century, under the Third Republic, the concept of solidarity was embodied in the doctrine of solidarity, and from then on constituted the basis for the social security system as a whole. It also dominates the RMI program, which, at the time it was implemented, was widely supported by the general public (Legros and Simonin, 1991). The parliamentary debates that preceded the adoption of the RMI focused on a distinctive ideal of solidarity, a "Anew solidarity" specifically directed toward the fight against exclusion. Insertion thus draws its meaning from the French *custom* of solidarity.

1.6 The field of application of the reciprocal relationship: the category-based approach or the universalist approach. Workfare goes hand in hand with a categorization of the poor: the obligations it imposes do not apply uniformly to all welfare recipients but are based, instead, on differences between recipients. This selective model is implemented using a formal system of exemptions, under which certain subcategories of recipients are relieved of their obligations. Two selection criteria stand out in this targeting process: the age of the children involved and the sex of the recipient. The selective U.S. model thus shows the interference that exists between recipients' status as mothers and as workers. In the *insertion* approach, the underlying universalist logic corresponds to the republican ideal, based on formal equality between citizens. In accordance with this principle of equality, one of the main components in the republican identity, no formal distinction is made between RMI recipients with regard to the duty of *insertion*. All recipients are required to sign a contract of *insertion*, a compulsory complement of the allowance. In terms of the duty of *insertion*, all receive the same treatment and all are equal. However, although the French model is not selective from a formal point of view, it is selective in its application. This shows one of the contradictions of the concept of citizenship, which, historically, is also demonstrated in the treatment of women: behind the formal political rights, the image of the "citizen" hides a differentiation between men and women. In this connection, we have identified, in the United States and France, two opposing processes for selecting recipients on the basis of their employability. The U.S. model uses "upstream employability selection," while the French model uses "downstream employability selection." The U.S. model has been described above: the selection of recipients is inherent in the design of the workfare program, with its precise delimitation of categories. In France, the categorization process is found at a later stage, namely when the *insertion* mechanism is applied. In the French system, the selective approach is found, first, in the differentiated application of the contractual process (signing of the *insertion* contract) and, second, in the typical trajectories followed by recipients under social or vocational *insertion* measures, and in employment policies.

1.7 Conceptions of the social integration of social assistance recipients: exclusively professional or professional and social. In the United States, the activities available to recipients as part of the workfare program have been connected exclusively to employment integration (job search activities, training, education, internships, community work, etc.). The activities did not extend, as is the case for the RMI, to "social *insertion*." In some cases, AFDC-TANF recipients are required to take action concerning health problems or drug addiction. However, these are in addition to and, at least formally, are not substituted for the workfare requirements. In France, the RMI law provides for two types of *insertion*: professional *insertion* and social *insertion*. Although the general reference remains professional *insertion*, in other words employment or training leading to employment (through job preparation, community interest, training, and internship activities, and so forth), the RMI law extends *insertion* activities to "actions to allow recipients to regain or develop their social autonomy, once provided with appropriate social support, and to participate in family and civic life and the life of society, especially within a neighborhood or municipality, and in activities of all kinds, especially cultural and sporting activities," to "actions providing access to housing, rehousing or home improvement," and "actions designed to facilitate access to (health) care" (MASSV, 1993: 62-63).

1.8 Interaction dynamics between assistance, employment, and the family: precedence of the family or of employment. Workfare is founded on the transformation of the family. The instability of family relationships is the primary cause of the *vulnerability* of welfare recipients. Social assistance has thus become a family policy by default, the United States being the only industrialized country never to have established a public system of universal family allowances. Low-quality employment, which prevents those who escape from welfare from establishing a durable wage-earning relationship, also explains their social condition. Employment retention problems are mainly caused by low pay and the insufficiency of health coverage in the jobs to which welfare recipients have access. Insertion is founded on a transformation of employment. The main constraints facing RMI recipients are a lack of jobs (a high level of unemployment in general, including *insertion* unemployment and long-term unemployment) and the restrictiveness of unemployment-insurance rules. With the RMI system, social assistance in France has become a system of second-tier unemployment compensation. The family is the second item in the explanation of the dynamics of poverty in France but, in this case, concerns mainly women recipients. Workfare is founded on the evolution of the family at a second level: family changes have directed the transformation of assistance into a reciprocal relationship. In general, the reciprocal nature of social assistance can be explained by the institution of new categories of "employable" individuals in the sphere of social assistance. Workfare emerged simultaneously with the social constitution of employability for AFDC recipients. This is clearly a social process of employability construction, since this new dimension in the identity of poor mothers does not stem from the acquisition of objective characteristics (skills, qualifications, etc.). Rather, it is the product of an evolution in the *institution* of paid employment for women, itself linked to the transformation of the family. For *insertion*, the new employability at the roots of the reciprocal relationship appears to be different: it comes, not from the evolution of the social norms connected with paid employment and family, but rather from the taking in charge by the assistance system of new "employable" individuals. In France, the transformation of employment and unemployment insurance are the main reasons behind the emergence of an employable population, in other words unemployed men and women whose economic status is no longer determined by wage or insurance relationships, but by an assistance relationship.

1.9 Links with employment policies: primarily selective or primarily universal. In the United States, workfare programs have more often been designed by social welfare agencies, consisting of measures exclusively targeting AFDC recipients (job search activities, unpaid work, job preparation activities, remedial classes, etc.) The links with other broader programs intended for a wider range of participants are less clear than in France. In addition, in the United States, even when social assistance recipients have taken part in programs designed for a broader clientele, such as the programs under the Job Training Partnership Act (JTPA) or offered by educational institutions, they have not had access to an effective manpower policy. Historically speaking, "employment policy" in the United States, if the expression can be used with reference to that country at all, has tended to target specifically the most vulnerable individuals within the general population. Insertion in France has gone beyond the boundaries of social assistance, far more so than in the United States. The professional *insertion* of RMI recipients is clearly connected with the employment policy measures administered by the public employment authorities under the *Agence Nationale pour l'Emploi* (ANPE). In this case, the status of the recipients who have access to this type of *insertion* changes since the activities are generally supported by genuine employment contracts offering the same *rights and duties* as those of other wage earners. The problem is that the employment contracts concerned are mostly for part-time jobs. However, French employment policy is more highly developed than employment policy in the United States

1.10 The current regression: a progressive reduction in the rights of social assistance recipients or a progressive reduction in the rights of wage earners. In the case of the United States, assistance programs have deteriorated because the status of a wage-earner is, in itself, a low-level status. First, low wage levels reduce the upper limit of assistance allowances. Second, the existence of a class of working poor, in its broad meaning, intensifies social polarization and destroys the solidarity existing between the "working poor" and welfare recipients, ruining any possibility of a broad alliance, the necessary prerequisite for a progressive reform of the assistance system. In France, the leveling down of collective protection measures seems to begin in the assistance sphere. Through the employment policy, the wage-earning relationship has, in part, been defined by the policy on the fight against exclusion, to the point where it has actually been transformed. The extent of the professional *insertion* measures has created a zone of intersection between assistance and employment, by gradually taking over *rights* areas through part-time jobs. The way in which poverty is regulated in France has dragged down the terms of the wage-earning relationship. The use of the situation of "excluded" individuals as a point of comparison with the "included" has been used as an excuse to reduce *rights* in the employment sphere. Since, in France, the pathology is sought within society rather than among the actual poor, those who are integrated—according to the ideology of *insiders* (*or insiders/outsiders*)—appear as the bad citizens when compared to the poor, since they have conserved their rights to the detriment of the excluded. In contrast to the U.S. vision, it is not the social assistance recipients whose behavior is at fault, but the "privileged" wage earners. In this way, the problem of exclusion has led to a curious reversal of the situation in which it is not the *rights* of the recipients, as in the United States, but rather the rights of the other citizens that have been called into question.

Some Key Changes since the Mid-1990s in the U.S. and French Social Assistance Systems

In this section, we will review some key changes that have occurred since the mid-1990s in state initiatives or research areas that reflect the transformation of social assistance in the United States and France. The American and French experiences will be presented successively. The points selected reflect our theoretical bias for the analysis of the *rights and duties* of social assistance recipients. Also, we must always bear in mind the extraordinary complexity of the situation investigated here, a complexity resulting from the scope of our research subject—two countries with vastly different institutional settings in employment and social security—and secondly, from the American case's particular features: a federal political system where jurisdiction over social assistance programs such as TANF is mainly state based[5] and where, furthermore, diversity between states has greatly increased as a result of the devolution process underway since the early 1990s.[6] Finally, we must be aware that describing state policy initiatives is one thing, while providing any sense of the implementation process is quite another: the variation of practices at ground level is a great source of complexity.

The enactment of PRWORA in 1996, after two years of strong debate, is undoubtedly the major event of the last years in the field of social assistance, bringing about a complete overhaul of the system.[7] We will look at the goals of the welfare reform, the initiatives taken by states since 1996, above all on employment related aspects, and new research areas.

A key component of the new welfare law is devolution, that is, shifting the control of cash assistance programs from the federal government to the states. Indeed, the purpose of TANF "is to increase flexibility of States in operating a program" designed firstly to "provide assistance to needy families so that children may be cared for in their own homes or in the homes of relatives" (U.S. HR, 2000: 354). But PRWORA "did not simply devolve functions to states: it established specific funding and policy rules, requirements, and signals to encourage and discourage particular state action" (Greenberg, 2001: 20). Thus, devolution also imposed constraints over the states which must follow federal goals primarily through penalties, bonuses, and rules on spending (Greenberg, 2001: 21). This devolution began with the state waivers but culminated with the PRWORA which permitted increased diversity among state welfare programs.

The reform strongly emphasized work. Indeed, the second goal of TANF was to "end the dependence of needy parents on government benefits by promoting job preparation, work, and marriage" (U.S. HR, 2000: 354). Particularly in the earliest stages of the TANF implementation, the "strongest message" of the 1996 law was caseload reduction: "states began to emphasize caseload constriction (strategically termed "dependency reduction") as a policy goal" (Edelhoch, Liu, Martin, and Wiseman, 2001: 2). Efforts to cut caseloads translated into many day-to-day practices, such as imposing new eligibility requirements, terminating grants when requirements were not met, and using sanctions (Greenberg, 2001).[8] This emphasis on work requirements and sanctions was a hardening of the welfare reform initiatives undertaken under the waiver system (Edelhoch, Liu, Martin, and Wiseman, 2001). This reflects the importance of work in the American society—"Americans who leave welfare for work gain the respect our society reserves for workers, even if they gain not a cent of income" (Kaus, 2001: 44). The emphasis on work also reflects public opinion about welfare mothers newly seen as "employable":

> Whenever Americans are polled about social welfare policies, two consistent themes emerge. Two-thirds or more of those surveyed say they support policies that help "the poor" who cannot help themselves, especially children, the elderly, and the disabled. And about two-thirds say that they do not support "welfare." Americans consistently want government to lend a hand to those who cannot provide adequately for themselves, but only if it can do so without discouraging work and promoting independence." (Berlin, 2001: 34)

Behavioral changes targeted not only work, but also family, as shown by the two last goals of TANF: "3. Prevent and reduce the incidence of out-of-wedlock pregnancies and establish annual numerical goals for preventing and reducing the incidence of these pregnancies; and 4. Encourage the formation and maintenance of two-parent families" (U.S. HR, 2000: 354). Supporters of the reform hoped that welfare reform would impact family structure. In a more extensive way, there was a broad spectrum of social problems that reformers were attempting to combat as recipients could be required to improve their lives, such as obtaining a high school diploma, enrolling in parenting education, entering drug treatment, or ensuring that their children are immunized and attend school (U.S. GAO, 2000). Even more radically, as Kaus (2001:1) points out, for "most proponents of reform, the goal was, as Bill Clinton put it, to 'break the culture of poverty' in America's ghettos":

> "...to take a culture characterized by welfare dependence, a high rate of births out-of-wedlock, high male unemployment, and crime and replace it with a new, more virtuous social dynamic, in which every family would be expected to have a breadwinner, and consequently young men and women would have better choices about schooling, marriage, and childbearing." The test for the reform's success, then, is whether in the long run the largely urban, largely minority, welfare-reliant "ghetto-poor" culture is absorbed into the mainstream America culture, whether "underclass" neighborhoods improve, employment rises, the out-of-wedlock birth ratio declines, the streets become safer, and children do better in school.

The description of the welfare policies states adopted after PRWORA reveal a wide diversity in policy choice with substantial variation in provision of entitlement to cash assistance, "diversion" practices, state time limits, work requirements, and the use of contracts to formalize the obligations between the recipients and the state (see table 5.2). Under AFDC, states were required to provide assistance to all families who applied and met the eligibility criteria established under the policy. This provision has been repealed by PRWORA, explicitly stating that Part A of the law "shall not be interpreted to entitle any individual or family to assistance under any State program funded under this part." Even if federal law explicitly denies entitlement to individuals, states, by statute or constitution (such as in New York), are free to create an entitlement to assistance, or to establish rules for the assistance provision in the case of no entitlement. We can see that even if only five states choose entitlement to cash assistance, the majority of states decided that cash assistance benefits "will be provided to all families who are eligible."

Welfare rolls can be reduced by speeding up exit rates, but also by lowering entry rates. To influence the initial openings, states have used what is called "diversion programs," that is, types of assistance provided to divert eligible applicants or recipients from ongoing AFDC/TANF receipt. Programs can include a one-time cash payment, support services (such as child care or medical care), or a combination of the two. Although some states apply a variety of strategies to divert applicants from ongoing AFDC/TANF receipt (such as requiring an applicant to participate in job search), only those programs that provide a cash payment are identified in table 5.2.

Time limits are one of the most radical changes brought about by federal law. While AFDC had no time limit, PRWORA prohibits states from using federal TANF funds to provide assistance to a family with an adult who has received assistance for 60 months in his/her lifetime; a 20 percent hardship exemption applies.[9] However, PRWORA also gave states the option to establish a lower maximum. State time limit policies vary in the time period for which assistance is terminated. In 1999, thirty-six states applied and imposed 60-month time limits, while twenty states had even shorter time limits. On the other hand, states can provide an "exemption" to time limits ("a circumstance under which a month of assistance does not count in determining whether the family has reached the time limit [the "clock stops"]) as well as an "extension" ("a circumstance under which aid may be continued even though the family has reached its time limit"). The majority of states have time limit exemption policies while the reverse holds for time limit extension policies. However, as families began to approach time limits in other states in late 2001 and 2002, it was expected that policies governing extensions would be developed.

According to Fender, McKernan, and Bernstein (2001: 7),[10] the following seven policy elements "might represent the leniency or stringency of state recipient work requirement policies: (1) what is an allowable work activity to meet the requirement; (2) the minimum hours of work required in order to count; (3) how quickly the requirement kicks in, in relation to the onset of cash benefits; (4) who can be exempt from a work requirement; (5) the dollar amount of the most severe sanction; (6) the duration of the sanction; and (7) the dollar amount of the initial sanction." On all these points, state policies vary significantly. Table 5.2 presents information on some of these points. One of the main questions is how states define "work" in order to meet the mandatory work participation rate requirements of the new federal law.[11] In fact, post-TANF welfare-to-work efforts have moved toward a "Work First" approach, even if in 1999, most states allowed all types of work activities to count toward recipient work requirements. This means that since the mid-1990s, state policies have reduced previous access to education (two- or four-year degree programs at postsecondary institutions).

TANF requires work after a maximum of 24 months (the work trigger rule) (U.S. HR, 2000). Only six states adopted PRWORA's maximum two-year time frame before a work requirement applies. Most states' (33) work requirements start immediately (Fender, McKernan, and Bernstein, 2001). Individuals who fail to cooperate without good cause with requirements established in exchange for cash benefits can lose all or part of their allowance and may jeopardize other public benefits as well.[12] Nine of the work activities listed in the statute are highly prioritized.[13] These activities reflect the "Work First" approach promoted by PRWORA. States have considerable flexibility in setting up their sanction policies and a wide variety has been adopted by states. According to the General Accounting Office, "although sanction rates in the states during 1998 were low, about 135,800 families nationwide were under sanctions in an average month during that year" (U.S. GAO: 2000: 38). Sanctioned families "tended to have adults with lower levels of education and less work experience than did the TANF population in general," and to have more than one of these "barriers to employment" (such as a lack of support services like child care and transportation) (U.S. GAO: 2000: 33-34). Also, sanctioned families have a greater incidence of domestic violence, disabilities, and other physical and mental health problems than other welfare families.

Some states require individuals to sign "employability plans" (EP), which are contracts limited to work-related activities or requirements. These differ from "personal responsibility contracts" (PRC), which cover any contracts other than separate employability plans. PRC may include a range of behavioral requirements such as requiring immunization of the child(ren) and can also include work-related requirements (SPDP, 1999). All states use these contracts.

Table 5.2
Description of Welfare Policies States Adopted after PRWORA

State Entitlement Policies

In 1999, five states indicated that they have an explicit entitlement to cash assistance in state statute. Seventeen states have state statutory language which explicitly states that there is no entitlement to cash assistance. Twenty-eight states have no explicit statutory language regarding entitlement. The majority of states (33) have opted to include explicit language in their state policies (statute or regulation), stating that cash assistance benefits will be provided to all families who are eligible. Twenty-three states report having explicit language in state policy that benefit payments are subject to state appropriation or funding (last updated August 29, 2000).

Formal Cash Diversion Programs

Under these programs, families receive an up-front, lump sum payment in lieu of ongoing cash assistance payments. Some twenty-three states operate such programs. For example, a state may give a family three months' worth of cash assistance in a single payment on the condition that the family will be ineligible for a prescribed period of time if the payment is accepted. Alternatively, a state may agree to make a payment on a case-by-case basis to address emergency needs, such as a car repair bill. Some twelve states limit how many times, or how frequently, a family can receive a formal diversion payment, and one state leaves this decision to county discretion. In fifteen states, recipients of diversion payments are ineligible for ongoing cash assistance for a certain time period, and two states permit counties to determine this policy.

State Time Limit Policies

Some states have either a *fixed period* (terminate or reduce assistance for a fixed period of time after which regular assistance can again be provided) or a *lifetime time limit* (terminate or reduce assistance permanently). Other states have both fixed period and lifetime time limits. State policies differ as to whether benefits to the family are terminated or reduced when the time limit is reached. Seven states impose the time limit only on the adult(s) in the family and continue benefits to the children in a reduced amount when the time limit is reached. Time limit policies differ among states in the length of time a family can receive assistance before the time limit is reached. A total of twenty states impose time limits shorter than 60 months that reduce or terminate assistance. A total of thirty-six states impose 60-month time limits. Families have already begun to reach time limits in eighteen states as of June 2000. By January 2001, families will begin to reach the time limit in three additional states. In twenty-eight states, families will not begin to reach time limits until October 2001 or thereafter. In some states, few or no families have lost benefits due to reaching the time limit, largely because of the state's exemption or extension policies. In other states, thousands and, in Connecticut, tens of thousands of families have lost benefits due to the time limit.

Eighteen states have no *time limit exemption* policies. The rest of the states have exemption policies that set forth circumstances under which a month will not count against a state-defined time limit even though an adult is receiving assistance as part of the family. The most frequent reasons for time limit exemptions are that a parent or caretaker is disabled (26 states) or is caring for a disabled household member (22 states). Other time limit exemptions include policies that stop the clock when an adult is caring for a young child (13 states); when an adult is pregnant (10 states); for victims of domestic violence (18 states), and so on. While some states, particularly those in which families are already reaching time limits, have adopted detailed *extension policies*, other states, particularly those that have adopted the TANF 60-month limit, have not yet developed policies governing the specific circumstances under which extensions will be granted. A number of states have adopted a general policy that extensions will be available for up to 20 percent of the caseload on the basis of hardship or domestic violence without further elaboration. Five states have policies that provide no extensions and three states do not yet have policies on extensions (last updated July 20, 2000).

Work Requirement Policies

Allowable activities. In all states, job search is an authorized work activity and counts towards meeting work participation rates. Some forty-two states authorize subsidized employment as a work activity; eight others do not authorize it, and one state allows localities discretion to authorize it. Almost all states (47) authorize vocational educational training as a work activity, with two states not authorizing it, and two states allowing localities to decide the issue. Almost all states (47) authorize adult basic education and English as a Second Language (ESL) as work activities, with three states allowing localities to decide the issue, and one state not authorizing it. Some forty-four states authorize education directly related to employment as a work activity, five do not authorize it, and two leave the issue to local discretion. Most states (45) authorize on-the-job training as a work activity, two leave the decision to local discretion, and four states do not allow it. Most states (47) authorize job skills training as a work activity. Unpaid community service is an authorized activity in thirty-four states and not authorized in fifteen. One state leaves the decision to local discretion. Unpaid work experience is an authorized activity in forty-four states and not authorized in five states. Almost all states (48) authorize job readiness as an activity, with one state not authorizing it, and two leaving it to local discretion. In nearly half the states (21), participation in postsecondary degree programs can meet the state work requirement for longer than the 12 months countable toward TANF participation rate requirements. Of the twenty-one states, nine allow participation in postsecondary education alone to meet the state work requirement. Twelve states allow participants to meet the state work requirement for more than 12 months by combining postsecondary degree programs with some work. In thirteen more states, postsecondary education can meet the work requirement for up to 12 months. Four of the thirteen states allow postsecondary degree programs as a stand-alone activity. In another thirteen states, participation in a postsecondary degree program does not meet the state work requirement. Most of these states do allow up to 12 months of vocational educational training, which, depending on the state's definition, may include community college training programs. Four more states leave it to counties to decide whether to allow participation in postsecondary degree programs to meet the work requirement.

Hourly Participation Requirements. Some thirty-nine states require that single adult recipients receiving TANF participate in work activities for a set number of hours per week. Ten states determine hours of participation on an individual basis and two states allow localities to set the required hours of participation. In FY 2000, the majority of states with a fixed hourly participation requirement set the number of hours at the federal participation rate level of 30 hours per week (27 of the 39 states), with three of these states allowing adult recipients with children under age six to work 20 hours per week. Some six states set the hourly requirement higher, ranging from 32 to 40 hours per week. Some five states set the hourly requirement lower, ranging from 20 to 29 hours per week. Most states (24) do not require a fixed sequence of work activities for recipients subject to the work requirement (last updated January 2, 2001).

Sanction
Partial sanctions result in a grant reduction by a percentage of the total grant or a flat amount. Thirty-six states impose partial sanctions for initial instances of non-compliance for some or all groups of families. In seventeen of the thirty-six states that impose partial sanctions at some point, the adult portion of the grant is removed and reduced benefits continue for the children for the duration of the sanction. In another seventeen states, the grant is reduced by a percentage, usually 25 to 50 percent. Two states reduce the grant by

a flat amount of $50 or $100. A full-family sanction terminates cash assistance to the entire family. Thirty-six states impose full-family sanctions at some point during the sanction process. In half of these states (18), full-family sanctions are imposed immediately for any instance of non-compliance for some or all groups of families. In nine states, sanctions are always lifted once the individual complies with the work activity. In thirty-nine states, sanctions are imposed for a set time period, which can go beyond the time the individual complies. In seven states, assistance can be terminated permanently for non-compliance. In most states, sanction durations increase after each instance of non-compliance or with continued non-compliance (last updated June 6, 2001).

Personal Responsibility Contracts and Employability Plans

All states require individuals to sign either a *personal responsibility contract* or an employability plan; some seventeen states require both. Of the thirty-five states that require a personal responsibility contract, two states require applicants to sign before filing an application, twenty-two require applicants to sign when they apply or while the application is pending, ten require signing after eligibility is determined, and in one state, the point at which signing is required varies depending on when the client attends an orientation session. Obligations included in personal responsibility contracts include participation in work activities, child and/or minor parent school attendance, cooperation with child support enforcement requirements, child immunization or preventive health measures, participation in life skills or parenting training, substance abuse provisions, and agreement to achieve self-sufficiency within a set time period. In twenty-seven of the thirty-five states, personal responsibility contracts include a state or county agreement to provide services to the individual. There are no exemptions from the requirement to sign a personal responsibility contract in nineteen of the thirty-five states. In the other sixteen states, exemption criteria include those exempt from work requirements, caring for a young child, and disabled caretakers. The sanction for not signing a personal responsibility contract is the same as the sanction for failing to comply with work requirements in sixteen states. Some fourteen states deny benefits to individuals who do not sign a contract. Four more states impose a partial benefit sanction, and one state does not impose a sanction for failing to sign a personal responsibility contract. Of the thirty-three states that require an *employability plan*, no state requires applicants to sign before filing an application, five require applicants to sign while the application is pending, eighteen require signing after eligibility is determined, and in ten states the point at which signing is required varies. One state did not provide this information. In twenty-three of the thirty-three states, employability plans include a state or county agreement to provide services to the individual. There are no exemptions from the requirement to sign an employability plan in three of the thirty-three states. In the other thirty states, exemption criteria include those exempt from work requirements, those caring for a young child, disabled caretakers, and those working in unsubsidized employment for some minimum number of hours per week. The sanction for not signing an employability plan is the same as the sanction for failing to comply with work requirements in twenty states. Six states deny benefits to individuals who do not sign a contract, and one state gives counties discretion to determine the sanction amount. Six states do not impose a sanction for failing to sign an employability plan (last updated March 3, 2000).

Source: Extracts from State Policy Documentation Project (SPDP); http://www.spdp.org; site inform. as posted on 1.11. 2002.

Beside restrictive measures, the 1996 reform also resulted also in increased support services that mirror the fact that TANF "is a funding stream for a variety of allowed purposes, not just a program of cash welfare aid" (U.S. HR, 2000: 354). Firstly, the 1996 law sharply expanded funding for child care (U.S. HR, 2000), even if TANF contains no child care guarantees.[14] TANF combined the major previous federal child care funding sources into a single Child Care and Development Fund (CCDF) block grant. The amounts appropriated for the new Child Care and Development Block Grant (CCDBG), which constitutes the mandatory funds of the CCDF, was $13.9 billion over six years, "more than $4 billion above spending levels estimated by the Congressional Budget Office for the repealed AFDC-related child care programs" (U.S. HR, 2000: 360). In fact, "public child care funding has grown from roughly $2 billion in 1990 to at least triple that level just a decade later, and, in contrast to ten years ago when some states basically had no subsidy system, every state now has a public child care subsidy system to help low-income families." (Adams, Holcomb, and Snyder, 2001: 1)[15] Secondly, states provide other post-employment benefits and services (case management services, retention bonuses, transportation allowances, etc.) designed to help welfare-leavers who find a job to remain employed or to find another job if they leave the first one. Thirdly, spending increased for substance abuse treatment, mental health counseling, domestic violence services, transportation, and related services (Greenberg, 2001). Increased spending on services "resulted probably from substantial new money for states coming from block grants reflecting the 1994-1995 peak federal spending and caseloads in the context of falling welfare rolls" (Greenberg, 2001). Finally, states have expanded their services to a much broader group of poor families and thus, a growing number are creating innovative initiatives (such as education and training, tuition assistance, individual training accounts, etc.) designed to assist working, low-income families in general, and not just TANF recipients.[16] Child care policy underwent a similar evolution as TANF expanded the CCDBG to apply to low-income families (U.S. HR, 2000). However, as for benefits related to cash assistance for TANF recipients, the problems were major: although many former recipients remain eligible for Medicaid and the Food Stamp program, "receipt of these benefits drops off precipitously when families leave welfare" (Loprest, 2001: 5). The federal and state governments have also set up major financial incentives to stimulate higher employment among welfare recipients. First, after TANF became law, many states (25) increased their earnings disregard, that is, the exemption of a part of recipient's earnings in calculating income for eligibility or benefit computation purposes, to "make work pay" (Fender, McKernan, and Bernstein, 2001). Secondly, employee-based subsidies, with the same goal of raising the job-related income, have been greatly expanded, whether at the federal level or at the state level. The federal Earned Income Tax Credit (EITC), the largest existing subsidy of this type,[17] which was increased in 1987, 1991,

1994, and 2001, continued to grow. In 1999, the EITC was claimed by 19.2 million families and individuals; in 2001, the maximum EITC benefit was $4,008 for families with two or more children (Johnson, 2001). With its constant expansion, EITC "has recently begun to attract more criticism as a 'welfare' program" (Bartik, 2001: 78). In addition to the federal EITC, in 2001, sixteen states offered state EITC's based on the federal credit (Johnson, 2001). Also, two federal employer-based subsidies, the Work Opportunity Tax Credit (WOTC) and the Welfare to Work Tax Credit (WWTC), were created in 1997 and 1998, respectively, in order to stimulate the hiring of target groups by the payment of a percentage of wages. In addition to these national wage subsidy programs, fifteen states had some sort of tax-based wage subsidy for private employers who hired disadvantaged groups (Bartik, 2001).[18]

In some segments of the labor market, welfare reform generated negative impacts. For example, in New York City, which was singled out as an area likely to exhibit a low-skill unemployment increase following the arrival of welfare leavers in the workforce (Lerman, Loprest, and Ratcliffe, 1999), paid positions were replaced through attrition by workfare workers assignments. The city's rapid expansion of its workfare program, the nation's largest with more than 35,000 welfare workers (Greenhouse, 1999), led the union representing municipal employees to assert in a lawsuit filed on April 15, 1999, "that the Giuliani administration has illegally replaced nearly 2,000 unionized clerical workers with unpaid welfare recipients for jobs once held by city workers" (Jacobs, 1999). For Diller (1998), workfare in New York did not help participants to find permanent jobs but offered a workforce that was low-cost and docile because of its vulnerability:

> The New York City Department of Sanitation, one of the principal "employers" of workfare workers in the city, has not hired a single workfare worker into a job. The two principal impacts of workfare have been a significant decline in public assistance caseloads, as the program drives individuals off the rolls, and improved municipal services. Parks, streets, vacant lots and municipal buildings have become cleaner during a period when the number of municipal employees has fallen by more than 15,000. In fact, municipal officials credit workfare workers with "saving" their agencies at a time of large budget cuts. In other words, workfare has enabled the City of New York to replace a portion of its well-paid unionized workforce with public assistance recipients, who are paid at a fraction of the amount and receive none of the "fringe" benefits, such as vacations, pension plans, and private health insurance, that City workers traditionally receive. It has been estimated that the WEP program saves the City of New York $600 million a year compared with the cost of hiring employees to perform the same work. Instead of helping welfare recipients obtain jobs, New York's workfare program is eroding the job base. (p.31)

This raises the issue of employment rights of workfare participants and displaced workers, which, although a problem long before the 1996 reform (Dietrich, Emsellem, and Kithan Yau, 1997), has taken on greater importance since then due to TANF's emphasis on work. Even if administrative rulings tend to guarantee participants in workfare programs the same level of protection as others who can establish an "employment" relationship protected under the federal statutes,[19] in "a given situation, there may be a question as to whether an employment relationship exists, or there may be an applicable exemption under the federal statute that is either generally applicable to employees in similar circumstances (such as public employees) or particularly applicable to welfare recipients in work programs" (Dietrich, Emsellem, and Paradise, 2000: 2). Lack of enforcement of employment rights is also "particularly problematic" for those in workfare programs (Dietrich, Emsellem, and Paradise, 2000). The unequal protection for welfare workers and unionized workers led unions to officially support the organization of workfare participants in order to grant them access to "the same rights as other workers" (Greenhouse, 1997). On the other hand, the problem of poverty despite work is still very worrisome: "In 2000, a greater percentage of the poor had one full-time worker in the family than in 1993 (44.5 percent compared with 36.0 percent). Thus, even though people with working family members were less likely to be poor in 2000 compared with 1993, the poor were more likely to have a working family member" (Dalaker, 2001: 8). Also, since 1994, the national "living wage" movement has seen great growth: today, more than seventy-five living wage campaigns are underway across the country (ACORN, 2002).[20]

At the implementation level of workfare, the privatization of workfare services is another clear change occurring within the welfare system. Devolution, which accelerated with the 1996 reform, granted states broad latitude to reorganize welfare delivery. States took advantage of this opportunity to restructure their institutional arrangements for policy delivery: "in the aftermath of welfare reform, there appears to be an explosion in the privatization of welfare delivery, as new contracting regimes shift responsibility for putting welfare recipients to work from public welfare agencies to private contractors" (Brodkin, Fuqua, and Thoren, 2001: 3). For example, in Chicago, before TANF, "services intended to prepare and place welfare recipients in paid employment were conducted largely in-house within the state welfare agency. Since TANF, over a four-year period, the number of private agencies receiving contracts nearly doubled, and, more significantly, the amount of public funds going to private contractors increased by 700 percent" (Brodkin, Fuqua, and Thoren, 2001: 1). The vast majority of private contractors were nonprofit contractors, but the relative share of for-profit contractors had increased in FY 2001 to make up 21 percent of the total (Brodkin, Fuqua, and Thoren, 2001). According to Park and Van Voorhis (2001: 192), TANF "promotes retrenchment of public delivery through privatization" which becomes an attractive option for states "faced with decreasing budgets and financial penalties for failure to meet new employment requirements." Thus, privatization reflects the "states' growing acceptance of important market principles, infusion of competition, maximisation of benefit for all parties, and the need for customized services—as a mean to effectuating lasting change" (Park and Van Voorhis, 2001: 192). The "market-driven world of corporate providers may create incentives to deny aid if the providers' profits are linked to reducing the welfare roll" (Park and Van Voorhis, 2001: 207). Another clear change in the welfare delivery system is the growing closeness between welfare and workforce services. Under the Workforce Investment Act (WIA) of August 1998, states may engage in unified planning allowed for welfare and workforce development programs, and that will ease the transition from welfare to work and also lead to the upgrading of low-income working parents' skills and provide access to better jobs (Strawn and Martinson, 2000). Thus, the Labor Department agencies are increasingly engaged in service delivery for welfare recipients.

With PRWORA, reform activity directed toward "strategies to promote responsible behaviour"—in effect a new strain of social engineering using welfare policies and rules to encourage socially desirable behaviors" (Maynard et al., 1998: 135)—reached its peak. The focus was put on the regulation of family behaviors, "personal decisions about marriage and cohabitation, decisions affecting family stability (for example, divorce and other family composition changes), fertility decisions, and the quality of parenting" (Maynard et al., 1998: 135). Policy initiatives to promote the family-related goals of TANF included imposing a family cap, that is, paying no benefit or a reduced benefit for a new baby born to a mother already on welfare.[21] PRWORA stayed silent on the family cap: implementation decisions regarding family cap policy were left to the states (Harris, 2001). In 2001, twenty-three states, representing around 52 percent of the nation's TANF caseload, had implemented some type of family cap (Harris, 2001). Only eight states had implemented the family cap policy after welfare reform; the fifteen remaining states implemented the policy under a waiver to the AFDC program (Harris, 2001). During an average month in 2000, twenty of the twenty-three family cap states reported that approximately 108,000 families received less in cash benefits than they would have if their benefits had not been capped, representing about 9 percent of TANF families in these states; the monthly loss was about 20 percent of the cash assistance (Harris, 2001: 13). However, on the whole, states were not as active on family issues as on employment-related issues; similarly, HHS's research efforts were focused on employment-related goals (Harris, 2001). Also, in view of the 2002 TANF Reauthorization, more than fifty state leaders recently wrote to Congress requesting that it designate 10 percent of welfare funds for pro-marriage and family-strengthening activities (Wetzstein, 2001).

What, ultimately, were the results obtained in terms of employment and marriage?[22] In 1999, the national TANF caseload was about half the size (48 percent) of AFDC peak level of 1994 (U.S. HR, 2000). The employment rate of single mothers rose from 57 percent in 1992 to almost 71 percent in 1999

(U.S. HR, 2000). But "welfare caseloads have fallen far more rapidly than child poverty, many families have lost their benefits without finding work, and many who have found work have had little or no increase in economic well-being" (Greenberg, 2001: 200). If poverty decreased among lone mothers, among the poorest mothers (the lowest quintile) income fell "because these mothers have lost more in cash welfare and food stamps than they have gained in earnings and the earned income credit" (U.S. HR, 2000: 1409). And between 1995 and 1999, among people in families headed by working single mothers, there was no progress in reducing poverty because reductions in poverty as a result of economic growth were entirely offset by increases in poverty due to contractions in government safety net programs (Porter and Dupree, 2001). During discussions on welfare reform, the proportion of out-of-wedlock births began to decrease after having risen for over a century (Harris, 2001). A substantial decline in teen pregnancy rates occurred in the 1990s (Edelhoch, Liu, Martin, and Wiseman, 2001). In sum, "ending dependency through job preparation, work, and marriage may be an elusive goal. It appears that welfare initiatives have little or no impact on marriage. And although welfare-to-work programs generally increase earnings and employment, they do not necessarily end dependence and raise income. At least in the short run, many TANF recipients will not be able to escape poverty through work unless taxpayers provide an earnings supplement of some kind" (U.S. HR, 2000: 1410-1411).

Lastly, the welfare reform, with its strong emphasis on employment, has caused the emergence of new research areas since the mid-1990s. This is the case, firstly, for the "welfare leavers" studies, which "constitute the bulk of research available since enactment of TANF" (U.S. HR, 2000: 1407). Welfare leaver studies show that those who are working usually have part-time, low-wage jobs, without important benefits such as paid sick days and health insurance. For these low wage earners, employment is often intermittent, involves nonstandard hours, and ever changing schedules; also, "many recipients remain poor or near poor, even years after leaving welfare" (Strawn and Martinson, 2000: 11, 12, 13). From that perspective, recent public policy initiatives and research have focused on "retention issues," that is, on increasing job tenure among TANF clients, as well as on career mobility and wage progression opportunities for low-wage workers. In addition, the TANF requirement that agencies work with the entire welfare caseload brought "a new urgency" to the question of how best to help welfare recipients move from welfare to work (Hamilton et al., 2001).

Research on labor market insecurity is also present. Therefore, considering that many studies emphasizing "employment barriers" "tend to locate employment instability within workers rather than workplaces," some researchers examine "the structure and nature of lower-wage work with particular attention to features that create instabilities for workers and that make it an unreliable source of income, especially in the absence of other income supports"

(Lambert, Waxman, and Haley-Lock, 2001: 3-4). Unemployment insurance, and its links with welfare, has been also a subject of renewed interest. As a higher percentage of women enter employment, employment-related social benefits take on greater importance. This is all the more true at the present time since unemployment insurance is particularly poorly suited to providing effective protection for the most vulnerable workers (part-timers, low wage earners, intermittent workers), such as former welfare recipients (Lovell and Hill, 2001). In a weakened U.S. economy, this situation is further worsened as unemployment insurance problems and policy challenges increase. Finally, TANF influenced the unemployment insurance reform. Indeed, in the second half of the 1990s, legislation dramatically altered the nature and functioning of the unemployment insurance system, with the emphasis overwhelmingly placed on the return to work (Corson and Spiegelman, 2001). Thus these changes in the unemployment insurance system were foreshadowed in the welfare reform: the WIA "includes many of the characteristics of the PRWORA for the (unemployment insurance) system. The emphasis on speedy reemployment, with training provided only if necessary to obtain employment; the philosophy is that the best training is a job" (Corson and Spiegelman, 2001: 5).

Child care continues to be the pivotal issue for women alone with children. This is an inevitable outcome of the emphasis put on women's employment and, consequently, of the child care needs of families moving from welfare to work. Thus, both in terms of policy and in the lives of individual families, public subsidies for child care are gaining importance (Adams, Holcomb, and Snyder, 2001). More broadly, work-family combination issues are becoming an increasingly pressing social issue in the United States not only for parents leaving welfare for work but also for working parents at large. A number of studies have indicated that work-family conflicts "are one of the principal reasons that parents who leave welfare for work are unable to keep their jobs" (Heymann and Earle, 1998: 314). Many researchers argue that it is not realistic to expect single parents living in poverty to combine full-time work with parenting as long as much of the employment increase in the United States has been in two-parent families, with both partners participating in child care and employment and where most of married mothers work only part time or part year (Heymann and Earle, 1998). Furthermore, "mothers who returned to work from welfare were significantly more likely than other working mothers to lack the benefits they needed to succeed at work while caring for their children" (Heymann and Earle, 1998: 316).

Under the investigation of the "barriers to employment," other crucial though previously neglected issues for women have come to the fore, namely violence against women and health issues. Again, these issues reflect the distinctiveness of situations experienced by women TANF recipients. Domestic violence, which seriously impairs the ability of welfare mothers to enter or remain in employment, and to collaborate with welfare agencies for child support payments are now being documented (Scott, London, and Myers, 2002). Health problems of welfare recipients, namely mental health in general and depression in particular, are also becoming a focus of attention (Lennon, Blome, and English, 2001). From that perspective, the relation of depression to welfare, employment, and job retention is investigated.

If we now turn our attention to France, we can observe major changes since the mid-1990s. A decade after the unanimous acceptance of the RMI, a significant new direction was taken by the French government in the implementation of public policies against exclusion. An overall approach to prevention and opposition to all forms of exclusion was introduced with a broad governmental program made up of a three-year action plan, adopted in March 1998, and a framework law on exclusion, enacted in July 1998: the *Loi d'orientation sur la lutte contre les exclusions* (LOLE) (orientation law on the battle against exclusion). By the nature of its goals and the ambitious scope of its means, the LOLE takes the intervention logic of the RMI even further. For the French government, this set of measures is inseparable from a broad range of economic and social measures in which employment plays a key role. Thus, we will look not only at the LOLE goals and the French government's initiatives concerning the exclusion policy but also in the related employment policy area, and at the new issues that have been central to the French debates: concerns about poverty and exclusion.

In France, as in the United States, a process of empowerment of local authorities through the transfer of power to the regions and the "local collectivities" (*collectivités locales*) is well underway, though designated differently than in the United States, as a "decentralization" process. In fact, regions have been strongly involved in the implementation of the personalized support services for the unemployed. But the decentralization process operates only on the insertion side, while on the benefit side, the RMI remains uniform across the country.

The RMI program had three goals: to guarantee a minimum income, access to social rights (health care, housing, work injury insurance for "insertion" activities), and finally access to *insertion*. The LOLE lends new resources and strengthens the public authority action plan which led to the RMI. The "anti-exclusion" law represents an integrated approach to the promotion of fundamental rights. The new scheme covers all aspects of the "excluded's" life, from employment to education, and including health, housing, debt, and even culture (see table 5.3). The spirit that led to the institution of *insertion* in RMI is dominant in the LOLE in two broad dimensions, occupational and social, and in all their multiple connections to a whole range of aspects of life in society. The first article of the LOLE reads as follows: "The combat against exclusions is a national imperative based on the respect of the equal dignity of all human beings and a priority of the whole of the public policies of the nation" (PNAFPES, 2001: 9).[23]

The objective of the LOLE is not to set up new rights but to give substance to the rights already existing in the legal system, according to the law's presentation (Liaisons sociales, 1998). It is argued that it is not permissible that poverty be allowed to decrease people's capability to exercise their rights (Liaisons sociales, 1998). As can be clearly seen in table 5.3, four broad directions are set out. Firstly, the objective of the program is to guarantee access to fundamental rights, understood as a springboard towards social reinsertion. The program states that it is pointless to try to put in place a real cohesion policy—the aim of public policies being to help social assistance recipients to no longer need assistance—if access to employment, decent housing, and health care continue to be theoretical principles without real efficacy. The second orientation is the prevention of exclusions. It is emphasized that this law represents a change of perspective in that intervention is imperative to prevent the problems that are the program's focus. The government states that this policy, aimed at improving the situation of the poorest of the poor, must be created in collaboration with the poor. Thirdly, the plan specifies that the state and its partners must be able to respond effectively to emergency situations, when all preventive measures have failed. Lastly, the fourth orientation affirms the importance of concerted action against exclusion, that is, the recognition that prevention and action demand the coordinated action of the various measures on the part of the policy's key players (Liaisons sociales, 1998).

With regard to occupational integration, which dominates social insertion in RMI, various measures have followed the introduction of the 1998 law. State's initiatives have focused on different plans of "pathways to employment," on job creation, and on financial incentives.[24] With regard to the pathways to employment, two broad sets of support measures for groups excluded from employment were put in place to enhance the "accompaniment" both towards and within employment. These programs were the *Nouveau Départ* (ND) (New Departure Towards Employment) program and the *trajet d'accès à l'emploi* (TRACE) (career path access to employment) program. Both programs were part of the first *Plan National d'action pour l'Emploi* (PNAE) (National Action Plan for Employment), which France presented in 1998 at the European level and which is partially funded by Social Europe funds. The ND program, inaugurated in October 1998, brings into reality a right that is laid out in the 4th article of the 1998 law, the right to an individualized path toward employment for some unemployed groups, in particular the long-term unemployed. The goal of the program is to promote a return to work through either job search assistance, vocational training or a personalized follow-up plan and combined with social support. The year 1998 saw 120,000 people enter the program.[25] In 1999, 800,000 citizens benefited from the ND program; 1 million in 2000 (PNAFPES, 2001). The complete implementation of the program has as its goal to assist 2 million job seekers.[26] On the other hand, the

TRACE program is designed for specific categories of hard-pressed young people in the 16 to 25 age range. It is to be noted that the RMI does not cover the poor under 25 years old, unless they have dependent children. The 5th article of the law against exclusions indicates that the state is taking the initiative to implement a stronger and more personalized insertion path plan for this group of young people at risk of being occupationally excluded. The TRACE program offers these young people an ongoing individualized support plan for the transition to regular employment over a maximum 18-month time period (Eironline, 2001b). The program helped 51,000 in 2000, while 60,000 more young people were to enter the program in 2001 (PNAFPES, 2001). The French Government has expressed satisfaction at the results obtained thus far: 54 percent of the young people who left the TRACE program are either employed or in training (PNAFPES, 2001).

Table 5.3
La loi d'orientation contre les exclusions **(LOLE)**

A Global Plan

Access to fundamental rights
Access to employment. Every young person or adult, any citizen facing long-term unemployment or problems of professional nature will have the right to personalized support service.... For young people, the *trajet d'accès à l'emploi* (TRACE) (career path access to employment) program will offer an individualized insertion path plan (*parcours d'insertion individualisé*), up to a maximum time period of 18 months (60,000 per year). Twenty percent of the "New Services-Jobs for Young People" program (*Nouveaux services-emplois jeunes*) will be set aside for young people living in underprivileged neighbourhoods... For adults, the overall service capacity and support mechanisms of the public service for employment will be strengthened; a work-study program (*formation en alternance*), on the model of the *contrat de qualification* (qualification contract), will be set up on a trial basis; the *contrats emplois consolidés* (consolidated employment contracts)[27] will be increased and adapted in order to benefit groups experiencing the greatest difficulty. At the same time, the service capacity of *insertion* enterprises will be doubled over a three-year period.

The right to housing. In addition to the increase in the intervention means of the *fonds de solidarité logement* (FSL) (housing solidarity fund), the program makes provision for an increase of housing availability for the disadvantaged (adoption of subsidized rental loans) and a tax on housing left vacant, requisitions and easier access to the social subsidized housing...

Access to care. Universal medical coverage (*couverture maladie universelle,* CMU) will be put in place in 1999, in order to enable anyone aged 16 years or over to be affiliated with the general Social Security regime. A supplementary protection will be implemented in order to guarantee free medical care to the most in need.

Access to education. The education priority zones (*zones d'éducation prioritaire*) will be reactivated, free school support and supervision services will be developed...

Access to culture. Contracts with objectives will be agreed upon with the local groups (*collectivités locales*) and associations in order to promote cultural practices.

The prevention of exclusions

- Means of existence will be guaranteed to the most needy.... Social minima will be price indexed. To encourage the return to employment, ASS, RMI, and API[28] recipients who return to employment will be authorized to combine for a one-year period, on a digressive basis, both their benefits and their earnings.

- A reform in the cure of overdebtedness will make it possible to allow a basic living allowance to the people concerned and to spread their debts over eight years instead of five.

- The remaining in housing will be encouraged by the prevention of evictions (a rehousing supply will be used before the use of police services).

- The exercise of citizenship will be made easier: the right to vote will be given to the homeless, the increase in "*maisons de justic*" (justice houses)...

- The access to sports and tourism will be reinforced: sport-tickets facilitating the membership for young people in sport associations, *solidarité vacances* (vacation-solidarity) fellowships...

Responses to emergency situations

Access to water, electricity, and natural gas will be guaranteed to the most needy. The scheme of social vigilance will become general and unified by the implementation of an emergency cell unit network. The emergency housing network will be strengthened and major renovations will make the centers more inviting.

The increased efficiency of public action

While mobilizing the involved parties, the state will make sure of the efficacy and coherence of the actions undertaken. This will translate into renewed training for the social professions, in the setting, at the end of 1998, of an *Observatoire des phénomènes d'exclusion* (Observatory of exclusion phenomena), and the implementation of an interministerial committee overseeing the negotiation of agreements between the local partners.

Source: Excerpt from J. Fenoglio (1998). *La France est le seul pays européen à se doter d'une loi contre l'exclusion, Le Monde,* 21 mai, *in* J. Damon, *Les politiques d'insertion, Problèmes économiques et sociaux,* Paris: La Documentation Française, No 807:72; translation by the writer.

Job creation has been a major strategy course for RMI recipients since the program's inception. This focus has translated into diverse types of contracts, which have differed along activity content, target groups, organizations involved, and so on. The *contrats emploi solidarité* (CES) (employment solidarity contracts) have been the major job creation initiative for RMI recipients.

CES are temporary, part-time contracts, subsidized contracts (20 hours per week, for a period of three months to two years) targeting the nonprofit sector. In 1992, the *contrats emploi consolidé* (CEC) (consolidated employment contracts) were created as a follow up to the CES for RMI recipients unemployed for one year. CEC contracts apply the same to employers as CES contracts but are targeted to groups with specific problems. The contracts can be either full or part time and can be extended to twelve months, renewable for a maximum of five years. In 1995, the *contrats initiative emploi* (CIE) (employment initiative contracts) were created. The CIE are regular labor contracts subsidizing private sector employers. In CES, CEC, or CIE, as specified above (1.9), welfare recipients gain regular employee status, with all the corresponding rights and duties.[29] The 1998 anti-exclusion law refocused CES and CEC even further on priority groups, including RMI recipients, and also allowed direct access to CEC. The spaces in CES were subsequently reduced (PNAFPES, 2001). More recently, in October 2001, in the face of an economic downturn that had begun a few months earlier—the unemployment rate, which had been declining rapidly since 1997, began to increase in April 2001—the creation of 30,000 new CES and 20,000 new training and employment insertion courses (SIFE) was announced by the Minister of Employment (Eironline, 2001a).

Since the mid-1990s, occupational integration of RMI recipients has been increasingly linked to French employment policy. First of all, the CES, CEC, CIE are administered by the public employment service, the *Agence nationale pour l'emploi*, ANPE (National Employment Agency). As well, the employment policy measures cover not only RMI recipients but many categories of users. Secondly, with the ND and TRACE programs, ANPE has been more intensely mobilized towards personalized aid for the unemployed experiencing the most difficulty. Since January 2001, the public employment service has set national and local monthly goals for the long-term unemployment exit rate of RMI recipients (PNAF-PEF, 2001). A third impetus contributing to the intensification of support measures for the excluded, implemented by the ANPE, stemmed from France's involvement at the European level.

In fact, French interventions against exclusion have also been increasingly linked to European initiatives. It was under the French presidency that the European Council (EC) became involved in October 1997 in the fight against exclusion (Liaisons sociales, 1998). At the Nice summit of December 2000, the new European strategy of a united combat against poverty and social exclusion was launched, as the fifteen Member States of the EU adopted common objectives in this area. Thus, along with other EU members, in June 2001, France presented a national action plan to carry out this strategy: the French National Action Plan against Poverty and Social Exclusion (*Plan national d'action français contre la pauvreté et l'exclusion sociale*). At the European level, these initiatives show the deepening of the Social Europe. For France, this national action plan is seen as a new step forward, after the triennial plan and the LOLE of 1998, in the public policies against exclusion, to "make it possible to improve the effective access to fundamental rights for everyone and to implement a true equality of opportunity (*égalité des chances*) in access to employment" (PNAFPES, 2001: 9).[30] The French plan reviews existing policies and presents those that are foreseen over the next two years in the four areas defined at the European level: universal access to fundamental rights, especially in matters of employment, the prevention of situations of exclusion, the protection of vulnerable groups, and the mobilization of society as a whole (PNAFPES, 2001). In accordance with this plan, a new public employment service, the *programme d'action personnalisé pour un nouveau départ* (PAP/ND) (Personalized Service for a New Departure Towards Employment) was set up in July 2001. This program expands on the previous individualized service of the ND program. Therefore, PAP/ND becomes a reality through the development of a personalized plan, set up with an ANPE counselor, based on an ongoing and increased social service availability continuing until the return to employment, instead of four months, as was previously.[31] This measure accompanies the new unemployment insurance agreement,[32] but will cover all unemployed, whether or not they are unemployment insurance recipients (PNAFPES, 2001). Under this second program to fight exclusion, the TRACE program is also extended through the doubling of the number of young people accepted into the program and the creation of a new grant for participants (Eironline, 2001b).

Job creation is also directed to young people. In October 1997, a new job creation program for those under the age of 26 was launched under the name of the *Nouveaux services-emplois jeunes* (NSEJ) (New Services-Jobs for Young People) program. Its purpose is to "create and develop new activities that have social utility and which correspond to emerging or as yet unsatisfied local needs and to allow 350,000 young people to perform these activities and gain professional experience of the corresponding employment environment."[33] The youth employment contracts signed under the NSEJ program are regular labor contracts that can be either of an unlimited duration or for a fixed term of 60 months.[34] This program considerably boosted the creation of jobs in the service sector. Between October 1997 and June 2001, more than 312,000 young people were employed under this program. At that point, it was predicted that the number of young people hired would exceed 350,000 by the fall of 2001 (MES, 2001).

The major job creation initiative in France since the mid-1990s and the best example of the high degree of development in French employment policy, has been the working time policy. The laws on negotiated workweek reduction have been the key event in the field of the employment policy in France since the 1980s. This law was aimed primarily at stimulating job growth in order to reduce unemployment. Competitiveness as well as improved working conditions and an improved balance between career and personal life were the other objectives pursued by these laws. In brief, these laws establish a new, legal workweek limit of 35 hours, spell out the rules governing overtime, and set forth new arrangements for organizing work hours. New tax breaks on employer contributions were also introduced. Finally, a wage guarantee system for minimum-wage employees was created.[35]

A striking tendency in France in recent years has been the growing use of financial incentives to stimulate employment of low-skilled workers, including RMI recipients. Firstly, on the employment policy side, the French government has taken initiatives in allowing social insurance contribution exemptions so as to decrease labor costs. Therefore, in 1996, while the amounts devoted to measures aimed at lowering labor costs amounted to 40 billion FF ($5.7 billion) (Cornilleau and Gubian, 1997), the exonerations of social insurance premiums for "low wage" earners reached 80 billion FF ($11.4 billion) in 1999 (Mills and Caudron, 2001).

With the additional tax breaks on employer contributions included in the laws on the 35-hour work week, the exonerations should exceed 100 billion FF ($14.3 billion) in 2001 and 2002 (Mills and Caudron, 2001). Secondly, previous RMI income disregards were strengthened by the 1998 law against exclusions:[36] the combining of the benefit and earnings was completely allowed during the first trimester (for the portion of the wage below half-SMIC[37]) and partially thereafter (50 percent of earnings were reduced during a maximum period of fifteen months) (Afsa, 1999). In 2001, the PNAFPES extended the length of the period for combining earnings and social assistance benefits, including RMI benefits, up to a 100 percent rate (PNAFPES, 2001). Thirdly, in January 2001, a new wage supplementation program for low wage earners was introduced—the *prime pour l'emploi* (PPE) (employment premium)—in order to incite the return to or the maintenance of employment. This tax credit covers wage earners whose wages do not exceed 1.4 times the SMIC (2.1 SMIC for lone-parents or for households with only one wage earner). Nine million workers should be eligible for this credit for a total of 25 billion FF ($3.6 billion) over a three-year period (Mills and Caudron, 2001: 227). The PNAFPES announced that PPE would double in 2002 and would apply to almost 10 million people in 2001 (PNAFPES, 2001).

With regard to the question of the occupational integration of the poor, a major change occurred in 2000 from within the unemployment insurance system. The negotiation of the new unemployment insurance agreement at the *Union nationale pour l'emploi dans l'industrie et le commerce* (UNEDIC) (National Union for Industrial and Commercial Employment) became a political milestone event in the field of social security in France. In 2000, a highly controversial debate was sparked by the reform proposals put forth by the *Mouvement des entreprises de France* (MEDEF) (French enterprises movement), the largest employer organization in France. Controversy was centered around the plan to create a new contract, the *contrat d'aide au retour à l'emploi* (CARE)

(Return to Employment Assistance Contract), which emphasized the principle of "tied aid" in the unemployment insurance program: both the funding for training and eligibility for the receipt of unemployment insurance benefits were to be conditional upon both the signature of the CARE contract and the participation in a training course that made a rapid return to employment possible (Yerochewski, 2001). This project drew almost unanimous opposition (Mills and Caudron, 2001).[38] As well, the government in the end negotiated that the benefit would be independent from the contract (Yerochewski, 2001). This is how a new agreement, signed for the period from July 1, 2000 to December 31, 2003, came to replace CARE: the *Plan d'aide au retour à l'emploi* (PARE) (Return to Employment Assistance Plan). The PARE "defines the reciprocal commitments of the compensation regime and of the job seeker eligible for compensation" (UNEDIC, 2000). With the PARE, each job seeker commits to participating in the evaluation of his or her professional capacities, to attending regular meetings making up a personalized "accompaniment," to mutually defined measures in a personalized action plan (*projet d'action personnalisé*, PAP), and to be effectively and permanently seeking a job" (UNEDIC, 2000). No sanction is imposed in case of the absence of a signed PAP. But in case of a refusal of either a job opening or of a training program, a sanction system is set up that may allow for a warning or even the decrease, suspension, and refusal of the benefit (Mills and Caudron, 2001).

The PPE as well as the PARE reflect the same logic in that both result from concern about work incentives for the unemployed (Mills and Caudron, 2001). For example, with the PPE, government aimed to limit "inactivity traps" "likely to hinder the return to employment of job seekers or of those in receipt of basic social benefits" as well as to raise the net income for employees in the lowest wage bracket. Indeed, a striking change of the last years in France is the rapid rise of the theme of work incentives, along with increasing focus on the "working poor." In fact, these same questions were almost nonexistent in the main French debates on poverty before the mid-1990s.[39]

Thus, in recent years, work incentives have become an ever greater priority in France: "the theme of 'work disincentive' is central in the analysis of unemployment in France since the economic recovery of 1998" (Mills and Caudron, 2001: 300). Recent reports on social minima (CGP, 2000; Join-Lambert, 1998) or on the question of full employment have attempted to put emphasis on the low level of extra income generated by the return to employment because of the high marginal tax rate or because of the loss of tied benefits (such as housing subsidies). The new popularity of work incentive issues does not stem simply from the influence of ideas coming from the Anglo-Saxon countries, channelled at the European level by countries such as the United Kingdom. The work incentive theme was a direct result of the direction taken by government labor market intervention, which, in turn, influenced labor market structure in such a way as to raise this type of concern. The public employment policy of the 1990s, with the exonerations of social security contributions and highly subsidized employment creation in the form of the CES and CEC, was a factor in contributing to the increase of contingent work, especially part-time jobs. In fact, part-time work (and above all involuntary part-time work) has increased at a rapid rate in France over the past twenty years: while at the end of the 1970s, part-time work accounted for only 6 percent of total employment. In November 2001, it made up approximately 14 percent of total employment (Eironline, 2001c).[40] The political choice to structure CES on a part-time basis (20 hours weekly), in order to maximize the effect on employment for a given budgetary cost (Concialdi, 2000), had two broad consequences, since this contract was a major channel through which RMI recipients entered employment.[41] First, it contributed to the formation of a sub-set of working poor; second, it contributed to legitimizing part-time jobs paid at the SMIC as the employment norm for RMI recipients (CGP, 2000). As a result, the net advantage of a return to employment involves earnings that amount to half the minimum wage, which appears to be, on a purely monetary basis, a work disincentive.[42] Thus, from that perspective, we can say that state intervention partly structured the debate on work incentives. However, we must add that since 1998 the trend has been reversed as a series of measures has decreased the advantages of part-time work and contributed to full-time job creation (Gautié and Gubian, 2000).

The recent discovery of the "working poor" phenomenon in France was also partially a byproduct of the prevalence of part-time employment in the French labor market, as reduced hours decrease earnings and contribute to increasing wage-earner poverty. The poverty level, or "very low wage threshold," corresponds to wages below half the median wage.[43] This category of very low wage employment increased in France from 5 percent of total employment in 1983 to 10 percent in 1999 (Concialdi, 2000). Part-time jobs were overrepresented in "low wage" employment[44] (Concialdi and Ponthieux, 2001). Also, if the poverty rate was on average 2.5 times higher in the United States than in France in 1995 (20.9 percent vs. 8.4 percent), the workforce poverty rate was 10.5 percent in the United States and 6.5 percent in France (Concialdi and Ponthieux, 2001). Working poverty stemmed primarily from the short duration of work in France, and from low hourly wages in the United States (Concialdi, 2000).

The broad scope of French anti-exclusion policy since the mid-1990s is undeniable. However, this does not mean that all the objectives pursued have become reality. On many points, the means of intervention are still well below what was expected. In this regard, the Achilles' heel of RMI policy is and has always been the lack of resources devoted to the implementation of the *insertion* contract (*contrat d'insertion*). Firstly, we must emphasize the fact that the issue of "contracts" is central to the insertion model. In addition to the occupational contracts described above, the *insertion* contract is the focal point of interest with regard to RMI. As the insertion component of the RMI is applied in the *insertion* contract, the contract becomes the visible symbol of the state's effective commitment towards the excluded. At present, the contract rate has always been far from being acceptable, with respect to the formal obligations of the law according to which every RMI recipient must sign an insertion contract within the three-month period following his or her arrival in the program.[45] The contract rate which varied between 40 percent and 50 percent during the first years of the program (DIRMI, 1994), reached a level of only 53 percent in 1998. The most recent data reveal, for 2000, a contract rate of 50 percent.[46] We might add that the data become increasingly strategic in political terms. To be specific, it is our opinion that the weakness of the RMI program contract rate does not mean that "RMI is not coercive scheme" (Barbier and Théret, 2001). In fact, the implementation problems must be examined separately from questions related to the program's nature. The "tied aid" nature of the RMI, that is, the obligation principle it contains, remains intact as the "duty of insertion" is linked, for the recipient, to an economic sanction.[47] In addition, as unemployment insurance and RMI programs are increasingly linked, via the public employment policy, problems of financing have arisen. Now UNEDIC is faced with the success of the PARE and cannot fund the new follow-up component while maintaining, at the same time, a decrease in unemployment insurance premiums (Yerochewski, 2001).[48] Thus, the ANPE could lack the financial means necessary to the implementation of its personalized action strategies for the unemployed (Yerochewski, 2001). These are several examples of the wide gap that exists between publicly announced objectives and actual practice in the insertion model.

Finally, public statements and policy concerns on poverty and exclusion have also developed since the mid-1990s. The French government now speaks in terms of all types of exclusions instead of exclusion, in the singular, as was typical of RMI beginnings. This change makes one think that the concept has been made more complex as the underlying reality inherent in the term of "exclusion" has been better understood as seen through various facets of the excluded person's life. Another line of reflection addresses the question of combining family life and employment, which has been altered by the French public intervention style of recent years. Indeed, this theme was influenced by the workweek reduction policy: debates on working time issues and the implementation of new laws instigated a broader reflection expressed in terms of "social times" (*temps sociaux*). This subject of social times, which also became current in other European countries such as Italy, has made it possible to consider the issue of time in all its various facets (Gauvin and Jacot, 1999). This perspective makes it possible to directly take into account the gender inequalities in the social division of work (Méda, 2000). Thirdly, another research area that has emerged since the mid-1990s is the "transitional labor markets" research program (Gazier, 1998). Closely developed in collaboration with German social science researchers, this new approach to employment policy deals with new ways to structure mobility perspectives for workers by instituting new rights. This is an ambitious research program in that it is aimed at the creation of a new labor market regulation mode. Fourthly, on the other hand, there is a noticeable overall net decrease in evaluation research since the mid-1990s in France. In contrast to the first years of the RMI program implementation, when the government was highly committed to encouraging evaluation research, this type of research has been neglected over the last few years. However, comparative research in the area of social security policies has grown rapidly.

Two Models of Reciprocity in Transformation

In this section, we will come back to the workfare and *insertion* models in light of the changes that have occurred since the mid-1990s in both the United States and France. We will synthesize the key points outlined in the last section as they relate to the different features of our reference models. Our aim is to examine the degree of transformation in the workfare and *insertion* models that has taken place over the last years in terms of *rights and duties* for the state and the recipients.

If we consider the welfare system structure (1.1), two conclusions can be drawn. First of all, with respect to the degree of centralization of social assistance systems, the initial characteristics of the workfare and the *insertion* models have been further accentuated. In effect, the decentralized feature of the U.S. welfare system has been carried further with the devolution process strengthened by PRWORA. In France, we can characterize the increasing role of the supranational level as being a centralization process—as France's national initiatives are increasingly intertwined with those of Europe—in the direction of French social assistance policies.[49] In the United States, the increasing process of decentralization is seen by some researchers as negatively affecting recipients' rights, since state control over redistribution leads, by a higher degree of interstate competition, to a "race to the bottom," in which "states successively reduce their welfare generosity in order to avoid becoming 'welfare magnets'" (Bailey and Rom, 2001: 2). According to Greenberg (2001), if the devolution has not yet led to growing restrictive welfare policy, if caseloads were to suddenly rise substantially, "states would be forced to cut other programs, restrict assistance, or commit more state funds. In such a context, the meaning of state discretion would be different" (pp. 21-22). According to Greenberg (2001), at the present time, the problem stems mostly from a lack of information about the way the system functions because the devolution process increases the system's opacity, causing "increased difficulty in tracking program rules and understanding program outcomes across states" (p. 23). Secondly, concerning the category-based or unified structure of the social assistance systems, the workfare model has faded while the *insertion* model has been reaffirmed. Thus, the category-based U.S. system has been broadened through TANF: as funding of a variety of services has been added to cash welfare aid, policies have become less focused on welfare recipients alone but have also included the working poor who benefit from the program. Conversely, in France, the social assistance system has become slightly more unified with the introduction of the 1998 law, as the treatment of social minima recipients (API, ASS) became closer to that of RMI recipients.

With regard to the representation of the social assistance "subject-citizen" (1.2), while the concepts of the "dependent" and the "excluded" continue to dominate in the United States and France, respectively, some gradual shifting can be seen at the level of poverty analysis in both countries. In the United States, as the concept of the worker gradually replaces the idea of the social assistance recipient, low-pay jobs and contingent work, shortage of fringe benefits and family-friendly policies, and the results they have on low wage earners, such as working poverty, retention problems, and instability, have truly begun to be recognized. This acknowledgment is certainly still hesitant, as was pointed out critically by a large number of groups who presented their comments on the TANF Reauthorization of October 2002 to the Congress. However, a change is noticeable in the tone of the general debate: "Broad agreement exist about some new goals: helping low-income parents keep jobs and advance through the workforce; expanding participation in programs, such as child care, food stamps, and Medicaid, that support working families; and helping families with the most severe barriers to employment" (Greenberg, 2001: 21). This change in perception could gain momentum if the economic downturn continues in the United States, the higher unemployment rate making the employment situation of former recipients even more precarious. On the other hand, in France, the excluded remains central to the poverty debates. However, as the question of work incentives and the "poverty trap" become an increased concern, the vision of the excluded begins to blur: considerations on an individual basis become more and more prevalent in the analysis of the causes of poverty.

The key objectives of workfare and insertion (1.3) remain identical. The fight against dependency or exclusion is still the *leitmotiv* of state action in dealing with social assistance recipients in the United States and France, respectively. In the first case, the predominance of the traditional goals of workfare translated into an obsession with a decline in welfare rolls, which became a hallmark of reform success. Many state initiatives were aimed primarily at decreasing caseloads, by a range of means ("work first" culture, lifetime limit, tougher work sanctions, and widespread adoption of diversion practices) (U.S. HR, 2000). Even policies directed at reducing out-of-wedlock births can be interpreted in this light, as indirect attempts to decrease the likelihood of initial openings (Edelhoch, Liu, Martin, and Wiseman, 2001). In addition, PRWORA strongly emphasized family reform, based on the moral principles accompanying the reestablishment of the traditional family structure. The argument was that "offering permanent help for needy children in single-parent families had encouraged family break-up, enabled nonmarital births, and fostered long-term dependency" (U.S. HR, 2000: 352). In a broader perspective, through these behavioral changes, a "long-term cultural transformation" (Kaus, 2001: 1) was the goal. On the French side, the initial objective of the fight against exclusion was reinforced, evolving into a fight against all forms of exclusion, and its overall ramifications in all areas of the excluded person's life. The goals of decreasing work disincentives and threshold effects resulting from the interplay of various policies directed towards the poor have also been more actively addressed. However, in contrast with the United States, these goals have been explicitly put in balance with social justice issues, and seen from the point of view of public policy coherence. Another difference in the French work incentives approach is that the limits of this perspective, as a pertinent analytical tool that may explain the employment behaviors of the poor, have been greatly acknowledged (CGP, 2000; Gautié and Gubian, 2000). There has been less interest in France than in the United States with measuring the effects of benefit reduction rate on labor force participation rate and employment rate. However, one must note some inconsistencies in the treatment of the various groups by social policies in France: labor force attachment was stimulated for social assistance recipients—RMI recipients, lone-mothers API recipients, and ASS recipients—while it was discouraged for some employed mothers, with the setting-up of the *allocation pour jeune enfant* (APE) (Young Child Benefit), which decreased the work participation rate of mothers (Bonnet and Labbé, 2000).

If we turn our attention to the *rights and duties* of the recipients and the state (1.4), the disparity between workfare and *insertion* has widened since the mid-1990s: the duty of the poor has been increased in the United States, while the collective duty of society in France has translated into new rights for the poor. This point, central to our problem, requires further development, which will be given above all for the American experience. In this way, TANF hardened previous trends of workfare by increasing work obligations for the poor. As the law's title indicates, "personal responsibility" is pivotal in the new system. Transitional aid, work trigger rule, increased "work participation" rates (instead of "participation" before), and priority given to work activities detrimental to other components of the previous *workfare* programs (mainly education and training), all amount to strengthening the stringency of the *contrepartie* principle inherent to workfare. This result stresses the cyclical evolution of workfare, which began with very punitive work assignments, during the era of California Governor Ronald Reagan, and then softened with the broadening of activities included, and with education playing the central role, with the Family Support Act (FSA) 1988 reform, to then revert to toughened obligations at this time. On the other hand, one trend has always remained constant since the very beginning of workfare, the latter has been extended to an ever-growing percentage of AFDC-TANF recipients. With TANF, the age of a dependant child qualifying for an exemption has been decreased to one year and welfare agencies are asked to work with the entire caseload. In New York, workfare has even been extended to the homeless.[50] Thus, overall, lone mother welfare recipients, newly considered "able-bodied" in employment instead of "able-bodied" in work at home, now bear the consequences of the deepening of a social norm of women's employability. The image of the undeserving welfare poor was hardened with the 1996 reform. And with it was reaffirmed the work ethic: "the moral judgments that we (society) make about welfare recipients are really addressed to us. They affirm our values of hard work and proper moral conduct. They make the U.S. feel better by punishing the victim" (Handler, 2001: 36).

Emphasis on work, instead of on educational activities—or "workforce attachment" approach as opposed to a "human-capital investment" approach (Hagen and Lurie, 1994)—as was previously the case in the FSA, merits special attention. Indeed, a major stake for women is what counts as "allowable work activities," to the extent that access to higher education is one of the most important issues for women. In effect, education is key to enabling poor women access to move to jobs that are better paid and offer more benefits: "The most effective welfare-to-work programs share a flexible, individualized approach that mixes job search, education, job training, and work" (Greenberg, Strawn, and Plimpton, 2000: 4). A recent extensive study on the relative impact of education-focused programs and employment-focused programs found disappointing results for the former, but still concludes that a mixed approach, blending both employment search and education or training, was the most effective strategy (Hamilton et al., 2001). On the other hand, research on factors related to job advancement for low-income parents shows that where these parents start in the workforce has an impact on their economic well-being in the future: firstly, "higher basic skills, and especially education beyond high school, are linked to higher wages later on," and, secondly, "starting out in higher-paying jobs is linked to higher wage growth over time" (Strawn and Martinson, 2000: 19). Thus, by limiting educational, particularly postsecondary education, and training activities, TANF may seriously impair welfare mothers' perspectives for long-term economic security. If many states now allow more TANF recipients to participate in postsecondary education, this is far from being sufficient to guarantee that single welfare mothers will no longer be highly concentrated in low wage sectors of the economy, and escape the gender-based occupational segregation still prevailing. Therefore, education and work supports are all the more critical issues at the present time as, with the decline in the welfare rolls, the stayers are now the most disadvantaged among welfare mothers.

We must also consider the fact that, from the point of view of advocates of the 1996 reform, this law expanded welfare recipients rights since the shrinking of the caseload means that a far greater percentage of welfare recipients improved their status through job entry instead of "dependency" on welfare. The "Work-First" approach is not only a means of reducing welfare costs. It is also "based on the belief that the workplace is the best place for workers to learn the skills and habits valued in today's labor market" (Lambert, Haley-Lock, 2001a: 13). However, from an institutionalist perspective, *rights and duties* of social assistance recipients must be judged by the quality level of their economic status, which, in turn, relies on the collective protection level or economic security provided to citizens. For economic security to be achieved, citizens must be provided with "security of expectations," since economic insecurity is not only a question of having a low or irregular income, but also of being uncertain about receiving an income at all (Gagliardo, 1949).

From that perspective, the situation of former welfare mothers is not very rosy. We have already stressed the economic fragility of welfare mothers, as demonstrated from the results of the leaver studies. We also saw that the situation of many working single mothers has not improved. This explains why a significant number of organizations recently recommended, in their comments on TANF Reauthorization, that the reduction of poverty, instead of the reduction of the welfare rolls, be the main objective of welfare reform. Moreover, even if, up to now, states have been able to offer a wide array of work supports, uncertainty remains as to what will occur in the future: having enough resources to meet service needs is "a story about how it is easier to make choices when resources are expanding. The same discretion would likely be exercised quite differently in a time of scarcity" (Greenberg, 2001: 22). As an economic downturn follows the strong economy of the 1990s,[51] caution is called for. Of course, state practices differ on many points and it is impossible to clearly set out a single workfare intervention pattern. But in fact, it is hard not to conclude that seldom in the last half century has the United States been so poorly prepared to assist individuals struggling with the effects of an economic weakening. In addition to time-limited social assistance, the unemployment insurance system is not at all adapted to address the unemployment needs of former welfare recipients. Lastly, the promotion of the traditional family, that is, the heterosexual, married couple, demonstrates the power of the "moral right" in the United States in the shaping of policy decisions governing family policy (Baker, 1997). In fact, promoting marriage not only "hasn't been proved to reduce poverty," as argues Hartman, but the promotion of marriage through welfare could also force low-income women to continue in relationships with violent men or would discount or overlook such family structures as homosexual unions (Wetzein, 2001).

In the same way, in France, the reform furthered the principles and the means of the initial model. LOLE did so by increasing the fronts for social intervention within the framework of a strategic and integrated approach to fighting poverty and social exclusion, including the setting of medium- to long-term targets. New ways to implement the existing rights of the poor were set up, as well as a new "right to accompaniment." In 2001, the European Commission singled out "as good examples of a strategic approach" to promote social cohesion the national action plans of the Netherlands, Denmark, and France.[52] The distinctive feature of the RMI, which is not based on the idea that assistance should be provided in exchange for some activity, remains unaltered. However, this does not mean that economic security for the poor in France has been guaranteed. A high unemployment rate still prevails among RMI recipients, wage-earning poverty has increased for a large percentage of those who entered into a subsidized work contract, and support measures to pursue in career path plans are lacking.

In as much as the *rights and duties* formulae were pushed further in both countries, the assistance customs (1.5) could only follow in the same direction. This is all the more true in that a custom can only be fully grasped over a time span. Therefore, the solidarity custom has seen a new extension with the 1998 reform—the values promoted in the law being identified as to the *"fondements même de la République"*[53]—as has been the custom of deservingness in the United States since 1996. Also, in the United States, public opinion continues to not support welfare, while in France, the most prevalent idea continues to be that social expenditures should be increased to help social assistance recipients. Here, in these opposite social assistance customs, the huge divergence between the two evaluation research "traditions" in the two countries (Morel, 1996) reflects a "societal coherence." In as much as the political discourse on solidarity does not require evaluation research demonstrating a high level of performance for programs for the poor, since this approach is anchored simply in the existence of a high level of expenditures devoted to the poor, similarly the American distrust for public policies and above all welfare policies, in conformity with the custom of deservingness, absolutely requires, in order for both welfare and workfare programs be politically sustainable, the seal of approval of the research and evaluation community through "scientific" research, whether it be impact studies or cost-benefit analysis.[54] Thus, the considerable volume of resources spent on evaluation of social policies in the United States only takes on its full meaning within the framework of the country's specific custom.

With regard to the application of the reciprocal relationship (1.6), the distance between the workfare and the insertion models has lessened. At the formal level, the American selective model has been considerably softened as the workfare obligations were imposed on almost the entire welfare caseload. Indeed, TANF gives no exemptions from work requirements, allowing states to exempt recipients with a child under the age of one (U.S. HR, 2001). For women, this means that their role as care givers has been gradually erased as their status as wage earners is becoming foremost. In France, the universalist logic of the insertion model, at least formally, has remained as prevalent as previously. However, at the implementation level, the evaluation of selection mechanisms remains to be done. We can see that the "downstream employability selection" that was observed in France, because of a selective process which applies at the implementation level of the *insertion* mechanism, is still partially existent. Indeed, the insertion contract applies only to half of the RMI caseload. However, to thoroughly evaluate the insertion model, we would need to know how the traditional paths followed by recipients under social or vocational *insertion* measures and in employment policies have changed. The U.S. model became more similar to the French model, not only in the broadening of the caseloads bound by obligations, but also in the means used to apply these obligations, with the practice of widespread contracting, by means of personal responsibility contracts" (PRC) and "employability plans" (EP). More research should be done on the distinct significance of the contract in both countries.

Both models continue to be very divergent on concepts of the social integration of social assistance recipients (1.7). In the United States, the links to employment integration have been tightened with PRWORA, while on the other hand, LOLE devoted more attention to all the dimensions of the excluded person's social life. Paradoxically, the almost exclusive attention that was put on employment services in workfare has been relaxed, as more services were added in helping the welfare poor to enter employment. In that sense, the meaning of occupational integration in the United States has been broadened. Services for welfare mothers experiencing domestic violence, which, under the family violence waivers, can be exempted from work requirement and time limits, is an example of what would resemble "social insertion" in France.

Concerning the dynamics of interaction between assistance, employment, and the family (1.8), we found that only the workfare model has changed, in that the precedence of family has been replaced by the precedence of employment. Thus, on that point, the workfare model has become closer to the insertion model. Indeed, with the dramatic decline of welfare rolls, employment became the main exit route from welfare. And as more welfare mothers enter jobs, the instability of employment relationships can be seen as the primary cause of their economic vulnerability. The ongoing development of research themes related to employment also reveal its importance. One must note that welfare is still a family policy by default, but increasingly tends to become also an unemployment policy by default (within time limits). In addition, the family continues to be pivotal under the PRWORA, where three out of four goals deal with family reform. In fact, it would not be surprising that family-related concerns increase significantly in the future, especially in the TANF Reauthorization debate. In France, RMI recipients are still mainly limited by the lack of jobs and the restrictiveness of unemployment-insurance rules. Finally, the issue of combining employment and family life is of growing importance and interest in both countries.

Both in the United States and France, the links between integration programs for social assistance recipients and employment policies (1.9) have tightened. Thus, the primarily selective character of workfare has lessened as welfare agencies and workforce development services have become increasingly intertwined. In addition, with the WIA, public employment policies have taken a new place in the United States. But, when one looks at the research programs focused on the issue of "transition," the gap in employment policy concepts clearly stands out in the United States, "transition" means passage between welfare and work, welfare and family, or from low-wage jobs to better-paid jobs, while in France, the term begins to be integrated into the global approach of the "transitional labor markets." In France, a contradictory dual change can be observed: on the one hand, the universal feature of the insertion model increased, with the growing involvement of the ANPE in follow-up services for RMI recipient employment, and yet, on the other hand, selectivity has also increased, as integration measures, namely subsidized contracts, have been more highly targeted on the least disadvantaged, such as the RMI recipients.

However, one key difference must be underlined: if, in France, insertion activities are more closely related to the public employment policy, in the United States, service delivery changes have been accompanied by the rise of private intermediaries. This trend could lead, in relation to the point discussed in 1.6, to new types of selective practices, as private providers are strongly encouraged to adopt "creaming" practices, that is, as a matter of priority, to offer services to the most employable among welfare recipients. In addition, the status of social assistance recipients in workfare and insertion has become closer, increasingly, to the status of wage earners. This occurred because of the massive entry of American welfare recipients into employment.

Finally, what has happened in regard to the interactive dynamics between the rights of social assistance recipients and the rights of wage earners (1.10)? In both countries, previous trends have been extended. In France, the weakening of the employment norm continued, following public employment policy orientations. The lowering of indirect labor costs, with the exoneration of social insurance premiums, had an "indubitable influence on the general functioning of the labour market" (Barbier and Thérêt, 2001: 166-67). Next, the growth of subsidized contracts intensified this trend. The dynamics at work here were, at least in the latter case, that of the impact of the social assistance area on employment. In the United States, the decrease in the rights of social assistance recipients has also continued, occurring rapidly, however, when the 1996 welfare reform ended welfare entitlement for individuals. In that case, the impetus towards the decrease of collective protection measures came from the employment area.

But, conversely, in the United States as in France, social assistance reforms also influenced, as a repercussion, the terms of the wage-earning relationship. This is illustrated by the New York City example where workfare placements replaced well-paying regular jobs. Here the effect of welfare on employment was clearly a downgrading effect on the work relationship. But social assistance reforms influenced the wage-earning relationship also through unemployment insurance policy. This was clearly seen in the United States, as the principles of the 1996 welfare reform were translated into the WIA. A similar effect also occurred in France, when the idea of contracting dominated MEDEF efforts to revamp the unemployment insurance system. Then, the figure of contract, prominent in RMI, influenced the new design projected of unemployment insurance. Therefore, with the PARE, a major change in direction was undertaken at the level of the economic security status of the unemployed. The whole debate on PARE "centers precisely on the portion of risk and responsibility that the collectivity must bear or the salaried worker, while modifying the initial principle of sharing of unemployment insurance based on the sole acquisition of the rights to benefits" (Morin, 2000: 734).[55] Even if some new protections have been granted to the unemployed, the new unemployment convention, according to Mills and Caudron (2001), "definitely confirms unemployment dualism," with the unequal protection of the unemployment of the short-term unemployed, and of the unemployment of the least employable who "will be more rapidly eliminated from unemployment insurance, forced to accept any job available or any training offered" (pp. 234-235).[56] Finally, in both countries, income supplementation has increased (with EITC and PPE). But it is primarily in France that this kind of policy has been analyzed as a way to subsidize employers and low-wage jobs, with the consequence of a possible degradation of the employment norm (CGP, 2000; Belorgey, 2001).[57]

Conclusion

The trend towards the establishment of a new reciprocal social assistance relationship has been observed in many countries (Barbier, 2000; Baker and Tippin 1999; Gilbert and Van Voorhis, 2001; Loedemel and Trickey, 2001), allowing us to consider this to be a convergence process among industrialized countries. This convergence, however, masks the differences existing between specific approaches of "reciprocal obligations." The United States and France clearly illustrate this situation: in the mid-1990s, these two countries represented opposing models and this is still the case today. In addition, on many aspects, the reasoning of the workfare and the insertion models have even been strengthened. Conversely, where the initial features have seemingly faded, it was chiefly because the workfare model had changed, matching the features of the insertion model.

The well-being of sole-mother recipients and their children is contingent upon whether these mothers enjoy access to a job and see their productive contribution through household and caregiving activities acknowledged, if employed; this holds true for all social assistance recipients, if work allows them both to escape poverty and to live with dignity by holding good jobs, and, finally, whether it is possible to count on a strong social security system, when employment earnings must be replaced, providing, as a very minimum, social assistance benefits. The specific situation of women recipients in regard to family and employment must also be taken into account, namely through support services such as child care, as well as measures to combat domestic violence, as in the American situation, but more broadly, by combining "social times" to facilitate the balancing of the dual-role for all parents. On all these points, in the United States above all, but also in France, there is still a long road ahead.

Notes

1. Social assistance should be differentiated from social insurance, which is an income replacement mechanism designed to provide a level of income continuity, and from universal benefits whose primary objective is compensation for specific charges.
2. AFDC (commonly called *welfare*) was a means-test program intended mainly for poor single-parent families.
3. RMI was created in 1988 and renewed in 1992.
4. In 1988, the RMI program added to a preexistent system of *social minima,* which already provided last-resort assistance to specific subgroups in the population. The RMI program has an ambiguous nature in that it has the characteristics of an assistance program (means tested) but is seen as resolutely different from a traditional assistance scheme, because of its "insertion" component. The insertion dimension is thus fundamental for understanding this new piece of the French system of "social minima." We can thus talk in terms of a real *insertion approach* when we examine the welfare-to-work programs for social assistance recipients in France. For a description of the RMI program, see S. Morel (1998).
5. This is not the case with all social assistance programs, such as, for example, the Food Stamps program.
6. The complexity of welfare policies began increasing by the mid-1990s, as states were granted waivers to experiment with new policies, such as, namely, time limits.
7. This reform changed the basic features of AFDC, as they were laid out in the 1935 Social Security Act.
8. In some states, the use of sanctions accounted "for a major part of the caseload decline" (Greenberg, 2001: 23).
9. States can extend assistance paid for by the Federal TANF funds beyond the five-year limit for up to 20 percent of their caseload.
10. Unpublished paper, cited with the permission from the authors.
11. States must achieve minimum rates of participation by adult recipients of TANF assistance. The rates were established in 1997 at 25 percent for all families (75 percent for two-parent families), at 40 percent (90 percent) in 2000 to reach 50 percent in 2002.

> Moreover, to be counted as a work participant, a recipient must be engaged for at least 30 hours a week on average in 2000-2002 (U.S. HR, 2000).

12. Apart from work-related sanctions, states must also sanction families who do not cooperate with child support enforcement requirements and can sanction individuals refusing "without good cause" to comply with their individual responsibility plan (U.S. HR, 2000).

13. They are: (1) unsubsidized employment; (2) subsidized private employment; (3) subsidized public sector employment; (4) work experience; (5) on-the-job training; (6) job search and job readiness assistance; (7) community service programs; (8) vocational education training (12 months maximum); and (9) providing child care for a community service participant (U.S. HR, 2000: 357).

14. The 1996 law eliminated the state obligation that existed under AFDC to guarantee child care to cash assistance recipients who needed child care in order to work or participate in education or training. States were also given increased discretion in designing and operating child care programs by TANF.

15. Unpublished paper, cited with permission from authors.

16. SPDP, 1999; State Policies Regarding TANF Work Activities and Requirements: Post-employment Benefits and Services; http://www.spdp.org/tanf/work/worksumm.htm.

17. EITC is a refundable income tax credit available to low- and moderate-income working families. As it increases with earnings, it creates an incentive for welfare recipients to earn income.

18. Most of them have been run "on an extremely small scale" (Bartik, 2001: 212).

19. Especially the guidance from the U.S. Department of Labor entitled *How Workplace Laws Apply to Welfare Recipients* (revised 02.29.1999), which states that federal laws apply equally to workfare and to all workers (Dietrich, Emsellem, and Paradise, 2000).

20. The living wage campaigns seek to pass local ordinances requiring employers who hold large city or county service contracts or receive substantial financial assistance from the city to pay their workers a living wage (ACORN, 2002).

21. Congress also established a "Bonus to Reward Decrease in Illegitimacy Ratio," permitting HHS to reward states that showed the greatest reduction in out-of-wedlock births while decreasing their abortion rates. States are also required by HHS to set goals to reduce out-of-wedlock pregnancies. The National Strategy to Prevent Teen Pregnancy and the Abstinence Program were also authorized (Harris, 2001).

22. A debate exists as to whether the decrease in welfare rolls is due to welfare reform or to the healthy economic situation. (How healthy is the economy currently?)

23. Author's translation.

24. In the fight against exclusion, many other measures, which it would take too long to present here, were implemented, such as the *couverture maladie universelle* (CMU) (universal medical coverage), set up in July 1999.

25. Agence Nationale pour l'Emploi (ANPE), Press release, 1 February 1999.

26. Id.

27. For a brief description, see below.

28. ASS and API are, respectively, the *allocation de solidarité spécifique* and the *allocation de parent isolé* programs.

29. RMI recipients may also obtain a trainee status.

30. Author's translation.

31. Ministère du travail (2001). Le renforcement de l'accompagnement des demandeurs d'emploi les plus en difficulté notamment les allocataires du RMI et du régime de solidarité, p. 1; www.social.gouv.fr/htm/actu/34_010718.htm (October 22, 2001).

32. See below.
33. *Ministère de l'emploi et de la solidarité;* http://www.nsej.travail.gouv.fr/index_en.html (January 22, 2002).
34. Id.
35. *Ministère de l'emploi et de la solidarité;* http://www.35h.travail. gouv.fr/texteang.htm (January 22, 2002).
36. Income disregards were also extended to other social minima programs (API, *allocation d'insertion, allocation de veuvage*).
37. In 2001, the *salaire interprofessionnel minimum de croissance* (SMIC), the French minimum wage was set at 43.72 FF per hour (7,388.68 FF per month (169 hours of work)); INSEE, *Les grands indicateurs;* http://www.insee.fr/fr/indicateur/smic.htm.
38. *The Confédération des syndicats français* (CFDT) (French Unions Confederation) was the only union confederation following the MEDEF on this point.
39. To be sure, the issue of incentive to work was raised once in a while but without significant echo in the political arena.
40. Since 1998, a downward trend in involuntary part-time work has been registered (Eironline, 2001c).
41. One out of three former recipients who found a job held a subsidized job (CES/CEC) (Afsa, Demailly, and Guillemot, 2000).
42. In 1999, the net monthly benefit for a single RMI recipient to be in a CES (an half-SMIC) was 216 FF lower, compared to RMI benefit (without earnings disregard), and 1,324 FF (with earnings disregard) (CGP, 2000). RMI leavers can also lose housing benefits.
43. The poverty threshold equalled 3,750 FF in 1999 (Concialdi, 2000).
44. The "low income threshold" must be distinguished from the poverty ("very low wage") threshold. It corresponds to wages below two-thirds of the median wage, and amounted to 5,000 FF (90 percent of the SMIC) in 1999 (Concialdi, 2000: 708).
45. Facts other than the lack of means can explain this situation, namely that many recipients leave the RMI program too quickly to have time to sign a contract (CNE-RMI, 1992).
46. Data obtained from the French Ministry of Employment and Solidarity (*Ministère de l'emploi et de solidarité*).
47. The RMI recipient must engage in insertion actions under penalty of being refused prorogation of the benefit after the first trimester period. The payment of the benefit is suspended "if and only if it is established that the cause is due to the person concerned and without legitimate motive" (DIRMI, 1994).
48. While the ANPE is in charge of the implementation of the PARE, the funding of the PAP, through which the unemployed project is given substance, is partly at charge of UNEDIC.
49. The United States is also part of a regional economic integration process, in the Americas, but, conversely to Europe, the social dimension of this process has been very poorly developed.
50. In October 1999, Giuliani's New York City administration "announced that homeless people in New York would be required to work as a condition of shelter" (Bernstein, 1999).
51. After having grown for the ninth consecutive year in 2000, with the unemployment rate falling to 4.0 percent in November 2001, in just thirteen months, the U.S. unemployment rate has risen from 3.9 percent to 5.4 percent; *Wall Street Journal Europe,* Vol. XIX, 193, 5 November 2001: 1.
52. "EU steps up fight against poverty and exclusion. Only a cohesive Europe can tap human resources," says Commissioner Anna Diamantopoulou; 10 October 2001;

http://www.unionnetwok.org/UNIsite/Sectors/Commerce/EU/ EU_against_poverty_and_exclusion.htm (January 22, 2002).
53. Speech of the Minister, Martine Aubry, in the National Assembly.
54. As J. M. Gueron indicates (1991), in the United States the legislator needs irrefutable data because it is deemed indispensable from a political viewpoint to justify expenditures devoted to manpower programs.
55. Author's translation.
56. Author's translation.
57. The proposal of the *allocation compensatrice de revenu d'activité* (ACRA) (income activity compensation benefit) in the Belorgey Report B (CGP, 2000), which was an increase and an extension of the existing RMI earning disregards, has provoked the same type of reaction (Gautié and Gubian, 2000; Belorgey, 2001).

References

ACORN, The Association of Community Organizations for Reform Now. (2002). *Living Wage Resource Center.* http://www.livingwagecampaign.org/; web site visited on January, 18, 2002.

Adams, G., Holcomb, P., & Snyder K. (2001). *Navigating the Child Care Subsidy System: Access and Utilization Issues for Welfare Families.* Washington, DC: Urban Institute.

Afsa, C. (1999). *L'insertion professionnelle des bénéficiaires du RMI.* Paris: CNAF, Recherche, Prévisions et Statistiques.

Afsa, C., Demailly, D., & Guillemot, D. (2000). "Les allocataires du RMI: diversité des trajectoires." *Droit social* 7, 8: 713-716.

Bailey, M. A., & Rom, M. C. (2001). "Interstate Competition in Health and Welfare Programs: A Research Note." Paper presented at the APPAM Fall Research Conference, Washington, DC. November.

Baker, M. (1997). "Women, Family Policies and the Moral Right." *Canadian Review of Social Policy/Revue canadienne de politique sociale* 40: 47-64.

Baker, M., & Tippin, D. (1999). *Poverty, Social Assistance, and the Employment of Mothers: Restructuring Welfare States.* Toronto: University Press of Toronto.

Barbier J.-C., & Théret, B. (2001). "Welfare to Work or Work to Welfare, the French Case?" In *Activating the Unemployed. A Comparative Appraisal of Work-Oriented Policies,* edited by N. Gilbert and R. A. Van Voorhis. International Social Security Series, Vol. 3. New Brunswick, NJ, London: Transaction Publishers.

Barbier, J.-C. (2000). "Workfare, Activation Policies and the Welfare State in the Age of Globalization: Lessons from the U.S.A, France and the UK." Paper presented to the French-South African workshop, Work and Globalisation (preliminary version), Paris.

Bartik, T. J. (2001). *Jobs for the Poor. Can Labor Demand Policies Help?* New York: Russell Sage Foundation.

Belorgey, J.-M. (Ed.). (2001). *Refonder la protection sociale. Libre débat entre les gauches.* Paris: Éditions La Découverte.

Berlin, G. (2001). "The 30-Year Tug-of-War. Can Reform Resolve Welfare Policy's Thorniest Conundrum?" *Brookings Review* 19, 3: 34-38.

Bernstein, N. (1989). "City Fires 3,500 Former Welfare Recipients." *New York Times,* 5 January.

Blank, R. (2001). "Declining Caseloads/Increased Work: What Can We Conclude About the Effects of Welfare Reform?" *Economic Policy Review* 7, 2: 25-36.

Bonnet, C., & Labbé, M. (2000). "L'activité des femmes après la naissance du deuxième enfant. L'allocation parentale d'éducation a-t-elle un effet incitatif au retrait du marché du travail?" *Recherches et Prévisions* 59: 9-23.

Brodkin, E. Z. (1999). "The Politics of Welfare Reform: Is Relief in Sight?" In *Families, Poverty and Welfare Reform*, edited by Joseph Lawrence. Urbana: University of Illinois Press.

Brodkin, E. Z., Carolyn Fuqua, C., & Thoren K. (2001). "A Map of a New World: The Changing Face of Welfare-to-Work Intermediaries." Working Paper of the Project on the Public Economy of Work. Paper presented at the APPAM Fall Research Conference, Washington, DC. November.

Cancian, M. (2001). "Rhetoric and Reality of Work-based Welfare Reform." *Social Work* 46: 309-314.

Cancian, M., & Meyer, D. R. (2000). "Work After Welfare: Women's Work Effort, Occupation, and Economic Well-Being." *Social Work Research* 24, 2: 69-86.

CGP, Commissariat général du Plan. (2000). *Minima sociaux, revenus d'activité, précarité.* Rapport du groupe présidé par J.-M. Belorgey. Paris: La Documentation Française.

CNE-RMI, Commission nationale d'évaluation du Revenu minimum d'insertion. (1992). *RMI, Le pari de l'insertion, Rapport de la Commission nationale d'évaluation du Revenu minimum d'insertion.* Paris: La Documentation Française.

Commons, J. R. (1934). *Institutional Economics, Its Place in Political Economy.* 2 vols. New Brunswick, NJ, & London: Transaction Publishers, 1990.

Concialdi, P. (2000). "Les travailleurs pauvres." *Droit social* 7, 8: 708-712.

Concialdi, P., & Ponthieux S. (2000). "Salariés à Abas salaires et travailleurs pauvres: une comparaison France-Etats-Unis." *Premières synthèses* 02.1.

Cornilleau, G., & Gubian A. (1997). "L'évaluation macroéconomique des politiques d'emploi," in DARES, *La politique de l'emploi*, La Découverte, Collection Repères: 52-74.

Corson, W. A., & Spiegelman, R. G. (2001). "Introduction and Background of the Reemployment Bonus Experiments." In *Reemployment Bonuses in the Unemployment Insurance System. Evidence from Three Field Experiment*, edited by P. K. Robins and R. G. Spiegelman. Kalamazoo, MI: W. E. Upjohn Institute for Employment Research: 1-23.

Dalaker, J. (2001). *Poverty in the United States: 2000.* Current Population Reports, Consumer Income, U.S. Census Bureau; U.S. Department of Commerce. http://www.census.gov/prod/2001pubs/p60-214.pdf

Dickert-Conlin, S., & Holtz-Eakin, D. (2000). "Employee-Based Versus Employer-Based Subsidies to Low-Wage Workers: A Public Finance Perspective." In *Finding Jobs. Work and Welfare Reform*, edited by D. Card and R. M. Blank, 262-295. New York: Russell Sage Foundation.

Dietrich, S., Emsellem, M., & Kithan Yau, K. (1997). *Welfare Reforming the Workplace: Protecting the Employment Rights of Welfare Recipients, Immigrants, and Displaced Workers.* New York: National Employment Law Project.

Dietrich, S., Emsellem, M., & Paradise, J. (2000). *Employment Rights of Workfare Participants and Displaced Workers.* New York: National Employment Law Project.

Diller, M. (1998). "Working Without a Job: The Social Meaning of the New Workforce," Stanford Law and Society Review 9, 1:19-43.

DIRMI, Délégation interministérielle au RMI. (1994). *RMI, N° Spécial, Bilan 1993*, 23.

Downey, T. (2001). "The Politics of Welfare Reform. Republicans with Hearts Give Democrats Hope." Brookings Review 19, 3:9-11.

Edelhoch, M., Liu, Q., Martin, L., & Wiseman, M. (2001). "The Impact of South Carolina's Family Independence Program on Movers, Stayers, and Those In Between." South Carolina Department of Social Services and George Washington University Institute of Public Policy, October 17. Paper prepared for APPAM Fall Research Conference, Washington, DC. November.

Eironline. (2001a). Unemployment begins to increase; European industrial relations observatory on-line; http://www.eiro.eurofound.ie/2001/10/Feature/FRO110107F.html

Eironline. (2001b). Government strengthens TRACE for youth employment assistance program; European industrial relations observatory on-line; http://www.eiro.eurofound.ie/2001/10/Feature/FRO110109F.html

Eironline. (2001c). Involuntary part-time work declines; European industrial relations observatory on-line; http://www.eiro.eurofound.ie/2001/11/Feature/FRO111124F.html

Fender, L., McKernan S.-M., & Bernstein, J. (2001). "Taming the Beast: Categorizing Welfare Policies for Use in Research A Typology of Welfare Policies Affecting Recipient Job Entry." The Urban Institute. Paper prepared for APPAM Fall Research Conference, Washington, DC. November.

Fenoglio, J. (1998). "La France est le seul pays européen à se doter d'une loi contre l'exclusion." *Le Monde*, 21 mai, *in Les politiques d'insertion, Problèmes économiques et sociaux*, edited by J. Damon. Paris: La Documentation Française, No 807: 72.

Gagliardo, D. (1949). *American Social Insurance*. New York: Harper & Brothers.

Gautié, J., & Gubian, A. (2000). "Réforme du RMI et marché du travail." *Droit social* 7, 8: 699-707.

Gauvin, A., Jacot, H. (1999). *Temps de travail, temps sociaux, pour une approche globale*. Paris: Groupe Liaisons SA.

Gazier, B. (1998). "Ce que sont les marchés transitionnels." In *Les politiques de l'emploi en Europe et aux Etats-Unis*, edited by J.-C. Barbier and J. Gautié. Presses universitaires de France, Collection Les Cahiers du CEE: 339-355.

Gilbert, N., and VanVoorhis, R. (2001). *Activating the Unemployed*. New Brunswick, NJ: Transaction Publishers.

Greenberg, M. (2001). "Welfare Reform and Devolution. Looking Back and Forward." *Brookings Review* 19, 3: 20-24.

Greenberg, M., Strawn J., & Plimpton, L. (2000). *State Opportunities to Provide Access to Postsecondary Education Under TANF.* Washington, DC: Center for Law and Social Policy. www.clasp.org/pubs/jobseducation/postsecondary.final.PDF

Greenhouse, S. (1997). "City Labor Director Backs Effort to Organize Workfare Participants." *New York Times*, 9 February.

Greenhouse, S. (1999). "Union to Sue Giuliani Administration Over Use of Welfare Recipients in Jobs." *New York Times*, 4 February.

Gueron, J. M. (1991). "Évaluation et action: les programmes pour l'emploi et la formation aux Etats-Unis." In Organisation de coopération et de développement économique (OCDE), *L'évaluation des programmes pour l'emploi et des mesures sociales, Le point sur une question complexe*, 191-199, Paris.

Hagen, J. L., and Lurie, I. (1994). *Implementing JOBS: Case Management Strategies*. Albany: Nelson A. Rockefeller Institute of Government, State University of New York.

Hamilton, G. et al. (2001). *National Evaluation of Welfare-to-Work Strategies. How Effective are Different Welfare-to-Work Approaches? Five-Year Adult and Child Impacts for Eleven Programs*. Executive Summary, U.S. Department of Health and Human Services, U.S. Department of Education.

Handler, J. (2001). "The Paradox of Inclusion: Social Citizenship and Active Labor Market Policies." Draft Paper for the Law and Society Annual Meeting, Budapest, 4-8 July.

Harris, G. (2001). *More Research Needed on TANF Family Caps and Other Policies for Reducing Out-of-Wedlock Births*. U.S. General Accounting Office. September. GAO-01-924.

Heymann, S. J., & Earle. A. (1998). "The Work-Family Balance: What Hurdles are Parents Leaving Welfare Likely to Confront?" *Journal of Policy and Management* 17, 2: 313-321.

Jacobs, A. (1999). "Union Again Files Lawsuit Seeking End to Workfare." *New York Times*, 15 April.

Johnson, N. (2001). *A Hand-Up. How State Earned Income Tax Credits Help Working Families Escape Poverty in 2001.* Washington, DC: Center on Budget and Policy Priorities.

Join-Lambert, M.-T. (1998). *Chômage: mesures d'urgence et minima sociaux. Problèmes soulevés par les mouvements de chômeurs en France fin 1997-début 1998,* Rapport au Premier Ministre. Paris : La Documentation Française.

Kaus, M. (2001). "TANF and Welfare. Further Steps toward the Work-Ethic State." *Brookings Review* 19, 3: 43-47.

Lafore, R. (1992). "La pauvreté saisie par le droit." In *Le revenu minimum d'insertion, Une dette sociale*, edited by R. Castel and J.-F. Laé, 67-91. Paris: L'Harmattan.

Lambert, S., Waxman, E., & Haley-Lock, A. (2001). "Against the Odds: A Study of Instability in Lower-Skilled Jobs." Working Paper of the Project on the Public Economy of Work. Paper presented at the APPAM Fall Research Conference, Washington, DC. November.

Lambert, S., & Haley-Lock, A. (2001a). "Opening the Door to Opportunity: Investigating Lower-Skilled Jobs from an Organizational Perspective." Project on the Public Economy of Work, University of Chicago. Paper presented at the APPAM Fall Research Conference, Washington, DC. November.

Legros, M., & Simonin, B. (1991). "Le revenu minimum d'insertion et l'accès à l'emploi: quelques éléments de réflexion sur la situation française." *Travail et Société* 16, 2: 214.

Lennon, M. C., Blome, J., & English, K. (2001). "Depression and Low-Income Women: Challenges for TANF and Welfare-to-Work Policies and Programs." Research Forum in Children, Families and he New Federalism. Paper presented at the APPAM Fall Research Conference, Washington, DC. November.

Lerman, R., Loprest, P., & Ratcliffe, C. (1999). *How Well Can Urban Labor Markets Absorb Welfare Recipients?* Assessing the New Federalism Policy Brief, No A-33. Washington, DC: The Urban Institute.

Liaisons sociales (1998). *Lutte contre les exclusions. Projet de loi d'orientation*, Série V, 35/98, 7 (avril): 1-14.

Loedemel, I., & Trickey, H. (2001). *An Offer You Can't Refuse. Workfare in International Perspective*. Bristol: The Policy Press.

Loprest, P. (2001). *How Are Families That Left Welfare Doing? A Comparison of Early and Recent Welfare Leavers.* Brief B-36. New Federalism Policy Brief, Series B, No. B-36. Washington, DC: The Urban Institute.

Lovell, V., & Hill. C. (2001). "Today's Women Workers: Shut Out of Yesterday's Unemployment Insurance System." *Fact Sheet,* # A127, Institute for Women's Policy Research.

Martinson, J. K. (2000). *Steady Work and Better Jobs: How to Help Low-Income Parents Sustain Employment and Advance in the Workforce.* New York: Manpower Demonstration Research Corporation.

MASSV. Ministère des Affaires sociales, de la Santé et de la Ville. (1993). Loi n° 88-1088 as amended by Loi n° 92-722 du 29 juillet 1992; *Revenu minimum d'insertion, Fascicule spécial,* Bulletin officiel, N°93-11 bis.

Matus-Grossman, L., & Tinsley Gooden, S. (2001). "Opening Doors to Earning Credentials: Impressions of Community College Access and Retention from Low-Wage Workers." Manpower Demonstration Research Corporation. Paper prepared for APPAM Fall Research Conference, Washington, DC. November.

Maynard, R. et al. (1998). "Changing Family Behavior Through Welfare Reform." In *Welfare, the Family, and Reproductive Behavior,* edited by R. A. Moffitt, 134-175. Washington, DC: National Academy Press.

Méda, D. (2000). "Les femmes peuvent-elles changer la place du travail dans la vie?" *Droit social* 5: 463-470.

MES, Ministère de l'emploi et de la solidarité. (2001). *Plan du gouvernement pour assurer l'avenir des Nouveaux services et des Emplois jeunes,* 6 juin, Communiqué; http://www.nsej.travail.gouv.fr/actualites/actualites_f.html.

Mills, C., & Caudron, J. (2001). *Protection sociale. Économie et politique. Débats actuels et réformes.* Paris: Éditions Montchrestien.

Ministère du travail. (2001). Le renforcement de l'accompagnement des demandeurs d'emploi les plus en difficulté notamment les allocataires du RMI et du régime de solidarité, p. 1; www.social.gouv.fr/htm/actu/34_010718.htm (October 22, 2001).

Morel, S. (1995). "Time-limited Benefits in France." *Focus* 17, 2: 21-22.

Morel, S. (1996). "L'évaluation des politiques sociales aux États-Unis: l'exemple des programmes de retour à l'emploi pour les allocataires de l'assistance sociale." *Politiques et Management Public* 14, 2: 33-58.

Morel, S. (1998). "The New Reciprocity in the Relation of Assistance: American *Workfare* versus French *Insertion* Policies." *International Review of Comparative Public Policy* 10: 77-97.

Morel, S. (2000). *Les logiques de la réciprocité: les transformations de la relation d'assistance aux États-Unis et en France.* Paris: Presses universitaires de France, Collection Le lien social.

Morin, M.-L. (2000). "Partage des risques et responsabilités de l'emploi. Contribution au débat sur la réforme du droit du travail." *Droit social* 7, 8: 730-738.

Park, N.-H., & Van Voorhis, R. A. (2001). "Moving People from Welfare to Work in the United States." In *Activating the Unemployed. A Comparative Appraisal of Work-Oriented Policies,* edited by N. Gilbert and R. A. Van Voorhis, 185-212. International Social Security Series, Vol. 3. New Brunswick, NJ, London: Transaction Publishers.

Paugam, S. (1991). "Le RMI, moyen d'intégration sociale?" *Projet, Réussir l'intégration* 227: 91-100.

PNAFPES, *Plan national d'action français contre la pauvreté et l'exclusion sociale.* (2001). Paris: La Documentation Française.

Porter, K. H., & Dupree, A. (2001). *Poverty Trends for Families Headed by Working Single Mothers 1993-1999.* Washington, DC: Center on Budget and Policy Priorities.

Sawhill, I. (2001). "From Welfare to Work. Making Welfare a Way Station, Not a Way of Life." *Brookings Review* 19, 3: 4-7.

Scott, E. K., London, A. S., & Myers, N. A. (2002). "Living With Violence: Women's Reliance on Abusive Men in their Transitions from Welfare to Work." In *Families at Work: Expanding the Bounds,* edited by N. Gerstel, D. Clawson, and R. Zussman. Nashville: Vanderbilt University Press.

Soss, J. et al. (2001). "Setting the Terms of Relief: Explaining State Policy Choices in the Devolution Revolution." *American Journal of Political Science* 45, 2: 378-395.

SPDP, State Policy Documentation Project. (1999). A joint project of the Center for Law and Social Policy and the Center on Budget and Policy Priorities, Washington DC; http://www.spdp.org.

Strawn, J., & Martinson, K. (2000). *Steady Work and Better Jobs: How to Help Low-Income Parents Sustain Employment and Advance in the Workforce.* New York: Manpower Demonstration Research Corporation (MDRC).

UNEDIC. (2000). *Convention relative à l'aide au retour à l'emploi et à l'indemnisation du chômage; http://www.assedic.fr*

UNIOPSS, Union nationale interfédérale des œuvres et organismes privés sanitaires et sociaux. (2001). *Exclusion sociale et pauvreté en Europe.* Ministère de l'emploi et de la solidarité. Paris: La Documentation Française.

U.S. DHHS, U.S. Department of Health and Human Services. (2000). *Temporary Assistance for Needy Families (TANF) Program.* Third Annual Report to Congress, Washington, DC; http://www.acf.dhhs.gov/programs/opre/annual3.doc

U.S. GAO. (2000). *Welfare Reform: State Sanction Policies and Number of Families Affected* HEHS-00-44. 31 March.

U.S. HR, U.S. House of Representatives, Committee on Ways and Means. (2000). *2000 Green Book.*Washington DC: U.S. Government Printing Office.

Wetzstein, C. (2001). "States Want Pro-Family Welfare Funds." *Washington Times,* 10 December.

Yerochewski, C. (2001). "Le Pare victime de son succès." *Alternatives économiques* 198: 30-32.

Zedlewski, S. (2001). *Former Welfare Families and the Food Stamp Program: The Exodus Continues. Assessing the New Federalism,* Brief B-33. Washington, DC: The Urban Institute.

Zoyem, J.-P. (1999). *Contrat d'insertion et sortie du RMI. Évaluation des effets d'une politique sociale,* INSEE, Document de travail de la Direction des Études et Synthèses Économiques, G 9909.

Part 3

The Evaluations of U.S. Welfare
Reforms and Their Implications

6

Assessing Welfare Reform in the United States[*]

Alan Weil

Introduction

The enactment of the Personal Responsibility and Work Opportunity Reconciliation Act of 1996 (PRWORA), commonly referred to as welfare reform, was accompanied by a flurry of research and evaluation activity. Congress took the unusual step of including funding in the law for the Census Bureau to expand the Survey of Income and Program Participation (SIPP) to gather new data on the effects of welfare reform (U.S. Congress, 1996). The U.S. Department of Health and Human Services (HHS, 2002) funded states to study the well-being of the millions of families that left the welfare rolls (so-called "leavers"). The private philanthropic community made an unprecedented financial commitment to a variety of research and evaluation projects designed to monitor and determine the effects of welfare reform and related policies (National Research Council, 2001).

More than idle curiosity lies behind this interest in research. The central provisions of PRWORA—time limits on benefits, the requirement that all welfare recipients be working or in state-approved work preparation activities soon after joining the rolls and quickly after giving birth, and provisions designed to increase marriage and decrease nonmarital births—were enacted with little evidentiary support to suggest that they would have the intended effects. Key figures, such as the 60-month lifetime time limit, the 20 percent of the caseload states were permitted to exempt from the time limits, the 90 percent work participation requirement among two-parent families, and the 80

*The opinions expressed are those of the author and do not represent those of the Urban Institute, its trustees, or its sponsors.

percent state financial maintenance of effort requirement, represented political compromises, not research-based conclusions about what would make the best welfare policy. The ideological tidal wave of welfare reform provided little opportunity for welfare recipients, advocates for the poor, or researchers to shape the legislation. The investment in research was viewed as a vehicle for improving policy choices as the new welfare system took shape.

In addition, many people and organizations to the left of center on the political spectrum lobbied hard against the bill and expected welfare reform to be a demonstrable failure. They drew upon modeling results that showed increased hardship if specific welfare provisions were enacted (Zedlewski et al., 1996) and research suggesting that states would compete to cut benefits when given the option of doing so (Peterson, 1995; Donahue, 1997). Of particular concern to some was repeal of the individual entitlement to benefits (Edelman, 1997). Research and analysis was viewed as essential for documenting the expected failure of welfare reform.

Funding for the existing Temporary Assistance for Needy Families (TANF) and Child Care and Development Fund (CCDF, also known as the CCDBG) block grants and the Food Stamps program expire on September 30, 2002. While it is possible that Congress will continue these programs ("reauthorize," in Congressional parlance) without making any substantive changes in the law or in the level of funding, advocates of all stripes view reauthorization as an opportunity for improvement.

This chapter presents some of the most important findings from the largest research project conducted in the wake of welfare reform. It draws almost entirely from the Assessing the New Federalism project (ANF), conducted by the Urban Institute, a nonprofit, non-partisan research organization based in Washington, D.C. This focus on ANF findings is a necessary limitation, given the large volume of research on the topic. Those who are interested in the broad range of research done on welfare will find every major study and many smaller studies catalogued by the Research Forum on Children, Families, and the New Federalism (2002) at Columbia University.

After providing a brief history of welfare policy in the United States, this chapter discusses the major challenges researchers face in determining the effects of welfare reform. The chapter goes on to report the major findings from the ANF project, describing how welfare policy has evolved, how the welfare caseload has shifted, the role of work in the new welfare system, how welfare fits within the broader social safety net, how family structure and child well-being have changed, and how certain populations have been affected by welfare policy. It concludes with a series of policy implications that emerge from these data.

Among the American public and politicians, the term "welfare" is generally used to describe only means tested, cash assistance programs that are not based upon the recipient having a disability. Thus, the American debate over welfare focuses on the old Aid to Families with Dependent Children (AFDC), enacted in 1935 as part of the Social Security Act, and its successor, TANF. While AFDC originally provided cash payments primarily to widows and divorced or abandoned women with children, over time the caseload came to be dominated by never-married women raising their children without the father present. This shift took place alongside a steady and dramatic increase in mothers' participation in the labor force. These two factors made welfare a political issue. Some characterized welfare as promoting nonmarital births and allowing unwed mothers to stay home with their children while other mothers had to go to work. The fact that federal expenditures on the AFDC program, which in 1995 reached its peak of $16.2 billion, represented less than 1 percent of the federal budget (U.S. House Committee, 2000), or that cash benefits in the median state in 1995 were insufficient to maintain a family at even half the federal poverty line (Zedlewski and Giannarelli, 1997), did not diminish the issue's political salience.

There were periodic efforts to remake AFDC into a work program. The Family Support Act (FSA) of 1988 established a new work program, Job Opportunities and Basic Skills Training (JOBS), and made other changes designed to promote work. The Act failed to achieve its objective, in part because states—as permitted by federal law—exempted a large portion of their caseload from work requirements and generally left the culture of the welfare system unchanged (Nathan, 1996). States took the lead in welfare reform in the 1990s, applying for waivers[1] with the encouragement of the Reagan, Bush, and Clinton administrations. Many of the provisions that appear in PRWORA—time limits, sanction policies, caps on benefits for families that have additional children—draw upon policies states put in place using federal waivers.

The major provisions of PRWORA can be found in many sources (Haskins and Blank, 2001; Weil and Finegold, 2002). Its best-known provisions are the five-year lifetime limit on benefits; the requirement that states impose financial sanctions on families who fail to follow program rules; the requirement that states move increasing portions of their caseload into work activities; and the block grant funding structure that fixes the federal contribution at historical levels. Other provisions radically restrict legal immigrants' eligibility for a variety of programs; increase funding and state flexibility in the area of child care; freeze eligibility for public health insurance, while giving states new options for expansions; restrict eligibility for the Food Stamps program; restrict children's eligibility for Supplemental Security Income (SSI); and require states to expand child support enforcement.

Major Challenges in Determining the Effects of Welfare Reform

An effort to determine the effects of welfare reform, or to evaluate welfare reform, quickly runs into a series of analytic challenges (Bell, 1999; Weil, 2002). The four challenges discussed in this section are: defining the policies to be included under the rubric of welfare reform, defining the populations of interest, obtaining the necessary data on welfare policies, and collecting sufficient data on how families are faring under welfare reform.

Defining the Policies of Interest

The enactment of PRWORA neither establishes the starting point for welfare reform nor captures all of the recent policy changes that might affect the success of welfare policy. While PRWORA represents a major change in national policy, as noted above, many of the law's provisions had been implemented by individual states under waiver provisions that existed in federal law prior to PRWORA's enactment.

Similarly, while the federal law was enacted in the summer of 1996, state welfare policies have taken some time to adjust to the new federal provisions. Those states that were leaders in welfare policy adopted state laws that fit within the new federal framework very quickly upon enactment of PRWORA. Other states were slower. Of particular importance, California, the largest state in the country, did not implement TANF until 1998 after protracted battles over the design of the new program (Geen et al., 1998).

Thus, a study of the effects of welfare reform that takes the world as it existed on August 22, 1996, as a well-defined pre-welfare baseline and considers all changes after that date to be attributable to welfare policy will fail to capture the reality of the evolutionary nature of much of welfare policy in the United States. By contrast, an effort to disaggregate welfare policy into its pieces and consider the timing of every provision in every state will lose the synergy implicit in welfare reform—that the effect of the policies is larger than the sum of the parts because the whole describes a qualitatively different system than what existed before.

A separate problem in describing the policies of interest is to determine which policies are sufficiently closely related to welfare that they must be included in an analysis of the program's effects. The problem is most obvious when one considers the Earned Income Tax Credit (EITC). The EITC provides a refundable credit against federal taxes for low-income families who have earnings. In 1999, a low-income family earning $6,800 with one child would receive a federal tax credit of 34 percent of their earnings or $2,312, the maximum available under the EITC. Families with earnings between $6,800 and $12,460 were eligible for the maximum credit, beyond which the credit decreased, phasing out entirely at earnings of just under $27,000 (U.S. House Committee, 2000). Thus, the EITC has a dramatic effect on the cash resources of low-income working families—a population that overlaps substantially with those that might be receiving welfare. In addition, the EITC was expanded significantly in the mid-1990s (Ross Phillips, 2001). The EITC costs the federal government more than the sum of all TANF grants to states (U.S. House Committee, 2000) and is credited with lifting more families out of poverty than any other public assistance program (Porter et al., 1998). A study of the effects of welfare reform must take into consideration this change in tax policy. Yet, to do so requires either of two approaches: an effort to "control for" the effects of the EITC when examining welfare, an endeavor that is neither conceptually nor analytically entirely possible, or the decision to include the EITC in the study of welfare policy, which by definition yields results that cannot isolate the effects of the welfare provisions in PRWORA.

The EITC example is replayed in many other areas. Federal appropriations for child care assistance were increased in PRWORA. The federal government and states have recently adopted policies that provide health insurance to more children and parents than were covered in the past. The federal minimum wage was increased in 1996 and again in 1997, the first increases since 1991. The child support system was given new enforcement tools in PRWORA. Ignoring these changes will give a skewed picture of the effects of welfare reform. Including them all redefines welfare reform to be so broad as to lose much of its meaning.

Defining the Population of Interest

Closely related to the challenge of defining the policies of interest is determining what populations should be included in an evaluation of welfare policy. One option is to treat those on welfare at the time PRWORA was enacted as the group of interest. Over time, these families can be divided into "stayers" and "leavers." The stayers are still on welfare and in a system that collects data on their work status, earnings, and benefits. The leavers can be identified and surveyed to gather information on their well-being, and data matches can be conducted to determine their earnings. As noted above, the federal government has supported a number of leaver studies.

Examining only those who were on welfare in 1996 ignores the effects of welfare policy on those who subsequently joined the rolls, or those who might have joined under the old system, but did not do so in the new system. This population is of particular interest because federal welfare law now permits states to divert potential applicants away from welfare. An effort to understand the effects of welfare reform should include an analysis of how those who are diverted fare. This suggests a broader population of interest than just stayers and leavers.

But how broadly should the population of interest be expanded? Early projections of the effects of welfare reform considered the possibility that the influx of former welfare recipients into the labor force would place downward pressure on wages and increase unemployment (McMurrer, Sawhill, and Lerman, 1997). A major goal of the federal welfare law is to reduce nonmarital births and to promote married-parent families. In addition, the law expands child support enforcement tools. These policies potentially affect the entire low-income population. The child care and health insurance expansions described above reach much further up the income scale than cash welfare does. Including these programs requires looking at families with incomes up to and above twice the poverty line—a group whose income greatly exceeds cash welfare eligibility standards.

Limitations of Policy Data

Under the AFDC program, other than through waivers, states had relatively few options in how they ran their programs. The basic program data, including income eligibility standards and income disregards, were readily available from the federal government. As states were given large new areas of authority, the number of dimensions of policy variation grew exponentially. Federal administration of the block grant did not require knowledge of all details of states' programs, so this information was not collected. Meanwhile, some states granted substantial flexibility in program rules to their counties.

Those who wish to determine the effects of policy are naturally drawn to typologies that summarize and condense the multiple dimensions. Yet, these efforts are difficult, subject to substantial criticism, and may or may not capture the reality of the underlying implementation of welfare policy (Weil, 2002). An alternative approach is one taken in most of the early studies that sought to differentiate the effects of welfare policy from the economy in welfare caseload reduction. These studies create time series and use the month or year of adoption of a waiver or a law as an analytic variable. However, they simplify most waivers to a dummy variable, neglecting all interstate differences in specific rules or methods of implementation.

The Urban Institute has made a major investment in collecting state welfare policies in the years since PRWORA's enactment. The compilation of policies is available on the Internet; a book that summarizes those policies runs more than 200 pages (Rowe, 2000). While these data miss some intrastate variation, and they cannot capture the differences between how program rules are written and how they are implemented, they represent the most comprehensive collection of TANF program rules available.

Limitations of Outcomes Data

An effort to study the effects of welfare reform must draw upon data that show the well-being of families. There are three limitations researchers face in obtaining these data. First, for many of the populations of interest, information is simply not gathered. Some administrative and survey data are available on welfare leavers and stayers, but these data miss other important populations, such as those who never apply for welfare. Second, state-level data are limited, and when they are available, they are unlikely to be comparable across states. The SIPP, designed to be a primary source of information related to the effects of welfare policy, is of limited use for state-specific analysis (National Research Council, 2001). Some other data sources provide state-level estimates, but they generally suffer from the third limitation: narrow content. A broad view of the possible effects of welfare reform includes at a minimum employment, economic well-being, program participation, child and family functioning, and family structure. This constellation of data cannot be found on any existing government survey that provides state-level estimates.

Approaches Taken

Despite these limitations, a report of the National Research Council of the National Academy of Sciences characterizes the body of welfare reform research projects as "impressive in scope, volume, and diversity" and "unprecedented in comparison with any prior era of welfare reform." The same report, however, concludes that these studies "have done a reasonable job of monitoring the progress of the low-income and welfare populations," but far less well in evaluating the effects of welfare reform (National Research Council 2001).

The largest privately funded study discussed by the NRC is the Assessing the New Federalism project (ANF). ANF is a multi-year, multi-subject research project designed to document the policy changes and consequences of the federal government transferring authority for safety net programs to the states. The project is national in scope, but focuses its case study and survey activity on thirteen states that together are home to more than one-half of the nation's population, while they represent a range of states in terms of geography, child well-being, and approaches to public policy. More information on the ANF project can be found in Kondratas, Weil, and Goldstein (1998) and in Dean-Brick et. al (1999).

The ANF project takes a broad view of welfare policy and the populations likely to be affected by these policies. Most of the project's work looks at the characteristics of the entire population of families with children with incomes below twice the federal poverty line. Additional work focuses on specific populations, such as those on welfare, those who recently left welfare, or those who receive public benefits such as health insurance, child care subsidies, or food stamps. The project has made a major investment in gathering information on states' policy choices, covering topics including cash assistance, child care assistance, and health insurance. The project's largest component is the National Survey of America's Families (NSAF), a survey of more than 42,000 households, which has been conducted in 1997 and 1999, and is being repeated in 2002. Consistent with other aspects of the ANF design, the NSAF has a national sample, but also includes large samples in thirteen states, permitting consistent, cross-state comparisons on many indicators. The NSAF also oversamples households with children with incomes below twice the federal poverty level—the population of primary interest in our work.

Ten Major Findings On Welfare Reform

Despite the limitations researchers face, there is much that we have learned about welfare policy and welfare reform over the past six years. This section highlights ten findings that capture the essence of our research.

Welfare Reform Has Taken Hold

PRWORA was not the first attempt at welfare reform. Yet, prior efforts had limited effects on the actual operation of the welfare system (Nathan, 1996). By contrast, PRWORA ushered in an era of substantial change.

In the immediate aftermath of PRWORA, states made four major and rapid changes in their welfare systems. First, they took clear steps to shift to "work first" welfare systems. That is, they designed their welfare programs to emphasize rapid labor force attachment, with less emphasis on skills development or long-term education. States overwhelmingly adopted narrower exemptions from work requirements than had existed under AFDC. Most notably, with the federal government's repeal of the work exemption for parents with children less than three years of age, most states limited the exemption to one year, while many states chose even shorter periods, and a few have no exemption at all (Rowe, 2000). States also required welfare applicants to participate in work-related activities, with most states requiring applicants to spend a specified number of hours searching for a job immediately upon applying for welfare. In some states the welfare application is not even processed until job search activities are completed.

Second, most states modified program rules to help make work pay. Thirty-one states quickly expanded earned income disregards, which allow welfare recipients to keep more of their cash benefits even as they begin having earnings from work (Gallagher, et al., 1998). Most states use higher income standards for testing eligibility among recipients than among applicants (Rowe, 2000). In 2001, sixteen states had earned income tax credits that supplement the federal EITC, providing additional resources to working families through the tax code (Johnson, 2001).

Third, states adopted a varied set of rules to comply with federal work-oriented requirements in PRWORA. States designed and implemented sanction policies that reduced or eliminated benefits for those families that failed to follow program rules. Thirty-six states adopted full family sanctions (Gallagher et al., 1998). States also implemented the federally imposed five-year time limit on benefits, with ten states adopting shorter lifetime limits (Rowe, 2000).

Finally, states took steps to communicate these changes to caseworkers, welfare recipients, and applicants. Most states required some form of orientation session for applicants before they could be approved for benefits. These sessions emphasized the temporary nature of cash assistance and the requirement that almost all applicants pursue and obtain employment.

The Welfare Caseload Remains Dynamic

Ellwood and Bane (1983) documented that the welfare caseload was composed of two groups: long-term recipients who, at any given moment, composed about half of those receiving welfare, and short-term recipients who were the majority of those who receive benefits from the program over time. Subsequent analysis showed the high frequency with which people leave and return to the welfare rolls (Pavetti and Acs, 1997).

Despite rapidly falling welfare caseloads under PRWORA, the dynamic nature of the welfare caseload remains. Loprest (2002) finds that, among those who left welfare some time between 1997 and 1999, 22 percent were back on the rolls when they were interviewed in 1999. Looking at caseload dynamics another way, of those on welfare in 1999, 47 percent had been on consistently for the prior two years, 26 percent were on for the first time, and 23 percent had returned to the rolls after a period off welfare (Zedlewski and Alderson, 2001).

Those who have been on welfare continuously for the past two years and those who have left the rolls and returned have characteristics that suggest their prospects for sustained, successful employment are limited. Among long-term recipients and those who returned to the rolls, the prevalence of poor physical or mental health is 39 and 46 percent, respectively. Similarly, among these two groups the percentage with less than a high school education is 50 and 38 percent, respectively (Loprest, 2002).

These data help us interpret the decline of more than 50 percent in the nation's welfare caseload between 1994 and 2000. One possible early interpretation was that the caseload was falling because very few new applicants were joining the rolls due to successful efforts to divert and discourage applicants. A second possible interpretation was that the "easy" welfare cases were leaving the rolls, leaving behind those who are hardest to serve. The data demonstrate that neither of these hypotheses explains the magnitude of the caseload decline. Rather, just as in the past, the caseload is composed of a combination of short-term and long-term recipients whose employment prospects range from excellent to very poor.

More on Welfare Are Working Than in the Past

One goal of welfare reform was to increase work activity among those who are receiving cash assistance, and, indeed, that has occurred. The increase is striking. In 1999, 32 percent of welfare recipients reported some amount of paid work, up from 22 percent in 1997 (Loprest, 2002). Administrative data show work participation increasing from around 7 percent in the early 1990s to 33 percent in 1999 (HHS, 2000). Wages for these working welfare recipients are low. Their median hourly wage of $6.65 is lower than the $7.15 per hour median wage for those who have left welfare (Loprest, 2002).

Of particular interest is the increased level of work activity among those who face barriers to going to work. Research has demonstrated that people with limited education or work experience, raising young children, in poor physical or mental health, caring for a severely disabled child, or with limited English proficiency are less likely to be working. This pattern remains, but between 1997 and 1999, NSAF data show work among welfare recipients facing two or more of these barriers increasing four-fold, from 5 percent to 20 percent (Zedlewski and Alderson, 2001).

Increased work among welfare recipients is due to a complex set of factors. A portion of the shift reflects a change in behavior among welfare recipients. This increase in work parallels a dramatic increase in work among single mothers, from 59 percent employed in 1993 to 73 percent employed just five years later (Lerman, 2001).[2]

Increased work may also reflect changed reporting incentives. Under AFDC neither families nor states had an incentive to report earnings. Families with earnings received lower benefits and states were not judged on the basis of whether or not recipients were working. Under TANF, families face work requirements, larger income disregards, and the potential benefits of the EITC, making it more advantageous to report earnings than was the case in the past. States are held accountable to the federal government for meeting work participation targets among their welfare caseloads. The degree to which this increase reflects more accurate data collection is not known.

A final reason for observing more work among welfare recipients is the effect of increased earnings disregards. Larger disregards mean welfare recipients who go to work in low-paying jobs are more likely to remain eligible for a cash payment than they were in the past. With workers staying on the welfare rolls longer, the percentage of the caseload made up of workers will increase.

Most Who Have Left Welfare Are Working, But for Low Wages

With rapid and large declines in the welfare caseload, much attention has been focused on the well-being of those who have left the welfare rolls. Indeed, the news generally seems good. Sixty-four percent of those who left the welfare rolls between 1997 and 1999 and remain off welfare were working in 1999, and 79 percent were in a family with someone working. The median wage for former welfare recipients in 1999 was $7.15, which places these families squarely in the lower end of the labor market (Loprest, 2002). Like other low-wage jobs, the jobs of welfare leavers offer few benefits. Only about a third of these employers offer health insurance, and a slightly larger share offer paid sick leave (Acs and Loprest, 2001).

Adults who leave welfare and work full-time for a full year at the median wage and receive all supplementary benefits for which they were eligible could move their families out of poverty (Acs et al., 1998). However, most do not receive all of these wage supplements. In addition, the 25th percentile hourly wage was just $6.05. Together these data demonstrate that many working welfare leavers live on resources below the poverty line (Loprest, 2002).

As noted above, 22 percent of those who left welfare between 1997 and 1999 were back on welfare. These families may get a second or third chance to find stable employment, moving on and off welfare a number of times before they leave for good. However, if these efforts fail or take more than five years, the families lose access to federally funded cash benefits unless they fit within the 20 percent of caseload exemption for the time limit as defined by the state.

In addition, one in seven adults who leave welfare report no visible means of support. These welfare leavers are not employed, are not in a family with someone who is employed, are not receiving disability benefits, and have not returned to the welfare rolls where they will obtain benefits. Little is known about how these families survive, and why they have completely disconnected from the welfare system. With several hundred thousand families with children falling into this category in 1999, this group warrants more policy attention in the future.

States Are Doing More to Support Work

One of the most interesting stories of welfare reform is how dramatically it has shifted resources into systems that support paid employment. In 2000, only 41 percent of TANF spending was on paying cash benefits, down from 76 percent in 1996 (Zedlewski et al., 2002). Almost 30 percent of TANF funds were going to child care and work activities, up from just 9 percent four years earlier. Additional funds were going to a combination of activities, including transportation support, tax credits for low-income families, and programs to promote marriage or reduce nonmarital births.

The extent of these shifts varies substantially from state to state. Under TANF's fixed grant structure, large caseload declines free up resources that can be used for other purposes. In 2000, nine states were devoting less than a quarter of their TANF spending to cash benefits, while three states, including California, spent more than 55 percent on cash benefits (Zedlewski et al., 2002).

Reports from case studies indicate that states are also increasing their spending on services that support those who have substantial barriers to work. The "hard-to-serve" include those with mental or physical disabilities, substance abuse problems, and those with limited English language proficiency. No systematic data are available to quantify spending on services for these populations, but they are certainly getting more attention under TANF than they did in the past.

These direct expenditures described above supplement two policy changes discussed earlier: increased income disregards that permit families to keep more of their cash benefits as they begin to have earnings, and the federal EITC. This combination of work supports and financial supplements to work represent a major commitment to making work pay.

An important question when examining these data on changing TANF spending is whether these patterns represent new expenditures, or simply the reporting of previously existing spending under a new guise. The U.S. General Accounting Office (2001) has attempted to answer this difficult question. It examined ten states and found that all were spending less on cash benefits and most were bearing a smaller share of the financial burden relative to the federal government than they had in the past. Two aspects of this finding are important to note. First, the reported degree of "supplantation" (using federal funds to replace prior state spending) varied substantially across the ten states they examined. Second, the extent of supplantation is sensitive to how broadly one defines social services spending; a narrow definition reveals supplantation, while a broad definition that includes health and other social services programs does not.

The Work Support System Often Does Not Meet the Needs of Workers

Despite an increased financial commitment to supporting work, the shift to supporting work has been plagued with administrative difficulties. The problem stems from two sources. First, traditional welfare bureaucracies, designed to serve those in dire need who are not working, were not well suited to meet the needs of working families that face substantial constraints balancing work, family, and bureaucratic obligations. Second, separate administrative systems designed around specific programs, services, and providers were not coordinated in a manner that provides a comprehensive package of assistance to meet the needs of families.

Analysis conducted just before the implementation of PRWORA documented the degree of fragmentation in the various work support systems. Burt, Pindus, and Capizzano (2000) found that those who enter the system through the door of the welfare office were quite likely to find connections to a panoply of other supports, such as food stamps, health insurance, and, to a lesser degree, child care and child support assistance. However, those who entered through the door of the employment agency or the child support agency were far less likely to be informed of, directed to, or have their services coordinated with other agencies.

The fact that these problems remain is apparent when one examines caseload data for the Food Stamps program and the Medicaid program in the years following welfare reform. Both programs experienced substantial and rapid drops in enrollment. Subsequent analysis demonstrated that people who left welfare and remained eligible for these other support programs failed to obtain these benefits (Davidoff, Garrett, and Yemane, 2002; Zedlewski and Brauner, 1999; Zedlewski and Gruber, 2001). The story of child care is different. The movements of so many from welfare to work yielded increased use of child care supports. However, in many sites the administration of child care subsidies places time and documentation demands on applicants who are inconsistent with the needs of someone holding a job and raising children (Adams, Snyder, and Sandfort, 2002).

Deep Hardship Has Increased

With political attention focused on how TANF has converted welfare into a work-oriented program, it is easy to forget that TANF retains the old AFDC role of serving as the ultimate cash safety net for the lowest income families with children. AFDC benefits were never sufficiently generous to lift these families above the poverty line. However, the benefits the program did provide averted deep poverty.

Recent evidence suggests that the safety net post-PRWORA is less effective at supporting the neediest families than AFDC was. Zedlewski (2002) analyzed the financial resources of independent single-parent families—those with a single adult caring for one or more children without any other adults in the household. Between 1996 and 1998, the percentage of these families with any earnings increased from 83 to 88, but the percentage receiving TANF fell from 34 to 24, and the percentage receiving food stamps fell from 48 to 40 percent.

The figures are starker when the analysis focuses on the bottom quintile of independent single-parent families—those with income below 70 percent of the poverty line. The percentage of these families with earnings rose 4 points between 1996 and 1998, but the percentage with TANF income and food stamps benefits fell 17 and 9 points, respectively. When the overall financial picture of these families is examined, the 1.3 million independent single-parent families in the bottom quintile are shown to have experienced an average net decline in financial resources of $630, or 8 percent (Zedlewski, 2002). These statistics are of particular concern because they took place during a period of unprecedented economic growth.

Not all states experienced an increase in deep hardship. Ironically, states with more generous cash grants are more likely to observe such an increase. This is because a family moving off the welfare rolls either without employment or in a low-wage part-time job moves from poverty into deep poverty. In low benefit states, families living on the welfare grant live in deep poverty, so when they leave the rolls without work, they do not increase the count of families in deep poverty.

Family Structure

States have made two kinds of efforts to achieve the family structure goals of welfare reform. First, they have attempted to realign financial incentives to eliminate preexisting disadvantages that married parent families faced. Second, they have designed and implemented programs to dissuade teenagers and unmarried women from having children.

The original AFDC program was only available to parents who met the deprivation standard, meaning the "continued absence, incapacity, death or unemployment" of one parent. Under this definition, even very low-income married parents were ineligible for benefits. The Family Support Act of 1988 required states to establish AFDC-U programs to serve families in which one parent had a work history but was currently unemployed. Under TANF, thirty-three states treat single and married parent families identically with respect to eligibility, and another twelve made the treatment more equal than it had been in the past (Rowe, 2000).

Despite the elimination of formal rules that barred married parent families from eligibility, TANF retains the fundamental structural problem of a means-tested program targeted at those at the bottom of the income scale. Marriage to even a low-earning partner increases family income, thereby reducing or eliminating benefits. Thus, family-structure neutral eligibility rules that include an income test continue to disadvantage married parent families. The federal EITC has a slightly different set of incentives, since it has a phase-in income range as well as a phase-out range. If two adults have sufficiently low income, they can experience an increase in EITC benefits if they marry; adults with higher incomes face a marriage penalty. Most states that have enacted EITCs have the same structure.

Enhanced child support enforcement efforts are another mechanism for reducing the financial incentives for giving birth to and raising children outside of marriage, and evidence suggests that active enforcement has an effect on parental behavior (Nixon, 1997; Huang, 2001). PRWORA increased child support enforcement requirements for states, continuing a trend of increased activity in this area that began more than ten years earlier.

States have been more cautious in adopting programs targeted directly at marital and childbearing behavior. Programs designed to discourage teenagers from having children have grown substantially in the 1990s. Broader efforts to reduce nonmarital childbearing by adults are less common. While fourteen states had programs in 1999 designed to encourage sexual abstinence before marriage, none of the ten most populous states were home to these programs (Wertheimer, Jager, and Moore, 2000).

All together, these efforts have yielded few behavior effects than can be measured in population data. Teen birth rates have been falling since 1992, and the share of children living in married couple families stopped declining in the mid-1990s (Lerman, 2002). Fewer children are living with single mothers; more are living with cohabiting partners (sometimes both of the child's parents), but there has been no statistically significant increase in the share living with married parents (Acs and Nelson, 2001).

Effects on Children Remain Unclear

While many aspects of welfare policy could improve or harm children's well-being, evidence to date shows few measurable effects. Across a variety of measures, children in families on welfare and those in families who have left welfare fared no better or worse in 1999 than they did in 1997 (Zaslow et al., 2002). Specific welfare experiments have shown positive results for some children when parents go to work and increase the financial resources available to the family and some negative results, especially for adolescents (Hamilton et al., 2001). These experimental results do not yet point the way to unambiguous conclusions about the relationship between welfare policy and child well-being.

The absence of strong findings may reflect data limitations. Comprehensive measures of child well-being require direct observation, which is time consuming and expensive; narrower measures are not part of most population surveys. Limited findings may also reflect how long it takes for a series of modest changes to accumulate in a manner that affects children's well-being. While parental employment and family income may change rapidly, aggregate measures of children's well-being are likely to change much more slowly.

Welfare's Effects on Subgroups Are Varied

Welfare policies designed to support work are being applied to a heterogeneous population, with possibly varied effects. Elimination of the federal entitlement to benefits implies greater discretion with regard to services and supports provided, expectations placed upon clients, and application of sanction policies. The welfare population also becomes subject to the practices of the labor market, with differential rewards for different levels of education, training and work experience; wages and benefits reflecting broader labor market conditions; and the possible effects of discriminatory practices.

Reductions in the proportion of the population receiving welfare have been large and fairly consistent across racial and ethnic groups. As Finegold and Staveteig (2002) note, these data tell us little about the presence or absence of discrimination, since such practices in the welfare office might reduce caseloads, while labor market discrimination could increase caseloads. Still, a few warning signs are present. A larger share of blacks than whites who have left welfare indicate that they did so for administrative reasons. Fewer blacks than whites report receiving government supports in the few months after leaving welfare. A few small-scale studies have shown disturbing evidence of differential treatment between blacks and whites (e.g., Gooden, 1998).

Immigrants were the target of a substantial set of new legal provisions designed to bar them from receiving certain benefits. Prior to welfare reform, participation rates in AFDC and food stamps among low-income families with children led by legal permanent-resident aliens were lower than they were among families led by citizens (Fix and Passel, 2002). These rates have fallen among legal permanent-resident alien families at about the same rate as they have fallen among citizen-led families. Studies have demonstrated that the immigrant provisions had a "chilling effect," meaning families that retained eligibility left or failed to apply for the program out of fear or confusion (Fix and Zimmermann, 1998). More recent evidence, showing substantial declines in TANF participation among refugees—a group that should have been unaffected by the PRWORA provisions—affirms the existence of this phenomenon.

The immigrant provisions of PRWORA contained a new federalism twist. For the first time, states were given authority to define the safety net for needy immigrants. State choices were quite varied, with California standing out as having adopted the most generous package of supports despite substantial anti-immigrant political rhetoric that existed at the time (Tumlin, Zimmerman, and Ost, 1999). Also of interest is the fact that recent growth in the immigrant population is larger in low benefit states than in high benefit states, offering evidence that counters the hypothesis that high benefits serve as a "magnet" for immigrants (Fix and Passel, 2002).

Policy Implications

The existing TANF grant expires on September 30, 2002. Before that date, Congress must enact and President Bush must sign a bill to reauthorize the program for the future. As of this writing, President Bush has developed a proposal for reauthorization, and Representatives Cardin and Mink have introduced bills. The U.S. Department of Health and Human Services solicited comments on reauthorization and received almost 700 over the Internet alone.

The Urban Institute is not an advocacy organization, and does not take positions on proposed legislation. Our research, however, points toward a few policy principles that should be considered as welfare reauthorization proceeds.

Importance of Stability

The most encouraging aspects of welfare reform have taken time to develop. States were reluctant to develop or expand work supports such as child care and health insurance, and they were slow to develop programs that help employ people with substantial barriers to work. However, as it became clear that caseload declines were going to last, and states faced pressure to spend their available funds, more of these programs emerged. Similarly, over time local program administrators have developed linkages with a variety of community-based service providers that can help families meet their basic needs and deliver contracted services such as job training or assistance with complex needs like substance abuse or low educational attainment. General stability in the program will allow these developments to continue.

Help States Support Work

States have taken seriously the goal of moving families from welfare into paid work. The flexibility built into the federal law gives states many options for how they want to approach this task, and varied state policy choices reflect this flexibility. However, two aspects of federal law restrict this flexibility in a manner that seems inconsistent with the overall principles that are found in PRWORA.

First, the clock is running on the federal five-year limit on benefits every month a person receives benefits, even if that person is working. In a state with generous income disregards, a person can follow all program rules, mix cash assistance with paid work, yet be using up her limited benefits. While states vary in their use of income disregards, they have good reasons for wanting to adopt them. These disregards can provide families with a longer transition to self-sufficiency, can reduce hardship among families as they enter the work force, and can be of particular importance in areas with a high cost of living. Yet, federal law limits the benefits a state, and its citizens, can accrue from having these disregards.

Second, federal work participation goals for states do not count certain activities that might prepare a person for work. The dynamics of this provision are similar to those related to income disregards. States are disadvantaged if they choose welfare policies that emphasize training or impose substantial non-work burdens such as language training or substance abuse prevention counseling on families.

During the first six years of welfare reform these two provisions had limited effect. Very few families have reached their five-year limit on benefits. States have been able to exempt the few families that have reached this limit, and they have used creative accounting methods to avoid spending federal funds on services for them. Similarly, rapidly falling welfare caseloads have rendered the work participation goals easy to meet.[3] Still, the fact that these provisions have not caused problems to date does not mean they should not be fixed. In a tighter economy, and as the welfare system evolves, these federal provisions place substantial limitations on state flexibility that may prevent effective welfare policies from being adopted by states.

Refine the Federal Government's Role

States are firmly in control of welfare policy today. Federal mandates and proscriptions are substantial, but they are minor compared to the overall breadth of options states have. Yet, the federal government is paying a larger portion of the welfare bill than it did prior to reform (Zedlewski et al., 2002). History tells us that over time the federal government resists playing the role of federal financier without having a concomitant degree of programmatic control. The federal government's support for block grants either erodes, since the grants have a less well-defined constituency than do more targeted programs, or the block grants accrete rules, regulations, and restrictions over time.

The best defense against an eroding or corroding federal role is an effort early on to define an appropriate one. Two needs stand out. First, the federal government should increase its commitment to funding welfare experiments—well-designed efforts to determine what works and what does not in emerging welfare policy. With this funding, states can play the role of laboratories envisioned by devolution proponents. Second, the federal government must continue to refine its definition of success in welfare policy. While states may bristle at greater federal oversight, they will benefit in the long run from a solid national commitment to TANF and related programs.

Conclusion

Welfare policy and practice continue to evolve more than five years after the enactment of federal welfare reform. Many localities have moved beyond the strictly work-first policies adopted immediately after PRWORA, now providing a mixture of work support services and helping clients overcome barriers they may face in going to work (Holcomb and Martinson, 2002). States are focusing increased attention on those on welfare who are hard to employ. States vary substantially in their treatment of this heterogeneous group, relying on a combination of exemptions from work requirements and enhanced services to help place them in jobs, but also sometimes losing them from the welfare system as they are sanctioned for failing to meet program rules (Burt, 2002).

Local welfare offices have taken on the challenge of building new relationships with community-based providers, mostly nonprofit organizations, but in some instances for-profit providers as well. Client advocates have found a new voice in the welfare system, identifying supports that are necessary if clients are to succeed in the new work-oriented welfare system. As the first clients reach the five-year lifetime limit on benefits, states and localities are considering exemption policies while they also develop more intensive assessment tools designed to prevent these families from facing serious hardship when their benefits run out.

Those looking for good news about welfare reform can find it easily. Caseloads have fallen dramatically, work among those on welfare is up, most of those who left the rolls are working, poverty is down, and there are no measurable negative trends in child well-being. Yet, all of this good news emerges from a period of unprecedented economic growth. Welfare has benefited from a virtuous cycle: work-oriented policies and a strong economy have led to falling caseloads, which, with funding fixed, means more money to spend on work supports, thereby improving employment prospects, and the cycle continues. A weaker economy, combined with tighter state fiscal conditions, could reverse the cycle.

Still, it is undeniable that welfare reform has made the welfare system more flexible. By giving more control to state and local officials, it has increased their commitment to its success. Together, these factors make it more likely that the system will respond to changed circumstances—which stands in stark contrast to the rigid welfare system of the past. It is too early to tell if increased flexibility and commitment are all that is necessary to weather an economic downturn. That will prove to be the next test of American welfare policy.

Notes

1. Section 1115 of the Social Security Act permits the federal government to waive certain statutory requirements at the request of a state. The provision was enacted in 1962, but few states took advantage of it until the federal government began encouraging waivers in the Reagan administration—a posture that was retained by subsequent presidents.
2. Some of this increase could be the result of welfare reform, and some of the increase in work among welfare recipients is reflected in this increase. The two phenomena are interrelated, with the direction of causation flowing both ways.
3. States get a credit against their work participation goal equal to the percentage reduction in caseload.

References

Acs, G., & Loprest, P. (2001). "Synthesis Report of the Findings from ASPE's 'Leavers' Grants.'" Washington, DC: U.S. Department of Health and Human Services.

Acs, G., Coe, N. B., Lerman, R. I., & Watson, K. (1998). *Does Work Pay? A Summary of the Work Incentives Under TANF. Assessing the New Federalism* Brief A-28. Washington, DC: The Urban Institute.

Acs, G., & Nelson, S. (2001). *"Honey, I'm Home." Changes in Living Arrangements in the Late 1990s. Assessing the New Federalism* B-38. Washington, DC: The Urban Institute.

Adams, G., Snyder, K., & Sandfort, S. (2002). *Getting and Retaining Child Care Assistance: How Policy and Practice Influence Parents' Experiences. Assessing the New Federalism* Occasional Paper 55. Washington, DC: The Urban Institute.

Bell, S. H. (1999). *New Federalism and Research: Rearranging Old Methods to Study New Social Policies in the States. Assessing the New Federalism* Discussion Paper 99-08. Washington, DC: The Urban Institute.

Burt, M. R., Pindus, N., & Capizzano, J. (2000). *The Social Safety Net at the Beginning of Federal Welfare Reform: Organization of and Access to Social Services for Low-Income Families. Assessing the New Federalism* Occasional Paper 34. Washington, DC: The Urban Institute

Burt, M. (2002). "The 'Hard-to-Serve': Definitions and Implications." In *Welfare Reform The Next Act*, edited by Alan Weil and Kenneth Finegold. Washington, DC: The Urban Institute.

Davidoff, A., Garrett, B., & Yemane, A. (2002). *Medicaid Eligibility, Takeup, Insurance Coverage, and Health Care Access and Use before and after Welfare Reform: National*

Changes from 1994 to 1997. Assessing the New Federalism Discussion Paper. Washington, DC: The Urban Institute.

Dean Brick, P., Genevieve, K., McCullough-Harlin, R., Rajan, S., Scheuren, F., Wang, K., Brick, J. M., & Cunningham, P. (1999). *National Survey of America's Families: Survey Methods and Data Reliability.* No. 1. Washington, DC: The Urban Institute.

Donahue, J. D. (1997). *Disunited States: What's at Stake as Washington Fades and the States Take the Lead.* New York: Basic Books.

Edelman, P. (1997). "The Worst Thing Bill Clinton Has Done." *Atlantic Monthly* 279, 3.

Ellwood, D. T., & Bane, M. J. (1983). *The Dynamics of Dependence: The Routes to Self-Sufficiency.* Cambridge, MA: Urban Systems Research and Engineering.

Finegold, K., & Staveteig, S. (2002). "Race, Ethnicity and Welfare Reform." In *Welfare Reform The Next Act,* edited by Alan Weil and Kenneth Finegold. Washington, DC: The Urban Institute.

Fix, M., & Passel, J. S. (2002). "Assessing Welfare Reform's Immigration Provisions." In *Welfare Reform The Next Act,* edited by Alan Weil and Kenneth Finegold. Washington, DC: The Urban Institute.

Fix, M., & Zimmermann, W. (1998). *Declining Immigrant Applications for Medi-Cal and Welfare Benefits in Los Angeles County.* Washington, DC: The Urban Institute.

Gallagher, L. J., Gallagher, M., Perese, K., Schreiber, S., & Watson, K. (1998). *One Year after Federal Welfare Reform: A Description of State Temporary Assistance for Needy Families (TANF) Decisions as of October 1997. Assessing the New Federalism* Occasional Paper 16. Washington, DC: The Urban Institute.

Geen, R., Zimmerman, W., Douglas, T., Zedlewski, S., & Waters, S. (1998). *Income Support and Social Services for Low-Income People in California. Assessing the New Federalism* State Report. Washington, DC: The Urban Institute.

Gooden, S. (1998). "All Things Not Being Equal: Differences in Caseworker Support toward Black and White Welfare Clients." *Harvard Journal of African American Public Policy* 4: 23-33.

Hamilton, G. et al. (2001). *National Evaluation of Welfare-to-Work Strategies.* Washington, DC: Manpower Demonstration Research Corporation.

Haskins, R., & Blank, R. M. (2001). *Welfare Reform: An Agenda for Reauthorization,* edited by Ron Haskins and Rebecca M. Blank, 3-32). Washington, DC: Brookings Institution Press.

Holcomb, P. A., & Martinson, K. (2002). "Putting Policy into Practice: Five Years of Welfare Reform." In *Welfare Reform The Next Act,* edited by Alan Weil and Kenneth Finegold. Washington, DC: The Urban Institute.

Huang, C. C. (2001). "Impacts of Child Support Enforcement on Non-Marital and Marital Births: Is It Different by Racial and Age Group?" Paper presented at the Joint Center for Poverty Research Conference, Washington, DC.

Internal Revenue Service. (2000). *Statistics of Income Bulletin* (Spring): Table 2.

Johnson, N. (2001). A Hand Up: How State Earned Income Tax Credits Help Working Families Escape Poverty in 2001. Washington, DC: Center for Budget and Policy Priorities. <http://www.cbpp.org/12-27-01sfp.pdf Washington, D.C.>. Accessed 11/02/02.

Kondratas, A., Weil, A., & Goldstein, N. (1998). "Assessing the New Federalism: An Introduction" *Health Affairs* (May/June): 17-24.

Lerman, R. I. (2001). "Jobs and Wages Up Sharply for Single Moms, Gains Especially High After Welfare Reform." In *Single Parents' Earnings Monitor.* Washington, DC: The Urban Institute.

Lerman, R. I. (2002). "Family Structure and Childbearing before and after Welfare Reform." In *Welfare Reform The Next Act,* edited by Alan Weil and Kenneth Finegold. Washington, DC: The Urban Institute.

Loprest, P. J. (2002). "Making the Transition from Welfare to Work: Successes but Continuing Concerns." In *Welfare Reform The Next Act*, edited by Alan Weil and Kenneth Finegold. Washington, DC: The Urban Institute.

McMurrer, D. P., Sawhill, I.V., & Lerman, R. I. (1997). *Welfare Reform and Opportunity in the Low-Wage Labor Market. Opportunity in America* Brief 5. Washington, DC: The Urban Institute.

Nathan, R. P. (1996). "The 'Devolution Revolution'—An Overview." *Rockefeller Institute Bulletin*. Albany, NY: Nelson A. Rockefeller Institute of Government.

National Research Council. (2001). *Evaluating Welfare Reform in an Era of Transition.* Edited by Robert A. Moffitt and Michele Ver Ploeg. Washington, DC: National Academy Press.

Nixon, L. A. (1997). "The Effect of Child Support Enforcement on Marital Dissolution." *Journal of Human Resources 32*, 1: 159-81.

Pavetti, L., & Acs, G. (1997). *Moving Up, Moving Out, or Going Nowhere? A Study of the Employment Patterns of Young Women*. Washington, DC: The Urban Institute.

Peterson, P. E. (1995). *The Price of Federalism*. Washington, DC: The Brookings Institution.

Porter, K., Primus, W., Rawlings, L., & Rosenbaum, E. (1998). *Strengths of the Safety Net: How the EITC, Social Security and other Government Programs Affect Poverty*. Washington, DC: Center on Budget and Policy Priorities.

Research Forum on Children, Families and the New Federalism. <http://www.researchforum.org/>. Accessed 07/02/2002.

Ross Phillips, K. (2001). *Who Knows about the Earned Income Tax Credit. Assessing the New Federalism* Brief B-27. Washington, DC: The Urban Institute.

Rowe, G. (2000). "State TANF Policies as of July 1999." In *Welfare Rules Databook. Assessing the New Federalism*. Washington, DC: The Urban Institute.

Tumlin, K., Zimmerman, W., & Ost, J. (1999). *State Snapshots of Public Benefits for Immigrants: A Supplemental Report to Patchwork Policies. Assessing the New Federalism* Occasional Paper 24. Washington, DC: The Urban Institute.

U.S. Congress. House Committee on Ways and Means. (2000). Green Book. In *Background Material and Data on Major Programs within the Jurisdiction of the Committee on Ways and Means*. Washington, DC: U.S. Government Printing Office.

U.S. Congress. House of Representatives. (1996). Personal Responsibility and Work Opportunity Reconciliation Act of 1996: Conference Report to Accompany H.R. 3754. Report 104-725, 104th cong., 2d sess. <http://frwebgate.access.gpo.gov/cgi-bin/getdoc.cgi?dbname=104_cong_report&docid=f:hr725.104.pdf>. Accessed 12/02/2002.

U.S. Department of Health and Human Services, Administration for Children and Families. (2000). *Temporary Assistance to Needy Families (TANF) Program: Third Annual Report to Congress*. Washington DC: U.S. Government Printing Office.

U.S. Department of Health and Human Services, Office of the Assistant Secretary for Planning & Evaluation. "Leavers" and Diversion Studies. <http://aspe.hhs.gov/hsp/leavers99/reports.htm>. Accessed 07/02/2002.

U.S. General Accounting Office. (2001). *Welfare Reform: Challenges in Maintaining a Federal-State Fiscal Partnership*. GAO-01-828. Washington, DC.

Weil, A. (2002). "Program Redesign by States in the Wake of Welfare Reform: Making Sense of the Effects of Devolution." In *For Better of For Worse: Welfare Reform and the Well Being of Children and Families*, edited by Greg Duncan and P. Lindsay Chase-Lansdale. New York: Russell Sage Foundation Press.

Weil, A., & Finegold, K. (2002). "Introduction." In *Welfare Reform The Next Act*, edited by Alan Weil and Kenneth Finegold. Washington, DC: The Urban Institute.

Wertheimer, R., Jager, J., & Anderson, K. (2000). *State Policy Initiatives for Reducing Teen and Adult Nonmarital Childbearing: Family Planning to Family Caps. Assessing the New Federalism* Brief A-43. Washington, DC: The Urban Institute.

Zaslow, M., Anderson Moore, K., Tout, K., Scarpa, J. P., & Vandivere, S. (2002). "How are Children Faring under Welfare Reform?" In *Welfare Reform The Next Act*, edited by Alan Weil and Kenneth Finegold. Washington, DC: The Urban Institute.

Zedlewski, S. (2002). "Family Incomes: Rising, Falling, or Holding Steady?" In *Welfare Reform The Next Act*, edited by Alan Weil and Kenneth Finegold. Washington, DC: The Urban Institute.

Zedlewski, S., & Alderson, D. (2001). *Do Families on Welfare in the Post-TANF Era Differ from Their Pre-TANF Counterparts? Assessing the New Federalism* Discussion Paper 01-03. Washington. DC: The Urban Institute.

Zedlewski, S., & Brauner, S. (1999). *Are the Steep Declines in Food Stamp Participation Linked to Falling Welfare Caseloads? Assessing the New Federalism* Brief B-03. Washington, DC: The Urban Institute.

Zedlewski, S., Clark, S., Meier, E., & Watson, K. (1996). *Potential Effects of Congressional Welfare Reform Legislation on Family Incomes*. Washington, DC: The Urban Institute.

Zedlewski, S., & Giannarelli, L. (1997). *Diversity among State Welfare Programs: Implications for Reform. Assessing the New Federalism* Brief A-1. Washington, DC: The Urban Institute.

Zedlewski, S., & Gruber, A. (2001). *Former Welfare Families and the Food Stamp Program: The Exodus Continues. Assessing the New Federalism* Brief B-33. Washington, DC: The Urban Institute.

Zedlewski, S., Merriman, D., Staveteig, S., & Finegold, K. (2002). "TANF Funding and Spending across the States." In *Welfare Reform The Next Act*, edited by Alan Weil and Kenneth Finegold. Washington, DC: The Urban Institute.

7

Work, Welfare, and Economic Well-Being After Welfare Reform: Do State Policies Make a Difference?

Jordan Matsudaira and Sheldon H. Danziger

In 1996, the Personal Responsibility and Work Opportunity Reconciliation Act (PRWORA) fundamentally changed the nature of public assistance programs in the United States. PRWORA ended the federal entitlement to cash assistance and ceded to the states an unprecedented degree of discretion in developing their own welfare programs. Prior to 1996, state programs differed primarily by the amount of benefits they provided to families. They now vary widely in terms of eligibility requirements, the length of time limits, the use and severity of sanctions, the scope of job search and training activities, the generosity of work supports, such as child care, and the extent of diversion activities.

In the wake of these reforms and in the context of the booming economy of the 1990s, welfare participation and employment outcomes have changed dramatically for single women with children—the group most heavily represented on the welfare rolls. From 1993 to 2000, the number of families receiving cash assistance across the nation declined by 53 percent, and the employment rate of single mothers rose from 58.0 to 71.5 percent between 1993 and 1999.[1]

It is difficult, however, to assess the degree to which these changes can be attributed to welfare reform rather than to a strong economy or to their interaction. Blank (2001) reviews recent studies that attempt to evaluate the impact of welfare reform policies controlling for changes in the macro-economy. She concludes that welfare reform per se contributed substantially to the decline in caseloads, and, to a lesser extent, to the rise in labor force participation and hours worked among low-income mothers. Fewer studies evaluate the impacts of welfare reform on income and poverty levels, and Blank (2001) concludes that those effects remain uncertain.

At the national level, it is clear that welfare reforms have increased employment and reduced welfare utilization among single-female headed families. Two issues, however, cloud the policy relevance of these conclusions. First, insufficient attention has been paid to changes in poverty, nutrition, and other aspects of family economic well-being. Reduced welfare use and increased employment reduce the adverse efficiency costs of the welfare system but might have negative consequences for well-being. As Wiseman (1999) notes, "if caseload reduction is genuinely the barometer of achievement, social assistance should be abolished altogether, since such a change would produce maximum caseload decline."

Second, the literature to date has not evaluated which specific welfare policy changes have been responsible for the observed changes in work, welfare receipt, and economic well-being. Because of the diversity of state policy innovations prior to and in response to PRWORA, there is no specific set of policies that can be identified as constitutive of "welfare reform." Studies that identify the effect of welfare reform by using dummy variables corresponding to implementation dates capture only the average effect of different policy changes across the fifty states. It is possible that these national averages mask considerable variation in outcomes across states. If this is the case, then it is important to analyze how this variation is related to the specific policy components adopted by different states. It is likely that some policies decrease welfare receipt and increase work, whereas others decrease both welfare receipt and work. If welfare receipt declines and work increases, income could rise or fall as a result; if both decrease, income is likely to fall.

To reify average welfare and work effects is to fail to distinguish between strategies that have positive and deleterious consequences for the well-being of single mothers and their children. Now that states have the discretion to design their own welfare programs, understanding the impact of different policies on the full range of economic outcomes is crucial to the formulation of thoughtful welfare policies.

This chapter aims to address gaps in the literature by estimating state-specific impacts of welfare reform policies on four outcomes of single mothers: welfare utilization, employment, personal earnings, and family income. Using microdata from the March Current Population Surveys (CPS) over the 1990s, we use a difference-in-difference estimation strategy that utilizes the variation in outcomes across time periods relative to a control group of single women without children to identify the impacts of state welfare policies on single mothers. We then explore the relationships among the impacts on different outcomes. Finally, we analyze how the estimated impacts differ according to several broad categorizations of state welfare policies.

Welfare As We Now Know It

As mentioned above, PRWORA allows each state to decide which families to assist, subject only to a requirement that they receive "fair and equitable treatment." PRWORA also reduced the total amount of spending required from the federal and state governments. The federal contribution changed from a matching grant to a block grant that is essentially capped for each state at its fiscal year 1994 spending level. Increased costs associated with population growth, recessions or inflation must be borne by state budgets or by the poor. Moreover, states are only required to spend 75 percent of what they spent in 1994 on AFDC, the Job Opportunities and Basic Skills Program (JOBS), child care, and Emergency Assistance.

States that have both the funds and the desire can choose to provide a more-supportive safety net than existed before 1996. Each state can pursue whatever policies it chooses, including mutual responsibility reforms that increase its commitment to help recipients find jobs. In practice, however, most states have worked harder to cut caseloads than to provide either work opportunities or support services to recipients, including those who have been unable to find work (Pavetti, 2002).

States may not use federal funds to provide more than a cumulative lifetime total of 60 months of cash assistance. However, they can grant extensions to the limit for up to 20 percent of the caseload. States also have the option to set shorter time limits. As of early 2001, twenty-eight states had chosen to use the 60-month cumulative limit; five states have shorter limits ranging from 21 to 48 months; thirteen states have more complicated policies that allow 60 months of lifetime benefits, but restrict the number of consecutive months in which cash assistance can be received. Michigan and Vermont have not adopted a time limit and plan to use state funds to assist recipients who exceed 60 months (Seefeldt, 2002).

Most importantly, PRWORA increased the level of work expectations. Single-parent recipients with no children under age one are expected to work at least 30 hours per week. States can require participation in work or work-related activities regardless of the age of the youngest child; some states now exempt a mother for only 13 weeks following childbirth.

PRWORA offers no opportunity to work in exchange for welfare benefits when a recipient reaches her time limit. Although the labor market prospects for less-skilled workers have greatly eroded since the early 1970s, the government is no longer responsible for providing a cash safety-net. Although states can exempt 20 percent of recipients from the time limit, a greater percentage of post-reform recipients are likely to need such extensions or a last resort work-for-welfare opportunity. This is because their personal attributes (e.g., a high prevalence of health, mental health, and skill problems) compromise their employment prospects (Danziger, 2002).

States have chosen a variety of policies. For example, consider Idaho. The state has a time limit of 24 months, employs full-family sanctions the first time a family is out of compliance, and does not exempt mothers who must care for young children from work requirements. A full-family sanction means that everyone in the caseload loses cash benefits. In contrast, New Hampshire uses the federal time limit of 60 months, employs partial family sanctions, and requires mothers to work only after their youngest child reaches 3 years of age. Under partial family sanctions, the cash benefit is reduced, usually by eliminating that portion which is intended for the adult (Seefeldt, 2002).

Previous Research

Several recent papers have analyzed the impact of the switch from AFDC to TANF on single mothers' welfare, employment, and income outcomes using nationally representative data.[2] Schoeni and Blank (2000) use 1977 to 1999 CPS data[3] to examine the impact of state waivers before 1996 and PRWORA on all women between ages 16 and 54. In contrast to many studies, including the present chapter, they do not restrict the sample to single mothers to allow for the possible endogeneity of marital status and fertility with respect to welfare policies.[4] They identify the effects of welfare reform by interacting education level dummies with their reform variables on the assumption that reform primarily affects women with low skills.

Schoeni and Blank find (2000) that among all women with less than a high school education, state waivers decreased welfare participation by 0.9 percentage points, increased the share of women working by 2.0 percentage points, and increased the number of weeks worked annually and the number of hours worked per week by 0.73 weeks and 0.97 hours, respectively. Also, waivers increased women's own annual earnings by 5.03 percent, and increased total family income by 6.07 percent. The authors conclude that PRWORA led to a 1.90 percentage point decline in welfare use and an increase in family income of about 6 percent, but its effects on employment, work, and earnings were statistically insignificant.

Grogger (2000) estimates a model similar to that of Schoeni and Blank (2000) and explores the effects of time limits, as well as general welfare reform, on female-headed families, controlling for the effects of the economy and changes in the Earned Income Tax Credit (EITC) and the minimum wage. Using March CPS data from 1979 to 2000, he uses state-level variation in the implementation dates of time limits and statewide welfare reform to identify the impacts on families who differ according to the age of the youngest child. This interaction is meant to reflect the fact that families where the youngest child is younger have a longer period of welfare eligibility ahead of them, and will thus be more likely to alter their behavior in response to reforms. Consistent with this idea, he estimates that welfare reforms reduced welfare use by 3.7 percentage points for single-mother families with infants, and, to a lesser extent, for families with older children. For all female heads, welfare reforms increased employment by 2.6 percentage points, increased earnings by 6.7 percent, but had no statistically significant impact on family income.

Meyer and Sullivan (2001) analyze changes in the consumption expenditures of single mothers using data from the Panel Study of Income Dynamics and the Consumer Expenditure Survey. They argue that given the volatility of income from year to year, and underreporting problems in the data, consumption expenditures are a more accurate reflection of the well-being of single mothers. To isolate the effects of welfare reform from those of economic conditions, they employ a difference-in-differences strategy using single women without children and married women as control groups for single mothers. The results suggest that relative to both groups, single mothers' consumption was 2 to 4 percent higher in 1996-1998 than in 1994-1995, suggesting that welfare reforms improved their well-being.

Methodology

All of these studies implicitly assume that the effects of welfare reform are the same across all fifty states. Because the essential feature of PRWORA was to grant states greater authority to pursue their own welfare strategies, we expect that welfare reform's effects will vary widely across states. Accordingly, our goal is to estimate state-specific impacts that control for economic conditions, and then to explore whether variation in these effects can be explained by observed state policy choices.

Data

Data for welfare participation, employment, work, and family incomes during the calendar year are obtained from the March Current Population Surveys fielded in 1995 to 1997 and 1999 to 2001. Because the Surveys gather data on the previous calendar year, our data covers two time periods: 1994 to 1996, the three years prior to the enactment of PRWORA; and 1998 to 2000, by which time all states had implemented their welfare reform plans.[5] We pool data into three-year periods in order to have sufficient sample sizes for each state. Our sample sizes for the entire six-year period range from a low of 556 women in Maine to 5,943 in California (these numbers are smaller in regressions that condition on positive values, e.g., for earnings). All earnings and income values were converted to 2000 dollars using the CPI-U-RS. The full sample for our analysis consists of all civilian, single, female heads of households between the ages of 18 and 54 in each survey year.[6]

Table 7.1.
Trends in the Outcomes of Single Mothers and Women without Children

	Single Mothers	
	1994-1996	1998-2000
Received cash welfare during year	27.9 %	15.6 %
Worked at any time during year	74.6 %	83.4 %
Ave. total hours worked during year	1099.0	1256.6
Median personal earnings	$10,931	$14,243
Median family income	$16,972	$19,641

	Single women w/o children	
	1994-1996	1998-2000
Received cash welfare during year	2.5 %	1.1 %
Worked at any time during year	86.7 %	86.2 %
Ave. total hours worked during year	1455.7	1442.5
Median personal earnings	$19,088	$21,000
Median family income	$22,456	$24,560

Source: Authors' tabulations from 1995-1997 and 1999-2001 March CPS. Data are for all civilian, single, female household heads between the ages of 18 and 54, and are weighted by March Supplement Person Weights. Income and earnings are expressed in constant 2000 dollars. Single women without children are not necessarily household heads.

Methodology

As shown in table 7.1, the enactment of PRWORA was associated with dramatic changes in single mothers' welfare receipt, employment, earnings, and family income. Between the two time periods 1994-1996 and 1998-2000, the percentage of single mothers receiving cash welfare at some point during the year dropped by 12.3 percentage points, from 27.9 percent to 15.6 percent, while the percentage of those who worked at some point during the year rose by 8.8 percentage points, from 74.6 percent to 83.4 percent. Similarly, the median annual personal earnings and family incomes of single mothers rose by roughly $3,312 (30 percent) and $2,669 (16 percent), respectively.

Given the extraordinary economic expansion of the 1990s, however, these trends cannot be solely attributed to welfare reform. As the lower panel in table 7.1 reveals, earnings and income grew for women without children as well, a group that was relatively unaffected by welfare policies. Note that despite the economic boom, the annual employment rate of childless women was virtually unchanged at about 86 percent, whereas the rate for single mothers increased by 8.8 percentage points. Similarly, the percentage growth in median earnings was only 10 percent for women without children compared to about

30 percent for single mothers. These simple difference-in-differences of the sample medians imply that welfare reform may have contributed to large increases in both work and earnings. It is also worth noting that poverty remains high for single mothers with children. In 2000, the official U.S. poverty line for a single mother with two children was $13,874, whereas the median family income for mothers in our sample was about $19,641 in 1998-2000.

In order to disentangle the effects of changing economic conditions from the impact of state welfare policies, we employ a difference-in-difference regression strategy using single women without children as a comparison group. Our estimates of the impact of welfare reform on single mothers thus represent their change in a given outcome relative to the change for single women without children.

For this difference-in-difference approach to be valid, two conditions must hold.[7] First, welfare policies must influence the outcomes of single mothers but not those of single women without kids. Given the fact that less than 2.5 percent of the childless women in our sample received welfare in the years prior to reform, this condition appears approximately satisfied.[8] Second, the outcomes for both groups should respond to changes in economic conditions in the same way. Meyer and Rosenbaum (2001) find that employment for single women without children and single mothers responded similarly to changes in aggregate unemployment over the period from 1984 to 1996. To the extent that the two groups' other outcomes (i.e., welfare participation, earnings, and income) are also similarly affected by economic conditions, deviations in their trends over time can be attributed to factors differentially affecting one group.

In this study, we make an upper-bound assumption that the difference in the changes in each outcome is solely attributable to welfare reform. In particular, we make no attempt to control for changes in the Earned Income Tax Credit or expansions in the minimum wage, which have the potential to differentially affect the labor supply of single mothers and childless single women. While our estimates probably overestimate the effect of welfare reform per se, they should not bias our conclusions about the differences in outcomes across states for single mothers.[9]

To implement this difference-in-differences approach, we use a regression model similar to that used in Meyer and Sullivan (2001):

$$Y_{it} = a_0 + a_1 SM_{it} + a_2 Period_{it} + a_3 Period_{it} * SM_{it} + b X_{it} + e_{it} \qquad (1)$$

We estimate this equation for four dependent variables Y_{it}: whether woman i received welfare in year t, whether woman i worked in year t, the log of annual personal earnings in year t, and the log of annual family income[10] in year t. Regression equations with earnings or family income variables were run two ways: (1) with zero or negative earnings or income values bottom coded so that the cases are included in the regressions, and (2) discarding observations with non-positive earnings or income values.[11] Unless otherwise noted in the text, the results reported for earnings are conditional on positive values, and thus eliminate effects on earnings due to increased labor force participation, whereas those for income use bottom coded values and include all women. Standard errors are computed allowing for correlation of the error term within years. SM_{it} is a dummy variable equal to 1 if woman i is a single mother and 0 otherwise; $period_{it}$ is a dummy variable equal to zero if the observation is in the period 1994 to 1996, and equal to one for the period 1998 to 2000; and e_{it} is a person-year error term. X_{it} is a vector of personal characteristics, including dummy variables for race and educational attainment, number of children, and a quadratic in age.

In this specification, a_3 is the difference-in-difference estimate of the impact of welfare reform on outcome Y in a particular state. To see this, ignore the X_{it} term, and note that the difference-in-differences estimate is the change in the average Y_{it} for single

$$E[Y_{it} | SM_{it}=1, Period_{it}=1] = a_0 + a_1 + a_2 + a_3 \qquad (a)$$
$$E[Y_{it} | SM_{it}=1, Period_{it}=0] = a_0 + a_1 \qquad (b)$$
$$E[Y_{it} | SM_{it}=0, Period_{it}=1] = a_0 + a_2 \qquad (c)$$
$$E[Y_{it} | SM_{it}=0, Period_{it}=0] = a_0 \qquad (d)$$

mothers minus the change in the average Y_{it} for single women without children. This is equal to (a-b)-(c-d) = a_3.

Results

State Variation in the Effects of Welfare Reform

We begin by following the literature and estimating equation (1) on the sample that includes single mothers who head families and all single women without children who are primary or secondary individuals. The results are reported in Table 7.2. As with most studies, we find that welfare reforms contributed significantly to the decline in welfare receipt. Our difference-in-differences estimate, the coefficient on Period*SM (column 1), shows that between 1994 to 1996 and 1998 to 2000, 10.7 percentage points fewer single mothers relative to single women without children received welfare.

The problem with calling this estimate "the" impact of welfare reform, however, is illustrated in the first column of table 7.3, which shows state by state estimates of a_3 derived from estimating 51 state-specific regressions where the dependent variable takes the value of 1 if a woman received public assistance and 0 otherwise. The estimated impacts of welfare reform differ dramatically from state to state—so much so that the point estimates of welfare reform's impact in thirty-two states lies outside of the 95 percent confidence interval

Table 7.2
Regression Results of Estimating Equation (1) for Entire Population

Variables	Welfare Receipt	Worked Last Year	Total Hours (zeros are bottom-coded)	Total Hours (hours>0)	Log Personal Earnings (zeros are bottom-coded)	Log Personal Earnings (earnings>0)	Log Family Income (zeros are bottom-coded)	Log Family Income (income>0)
	(1)	(2)	(3)	(4)	(5)	(6)	(7)	(8)
Hispanic	0.034	-0.067	-101.880	-32.195	-0.367	-0.091	-0.225	-0.085
	(0.009)	(0.009)	(22.475)	(9.653)	(0.047)	(0.012)	(0.014)	(0.014)
Black	0.048	-0.061	-124.299	-14.905 NS	-0.369	-0.095	-0.189	-0.154
	(0.007)	(0.007)	(18.112)	(8.883)	(0.043)	(0.023)	(0.017)	(0.017)
Other non-white	0.017	-0.094	-217.035	-45.235	-0.577	-0.158	-0.261	-0.120
	(0.005)	(0.013)	(23.883)	(14.234)	(0.065)	(0.021)	(0.039)	(0.026)
<HS degree	0.136	-0.271	-688.077	-201.804	-1.913	-0.848	-1.115	-0.855
	(0.014)	(0.014)	(17.226)	(8.887)	(0.053)	(0.011)	(0.024)	(0.010)
HS degree	0.033	-0.074	-214.947	-39.714	-0.691	-0.355	-0.518	-0.416
	(0.004)	(0.004)	(1.813)	(9.244)	(0.016)	(0.008)	(0.011)	(0.005)
Number of Kids	0.074	-0.044	-118.565	-59.702	-0.287	-0.143	-0.016	-0.035
	(0.004)	(0.008)	(9.946)	(3.944)	(0.037)	(0.017)	(0.006)	(0.008)
Age	-0.012	0.008	117.271	96.216	0.225	0.189	0.137	0.122
	(0.002)	(0.002)	(2.982)	(2.443)	(0.011)	(0.006)	(0.006)	(0.008)
Age^2	0.000	0.000	-1.453	-1.164	-0.003	-0.002	-0.001	-0.001
	(0.000)	(0.000)	(0.041)	(0.034)	(0.000)	(0.000)	(0.000)	(0.000)
Period	-0.014	0.001 NS	-0.251 NS	2.644 NS	0.020	0.010	0.013	0.017
	(0.002)	(0.003)	(10.122)	(6.365)	(0.052)	(0.066)	(0.030)	(0.069y)
Single Mom	0.098	-0.001 NS	-80.644	-71.517	-0.134y	-0.130	0.089 NS	-0.019
	(0.014)	(0.016)	(22.494)	(6.400)	(0.064)	(0.026)	(0.012)	(0.012)
Period * SM	-0.107	0.083	157.124	44.232	0.449	0.110	0.058 NS	0.034y
	(0.016)	(0.013)	(28.996)	(5.115)	(0.070)	(0.025)	(0.029)	(0.023)
Constant	0.250	0.674	-552.164	136.443	5.537	6.350	7.129	7.572
	(0.045)	(0.037)	(42.640)	(42.213)	(0.198)	(0.107)	(0.122)	(0.083)
N	60927	60927	60927	42867	60927	50870	60927	58937
R-square	0.209	0.110	0.137	0.087	0.190	0.197	0.175	0.188

Values represent coefficient estimates that result from estimating equation (1) with ordinary least squares. Robust standard errors in parentheses are calculated allowing error terms to be correlated within years. All coefficients are statistically significant at the 5 percent level with the exception of those marked with y (significant at 10 percent) or NS (not statistically significant). These are the only coefficients in this table that are not significant at the 5 percent level.

Table 7.3
Estimates of a₃ for Welfare Utilization and Employment

State	Point Est.	95% CI Low	95% CI High	State	Point Est.	95% CI Low	95% CI High
	Welfare Receipt				Employment Rate		
CT*	-0.243	-0.305	-0.181	ID*	0.225	0.109	0.341
ID*	-0.218	-0.285	-0.151	CT*	0.221	0.141	0.301
MD*	-0.203	-0.242	-0.165	DC*	0.202	0.069	0.336
MN*	-0.203	-0.290	-0.116	MD*	0.197	0.106	0.288
NJ*	-0.192	-0.239	-0.145	NJ*	0.177	0.108	0.247
MS*	-0.173	-0.225	-0.121	PA*	0.171	0.135	0.207
PA*	-0.173	-0.248	-0.097	RI*	0.150	0.065	0.235
DC*	-0.168	-0.218	-0.117	FL*	0.141	0.107	0.175
SD*	-0.167	-0.238	-0.096	IN*	0.135	0.032	0.238
OR*	-0.154	-0.254	-0.055	IL*	0.129	0.081	0.178
WI*	-0.147	-0.185	-0.110	AZ*	0.125	0.025	0.224
KS*	-0.146	-0.208	-0.083	TN	0.121	-0.007	0.248
HI*	-0.145	-0.308	0.018	LA*	0.113	0.035	0.191
TN*	-0.145	-0.249	-0.041	CA*	0.112	0.084	0.140
FL*	-0.145	-0.173	-0.116	HI*	0.101	0.013	0.190
SC*	-0.141	-0.195	-0.087	NY*	0.099	0.045	0.153
IL*	-0.138	-0.170	-0.105	SC*	0.099	0.040	0.157
OK*	-0.133	-0.239	-0.028	AK*	0.097	0.024	0.171
MI*	-0.131	-0.146	-0.117	NC*	0.094	0.053	0.135
AK*	-0.126	-0.210	-0.041	AL	0.090	-0.002	0.182
IN*	-0.121	-0.224	-0.018	NE*	0.086	0.024	0.148
MA*	-0.119	-0.174	-0.064	**ALL US***	**0.083**	**0.057**	**0.109**
CO*	-0.118	-0.159	-0.076	OH*	0.081	0.019	0.143
NC*	-0.112	-0.185	-0.039	MT	0.077	-0.024	0.178
NY*	-0.109	-0.136	-0.083	SD	0.076	-0.069	0.222
ALL US*	**-0.107**	**-0.139**	**-0.075**	WA	0.076	-0.069	0.221
MT*	-0.106	-0.186	-0.026	UT	0.076	-0.016	0.167
WV*	-0.104	-0.170	-0.037	WV	0.072	-0.015	0.158
VT	-0.099	-0.278	0.081	CO	0.066	-0.030	0.163
AL*	-0.093	-0.160	-0.025	MN	0.056	-0.052	0.164
GA*	-0.090	-0.154	-0.026	WY	0.051	-0.051	0.152
WA*	-0.090	-0.168	-0.011	OK	0.050	-0.012	0.111
WY	-0.083	-0.167	0.001	MS	0.048	-0.059	0.155
OH	-0.081	-0.188	0.026	AR	0.046	-0.041	0.133
NH	-0.080	-0.190	0.029	KY	0.046	-0.097	0.189
CA*	-0.079	-0.112	-0.045	VA	0.045	-0.047	0.136
TX*	-0.072	-0.124	-0.020	MA	0.041	-0.037	0.118
VA	-0.071	-0.178	0.036	OR	0.037	-0.073	0.148
AZ	-0.065	-0.143	0.013	MI	0.025	-0.005	0.055
NE*	-0.063	-0.105	-0.021	IA	0.016	-0.098	0.131
IA	-0.062	-0.148	0.023	WI	0.014	-0.105	0.132
KY	-0.060	-0.123	0.004	NM	0.004	-0.092	0.100
NM	-0.055	-0.115	0.005	GA	0.003	-0.035	0.040
LA	-0.053	-0.163	0.057	DE	0.001	-0.063	0.065
DE	-0.049	-0.123	0.024	NV	-0.014	-0.058	0.031
NV	-0.040	-0.093	0.013	TX	-0.022	-0.048	0.005
RI	-0.024	-0.082	0.035	KS	-0.028	-0.154	0.098
AR	-0.008	-0.049	0.034	NH	-0.028	-0.079	0.022
MO	0.012	-0.085	0.109	MO	-0.038	-0.100	0.025
UT	0.022	-0.058	0.101	ME	-0.058	-0.128	0.011
ND	0.042	-0.081	0.165	ND*	-0.083	-0.136	-0.031
ME	0.059	-0.041	0.159	VT*	-0.093	-0.174	-0.012

Values represent the point estimates and 95 percent confidence interval for a₃ from estimating equation (1) separately for each of the 51 states. States are ranked by the value of their point estimates, from greatest welfare receipt deduction and from largest employment rate increase to smallest. "*" indicates that the estimate of a₁ is statistically significantly different from zero at the 5 percent level.

for the United States as a whole.[12] In four states, our model attributes declines in welfare receipt of over 20 percentage points to welfare reform—Connecticut, Idaho, Maryland, and Minnesota. And the point estimates for four states were actually positive, though insignificant, with Maine and North Dakota showing increases in welfare receipt due to welfare reform of 5.9 percent and 4.2 percent, respectively. The estimated impact of welfare reform on welfare participation is statistically significantly less (more negative) than −10.7 percentage points for ten states, and significantly greater than that for another eight states. It is clear that a national estimate of welfare reform's average impact on welfare utilization is not representative of "the" impact of welfare reform, because the impact varied so widely across states.

The state by state results of estimating equation (1) for employment rates is also shown in table 7.3; the results for annual earnings of positive earners and family income are displayed in table 7.4. For the entire United States, we estimate that welfare reform led to a 8.3 percentage point increase in the employment rate of single mothers relative to that of single women without children (table 7.2, column 4). Again, however, this average effect masks variation across states. Six states have point estimates for employment that are more than double this average, led by the 22.5 and 22.1 percentage point gains in Idaho and Connecticut. At the other extreme, the estimated impact of welfare reform is actually negative in eight states. For two of these states, North Dakota and Vermont, the negative coefficient is statistically significant.

The same general pattern is borne out in our regression analyses of personal earnings for women with earnings. For the United States as a whole, we estimate that welfare reform led to a 11 percent increase in the earnings of single mothers relative to those of single women. If the same regression is estimated including women with earnings (compare columns 5 and 6 in table 7.2), a much larger estimate is obtained (about 45 percent). This difference reflects both increased participation effects (column 2, table 7.2) in addition to increased hours worked among those already working (column 4, table 7.2). The range of the point estimates for earnings is even wider than for welfare receipt or employment. Single mothers in twelve states experienced relative earnings gains more than twice the 11 percent average. And at the opposite extreme, the point estimates for Utah, California, North Carolina, Arizona, Maryland, Mississippi, Missouri, Kansas, Georgia, North Dakota, Nevada, and Louisiana all suggest that earnings fell in response to welfare reform in those states. However, none of the negative coefficients are statistically significant.

Our results for the entire United States suggest that the average family income of single mothers rose relative to single women without children by 5.8 percent, and the estimate is marginally statistically significant. This average estimate, however, is not representative of the experience of all states. We estimate statistically significant gains (table 7.4, right panel) in income due to welfare reform in nine states: Idaho (53.5 percent), Tennessee (50.5), Arizona

Table 7.4
Estimates of a_3 for Log Personal Earnings and Log Total Family Income

Log Personal Earnings (conditional on positive earnings)				*Log Total Family Income (negative & zeros values are bottom-coded)*			
State	*Point Est.*	*95% CI Low*	*95% CI High*	*State*	*Point Est.*	*95% CI Low*	*95% CI High*
ID*	0.453	0.216	0.690	ID*	0.535	0.359	0.710
MT*	0.389	0.117	0.661	TN*	0.505	0.057	0.952
WY*	0.387	0.139	0.635	AZ*	0.408	0.279	0.537
TN*	0.356	0.111	0.601	MD*	0.301	0.171	0.432
WV	0.340	-0.127	0.807	WV	0.274	-0.031	0.579
RI*	0.325	0.097	0.553	RI	0.273	-0.082	0.627
IA*	0.303	0.009	0.597	SC	0.266	-0.056	0.589
PA*	0.288	0.086	0.489	MT	0.265	-0.084	0.615
AZ*	0.255	0.021	0.489	CT*	0.261	0.132	0.390
MN	0.250	-0.160	0.661	PA*	0.251	0.043	0.458
CT	0.238	-0.183	0.660	UT	0.245	-0.102	0.592
MI*	0.237	0.012	0.462	IL*	0.225	0.033	0.417
DE*	0.220	0.022	0.419	OH*	0.222	0.071	0.373
FL*	0.220	0.085	0.355	FL*	0.220	0.125	0.315
OH	0.202	-0.061	0.465	NE	0.204	-0.225	0.633
IL*	0.200	0.100	0.301	IN	0.189	-0.176	0.554
IN	0.195	-0.115	0.504	NJ	0.146	-0.135	0.427
NJ*	0.180	0.070	0.291	WI	0.141	-0.193	0.47
KY	0.173	-0.075	0.422	NC	0.135	-0.140	0.410
WI	0.160	-0.220	0.539	AL	0.129	-0.089	0.347
OK	0.147	-0.074	0.369	ME	0.099	-0.335	0.533
ME	0.145	-0.197	0.487	WA	0.098	-0.267	0.46
TX*	0.139	0.025	0.254	WY	0.087	-0.204	0.39
NE	0.135	-0.153	0.422	AR	0.074	-0.270	0.418
OR	0.123	-0.130	0.377	**ALL US***	**0.058**	**0.001**	**0.115**
VA	0.111	-0.104	0.326	LA	0.033	-0.313	0.380
ALL US*	**0.110**	**0.060**	**0.161**	CO	0.033	-0.225	0.292
VT	0.104	-0.206	0.414	SD	0.031	-0.280	0.342
AL	0.100	-0.271	0.470	AK	0.020	-0.044	0.084
DC	0.070	-0.286	0.426	DE	0.008	-0.013	0.029
CO	0.069	-0.139	0.277	CA	0.003	-0.065	0.071
SD	0.065	-0.302	0.432	DC	0.003	-0.290	0.296
AK	0.064	-0.109	0.237	MI	0.001	-0.201	0.203
WA	0.060	-0.227	0.347	NY	-0.001	-0.165	0.163
NM	0.058	-0.163	0.280	VA	-0.003	-0.227	0.221
SC	0.058	-0.284	0.400	KY	-0.022	-0.508	0.46
NY	0.024	-0.079	0.127	OK	-0.029	-0.341	0.283
MA	0.020	-0.139	0.180	HI	-0.031	-0.375	0.312
NH	0.010	-0.419	0.438	MS	-0.055	-0.408	0.297
HI	0.001	-0.342	0.343	IA	-0.071	-0.515	0.373
UT	-0.030	-0.233	0.174	MA	-0.079	-0.243	0.085
CA	-0.032	-0.118	0.054	MN	-0.117	-0.300	0.065
NC	-0.043	-0.172	0.086	VT	-0.125	-0.371	0.122
AR	-0.064	-0.305	0.178	OR	-0.129	-0.368	0.110
MD	-0.080	-0.287	0.126	NV	-0.146	-0.579	0.287
MS	-0.081	-0.413	0.250	TX*	-0.180	-0.232	-0.128
MO	-0.091	-0.484	0.303	ND*	-0.195	-0.346	-0.044
KS	-0.097	-0.371	0.177	NM*	-0.260	-0.476	-0.04
GA	-0.108	-0.354	0.138	KS	-0.274	-0.551	0.002
ND	-0.110	-0.435	0.214	NH	-0.317	-0.673	0.039
NV	-0.196	-0.469	0.077	GA*	-0.371	-0.506	-0.237
LA	-0.220	-0.477	0.037	MO*	-0.381	-0.475	-0.288

Values represent the point estimates and 95 percent confidence interval for a_3 from estimating equation (1) separately for each of the 51 states. States are ranked by the value of their point estimates, from largest increases in personal earnings and family income to smallest. "*" indicates that the estimate of a_3 is statistically significantly different from zero at the 5 percent level.

(40.8), Maryland (30.1), Connecticut (26.1), Pennsylvania (25.1), Illinois (22.5), Ohio (22.2), and Florida (22.0). On the other hand, five states experienced statistically significant declines in family income: Texas (-18.0 percent), North Dakota (-19.5), New Mexico (-26.0), Georgia (-37.1), and Missouri (-38.1).

Haskins and Primus (2001) report that for some low-income single mothers, losses in income from welfare benefits offset much of the post-PRWORA earnings increases. They report that the poorest 40 percent of single-mother families increased their earnings by about $2,300 between 1995 and 1999, but their disposable income increased on average by only $292 due to the reductions in cash welfare and food stamps.

Relationships among Outcomes across States

We turn next to examining the extent to which there are consistent relationships among the estimated impacts of welfare reform on different outcomes. For example, do states with large reductions in welfare caseloads have large increases in employment rates or family income? We address these questions by running simple regressions of the form:

Impact on outcome i_s = constant + b(-1* Impact on welfare receipt)$_s$ + e$_s$
where we ignore issues involving the precision of generated regression coefficients and use the point estimates of the impacts for each state reported in tables 7.3 and 7.4 as the dependent and independent variables. We estimate b using ordinary least squares.

As we expect, declines in welfare receipt are most strongly linked to increases in the proportion of women working during the year. The slope coefficient in this regression is 0.68 (t=5.16), suggesting that a state that achieved a 10 percentage point reduction in the caseload also experienced a 6.8 percentage point increase in the employment rate for single mothers; the R^2 is 0.35. It should be noted, however, that the relationship described here is between percentage point change in the proportion of single mothers receiving welfare at any point during the year, and the proportion who worked for pay at any point during the year. Being employed during the year does not necessarily imply substantial labor force attachment.

The relationships between the declines in welfare receipt and increases in earnings (conditional on positive values) and family income due to welfare reform are much weaker. While the point estimates for b in each regression suggest that declines in welfare receipt are associated with rises in earnings (estimated b = 0.68) and income (estimated b = 0.90), each of these estimates is only marginally significant at the 5 percent level (p-values are 0.048 and 0.044, respectively). The R^2 statistic is 0.078 for the earnings regression, and 0.080 for the family income regression.

Table 7.5
State Rankings for Components of Welfare Programs

State	Benefit Generosity	Earnings Disregards	Sanctions	Time Limits	Overall Work Incentives
Alabama	Low	Low	Strict	Moderate	Mixed
Alaska	High	Medium	Lenient	Moderate	Weak
Arizona	Medium	Low	Moderate	Lenient	Weak
Arkansas	Low	Medium	Lenient	Strict	Mixed
California	High	High	Lenient	Lenient	Mixed
Colorado	Medium	Low	Moderate	Moderate	Weak
Connecticut	High	High	Moderate	Strict	Mixed
Delaware	Medium	Low	Strict	Strict	Mixed
District of Columbia	Medium	Medium	Lenient	Moderate	Weak
Florida	Medium	High	Strict	Strict	Strong
Georgia	Medium	Low	Strict	Strict	Mixed
Hawaii	High	High	Strict	Moderate	Mixed
Idaho	Medium	Low	Strict	Strict	Mixed
Illinois	Medium	High	Moderate	Moderate	Strong
Indiana	Medium	Low	Lenient	Lenient	Weak
Iowa	Medium	High	Strict	Moderate	Strong
Kansas	Medium	Medium	Strict	Moderate	Strong
Kentucky	Low	Low	Moderate	Moderate	Mixed
Louisiana	Low	High	Strict	Strict	Strong
Maine	Medium	High	Lenient	Lenient	Mixed
Maryland	Medium	Low	Strict	Lenient	Mixed
Massachusetts	High	High	Strict	Strict	Mixed
Michigan	Medium	Medium	Strict	Lenient	Mixed
Minnesota	High	Medium	Lenient	Moderate	Weak
Mississippi	Low	High	Strict	Moderate	Strong
Missouri	Medium	Medium	Lenient	Moderate	Weak
Montana	Medium	Medium	Lenient	Moderate	Weak
Nebraska	Medium	Low	Strict	Strict	Mixed
Nevada	Medium	Medium	Moderate	Strict	Strong
New Hampshire	High	High	Lenient	Moderate	Mixed
New Jersey	Medium	Medium	Strict	Moderate	Strong
New Mexico	Medium	High	Moderate	Moderate	Strong
New York	High	High	Lenient	Lenient	Mixed
North Carolina	Low	Medium	Moderate	Strict	Strong
North Dakota	Medium	Low	Strict	Moderate	Mixed
Ohio	Medium	High	Strict	Strict	Strong
Oklahoma	Medium	Medium	Strict	Moderate	Strong
Oregon	Medium	Medium	Moderate	Strict	Strong
Pennsylvania	Medium	Medium	Moderate	Moderate	Mixed
Rhode Island	High	High	Lenient	Lenient	Mixed
South Carolina	Low	Low	Strict	Strict	Mixed
South Dakota	Medium	Low	Strict	Moderate	Mixed
Tennessee	Low	Low	Strict	Strict	Mixed
Texas	Low	Low	Moderate	Moderate	Mixed
Utah	Medium	High	Strict	Strict	Strong
Vermont	High	Medium	Moderate	Lenient	Weak
Virginia	Medium	Low	Strict	Strict	Mixed
Washington	High	High	Lenient	Moderate	Mixed
West Virginia	Medium	Low	Moderate	Moderate	Weak
Wisconsin	High	Low	Strict	Moderate	Mixed
Wyoming	Medium	Low	Strict	Moderate	Mixed

Source: Reproduced from Blank and Schmidt (2001).

Welfare Policies and Their Impact

Thus far we have demonstrated that there is wide variation across the states in the impact of welfare reforms on welfare participation, employment, earnings, and income. It also appears that states that have reduced their welfare rolls the most have also seen the biggest increases in single mothers' employment and earnings. A natural question to ask then is, what specific policies are associated with declines in welfare receipt and increases in employment, earnings, and income, and which policies are not?

To address this question, we employ a scheme for categorizing the welfare policies of each state reported by Blank and Schmidt (2001), and reproduced in table 7.5. The scheme ranks states according to how their policies differ from the median state's policy in five categories: (1) benefit generosity; (2) earnings disregards; (3) sanctions; (4) time limits; and (5) a combination of all of these policies, or "overall work incentives." For example, a state will have "low" benefit generosity or "strict" time limits if its benefits are lower, or if time limits are shorter, than the median state policy. Policies that are similar to the median policy are classified as medium or moderate.

Using this classification scheme, we explore the extent to which variations in each policy are systematically related to differences in the impact of welfare reform on each of the four outcome measures. We do this by computing the simple (unweighted average) of a_3—our estimates of welfare reform's impact in tables 7.3 and 7.4—across the states in each policy category. To the extent that any one set of policies (e.g., sanctions) has a decisive impact on women's outcomes, we expect to observe states that implemented different policies to realize different impacts due to welfare reform. For example, we might expect to see a larger reduction in welfare receipt in states with stricter sanction policies as compared in those with more lenient policies. One problem, however, is that the Blank-Schmidt categorization does not account for implementation differences. That is, one state may have a very strict sanction policy in its rulebook, but might rarely use it, whereas another state might more frequently impose sanctions that appear to be more lenient. Not accounting for implementation differences may make it difficult for us to evaluate the effect of policy differences on welfare reform outcomes. In addition, finding a lack of a pattern in a_3 for a specific policy is not indicative of a lack of a relationship between policies and outcomes since the analysis does not simultaneously control for differences in other policies (e.g., strict sanctions and generous earnings disregards in a given state) that may have offsetting effects.

Our results are reported in table 7.6. Starting with column 1, a striking finding is the lack of a systematic relationship between specific policies and the reduction in welfare participation, the outcome that is most directly affected by welfare reform.[13] We expect that other things being equal, states with lower benefit generosity, stricter sanctions and time limit policies, and stronger overall work incentives to experience the greatest declines in welfare receipt. In fact, the states with high benefit generosity, states with moderate time limit policies, and *weak* overall work incentives had the greatest average drop in welfare receipt. Only the results for sanctions appear to accord with our prior hypothesis that stricter policies should lead to greater declines in caseloads.

Table 7.6
Estimates of Impact of Welfare Reform by State Policy Category

State Welfare Policy		Number of States	Welfare Receipt	Worked Last Year	Log Earnings (earnings>0)	Log Earnings (bottom-coding)	Log Fam Income (bottom coding)
All States	all	51	-0.103	0.069	0.112	0.391	0.057
Benefit Generosity	low	9	-0.095	0.071	0.046	0.356	0.098
	med	30	-0.098	0.068	0.136	0.404	0.063
	high	19	-0.122	0.070	0.102	0.385	0.010
Earnings Disregards	high	17	-0.089	0.078	0.085	0.417	0.051
	med	15	-0.119	0.057	0.091	0.309	-0.020
	low	19	-0.104	0.071	0.154	0.432	0.123
Sanctions	strict	25	-0.112	0.071	0.105	0.412	0.079
	moderate	13	-0.110	0.064	0.135	0.368	0.056
	lenient	13	-0.080	0.071	0.103	0.373	0.016
Time Limits	strict	17	-0.101	0.083	0.087	0.459	0.116
	moderate	25	-0.111	0.057	0.123	0.337	-0.009
	lenient	9	-0.086	0.077	0.130	0.412	0.128
Overall Work Incentives	strong	14	-0.105	0.066	0.055	0.364	0.019
	mixed	27	-0.100	0.071	0.123	0.397	0.077
	weak	10	-0.110	0.070	0.165	0.412	0.057

Values represent the unweighted average of a_3 for the states in each policy category. Welfare policy categories are from Blank and Schmidt (2001).

There is very little difference in the average impact of welfare reform on employment across states in different policy categories. For all policy categories, there is at most a 0.007 difference in the average increase in employment between states with strict policies and states with lenient policies (i.e., this difference represents only about one-tenth of the typical a_3, which is 0.07). The patterns for the estimated impact of each of the policies are also non-monotonic, with the estimates of a_3 roughly equivalent between strict and lenient policy states, but smaller for states in the moderate policy category. Not surprisingly, the pattern of estimates for earnings that captures participation effects by including women with no earnings in the model (column 4) follows essentially the same pattern.

The results for earnings conditional on positive values and family income are similarly counterintuitive. In particular, where relationships appear to exist they tend to be either non-monotonic, or completely the opposite of what we would expect. It should be noted, however, that all of the means reported in table 7.6 are estimated with very large standard errors, suggesting that any patterns that do exist may be spurious.

One possible explanation for the lack of systematic relationships between state policies and outcomes may be that our static categorization of welfare policies is ill suited to capture the changes in welfare policies that occurred over the 1994-1996 to 1998-2000 period that we use to estimate impacts. In particular, it may be that states adopted certain policies prior to 1996 under a waiver program, and that the effects of those waivers were already reflected in the outcomes of single mothers in our pre-PRWORA period. To the extent that this is true, our estimates may underestimate the effect of welfare reform in states that had significant waiver programs in place.

In order to check the sensitivity of our results to this kind of effect, we re-estimated the effects shown in table 7.6 on a restricted sample of states that includes only those states that did not have a waiver program implemented prior to 1996.[14] Of the thirty-two states that remain (data not shown), we are reasonably confident that their welfare programs were sufficiently similar in the pre-PRWORA period that the policy taxonomy provided by Blank and Schmidt is an acceptable proxy for their policies' changes over our analysis frame. Restricting the sample in this way does not significantly alter the qualitative conclusions above.

Discussion

In the wake of the passage of PRWORA, states have implemented a myriad of welfare policies that have reshaped the social safety net for single mothers and their children. In this context, evaluating the impact of specific policies on the economic behavior and well-being of poor women becomes not only more complicated, but also more important. Now that states can design their own welfare programs, research should focus on assessing the impacts of specific policies and how the impacts of different policies tend to reinforce or negate one another. As the end of the economic boom of the 1990s makes clear, research must also focus on how local economic conditions affect the relative effectiveness of different policies.

In this chapter, we show that the impact of welfare reform policies on welfare utilization, employment, personal earnings, and family income of single mothers varied widely across states. The point estimates for the change in welfare receipt across states ranged from –24.3 to +5.9 percentage points. And the range was just as wide for the other outcomes: +22.5 to –9.3 percentage points for the change in employment rates; +45.3 to –22.0 percent for earnings growth; and +53.5 to –38.1 percent for the change in total family income. It is clear that the national averages we estimated for these outcomes (table 7.2) mask a great deal of heterogeneity among states. Explaining the relationship of this variation to the specific policies adopted by different states should be a priority for future research on the effects of welfare reform.

Having established the importance of examining the link between specific policies and groups of policies and single mothers' outcomes, we recognize that it is a formidable task. Given the simple nature of our analysis relating welfare reform impacts to specific policies, it is not surprising that we did not observe strong relationships between policies and outcomes. There are literally scores of dimensions along which welfare programs differ, and failing to control for the configuration of other policies or implementation differences in the policies we do evaluate will make it very difficult to determine the effects of a particular policy.

At the same time, the lack of relationship between our estimated outcomes and any one policy shown in table 7.5 is problematic. Ultimately, multivariate analyses of the effects of specific policies must rely heavily on cross-state variation in policies, limiting the effective sample to the number of states for which we have data. In the absence of other sources of variation, few policy variables can be included simultaneously in the regression model. In the absence of strong relationships between these policies and outcomes, then, there may not be enough degrees of freedom to identify their effects.

Despite these difficulties, we believe that research must attempt to assess welfare reform policies at this degree of detail in order to be relevant to policymaking. If researchers continue to "evaluate" welfare reform policies by estimating its average effects on poor women, they will be like the third statistician in the joke:

> Three statisticians go deer hunting with bows and arrows. They spot a big buck and take aim. One shoots and his arrow flies off three meters to the right. The second shoots and his arrow flies off three meters to the left. The third statistician jumps up and down yelling, "We got him! We got him!"

Notes

1.   Welfare statistics are from U.S. Department of Health and Human Services, Administration for Children and Families; employment figures are from Burtless (2000).
2.   For an extensive review of recent welfare reform evaluations, see Blank (2001).
3.   The dates refer to the year in which the survey was fielded, not to which the data corresponds; for example, the March 1998 CPS reports income during calendar year 1997.
4.   The relative merits of restricting the sample to female family heads are discussed by Grogger (2000).
5.   We omit 1997 since many states did not implement their TANF programs until sometime in that year. All states had implemented TANF by the beginning of 1998, with the exception of California which implemented its program in January of that year (see Schoeni and Blank, 2000, table A1).
6.   Women who are the heads of "related-subfamilies" and single women living with their parents or other relatives are excluded because the CPS does not report their

own incomes. Family income for these individuals includes the income of all related persons residing in the same housing unit.

7. An additional condition concerning when the implementation of reforms took place relative to our pre- and post-time periods is discussed below.
8. It is possible, however, that there may be spillover effects on the wages of non-mothers due to the increased labor supply of mothers. Endogenous fertility and marital decisions would also compromise this assumption. Further research is necessary to gauge whether these effects are significant.
9. A potential bias may be caused by the existence of state EITC programs that differ in their generosity across states.
10. Family income includes money income from all sources (e.g., wages and salaries, welfare benefits, property income, etc).
11. Negative and zero values were set to $100.
12. The coefficient from the U.S. is shown in bold; the 95 percent confidence interval ranges from -.139 to -.075.
13. We do not report standard error estimates for sample averages, but it should be kept in mind that the true error is related to the precision with which a_3 is estimated, as well as to variation in the point estimates across states within the same policy categories.
14. We use the implementation date of the first major waiver reported in Table A1 of Schoeni and Blank (2000).

References

Blank, R. M. (2001). "Evaluating Welfare Reform in the United States." University of Michigan: Unpublished mimeo. Forthcoming in the *Journal of Economic Literature*.

Blank, R. M., and Schmidt, L. (2001). " Work Wages, and Welfare." in *The New World of Welfare*, edited by R. M. Blank and R. Haskins, 70-102. Washington DC: Brookings Institution.

Burtless, G. (2000). "Can the Labor Market Absorb Three Million Welfare Recipients?" March 2001. Washington, DC: Brookings Institution. http://brookings.edu/views/papers/burtless/20000301.htm.

Danziger, S. (2002). Comment on "TANF and the Most Disadvantaged Families' Well-Being" by S. Zedlewski and P. Loprest in *The New World of Welfare*, edited by R. Blank and R. Haskins, 410-417. Washington, DC: Brookings Institution.

Grogger, J. (2000). "Time Limits and Welfare Use." National Bureau of Economic Research Working Paper 7709. Cambridge, MA: NBER, www.nber.org.

Haskins, R., & Primus, W. (2001). "Welfare Reform and Poverty." *Welfare Reform and Beyond*. Policy Brief No. 4. July. www.brookings.edu.

Meyer, B. D., & Rosenbaum, D. T. (2001). "Welfare, the Earned Income Tax Credit, and the Labor Supply of Single Mothers." *Quarterly Journal of Economics* 116: 1063-1114.

Meyer, B. D., & Sullivan, J. X. (2001). "The Effects of Welfare and Tax Reform: The Material Well-Being of Single Mothers in the 1980s and 1990s." National Bureau of Economic Research Working Paper 8298. Cambridge, MA: NBER, www.nber.org.

Pavetti, L. (2002). "Welfare Policy in Transition: Redefining the Social Contract for Poor Citizen Families with Children and Immigrants." In *Understanding Poverty*, edited by S. H. Danziger and R. H. Haveman, 229-277. Cambridge, MA: Harvard University Press.

Schoeni, R. F., & Blank, R. M. (2000). "What Has Welfare Reform Accomplished? Impacts on Welfare Participation, Employment, Income, Poverty, and Family Structure." National Bureau of Economic Research Working Paper 7627. Cambridge, MA: NBER, www.nber.org.

Seefeldt, K. S. (2002). *CQ Vital Issues Series: Welfare Reform*. Ann Lin, series ed. Washington, DC: Congressional Quarterly Press.

Wiseman, M. (1999). "In Midst of Reform: Wisconsin in 1997." Assessing the New Federalism Working Paper 99-03. Washington, DC: The Urban Institute.

8

Issues in the Design and Evaluation of U.S. Welfare Reforms

Christel Gilles and Antoine Parent

Introduction

In the form of a brief conclusion to Part 3, this chapter first highlights some basic issues raised by the design of the U.S. welfare reform: What is the intent of time limits? Does the reform imply a risk of polarization? Secondly, we question the nature of the approach to evaluation: What about evaluating targeted programs versus antipoverty alternatives? Do the existing evaluations of the reforms provide any understanding of the agents' economic behavior? Finally, we explore the lessons for the French system.

The Sustainability of the Welfare Reform

Revealed Preferences of the Legislator:
What Sense Can be Given to Time Limits?

If there is a question "open to discussion" about the U.S. reform, it is probably the question of "time limits." What did the legislators have in mind with regard to the implementation of time limits? The welfare reform is difficult to interpret when considering the role played by time limits: Was it merely an experimental reform with a short-term framework, aiming for immediate results? Was the goal of time limits only to take advantage of economic growth? Or was it to help or force recipients to project themselves in the long run? Questioning time limits leads to questioning the general meaning of the reform and its time consistency. We see at least four readings of the time limits.

When referring to the law, one of the goals of PRWORA is to reduce "dependency." The time limits are intended to reduce dependency in a straight line by providing temporary assistance to needy families. One can assume that there is simply an implicit hypothesis made by the legislator that welfare recipients are able to become "self-sufficient" after five years or less on the rolls. Assessing the effects of time limits ex post supposes a wait for the limit to be reached in all states and nothing can be observed and said before. Assessing time limits ex ante leads to a third perspective. On the one hand, imposing time limits could mean that the legislator was waiting for immediate results; the very short time horizon of the evaluation may reveal that the reform should imply immediate effects; five years is indeed a very short period of time and this may assume that the reform implies immediate results; on the other hand, time limits compel the economic agent to adopt a long-term perspective and to anticipate his life cycle.

Can we test the effects of time limits on economic behavior? Grogger (2002) recently made an evaluation of time limits.[1] He found that time limits have important effects on recipients' economic behavior. Using econometric modeling, the author found that since their implementation and until 2000, time limits explained 12 percent of the decrease in welfare participation and 7 percent of the increase in employment of single mothers. They did not have an effect on income and earnings of female-headed families. How can the fall in welfare participation be understood? These results suggest that time limits pushed recipients into work. Was it the expected goal of the legislator and can we rely on that kind of empirical data to know more about the inferences of time limits?

What drove caseloads to decline? According to Grogger (2002), time limits explained 12 percent of the drop in caseloads, the EITC 16 percent, changes in benefit level accounted for 5 percent, the rise in minimum wage 1 percent, employment conditions 10 percent, and finally, other welfare reforms 2.5 percent. All these factors explained 45 percent of the total variance. What are the other major excluded factors (55 percent) affecting welfare participation? As expressed by J. K. Sholtz (during a meeting of the American Economic Association in January 2002), there might be some methodological problems in considering time limits as an explanatory variable: Time limits are just one of a complex combination of policies that include sanctions, work requirements, and disregards. It is unlikely that the welfare reform and time limit dummies capture all these effects. Reform can vary across the states and it is not clear if the welfare reform and time-limit-dummy variables reflect the complexity of the economic behavior of recipients (see Matsudaira and Danziger, chap. 7).

More generally, does this type of empirical study help to define the nature (structural or temporary) of the changes in the agents' economic behavior induced by the implementation of times limits? We have, in fact, no certainty regarding the permanence of these changes.

The Risk of a "Polarization Scenario" Inferred by the Welfare Reform

Many observers underline that the outcome of the welfare reform has been particularly striking with regard to family structure. PRWORA stipulates that the reform aims at creating two-parent families and at reducing nonmarital child birth. We wonder if the major *economic goal* pursued by the legislator was not, by encouraging single mothers to work and to live in couples, to increase their standard of living. In this section, we discuss the risk of a spillover effect: solving the problem of individual poverty of single women by moving it to the household level may accentuate polarization between households. It is quite obvious that in lone mother households, maternal employment is a solution to reduce the risk of poverty. It is a well-known fact that poverty declines with the intensity of employment in the household to almost zero among dual earner families. On the surface, this suggests that women's employment is a decisive factor to fight against households' poverty and, to that extent, PRWORA appears to be the right strategy. In fact, this is not so clear: in OECD countries, during the past decades, the polarization[2] of households increased, reflecting new forms of inequalities among households. Could the AFDC/TANF reform contribute to reduce this kind of dualism?

Polarization describes a phenomenon where job joins job within household. The increase in women's participation rate appears to have a significant influence on the emergence of two-earner households while one major source of inequalities today relies on the development of two-earner households. Unemployment can decline and poverty grows because households are polarizing in terms of employment chances. Thus, unemployment risk added to marital endogamy may raise income inequalities among households.

Could TANF limit this secondary effect concerning single mothers? Actually, TANF can limit the effect of increasing polarization only if it helps single women with children to get out of their social conditions, by reducing their marital endogamy and reducing their unemployment risk. However, this is difficult to take for granted. Because of the higher risk of unemployment among less qualified women and the phenomenon of social endogamy, the probability for single mothers to belong to stable two-earner households is lower. If such a scenario occurs, welfare reform would just have transferred the disequilibrium to the level of household.

Questioning the Evaluation

What about Evaluating Targeted Programs versus Antipoverty Alternatives?

A first set of reservations can be made concerning targeted programs, a second concerning the lessons that are delivered by their evaluations.

Is targeting an argument in favor of the efficiency of TANF? Three levels of reservations can be made in relation to the targeted populations, the "control" of this population and the "principal-agents' relationship" in the presence of information asymmetries.

As emphasized by Sen (1995), targeting may negatively affect the self-respect of the poor; moreover, the sustainability of targeted programs is doubtful, as the potential beneficiaries are politically weak. Secondly, who defines the rules of eligibility? Do social workers responsible for recipients receive appropriate training and can they be deemed "qualified social workers?" Are programs implemented with equal accuracy within the states? Thirdly, hidden administrative costs can, in the presence of imperfect information, arise from the selection of projects, their execution, and monitoring. One of the major complexities concerns the identification of the poor; generally speaking, information asymmetries reduce the effectiveness of targeting when "cheating" occurs.

Thus, at the first level, targeted policies present some limits that cannot be overruled. The outcomes of the evaluations are partly dependent from this point. The multiple evaluations conducted at a state or county level deliver a very precise picture of the populations concerned with forms of strong poverty (*despite the reservations made above*) and of the efficiency of anti-poverty-targeted programs: the first step of the evaluations consists of identifying the characteristics of the population least attached to the labor market, with incomes below the poverty line, in order to test whether the measures implemented *in the framework of the reform* are efficient. Therefore, focusing on the policies implemented, the evaluations do not aim at discussing other social policy options. In particular, the evaluations omit any general thinking about political alternatives to targeted programs; for example, the implementation of a universal safety net, which might prove anti-poverty efficient should the objective be to reduce poverty. As we know, poverty is explained by structural factors. International cross-section analysis is useful to highlight the factors of the poverty gap between industrialized countries: it mainly depends on wage inequality, on domestic labor markets, on the degree of social coverage, and on the generosity of social protection systems. Since the evaluations focus on the U.S. experience, they do not provide any information on the comparative efficiency of targeted programs versus, for example, universal safety net programs. By no means do they question the fact that the very same results could be reached in terms of poverty reduction through a minimum wage revaluation, a better social coverage and more generous benefits, and neither do they test other anti-poverty options. Thus, if a criticism can be made of the existing evaluations, it is that they do not deliver any comparative assessment of the efficiency of alternative poverty-reducing policies.

More generally, these evaluations do not question their own objects, the nature of the reform implemented. In sum, it appears that the evaluation of targeted policies seems paradoxically to avoid the debate about the bases of an optimal poverty-reducing policy. Lastly, one has to keep in mind that as the law includes a dimension of compulsory counterpart, the evaluations may only reveal whether the law is well applied in the states or not.

Does Evaluation Highlight the Economic Behavior of Recipients?

First of all, it must be noted that since the welfare system was implemented, the sum of evaluation work done has been simply remarkable and to that extent, the evaluation of welfare reform in the United States has probably no equivalent in the world. Nevertheless, the extreme standardization of the evaluations can be underlined. The output is abundant and illustrates the explicit consensus in the American economic community on the methodology to adopt. Adding a new characteristic makes a new paper. The selected topics become increasingly narrow. The profusion of evaluation studies with very proximate content and methods gives the idea that there is just one way to deal with these phenomena.

To that extent, four questions can be formulated: Can the results be generalized? What are the implicit assumptions adopted when choosing an outcome indicator? To what extent can the results be mobilized? Does the evaluation explain the economic behavior of the recipients?

The difficulty in generalizing the results of the evaluations is particularly salient because of the diversity of local programs. The selection of states, where evaluations are mainly conducted, may compromise the outcomes of a generalization (see Matsudaira and Danziger, chap. 7). The choice of the outcome indicators is not neutral and not exempt from criticism. For instance, earning gains or income aim at determining if the recipient leaves poverty. Since the effects of the reform are measured over a short period of time, it seems clear that the "make work pay" strategy has more immediate results than a "human capital strategy" whose rates of return are made available in the long run. Gains from general training are negative at the beginning of the period and increase over time, whereas employment induces immediate gains. Any conclusion on the superiority of one strategy over the other is partly biased by the choice of the indicators, especially when they rely on gains' functions.

Moreover, the hourly wage is often regarded as the major indicator of employment quality: what is here assessed does not give any information about the stability in employment of people who have left the rolls, nor does it inform about the prospects of professional mobility. With regard to income indicators, very few studies deal with the issues of equity and well-being. To what extent can the results be mobilized? For example, what do we learn from the fact that a given explanatory variable is responsible for x percent of the decline in caseloads? How to interpret it? Will a weak statistical relationship between the reform and the results lead us to put into question the continuation of the reform? Do evaluations explain the economic behavior of the recipients? Evaluations do not give any information on the reasons for individual success or failure. We do not suitably know the reasons why one agent takes more advantage of the reform than another.

Conclusion: What are the Lessons for the French Experience?

Although evaluation is highly developed, advanced, and institutionalized in the United States, it is not in France. "Evaluation" has become a profession for which there is a market in the United States. Evaluation is taught at universities, which is not the case in France, and think tanks have no equivalent in France" (Perez, 2001). This difference may be due to the devolution of the welfare system as opposed to a centralized implementation of reforms in France. The difference in the use of evaluation between France and the United States may as well reveal a different conception of the role of the state in society: in a decentralized country, evaluation, by giving some guidance to public programs, can be seen as a means of inflection of social policies. In the French "Jacobin" tradition, evaluation may be considered a first step of public disengagement. The political and institutional context may explain why the recourse to evaluation is not so extensive in France. Other arguments can be mobilized: in the United States, eligibility rules for many social programs are strictly defined and social policies are targeted toward specific categories such as "ethnic groups"; this last distinction is absent in France where it tends to be considered "politically incorrect." In the United States, long-established affirmative action has been a favorable factor for the development of evaluation. In France, the implementation of targeted programs has often been rejected because of the stigma it might create. Lastly, in the United States, the continuation of a program is more or less conditional on the results of the evaluation. The notion of accountability is less generalized in France than it is in the United States. As a consequence, the use of evaluations is less developed. In our comparative assessment of French and U.S. experiences, these arguments explain why we cannot rely, on the French side, on a comparable system of evaluation.

What transpires from the comparative assessment of French and U.S. experiences is that normalized solutions exist on both sides of the Atlantic: there is a belief in incentive policies (see Dollé, chap. 4). In France, a correction of the marginal tax rates at the low end of the income distribution, completed by the increase of earning disregards for RMI recipients and the creation of an "income tax credit" for people earning less and slightly more than the minimum wage (the *Prime à l'emploi*), corresponds to the EITC and TANF. In both countries, the boundaries for program efficiency are set by the marginal tax curves, the employment rate, the level of unemployment, the nature of unemployment, and by the change in the demand for low-skilled workers. The differences between France and the United States regarding employment rate and the level of unemployment indicate that "room for maneuver" towards more work incentive policies exists in France. Nevertheless, the limit of the welfare reform in reducing the "core" of poverty, even in a favorable context of economic growth, suggests that a "make work pay" is not a sufficient strategy. Do we need a two-tier system in both countries? Which mechanisms should we then invent to correct the limits of incentive policies?

Notes

1. "The Effects of Time Limits on Welfare Use, Work and Income Among Female Headed Families" (AEA, 2002). In this model endogenous variables are, respectively, "welfare use" or "hours worked" or "income" of Female Headed Families, and exogenous variables are "time limits," "differences in reform implementation dates," "Unemployed rate by State," "log (max benefit)," "State year dummies."
2. Gregg and Wadsworth (1996), Esteban and Ray (1994), Wolfson (1994), Echevin and Parent (2002).

References

Echevin, D., & Parent, A. (2002). "Les indicateurs de polarisation appliqués à la France." *Economie et Prévisions*, 155.

Esteban, J. M., & Ray, D. (1994). "On the measurement of polarization." *Econometrica* 62, 4 (July): 819-851.

Gilles, C. (2001). "La réforme de l'aide sociale aux Etats-Unis. Un bilan après 5 ans d'application." Etudes et Résultats, DREES, No. 137, September.

Gregg, P., & Wadsworth, J. (1996). "It Takes Two: Employment Polarization in the OECD." Discussion paper No. 304, September. CEPR.

Grogger, J. (2002). "The Effects of Time Limits on Welfare Use, Work and Income Among Female Headed Families." Paper presented at the American Economic Association, Atlanta.

Heckman, J. J., & Smith, J. A. (1995). "Assessing the Case for Social Experiments." *Journal of Economic Perspectives* 9, 2 (Spring).

Perez, C. (2001). "Evaluer les programmes d'emploi et de formation, L'expérience américaine." Centre d'Etudes de l'Emploi, dossier 18, Paris.

Sen, A. (1995). "The Political Economy of Targeting." In *Public Spending and the Poor*, edited by D. van de Walle and K. Neat. Baltimore, MD: John Hopkins University Press.

Wolfson, M. C. (1994) "When Inequalities Diverge." *American Economic Review* (May): 843, 353-358.

Part 4

The Relationship between Economic Growth and Poverty

9

Welfare Reform, Economic Growth, and Poverty in the U.S.

Christel Gilles and Antoine Parent

Introduction

The aim of this chapter is to examine the national outcomes of the U.S. welfare reforms through the prism of the relationship between growth and poverty. Several economic indicators suggest that the reforms have been "a success": AFDC/TANF caseloads have been cut by nearly half since 1994; the employment rate of single mothers increased from 60 percent in the early 1990s to nearly 75 percent in 1999; and the poverty rate among lone mothers decreased from 37.2 percent in 1990 to 30.4 percent in 1999.

An extensive amount of research has been conducted on the evaluation of the U.S. welfare reforms. In this chapter, we survey the literature that focuses on the respective role played by the U.S. business cycle and the reforms on caseloads, employment, and poverty rates of single mothers. We deliberately omit discussing the effects of the reforms on the well-being of welfare leavers (see Weil, chap. 6), their family structure (see Burtless, 2000 and chap. 1) as well as on the effects of specific policy components of the reforms (see Matsudaira and Danziger, chap 7.). We find that the literature provides no clear-cut answer to the question of the respective contributions of economic growth and the reforms to the changes in welfare participation, employment, and income of single mothers. We attribute this finding to the differences in the methodologies employed in disentangling the effects of the reforms from other changes.

In a second section, we examine the short-term risks implied by the reforms: What would have been the results of the reforms in a weak labor market situation? What could be the outcome of an economic slowdown in the level of poverty among single-headed families? Will a reverse of the business cycle leave the structural changes engendered by the reform secured or not? We argue that, in a weak macroeconomic environment, the effects of the labor market dynamics on AFDC/TANF leavers remain uncertain, based on the analysis of the safety-net left to the working poor since the 1996 Reform.

Five Years Later: The Welfare Reform and Its Outcomes

Scope and Limits of Theoretical and Quantitative Approaches

Evaluations of the U.S. welfare reforms mainly question the existence of a causal relationship between the reforms and their goals which we arbitrarily reduced to three objectives: the decline in welfare participation, the rise in employment rate, and the fall in poverty among single mothers. Disentangling the effects of the reform from other changes (macroeconomic conditions, demographic and political changes) and controlling for these changes are the major issues encountered when conducting the evaluation. Specific methodologies are employed to this end, which, however, raise various problems of identification. Finally, in order to illustrate the anti-poverty efficiency of the programs reformed as well as the distributional effects engendered by the recent tax and social policy changes on single mothers' income, a third body of research will be mobilized which present other methodological limits.

Results Are Highly Dependent on the Methodologies Adopted

Two methods are commonly used when disentangling the effects of the U.S. reforms on caseloads, employment, and poverty rates from other changes: the differences in differences estimator (1) and econometric estimations of time series of cross sections (2).

The differences in differences estimator (1) consists mostly in studying the change of an outcome indicator of a treatment group, before and after the date of appearance of the event under scrutiny (the reform), and to compare this change to the change in the same outcome indicator of a comparison group. To be valid, the control group has to show similar socioeconomic characteristics to the treatment group in order to react comparably to changes other than the reform while being exempt from the influence of welfare reforms. Moreover, both groups should not be individually affected by any other unobservable variable. The comparability between these two groups is determinant in studying *ceteris paribus*. Once all these conditions are met, the evaluation delivers the marginal contribution of the reforms and enables us to assess their efficiency. In addressing the effect of welfare reform, single mothers are commonly considered the treatment group and compared with women without children. In general, the welfare reforms cover the reforms of six programs (Meyer and Rosenbaum, 2000) consisting of the EITC, AFDC/TANF, Food Stamps, Training Programs, Medicaid, and Child Care, although extensive amount of research focuses on the AFDC/TANF scheme only.

The differences in differences methodology presents a number of risks that could lead to biased results. The "selection bias" results from the existence of unobservable factors that may influence or sometimes explain the results. As shown by Blank and Schoeni (2000), waivers were implemented in states having a worse economy than non-waiver states, reflecting that the reforms were endogenous to economic conditions. An "attrition bias" emerges when the treatment group is not representative of all potential recipients. Finally, a "substitution bias" (Heckman and Smith, 1995) comes up when the control group can benefit from a proxy of the evaluated program. Finally this approach, like econometric estimations, reveals some problems of identification.

The second method (2) consists of econometric estimations based on time series of cross sections. This method has been applied essentially to analyze the effect of the Reform on caseloads (caseload studies), and to a lesser extent, to study the effect of the reform on other outcome indicators (Blank and Schoeni, 2000; Grogger, 2002).

With regard to caseloads studies, the models surveyed (estimated by the Weighted Least Square method) show different specifications: depending on the models, the dependent variable can take the form of the percentage of AFDC/TANF beneficiaries in the whole population (CEA, 1997) or the percentage of beneficiaries in the population of women between 16 and 54 years of age (Moffitt, 1999), with or without autoregressive terms. The dependent variables are welfare Indicator variables (taking the value of 1 for the month the waiver or PRWORA has been approved, (lagged) state unemployment rates or (lagged) employment rates capturing the impact of the business cycle and State, Year, and Trends Fixed Effects controlling for time and geographic differences among states. Some of the surveyed models include financial variables such as the minimum wage (CEA, 1999) and the benefit level (Ziliak et al., 2000), which reflect changes in financial incentives to work. The source of data (administrative or surveys), the sample period, the period of decomposition of the effects, and finally the dynamics might differ as well from one estimate to the other and contribute to the difference in results obtained.

The CEA (1999) estimate[1] presented below, is an illustration of the equations surveyed in the literature aimed at dissociating the effects of the welfare reforms on AFDC/ TANF caseloads from other changes.

CEA (1999) caseloads' estimate

$$ln\mathbf{R}_{st} = \mathbf{Waiver}_{st} + \beta_w + \mathbf{TANF}_{st}\,\beta_{tanf} + ln\mathbf{Benefits}_{st}\,\beta_b + ln\mathbf{Minwage}_{st}\,\beta_{mw} +$$
$$\mathbf{Unemployment}_{st}\beta_u + \gamma_s + \gamma_t + \mathbf{trend}{*}\gamma_s + \varepsilon_{st}$$

R$_{st}$: the ratio of the number of recipients to the population under 65 years of age in time "t" and state "s";

Waiver$_{st}$ **and TANF**$_{st}$: indicator variables that takes the value of one if the state "s" had a major waiver in effect, and one if TANF was in effect, at time "t" (for TANF implementation date varied across states);

Benefits$_{st}$: the maximum monthly benefit for a family of three on AFDC/TANF at time "t" in the state "s";

Minwage$_{st}$: the value of the state-specific minimum wage expressed as a monthly amount assuming employment for 30 hours per week for 4.33 weeks, at time "t";

Unemployment$_{st}$: the unemployment rate (current, lagged one year, lagged two years);

γ_s **and** γ_t: state and year fixed effects; and

trend*γ_s: linear state-specific time trends.

A similar approach was taken by Blank and Schoeni (2000). They employed pseudo-Panel Data econometric techniques to assess the effects of welfare reforms (Waivers and PRWORA), not only on caseloads but on a wide array of outcome indicators including welfare participation, employment rate, earnings, income and poverty, and family structure. They developed a set of reduced forms models where the dependent variable was explained by policy variables (dummies) and additional control variables which held unchanged the economic, demographic, and the political differences among states. These models take the following general form:

$$Y_{aest} = \mathbf{Waiver}_{st} * \mathbf{Educ} * \beta_{eWaiver} + \mathbf{TANF}_{st} * \mathbf{Educ} * \beta_{eTANF} + \gamma_s + \gamma_t + trend * \gamma_s + Z_{aest} * \beta_z + \varepsilon_{aest}$$

- For each of these variables, "a" stands for the age group, "e" for the education group, "s" for the state, and "t" for the calendar year.
- Y: one of the outcome variables listed above.
- The dependent variables are: -indicator variables for the Waivers and TANF that take the value of one when a major waiver and TANF were in effect or zero otherwise; indicator variables for education groups (*Educ*)—state and year fixed effects (γ_s, γ_t), linear state-specific time trends to control for demographic shifts (*trend*γ_s*) and finally, a vector of control variables (Z_{aest}) that correct for state characteristics regarding demography, policy, and economy.

These econometric estimations present different types of methodological problems: some problems of identification of the effects due to the heterogenity among states of the reforms and of their dates of implementation; some problems due to unobserved variables; and some problems of endogenity. Finally, econometric estimations raise the problem of comparability of their results since their specification can be very dissimilar.

The problem of identification is particularly severe when estimating the global effect of TANF since the federal reform has been implemented in all states on a 17-month period of time whereas waivers have been activated over a five-year period in some states. The identification of the effects of the components of welfare reforms is also problematic. The coding of the components varies across studies, the available information on TANF is limited, and the related number of observations sometimes too small to allow an econometric estimation of their effects. Finally, the choice and the number of the components of welfare reforms are not neutral on the assessment of their individual effects since they are not independent: for example, assessing the effect of a cut in benefit levels without taking into account a rise in child care benefits would lead to biased results (Blank, 2002).

The variety of specifications contributes to the differences in results. The treatment of the dynamics, in particular, varies significantly across studies. According to the model retained, the lag structure of the independent variables and of the dependent variable is very different across studies. Since authors do not always present the related statistical tests, judging the quality of the treatment of the dynamics in particular is not a sure bet. Moreover, in this literature, the treatment of dynamics happens to be justified by economic assumptions made by the authors rather than by econometric tests (Bell, 2001). To that extent, Blank (2002) suggests that the lag structure, often warranted by the assumption of a hysteresis effect hitting all welfare recipients, hides fundamental economic mechanisms that need to be studied.

More generally, the omission of important explicative variables (labor force participation, take up rate, etc. even though offset by the introduction of numerous fixed effects, limits the understanding of fundamental mechanisms underlying the changes in caseloads.

Both of these methodologies aim at assessing the impact of welfare reforms on a certain number of outcome indicators. Both approaches evaluate "mean impacts" of the program and deliver a limited appreciation of the effects of specific policy components implemented by various states (see Matsudaira and Danziger, chap. 7) and provide no information on the heterogeneity in response to the reforms (Heckman, Smith, and Clements, 1997). Finally, these empirical methods give a restricted understanding of the mechanisms originating these results.

Welfare Reforms and Labor Supply:
Theory Predicts an Ambiguous Global Effect

One of the difficulties in evaluating the effect of welfare reforms on labor supply comes from the fact that all programs do not, in theory, exert an impact similar in sign and scope. Literature[2] on the impact of the EITC on labor supply of single mothers is relatively straightforward since this benefit is a tax credit and concludes to a net positive effect. The AFDC and Food Stamp programs have a negative impact[3]: since these cash benefits are differential, recipients are particularly sensitive to the income effect they engender and are heavily penalized by the high implicit tax rate imposed when moving to work.[4] In advocating a "make work pay" strategy, the 1996 welfare reform materialized into higher income disregards for TANF recipients. The overall incidence on labor supply therefore turns more ambiguous[5]: whereas the effect is positive on the labor supply of recipients, it is negative for those newly eligible to the program and negative for those experiencing higher income levels. The overall effect depends in theory on the distribution of the number of people among then recipients, those newly eligible, and finally those having higher income. This uncertainty is more generally inherent in targeted benefits.[6] With regard to the extension of Medicaid to working single mothers, the effect on labor supply is considered strictly positive and so is the effect produced by the extension and increase of child care benefits for working lone mothers. Finally, the incidence of general or professional training programs extension is left unclear: it depends on the perception of the recipient vis à vis the mandatory aspects attached to the program. If considered a way to increase future earnings, the beneficiary will reduce his labor supply; an opposing view will lead to an increase in labor supply.

Do We Have a Clear Picture of the Effects of the Reform?

The effects of the reforms on caseloads and employment rate of single mothers. Caseloads studies (see table 9.1) agree that the business cycle and welfare reforms have both played a role in the decline of the number of AFDC/TANF recipients. However, when addressing the question of identifying the most influential factor between the two, research delivers no definite answer. According to the studies surveyed in this chapter, between 20 percent and 80 percent of caseload declines are attributed to the business cycle prior to 1996 and between 8 percent and 12 percent after; between 0 percent and 30 percent are attributed to the welfare reforms[7] before 1996 and between 35 percent and 75 percent after 1996. These studies provide highly different results (partly stemming from differences in the specification of the models) and a few only evaluate the effects of TANF. However, some general findings presented below can be addressed:

- over the 1993-1996 period, prior to the federal welfare reform, all studies surveyed show a prevailing effect of the business cycle on caseloads;
- after 1996, the two studies surveyed show an opposite result: the 1996 welfare reform had a larger effect on caseloads than on the business cycle;

- over a long period of time (1976-1998), caseloads became increasingly sensitive to the business cycle. According to the CEA (1999), a 1 point increase in unemployment rate leads (over the 1976-1980 period) to a 1.5 percent rise in the ratio of caseloads to the whole population; to a 3.2 percent increase over the 1981-1986 period, to 3.9 percent over 1987-1992, and finally to 4.4 percent since 1993.

Table 9.1

The Relative Importance of Policy versus the Economy on Caseloads

This table is taken from Blank (2000) and Bell (2001); we selected studies that give a decomposition of the effects originated by the business cycle and the welfare reforms.

Studies	Percentage of change attributed to the business cycle (employment and/or unemployment variables)	Percentage of change in caseloads attributed to the reforms	Period of decomposition of the effects	Sample period
CEA (1997)	between 31% et 45%	between 13% et 31%	1993-1996	1976-1996
Figlio and Ziliak (1999)	between 18% et 76%	between -7% et 1%	1993-1996	1976-1996
Ziliak & al. (2000)	78%	6%	1993-1996	1987-1996
Moffitt (1999)	47%	15%	1993-1996	1977-1996
Blank (2001)	59%	28%	1994-1996	1977-1996
CEA (1999)	between 26% et 36%	between 12% et 15%	1993-1996	1976-1998
	between 8% et 10%	between 35% et 36%	1996-1998	
Wallace and Blank (1999)	47%	22%	1994-1996	1980-1998
	12%	75%	1996-1998	

Source: Blank (2000) and Bell (2001).

Finally, one has to recall that in the CEA (1999) study, the increases in the federal minimum wage[8] and in its purchasing power (which stands as an explanatory variable different from the reforms and the business cycle) explained 10 percent of the decline in caseloads after 1996. However, the share of caseload changes unexplained by these estimates is sometimes high and leads to a cautious interpretation of their results: over the 1996-1998 period, 56 percent of the changes in caseloads is left unexplained in the CEA modeling (1999).

Whereas extensive amounts of research focused on the effects of welfare reform on caseloads exists, research on the causal effects reforms on employment rates has proved less abundant. We examine the studies of Blank and Schoeni (2000) and Meyer and Rosenbaum (2000), which provide accurate answers based on the two methodologies presented above.

Blank and Schoeni (2000) assessed the effectiveness of the recent welfare reform, examining the impact of both state-specific waivers in the early 1990s and PRWORA. They evaluated the impact of the reform on eleven outcome indicators including employment rate. Both methodologies have been employed, namely the difference in differences estimates and econometric estimations based on time series of cross sections using aggregated individual data on adult women from the Current Population Survey over the 1977-1999 period. In order to evaluate the incidence of the reforms on marital status, the authors studied the incidence of the reforms on low-educated women rather than on single mothers. For each of the eleven dependent variables, the authors calculated a mean, by state and year, for three distinctive education levels (less than twelve years, twelve years, and more than twelve years) and for four age groups (16-25, 26-34, 35-44, 45-54). They initially compared changes in the employment of low-educated women before and after the enactment of waivers to changes occurring in non-waiver states for the same group. The results, however, were biased, for non-waiver states did not represent a valid comparison group, the authors found waiver states to have weaker economic conditions than non-waiver states (reflecting that the dependent variable and the policy explanatory variable were endogenous). To better control for any endogenity bias, the authors developed an econometric model including various control variables and found that waivers had contributed to increase by two percentage points (see table 9.2), the employment rate of low-qualified women versus virtually no impact produced by PRWORA. According to the authors, the federal welfare reform did not influence the employment rate of single mothers (represented by low-educated women in this study), but economic expansion did. However, the same paper argued that PRWORA did play a prominent role in the decline in caseloads, inferring that the sanctions voted by the law (financial sanctions and time limits) acted as a catalyst for leaving the rolls.

Using the difference in differences methodology, Meyer and Rosenbaum (2000) examined whether the changes in policies had a causal effect on the changes in employment rates of single mothers over the 1984-1996 period.

Table 9.2
Effect of Waivers and TANF on Welfare Participation,
Employment Rates, Annual Weeks Worked and Poverty Rate of
Low-Educated Women (less than twelve years of education)

Dependent variables	Effects of the Reforms.		
	Waivers	TANF [1]	TANF [2]
Welfare participation	-0,8 point	-4,5 points	-3,3* points
Employment rate	+ 2 points	+0,6* point	+0,4* point
Annual weeks worked	+ 0,732	+ 0,77	+ 0,236*
Poverty Rate	-2,6 points	-2 points	-1,6 points

(1) Estimate based on the differences of residuals.
(2) Estimate based on the differences in differences.
Source: Blank and Schoeni (2000), results are not statistically significant at 10%.

Compared with Blank and Schoeni (2000), this study does not disentangle the effects of the reforms from other changes but gives an additional analysis of the causal effect of the reforms on employment rate. To a lesser extent, the authors assess the individual contribution to the changes in employment rate among single mothers of the major programs reformed (EITC, MEDICAID, AFDC).

Reporting here the results based exclusively on March CPS Data, the authors showed that between 1984 and 1996, single mothers' employment rate rose by 8.7 percentage points from 58.5 percent to 64.5 percent, compared to a 1 point decline to 79.5 percent for single women without children which, according to the authors, suggests that changes in employment regarding the treatment group did not result from better economic conditions. Furthermore, most of the change occurred between 1991 and 1996, which stands as the period of implementation of the Social and Tax reforms. As mentioned before, these results depend on the choice of the control group, which according to the authors, could have been differentially impacted by economic growth and could have incurred differential modifications over time in characteristics such as, age and education. In order to correct for such biases, the authors applied the difference in differences methodology to various control groups consisting of low-paid workers, high school dropouts, married mothers, and finally black men (this last group aims at correcting for the effect of the business cycle on employment of disadvantaged groups). Their findings were left unchanged, the authors therefore concluded on the outstanding influence of Tax and Social Policy changes on employment of single mothers. When examining the individual effects of the major Social and Tax reforms to the shift in single mothers' employment, the authors, with a similar approach, identified the effect of the Earned Income Tax Credit (EITC) and, to a less extent, the effect of Medicaid.

Disentangling the Effects of the Reform from Other Changes in Poverty

A direct causal effect. Blank and Schoeni (2000) established a causal effect of welfare reform on the decline of poverty among high school dropouts, defined in their study as a proxy of single mothers. Using econometric estimates of cross sections combined with the differences in differences method, the authors found that the waivers and PRWORA engendered a 2 percentage point decline in the poverty rate of high school dropouts. Neither the waivers nor PRWORA lead to a significant effect on women's own earnings; however, the waivers did contribute to raising family's earnings by 9 percent and family's income by 6 percent compared to an increase of 3 percent and 6 percent, respectively, due to PRWORA. A fall in social transfers could explain the spread between the changes of family earnings and income. While Blank and Schoeni (2000) set up a causal effect of welfare reforms on poverty, the Congressional Research Service, adopting a descriptive approach, assessed the contribution of each major income support program to the recent decline of poverty among single mothers.

The role played by each program in the decline of poverty among single mothers. The Congressional Research Service assessed the contribution of the major income support programs to the decline of poverty rate among single mothers (see table 9.3). According to the CRS, the EITC became, over the 1993-1998 period, the most efficient anti-poverty program. Its major expansion, voted on by Congress in 1993 and implemented over the 1994-1996 period, resulted in a substantial increase in the amount of the EITC bonus allocated as well as in a larger coverage of the population. Its contributions to the decline in the poverty rate has been multiplied by nearly 4 between 1993 and 1998. In 1998, it helped to reduce the poverty rate by 5.5 points compared to 2.2 in 1993. Comparatively, the anti-poverty efficiency of cash welfare and food assistance decreased over time: when added to other cash income, cash welfare pushed single mothers' poverty rate downward by 1.5 points from 38.8 percent to 37.3 percent in 1998 versus 2.2 points in 1993. Food Assistance had a comparable contribution in reducing poverty. When added to cash income including cash welfare, the poverty rate declined by 2 and 3 points in 1993 and in 1998, respectively.

Table 9.3
**Poverty Rates among Single Mothers in Percent Calculated
for Different Definitions of Income**

Definitions of income	1993	1998
Cash Income except Cash Welfare = (1)	47,4	38,8
(2) = (1) + Plus Cash Welfare = Official Income Definition For Measuring Poverty	45,2	37,3
(3) = (2) + Plus Food Assistance	42,7	35,2
(4) = (3) + Plus EIC	40,7	29,7

Source: Greenbook, 2000.

Although these results neither take into account the effects of the business cycle nor the incidence of the change over time in the structure of the poor population, they, however, support Meyer and Rosenbaum's (2000) findings on the prominent role played by EITC in the increase of single mothers' employment rate and in the decrease in their poverty rate. But how are those gains in income distributed among single mothers? We now address the question of the distributional effects of welfare reforms and present the results of research achieved by CRS and Primus (2000).

Table 9.4
Change in Poverty Gap per Poor Person

In 1999 $	1993	1995	1999
Per person			
Poverty Gap	3673	3689	3729
Poverty Gap after tax and transfers	2104	2142	2416
Per children			
Poverty Gap	2840	2696	2475
Poverty Gap after tax and transfers	1501	1503	1640

Source: Primus (2000), mimeo.

Some distributional effects engendered by welfare reforms. According to the CRS, while the majority of "earning poor" single mothers have experienced higher incomes since 1991, most of the gains occurred in 1994 and in 1995, prior to federal welfare reform. Since 1996, the bottom two quintiles have been no better off relative to poverty, whereas the first quintile has exhibited a net decline in income. For this most disadvantaged group, the structure and the level of income have noticeably altered. Their average total family income was lower in 1997-1998 than in 1994-1996 although higher than in any years before 1994. Their average cash welfare assistance received in 1998 was more than 40 percent lower than in 1994 and 30 percent lower for food stamps for the same years. In contrast, net earnings of the bottom quintile increased by nearly 70 percent between 1994 and 1998 and together with the Earned Income Tax Credit, it offset a little more than 50 percent of the loss incurred by the fall in cash welfare assistance and food stamps. Since the amount of public assistance programs is a due proportion of the number of people in the household as opposed to earnings, it contributes to some extent to penalize recipients moving to work.

Using the indicator of poverty gap and the distribution of annual income of single mothers, Primus (2000) confirmed the above results. The author showed that over the period of implementation of welfare reforms (1993-1999), poverty declined among households with children and single mothers. However, the poverty gap after tax and transfers for single mothers declined less than for all households with children respectively: -20 percent between 1993 and 1995 versus −27 percent and −7 percent between 1995 and 1999, versus -8 percent for all households with children. Secondly, the author showed that along with a global decline in poverty, measured by the poverty gap before and after tax and transfers, the situation of the poorest deteriorated between 1993 and 1999: per person, the poverty gap after tax and transfers increased by 15 percent (see table 9.4) and by 10 percent per children.[9]

Table 9.5
Annual Income Distribution of Single Mothers

In 1999 $	1993	1995	1999	Change in % 1993-1995	1995-1999
Quintile 1	7877	8721	8405	10,7	-3,6
Quintile 2	13954	16069	17109	15,2	6,5
Quintile 3	18633	21126	22507	13,4	6,5
Quintile 4	26735	28965	31491	8,3	8,7
Quintile 5	45903	48095	55867	4,8	16,2
				Change in %	
Quintile 1				1993-1995	1995-1999
earnings	1322	1744	2360	422	616
Means tested benefits	5547	5614	4279	68	-1335
Disposable Income	7877	8721	8405	843	-316

Source: Primus (2000), mimeo.

Finally, the impoverishment of some, highlighted by the rise in the poverty gap per capita, applied to single mothers. Primus (2000) showed that (see table 9.5) the bottom quintile of the annual income distribution of single mothers suffered from a loss (-3.6 percent) over the 1995-1999, period resulting from a fall in means tested benefits larger than the rise in earnings. Like the *CRS* analysis, this study does not take into account the change in the composition of the poor population, thus leaving a possible bias of attrition, nor does it correct for changes in the economic conditions occurring over the sample period. However, these studies underline that the welfare reforms might have inferred some distributional effects, a result that has not been evoked in quantitative research surveyed above.[10] In the following section, we question the viability of the welfare reform considering short-term and long-term risks attached to them.

The Effects of the Business Cycle

An Unstable Relationship between Economic Growth and Poverty

In order to assess the effect of the business cycle on welfare recipiency, an initial step is taken here consisting of the study of the relationship between economic growth and poverty. Freeman (2001) addressed this issue and evaluated the nature of this relationship over the 1960-1999 period in the United States. Since macroeconomic performance happened to be an unstable indicator of poverty development, the author tested the existence of other factors liable to distort over time the macroeconomic relationship between economic growth and poverty.

Based on elasticities of poverty rate to economic growth over the 1990-1999 period, Freeman (2001) found that on the whole, poverty has not responded to economic growth over the entire period with one exception however: in the late 1990s, economic growth rekindled its strong influence on poverty, comparable to that observed in the late 1970s.

According to the author, poverty presents cyclical patterns. However, while poverty rises during periods of recession, the magnitude of the change in poverty is left unclear during periods of economic growth: a drop of unemployment proved to be accompanied with either a weak or strong decline in poverty. Macroeconomic performance does not stand as accurately predictive of the trends in poverty.

According to Freeman (2001), three variables could be at the origin of the change over time of the incidence of economic growth on poverty: demographic changes, the shape of the income distribution, and finally the levels of real wage and wage inequalities.

Based on past observations, Freeman (2001) pinpointed the rise in single parenthood as a contributory factor to the decline between 1960-1999 in the relationship between economic growth and poverty, since this group emerged as particularly hard hit by poverty. All else being equal, an increase in single parenthood engenders a rise in poverty. Then, the author showed that the dispersion of income is responsible for the distortion of the link between economic growth and poverty rate. The wider the dispersion of income, the larger the incidence on poverty rate. Finally, considering striking changes in the combination of economic growth and trends in real wages and wage inequalities, Freeman (2001) tested the hypothesis that real wages and wage inequalities could affect poverty.

He tested this hypothesis and estimated an equation where the dependent variable, the poverty rate, was explained by the unemployment rate, real earnings, and finally earnings dispersion measured by, respectively, a Gini coefficient of family income and the ratio D5/D1 (median family income to the income of families in the bottom quintile). Using times series, and cross-section time series, and after controlling for state effects, Freeman (2001) concluded on the explanatory role of each of the three variables with regard to the level of poverty.

Freeman's (2001) main findings are that an increase in employment, illustrative of a strong economy, can lead to a decline in poverty only if real wages rise. The mid-1990s, characterized by, respectively, historically low unemployment and by improving real wages (+6.6 percent over the 1995-1999 period), contributed to the reduction of poverty. This specific combination of low unemployment and boosting real wages stood, according to the author, as the main explanation of the outcome of the 1996 welfare reform. From there, Freeman (2001) underlined the risks of negative consequences of welfare reform on poverty in a different macroeconomic environment.

Will the Labor Market Absorb TANF Leavers When the Economic Cycle Reverses?

The reform in causing a rush of lone mothers into the labor market should have implied, in theory (Solow, 1998), an increased competition between low-skilled workers (termed a substitution effect) and/or exerted a downward pressure on low wages.

Burtless (2000) surveyed three kinds of evidence to answer this question: the Bureau of Labor Statistics' estimates of employment growth; employers' answers to surveys on the availability of jobs and the necessary skills to qualify for these jobs, and the historical capacity of the U.S. labor market to absorb shocks on labor supply. The two first sources of information led to a pessimistic assessment since the majority of welfare recipients are high school dropouts and their occupations are low-skilled jobs, with a major difficulty to secure a stable job. On the contrary, the long-term capacity of the U.S. labor market to create jobs delivers a more encouraging message. Burtless (2000) assumed that the flow of recipients forced to accept jobs should imply a fall in wages of less-skilled workers. In response to this change, the output should be, in the long run, more unskilled labor oriented. Thus, through this possible channel, the labor market could continue to "absorb former recipients." According to empirical studies led at a general level over the 1996-2000 period, competition among low-skilled workers did not materialize. Lerman[11] (2000) explained the lack of low wages' adjustment by a higher demand for low-skilled workers than the supply. Lerman (2000) tried to gauge what would have happened to low wages should lone mothers not have entered the labor market. In doing so, he compared employment rates among low-skilled workers in two geographical areas: an area where the number of lone mothers entering the labor market was particularly high versus an area where it was not. Should a substitution effect have materialized, the employment rate of low-skilled workers in the first area would have dropped substantially relative to the one in the second area. The author did not find such an effect. This result can be interpreted as the effect of the business cycle on employment of former recipients.

In order to appreciate the degree of exposure of former welfare recipients to an economic downturn, the elasticity of the total number of recipients to unemployment rates can be employed: Figlio and Ziliak (1999) estimated that the elasticity of the number of recipients to unemployment rate varied from 6 to 8. Wallace and Blank (1999) and Blank (2001) obtained comparable elasticity rates. Accordingly, welfare recipients and presumably leavers are particularly exposed to economic downturns, which leads to question their access to unemployment benefits.

What About Unemployment Coverage?[12]

Three major research papers apprehend this question. First, Gustafson and Levine (1998) and Vroman (1998) who considered that the ratio of insured unemployment to total unemployment differed strongly between unemployed people formerly on welfare and other categories of unemployed. Then Holzer (2000) who showed that since welfare reform, with the employment characteristics of former recipients have converged with those of other low-skilled workers, allowing for a comparable eligibility to unemployment benefits. Despite these differences, these authors agreed that the difficulty faced by former recipients in obtaining unemployment benefits results from the existence of non-monetary requirements (30 percent of the unemployed met only non-monetary requirements).

Gustfason and Levine (1998) pointed out that the probability of obtaining unemployment benefit is not cyclical and does not mechanically improve during economic slowdown. They stressed that former welfare recipients were discriminated against other categories of low-skilled women when considering monetary requirements. Accordingly, the current system of unemployment benefit does not appear to be an adequate safety net for welfare leavers. Vroman (1998) found that only 20 percent of former recipients could claim unemployment benefits because of the four major restrictions attached to their payments: low earnings and short work history, a definition of the reference period, which does not include earnings of the quarter preceding unemployment registration, some disqualifying break-ups of the job contract (for instance, care for a sick child), and finally a definition of employment availability based on full-time work.

Thus, former welfare recipients do have limited access to unemployment benefits. Should they lose their jobs, they might be eligible for TANF only if they did not overpass the five-year time limit. In this literature, several solutions are considered regarding the reforming of the Unemployment Insurance System: the creation of an assistance unemployment system for those ineligible for the insurance system, changing the reference periods, smoothing some TANF rules and especially time limits, and finally raising financial supports for government assisted jobs.

Conclusion

This chapter reviews the literature focusing on the outcomes of welfare reform in terms of poverty in the context of the 1990s strong economy. We have tried to assess and question the definite statements according to which the reforms have been "a success."

We argue that there is no clear-cut answer to the question of the respective contributions of economic growth and the reforms to the changes in welfare participation, employment, and income of single mothers. Mainly, it appears that the new welfare policies outcomes in terms of poverty reduction cannot be isolated from the context of a strong labor market.

In a weak macroeconomic environment, an increased precariousness of leavers driven by the lack of safety-net for the working poor appears to be an important consequence of the structural changes induced by reforms.

Notes

1. This equation is, according to the authors, the most statistically robust to measure the global effects of Waivers and TANF on caseloads. However, a second equation, not presented in this chapter, is tested which aims at measuring the effects of five components of welfare reforms: time limits, family cap, exemptions, sanctions, and earning disregards.
2. See Eissa and Leibman (1996), Scholtz (1996). Over the EITC phase-out range, B. Meyer (2001, 2002) found that the labor supply disincentives are exaggerated and merit probably less concern by policymakers.
3. See Meyer and Rosenbaum (2000).
4. Wolfe (2000) found that once earning-disregards ended, the marginal tax rate was around 70 percent in Alabama, Mississippi, and Pennsylvania.
5. See Moffitt (2002).

6. The theoretical effect of TANF on labor supply is more complex however since it involves a sets of simultaneous changes which we do not evaluate here (earning disregards, time limits, training programs, etc.).

7. Depending on the caseload study, these reforms consist of the major Waivers implemented in twenty-six states (Ziliak et al., 2000) or consist in the major Waivers and PRWORA (CEA, 1999; Wallace and Blank, 1999).

8. Over the two periods of decomposition of the effects, 1993-1996 and 1996-1998, the federal minimum wage has been increased twice by 11.8 percent in 1996 and by 8.4 percent in 1997, which translated into an 8.5 percent and 6.2 percent rise in constant dollars. Prior to 1996, the federal minimum wage had been increased in 1978, 1981, and 1990. Over the 1978-1989 period, the real minimum wage decreased by one-third; it has stabilized since 1990 (source: BLS).

9. For research on the effect of the welfare reform on children, see S. Danziger (2001).

10. Excepted in Blank and Schoeni (2000), who found that PRWORA did not benefit less-skilled women at the bottom of the income distribution.

11. The author studied the effect of 230,000 new coming lone mothers into the labor market over the 1996-2000 period in twenty big cities.

12. Unemployment insurance is a federal program funded entirely by employers'contributions. States do have autonomy in the definition of their program, by fixing the conditions of eligibility, the reasons for benefits' exhaustion, the benefit level and spell. Allocation granting depends on monetary and non-monetary conditions. Monetary conditions concern previous earning gains perceived during the reference period, defined as the four prime quarters of the five preceding unemployment registration. In 1999, to be eligible, a person had to earn $ 1,730 during the period of reference, which was the equivalent of two months full time at the minimum wage ($5.15). Non-monetary conditions are many. An unemployed person should, on the average (in 1999) have worked two quarters during the period of reference and be available for a full-time job, be able to prove his job search and to argue for job losses and job refusals. If unemployment insurance covered, in 2000, 125 million people (97 percent of workers), the percentage of unemployed receiving the benefit is low (38 percent in 1999). Vroman (1998) had two reasons: a weak "resort" to unemployment insurance, estimated to 50 percent only, and a high ratio of "rejection," estimated to 30 percent.

References

Bell, S. (2001). "Why Are Welfare Caseloads Falling?" Discussion Paper No. 01-02. Washington DC: Urban Institute

Blank, R. (2000). "Declining Caseload/Increased Work: What Can We Conclude about the Effects of Welfare Reform." Paper prepared for the conference "Welfare Reform Four Years Later: Progress and Prospects" at the Federal Reserve Bank of New York. October.

Blank, R. (2001). "What Causes Public Assistance Caseloads to Grow?" *Journal of Human Resources* 36: 1.

Blank, R. (2002). "Evaluating Welfare Reform in the United States." Working Paper 8993, NBER. June.

Blank, R., & Schoeni, R. (2000). "What Has Welfare Reform Accomplished? Impacts on Welfare Participation, Employment, Income, Poverty, and Family Structure." Working Papers 7627, NBER. March.

Blank, R., Card, D., & Robins, P. (1999). "Financial Incentives for Increasing Work and Income Among Low-Income Families." Working Paper 6998, NBER. March.

Burtless, G. (2000). "Can the Labor Market Absorb Three Million Welfare Recipients?" In *The Low-Wage Labor Market,* edited by K. Kaye and D.S. Nightingale. Washington, DC.: Brookings Institution

Cancian, M., Haveman, R., Kaplan, T., Meyer, D., & Wolfe, B. (1999). "Work, Earnings, and Well-Being After Welfare: What Do We Know?" Institute for Research on Poverty. University of Wisconsin-Madison.

Council of Economic Advisers. (1997). "Technical Report: Explaining the Decline in Welfare Receipt, 1993-1996." Washington, DC: Executive Office of the President. April.

Council of Economic Advisers. (1999). "Economic Expansion, Welfare Reform, and the Decline in Welfare Caseloads: An Update. Technical Report." Washington, DC: Executive Office of the President. September.

Danziger, S. (2001). "After Welfare Reform and Economic Boom: Why is Child Poverty Still So Much Higher in the U.S. than in Europe?" Paper presented at the 8th International Research Seminar of the Foundation for International Studies on Social Security.

Danziger, S., & Haveman, R. (2001). "Understanding Poverty." Russell Sage Foundation, Harvard University Press.

Dollé, M. (2000). "La réforme du Welfare aux Etats-Unis: une tentative d'évaluation." *Revue Française d'économie 3.*

Eissa, N., & Liebman, J. (1996). "Labor Supply Response to the Earned Income Tax Credit." *Quarterly Journal of Economics* 61, 2: 605-637.

Eissa, N., & Hoynes, H. (1998). "The Earned Income Tax Credit and the Supply of Married Couples." Working Paper 6856, NBER. December.

Figlio, D., & Ziliak, J. (1999). "Welfare Reform, The Business Cycle, and the Decline in AFDC Caseloads." In *Economic Conditions and Welfare Reform,* edited by Sheldon H. Danziger. Kalamazoo, MI: W. E. Upjohn Institute for Employment Research.

Freeman, R. (2001). "The Rising Tide Lifts…" In "Understanding Poverty," edited by S. Danziger and R. Haveman. Russell Sage Foundation, Harvard University Press.

Gilles, C. (2001). "La réforme de l'aide sociale aux Etats-Unis. Un bilan après 5 ans d'application." Etudes et Résultats, DREES, No 137. September.

Grogger, J. (2002). "The Effects of Time Limits on Welfare Use, Work and Income Among Female Headed Families." American Economic Association, Atlanta. January.

Gustafson, C., & Levine, P. (1998). "Less-skilled Workers, Welfare Reform, and the Unemployment Insurance System." Working Paper 6489, NBER.

Heckman, J. J., & Smith, J. A. (1995). "Assessing the Case for Social Experiments." *Journal of Economic Perspectives* 9, 2 (Spring).

Heckman, J., Smith, J., & Clements, N. (1997). "Making the Most Out of Programme Evaluations and Social Experiments: Accounting for Heterogeneity in Programme Impacts." *Review of Economic Studies.* May.

Holzer, H. (1998). "Will Employers Hire Welfare Recipients? Recent Survey Evidence from Michigan." Discussion Paper No. 1177-98. Institute for Research on Poverty. October.

Holzer, H. (2000). "Unemployment Insurance and Welfare Recipients: What Happens When the Recession Comes?" Discussion Paper, Series A, No A-46. The Urban Institute. December.

Lerman, R., & Ratcliffe, C. (2000). "Did Metropolitan Areas Absorb Welfare Recipients Without Displacing Other Workers?" Discussion Paper, Series A, No. A-45. The Urban Institute. November.

Loprest, P. (2002) "Making the Transition from Welfare to Work: Success but Continuing Concerns." In *Welfare Reform. The Next Act,* edited by Alan Weil and Kenneth Finegold. Washington, DC: The Urban Institute Press.

Meyer, B., & Rosenbaum, D. (2000). "Making Single Mothers Work: Recent Tax and Welfare Policy and Its Effects." Working Papers 7491, NBER. January.

Moffitt, R., (1992). "Incentive Effects of the U.S. Welfare System: A Review." *Journal of Economic Literature* XXX (March).

Moffitt, R. (2002). "The Temporary Assistance for Needy Families Program." Working Paper 8749, NBER. February.

Moffitt, R., & Roff, J. (2000). "The Diversity of Welfare Leavers." Working Paper 00-01. Johns Hopkins University. October.

Morel, S. (2000). "Les logiques de la réciprocité. Les transformations de la relation d'assistance aux Etats-Unis et en France." Collection PUF.

Primus, W. (2000). "Preliminary Impacts." Mimeo. Center on Budget and Policy Priorities. Washington, DC. October.

Primus, W., Rawlings, L., Larin, K., & Porter K. (1999). "The Initial Impacts of Welfare Reform on the Incomes of Single-Mothers Families." Center on Budget and Policy Priorities, Washington DC.

Scholtz, J. K. (1996). "In-Work Benefits in the United States: The Earned Income Tax Credit." *The Economic Journal* 106: 156-169.

Solow, R. (1998). *Work and Welfare.* Princeton, NJ: Princeton University Press.

U.S. Department of Health and Human Services. (2000). TANF, Third Annual Report to Congress.

U.S. House of Representatives. (2000). Committee on Ways and Means, Greenbook.

Vroman, W. (1998). "Effects of Welfare Reform on Unemployment Insurance." Discussion Paper, Series A, No. A-22. The Urban Institute. May.

Wallace, G., & Blank, R. (1999). "What Goes Up Must Come Down? Explaining Recent Changes in Public Assistance Caseloads." In *Economic Conditions and Welfare Reform,* edited by Sheldon H. Danziger. Kalamazoo, MI: W. E. Upjohn Institute for Employment Research.

Weil, A., & Finegold, K. (2002). *Welfare Reform. The Next Act.* Washington, DC: The Urban Institute Press.

Weil, A. (2003). "Assessing Welfare Reform in the United States." In *Welfare Reform: A Comparative Assessment of French and U.S. Experiences,"* International Social Security Series Vol. 10. New Brunswick, NJ: Transaction Publishers. Washington, DC.

Wolfe, B. (2000). "Incentives, Challenges, and Dilemmas of TANF." Discussion Paper No.1209-00, Institute for Research on Poverty. May.

Ziliak, J., Figlio, D., Davis, E., & Connolly, L. (2000). "Accounting for the Decline in AFDC Caseloads: Welfare Reform or the Economy." *Journal of Human Resources* 35 (3): 570-86.

10

Growth and Poverty in France

Christel Gilles, Christian Loisy, and Antoine Parent

Introduction

Is This Topic Relevant?

Does research give credit to the intuition of a consistent negative correlation between real economic growth and poverty? Does the economic literature give evidence of a business cycle effect on poverty?

We will not deal here with the problem of determining the factors of growth (exogenous or endogenous). We will use here the expression "economic growth" in its wide sense, including both growth in the short run (as a transitory or cyclical phenomenon) and in the long run ("steady growth"). It is probably true that long-term economic growth is required in order to have a significant impact on poverty. The question of steady growth and its impact on poverty might be more relevant to the case of developing countries whereas addressing the issue of the effect of the business cycle on poverty relates more to developed countries. In order to assess the interactions between economic growth, inequality, and poverty, we will refer in this section to the GDP indicator.

Conventional analyses of the relationship between growth and poverty refer to the effect of growth and the business cycle on absolute poverty as opposed to relative poverty, which infers the notion of inequality. Absolute poverty rate, as used in the United States, defines the number of people as a percentage of the total population living below a given income threshold that is independent of the income distribution. The main issue is that economic growth, by raising average income could decrease the percentage of people living below an absolute poverty line. Thus, using an absolute poverty index may lead to evidence of a negative correlation between growth and poverty, or said differently, of a strong link between a decrease in absolute poverty and a steady growth of total income.

If we examine the relationship between economic growth and relative poverty index as used in France, we actually question the existence of a relationship between economic growth and inequality. Economic literature focuses largely on this particular topic and provides, however, less clear answers about the sign of the causal relation than results of studies focusing on the growth-poverty relationship.

The choice of an indicator is the first issue to deal with that can bias the nature of the link to be found between growth and poverty. But the problem cannot be as simple as the matter of an indicator. Changes in the shape of the income distribution may also have an influence on the level of poverty.

Growth–Inequality–Poverty: A Complex Issue

First of all, the complexity of the relationship between growth, inequality, and poverty results from *endogenous consequence* of fundamental economic and social processes in nations. Growth, inequality, and poverty may be jointly determined by endogenous variables through relationships that can vary in time and space. It comes that the causal relationship between growth and poverty, which we attempt to test for in the case of France (in this chapter), and is inevitably hazardous without any detailed analysis of other mechanisms that might influence this relationship. More basically, when dealing with the relationship between growth and poverty, one has to consider the effect of income inequality on both growth and poverty, which overall, depends on how changes in income distribution relate to the business cycle. Is it correct, for instance, to assume that income distribution widens when economic growth decelerates and narrows when it grows?

Furthermore, other issues complicate the assessment of the "growth–poverty" relationship: poor people represent an heterogeneous population (we can probably assume that some households are less affected by economic cycles than others—logically, groups that are more marginally attached to the labor force are supposedly less sensitive to the business cycle); their income is also heterogeneous (including both wages and transfers); one also has to take into account the cyclicity of the different components of household incomes among various demographic groups. One can suppose that real wages, hours worked, and labor force participation are pro-cyclical, but benefits are not.

The above elements make it difficult to establish any theoretical prediction of the nature of the link between growth and poverty.

The Recent Theoretical Consensus Challenging the "Trade Off" between Growth and Inequalities

New theoretical developments that question both the Kuznets and Kaldor growth models[1] hypotheses and challenge the "trade off" between growth and inequality, have their roots in the so-called "political economy" approaches (see Alesina and Rodrik, 1994). This analysis predicts a negative relationship between income inequality and growth.[2]

The imperfect capital market hypothesis (including moral hazard) provides other convincing arguments (see Aghion et al., 1999; Benabou, 1996). Inequality has a negative impact on growth via imperfect capital markets, to which the poor have a limited access. If capital markets discriminate against the poor, then potentially profitable activities are constrained by the lack of credit. Since the marginal productivity of capital is higher for the poor, redistribution from the rich to the poor is efficient. The imperfect capital market argument consists in advocating redistribution, which, by reducing inequality, fosters growth and reduces poverty. This approach leads to an extremely important conclusion: reducing inequalities strikes a double blow against growth and poverty, both in the short run (incentive policies that benefit the poor increase the rate of return of their investment, which is a growth process) and in the long run (decreasing inequality creates for each period an "initial condition" for the future, which is growth enhancing). In this framework, the main conclusion is that redistribution is a path towards growth, which reduces inequality and poverty at the same time. If the negative effects of increasing inequalities on growth are strongly established on a theoretical basis, empirical evidence is less convincing.

Some Empirical Evidence

Barro (1999) found the relationship to be negative in developing countries and positive in developed countries (an increase in inequalities fosters growth). Forbes (2000) tested a model where growth depended notably on income inequalities (measured by a Gini coefficient) and on the level of income and education. The author showed a positive effect of income inequality on growth in the short run, but underlined that this result did not contradict the existence of a negative relationship in the long run. Banerjee and Duflo (2000) concluded that the growth-inequality relationship was not linear and crucially depended on two variables, namely the degree of conflict for wealth accumulation and the initial level of inequalities in the society.[3] Because of this nonlinear relationship between growth and inequalities, it happens that any change in inequalities, whatever its sign, leads to lower economic growth in the future. Concluding with economic policy statements based on this research is not an easy task, for it asserts that any change in inequality leads to some distortions and penalizes economic growth. Nevertheless, the authors insisted on the short-term dimension of this effect: in the long run, social conflicts are pacified and the economy reaches an intermediary stage of inequalities, which corresponds to higher rates of economic growth. As a result, reducing inequalities may be, in the long run, growth enhancing.

In the field of Development Economics three main results emerge:

- first, there is no systematic relationship between growth rate and inequality; economic growth can be associated with both growing and falling inequality (see Deininger and Squire [1998], Ravallion and Chen [1997], who underlined this point through large data sets of cross-section developing countries);
- second, the initial level of inequality influences the change in the level of poverty: the lower (higher) the initial level of inequalities, the greater (weaker) the impact of growth on poverty.
- third, Economic Policy has to play a major role in compensating for inferior initial income distribution; Lal and Myint (1996) found that differences in performance in terms of poverty reduction are largely due to the choices of policy. Therefore, growth is not the only component of a "pro-poor strategy."

We gave theoretical and empirical evidence of the way inequalities intervene in the complex growth–inequality–poverty relationship. We now examine the direct effect of growth on poverty. Empirical literature is mainly composed of comparative studies, using large samples of countries and periods. Results are very often debatable because of the heterogeneity of the quality of statistics among countries. Hence, we focus on the comparative study of Dollar and Kraay (2000).

Growth Direct Effect on Poverty

Dollar and Kraay[4] (2000) estimated variants of the following regression of the logarithm of per capita income of the poorest fifth of the income distribution (Y^p_{ct}) on the logarithm of per capita income (y_{ct}):

$$Y^p_{ct} = \alpha_0 + \alpha_1.y_{ct} + \alpha_2 X_{ct} + \mu_c + \delta_{ct},$$

Where c and t stand for country and year indexes, X_{ct} is a vector of other determinants of the average income of the poor (like reducing inflation, openness to trade, democracy, social spending)[5]; $\mu_\chi + \delta_{\chi\tau}$ is a composite error term including unobserved country effects. The two key parameters are α_1, which measures the elasticity of income of the poor with respect to mean income and α_2, which measures the impact of other determinants of income of the poor over and above their impact on mean income.

Dollar and Kraay (2000) found α_1 to be very close to one. This result shows that global economic growth benefited identically for the poor and the rich. Dividing data points into different groups (rich and poor countries, periods of negative and positive economic growth, periods of "normal" and strong growth) did not change the basic relationship between the income of the poor population and growth, which came out positive and robust.[6] The Dollar and Kraay's study concluded on a number of firm assertions: the growth-poverty relationship did not change over time, it did not vary with the business cycle, and it appeared to be similar in developed and less developed countries. The authors summarized these results by "growth is good for the poor," an outcome that we test for the case in France.

The French Debate

In France, we see a fear of an "American future," where the rise in inequality would be the consequence of a change in redistribution policy and the result of a shift in labor market, characterized by a relative decrease of low wages. Nevertheless, this conception ignores some French characteristics: historically, France has followed a different path concerning both the labor market regulation (with regular minimum wage increases) and the social policy context (a wide coverage of all risks by insurance programs and the existence of assistance programs less targeted and much less attached to counterpart requirements). Does growth reduce poverty in France? One of the most debated questions in France concerns the double dimension, structural or transitory, of poverty. For the population concerned by transitory poverty, the assessment of the growth–poverty relationship is crucial. This question has known a vivid interest in France since the strong economic recovery, initiated in 1997. We try to answer this question on an empirical basis, using different kinds of poverty indicators: monetary relative and semi-relative poverty indexes, as well as living condition indicators and administrative poverty indicators in the form of the number of RMI minimum income recipients.

Poverty and Economic Growth: An Assessment with Conventional Poverty Indicators

In France, over the 1997-2000 period, economic growth reached 3 percent per year after a period of low economic growth (between 1 percent and 2 percent a year) in the beginning of the 1990s. This economic recovery led to more job creation and to an important decrease in unemployment. Between March 1997 and March 2001, the working population increased by 1.5 million people to 23.76 million. Over this period, creations of "stable jobs" prevailed and the proportion of short-term contract jobs decreased, following a period of high growth of temporary employment. The number of unemployed fell by 820,000 units and the unemployment rate reached 8.8 percent of the working population at the end of the period, the lowest rate since 1984.

Moreover, in March 2001, the proportion of long-term unemployed people (> 1 year) reached 35 percent according to the Labor Force Survey, close to the level attained in 1994, against 39 percent in 1997. Women and young people (under 25) are the two categories that benefited the most from the decline of long-term unemployment.

However, despite many job creations over the recent period, the relative poverty rate hardly changed. This can be explained by the fact that not all poor households are affected by unemployment whereas poverty also hits elderly people and single parent families. To some extent, it is also a consequence of the way poverty is assessed in France: it is a notion of relative poverty that actually measures inequalities in income distribution. The change over time of this type of indicator is very slow. Even over a longer period of time (1977-1994) it is difficult to point out the link between the business cycle and the poverty rate. Nevertheless, during the more recent period poverty has seemed to be more correlated to the business cycle than previously. Poverty contains several dimensions and its monetary and non-monetary aspects neither concern the same population nor exhibit similar patterns over time. Studying the relationship between poverty and economic growth implies analyzing poverty in its major components and dimensions. Despite a lack of information for a long sample period on household incomes and living conditions, we find that the effect of the business cycle on poverty is highly dependent on the choice of the poverty indicator and therefore on the notion of poverty it is associated with: indicators based on an absolute notion of poverty (like some indicators of living conditions) seem to react to economic fluctuations whereas others, based on a relative notion of poverty, do not directly relate to the business cycle.

The Data

The statistical system in France has carried out, only for a few years, annual surveys on households' income and living conditions, which allow a recent follow-up of poverty. This kind of data has existed since 1997 and delivers information on: type of housing, deprivations of consumption, perceived financial standing, and, of course, households' income. These surveys are carried out on a sample of 6,000 households. Theoretically, they measure all categories of income: earnings, capital income, social transfers, etc. Incomes are declared in brackets so in order to obtain a continuous distribution of income, we estimate a PROBIT model using social and economic characteristics of households: the age of the family head, social category, composition of household, education level, and housing status. We simulate a residual from a normal distribution, which is added to the previous result under the constraint that the estimated income finally remains in the brackets declared by the household. The process is iterative; a residual is simulated until the condition is respected, except for the last bracket for which there is no upper bound. This process led to a continuous distribution of income for the years 1997 to 2000. A similar process was used for the years 1977 to 1994, but with less detailed information.[7] Finally, we obtain a distribution of income using a non-parametric estimation of density. The results are presented separately in figures 10.1 and 10.2. The long-term change in income distribution shows an increase in income and an apparent declining trend of inequalities.

Figure 10.1
Distribution of Income by Consumption
Unit in Constant Francs
1977-1994

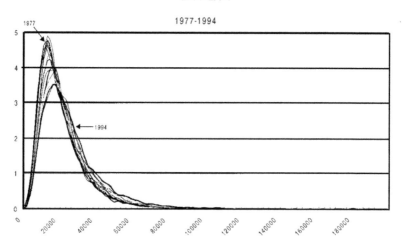

Figure 10.2
Distribution of Income by Consumption
Unit in Constant Francs
1997-2000

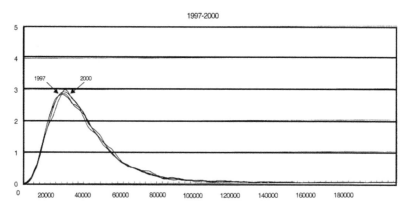

Choosing the Poverty Indicator

The poverty indicator commonly used in France is the monetary poverty rate. It depends on the distribution of income and on the choice of the poverty line. The poverty line is fixed at 50 percent of the median income by consumption unit. The equivalence scale used in France consists of considering the first adult as one consumption unit and each additional adult for 0.5 and finally 0.3 for each child (less than 14 years old). The choice of this scale, which is less progressive than the traditional Oxford scale (1, -0.7, -0.5), is a consequence of the structure of household consumption, which contains less individual goods, particularly food, and more collective consumption shared by all the members, like housing. This evolution of consumption justifies the preference for the new equivalence scale (Hourriez and Olier, 1998). The poverty line itself is traditionally fixed in France at 50 percent of median income by consumption unit. This choice is arbitrary, while in other European countries a level of 60 percent is preferred, which is the level used for European comparisons. This poverty line is relative because it depends each year on the distribution of income and is not based on the estimation of a set of essential goods like the federal poverty line used in United States (Orshansky, 1965). The poverty rate can be written as a function of y, the vector of income, and z the poverty line:

$$P = \frac{1}{N} \sum_{i=1}^{N} 1(y_i < z) \quad (1)$$

where N is the global number of households, y_i is the income by consumption unit of household i, z the poverty line, 1 is a dummy variable indicating if $y_i < z$.

This indicator gives information only on the proportion of poor households. To get information about intensity of poverty we must use another indicator called poverty gap. Formally, the poverty gap indicates the difference between the poverty line and the average income of the poor households. It can be written:

$$I = \frac{1}{N} \sum_{i=1}^{N} 1(y_i < z).(z-y_i) \quad (2)$$

with the same notations.

Evolution of Monetary Poverty Indicators (1977-1994, 1997-2000)

Figures 10.3 and 10.4 show the development of the poverty rate over two sub-periods, 1977-1994 and 1997-2000. It can be seen in figure 10.4 that the change in poverty indicator, and not its level as depicted in figure 10.3, could indeed be related to economic growth.

This poverty indicator did not seem to closely map the business cycle at least until the late 1980s and the beginning of 1990s. This inertia comes from the definition of the poverty indicator based on a notion of relative poverty. A relative poverty rate might decrease only when the income of poor households increases more than for the whole population and when their rise in income is large enough to lift part of them out of poverty (make some of them pass above the poverty threshold). An example can be given by the years 1981 and 1982.

Figure 10.3
Poverty Rates and GDP Growth

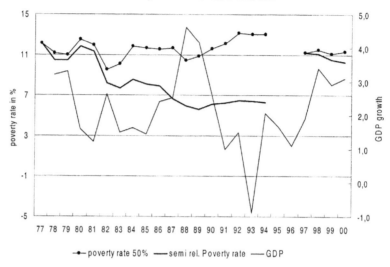

Figure 10.4
Change in Poverty Rate and GDP Growth

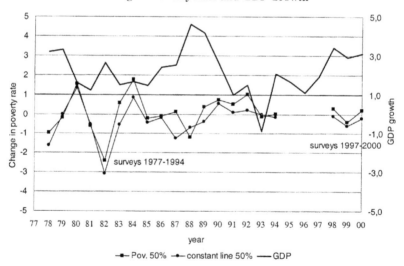

During these two years, the poverty rate decreased sharply (from 12.5 to 9.5 percent); the reason for this was not the economic growth, which stood only at 1.2 percent in 1981 and 2.6 percent in 1982, but was the important revaluation of minimum wage and social benefits, like the minimum pension for the elderly.

Besides, the income of old people, mostly composed of pensions, is not directly related to the economic conditions. This category of the population benefited the most from the revaluation of social allowances in 1982: the poverty rate diminished from 16 percent to 10 percent for elderly people (70 years and more). Moreover, at the beginning of the period, poverty among old people was important (21 percent for those above 70 years old and 14 percent for those between 60 and 70 years old) while the elderly people represented between 35 and 40 percent of the poor households. On the contrary, young households (under 30 years old) represented only 8 percent to 10 percent of poor households at the beginning of the 1980s and exhibited a low poverty rate (6 percent). This structure changed during the 1980s and 1990s, the poverty rate of young people reached almost 20 percent in the middle of the 1990s while they represented 16 percent of poor households when simultaneously elderly people's poverty rate decreased to 9 percent (see figure 10.5). This change in the structure of poverty by age is an important feature when assessing the relationship between poverty and economic growth since poverty among young households is more dependent of the conditions of the labor market than it is with other age groups.

Figure 10.5
Poverty Rate by Age

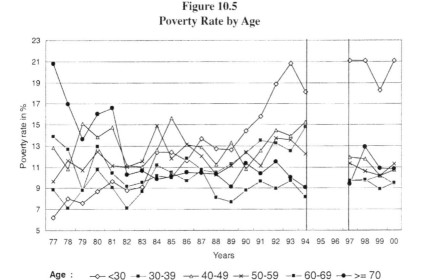

During recent years (1997-2000), the poverty rate has remained stable despite an acceleration of economic growth. The proportion of poor households has stayed at around 11-12 percent (with a poverty line set at 50 percent of the median income). A stable poverty rate does not imply that the income of poor households does not increase. In fact, between 1997 and 2000, their average income increased by 3.5 percent. But since over the same period, the income of other categories of households rose in the same proportion, and the median income and poverty line also increased.[8] Consequently, the poverty rate and the poverty gap remained rather stable over this period. The poverty gap remained around 24-25 percent of the poverty line between 1997 and 2000. For this last year, the annual income by consumption unit of poor households reached 4,573€.

Economic Growth is Correlated More with the Poverty Gap Than with Poverty Rate

Over a longer period of time, it seems that the link between poverty gap and economic growth has been stronger than with the poverty rate itself (see figure 10.6). This phenomenon has occurred especially since the middle of the 1980s. For the 1985-2000 sample period, the correlation between the poverty gap and GDP growth is about -0.9 and the elasticity of poverty gap to GDP growth is significant and negative (-0.55). The correlation with poverty rate is only -0.3.[9] The higher correlation between the poverty gap and economic growth may be a result of the distribution of incomes under the poverty line and therefore because of changes in the income of the poor households. If the period of high economic growth lasts a few years, poor households can benefit from it, which explains why the poverty gap diminished at the end of the 1980s. But, at the same time, the relative poverty line might also increase. This is why for an important share of poor households (around 50 percent), this change is not sufficient to raise their income above the poverty line and contributes therefore to a more stable poverty rate.

Figure 10.6
Poverty Gap and GDP Growth 1977-1994 and 1997-2000
(poverty line: 50 % of median income)

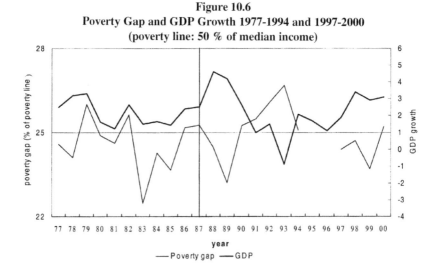

Table 10.1
Poverty Rate Calculated with a Fixed Poverty Line

	1997	1998	1999	2000
Poverty rate (50%)	11,2	11,1	10,5	10,3
Conf. Int. 95%	[10,4 – 12]	[10,2 – 11,8]	[9,7 – 11,3]	[9,5 – 11,1]
Poverty rate (60%)	17,9	18,4	16,5	16,5
Conf. Int. 95%	[16,9 – 18,9]	[17,4 – 19,4]	[15,5 – 17,5]	[15,5 – 17,5]

Source: INSEE, Living Conditions survey, May 1997-2000.

The Effect of Unemployment on Poverty Risk

We analyze now the effect of unemployment and inactivity on the risk of poverty. We use the last four surveys (1997-2000). The data related to 1977-1994 does not contain enough information on employment to carry out the same estimate for these years. The point of view adopted here is different than in the previous section. We are using microeconomic data to estimate a probability of being poor, explained by different characteristics of households. We estimate a LOGIT model taking for reference a household composed of two working adults with one child:

$$Y_i = k + \alpha X_i + \beta Zi + \varepsilon_t$$

where: Y_i is a dummy variable indicating if household i is poor, X_i are employment variables, and Z_i other socioeconomic variables. The effect of employment is introduced in the model with variables indicating the presence of one or two nonworking adults and of one or two unemployed persons. We control for other variables like family size, age, and social category, etc. The sample used contains only households under 60 years old (the legal age of retirement in France). The poverty line used is the relative one with a level fixed at 60 percent of the median income. With a level of 50 percent, the sample does not contain enough observations to make reliable estimates. Table 10.2 summarizes the results.

Table 10.2
Variation of Poverty Risk with Employment Factors

	1997-2000
Poverty risk for the group of reference	4.9
1 unemployed person	+6.2
2 unemployed persons	+20.5
1 nonworking person	+6.1
2 nonworking persons	+14.3

Source: INSEE, Living Conditions survey, May 1997-2000.

The reference is a couple, 30-39 years old, with two working adults and one child. The poverty risk for this category is very low (4.9 percent). The presence of one unemployed person adds 6.2 percent to the risk of poverty. Therefore, the same type of household with one unemployed individual will have a higher risk of poverty (11.1 percent). When the two adults are unemployed, the risk of poverty surges to 25.4 percent.

The variables selected to represent the link with the labor market are significant each year for the poverty risk. Nevertheless, it seems that the effect of unemployment on poverty is less important in 2000 than during the previous years. It is not easy to explain this evolution, because we have little information about unemployment and no information at all about the previous job of individuals in the survey, but we know from other sources that unemployment duration decreased between 1997 and 2000. Unemployed people in 1997 were probably more concerned with long-term unemployment than in 2000, a year of intense job creation.

Between 1997 and 2001, Living Conditions Indicators Evolved More in Phase with Economic Fluctuations

To complete the analysis of poverty based on monetary indicators, the French National Institute of Statistics and Economic Studies (INSEE) calculates some indicators of living conditions. These indicators, at least some of them, seem to be linked with economic growth during the period 1997-2001. Unfortunately, these data are homogeneous between 1997 and 2000, which only prevents us from making any analysis on a longer period. Living conditions indicators are constituted by an aggregation of twenty-seven items or "difficulties" which can be put together in four fields: six indicators belong to the domain of "budget difficulties" declared by households (like the share of repayments in income, having no savings, difficulties in making ends meet...); three for "late payments" (for gas, electricity, or telephone bills, rents and income taxes); nine for "consumption restrictions" in different fields (food, clothing, holidays, pieces of furniture...); and nine for "housing conditions" (size, equipment, and general opinion). The global indicator consists in isolating the share of the population facing eight difficulties or more in the four fields. With the same method four specific indicators can be obtained, one for each field of living conditions, with appropriate poverty lines: three difficulties or more (out of six) for "budget difficulties," one (out of three) for "late payments," four (out of nine) for "consumption restrictions," and three (out of nine) for "housing comfort." For the global indicator, the proportion of households concerned with eight difficulties or more decreased slightly between 1997 and 2001, from 13.1 percent to 11.5 percent. The most important and significant decrease occurred between 1997 and 1998 (see table 10.3).

Table 10.3
Living Conditions 1997-2001

	1997	1998	1999	2000	2001	Evolution 1997-2001	
	%	%	%	%	%	Difference	Significance
Global indicator	13.1	11.8	11.9	12.1	11.5	-1.6	Yes
(*)	(12.2 ; 14.0)	(10.9 ; 12.7)	(11.1 ; 12.7)	(11.2 ; 13.0)	(10.6 ; 12.4)	(-2.8 ; -0.4)	
Financial difficulties	11.4	12.5	12.6	13	12.5	1.1	Yes
	(10.6 ; 12.2)	(11.6 ; 13.4)	(11.7 ; 13.5)	(12.1 ; 13.9)	(11.6 ; 13.4)	(-0.1 ; 2.3)	
Consumption restrictions	12.9	10.5	10.4	10.8	9.7	-3.2	Yes
	(12.0 ; 13.8)	(9.7 ; 11.3)	(9.6 ; 11.2)	(10.0 ; 11.6)	(8.9 ; 10.5)	(-4.4 ; -2.0)	
Late payments	8.1	7.1	6	7	6.5	-1.6	Yes
	(7.4 ; 8.8)	(6.4 ; 7.8)	(5.4 ; 6.6)	(6.3 ; 7.7)	(5.8 ; 7.2)	(-2.6 ; -0.6)	
Housing conditions	12.3	12.5	12	12	11.9	-0.4	No
	(11.4 ; 13.2)	(11.6 ; 13.4)	(11.2 ; 12.8)	(11.1 ; 12.9)	(11.0 ; 12.8)	(-1.6 ; 0.8)	

Source: INSEE surveys on living conditions, May 1997-2001.
(*) Confidence intervals 95 percent; results are significant at 5 percent.

Before analyzing the link of these indicators with economic growth, it must be noted that "households facing difficulties" and "poor households" (according to the monetary approach) are not exactly the same population. Only two households out of five facing eight difficulties or more belong to the first decile of income by consumption unit. Nevertheless, income is the most important factor in bad living conditions, and most factors which explain monetary poverty also explain bad living conditions: for instance, the risk of bad living conditions is higher for households with unemployed or nonworking adults and for a single-parent family.

Between 1997 and 2001, While GDP Growth Accelerated, Consumption Restrictions Decreased Sharply But the Indicator on "Housing Conditions" Remained Stable

The most important change regarding the indicators of living conditions relates to the "restrictions on consumption"; it measures the ability to buy goods that are nowadays considered essential for French household living. This indicator seems to be close to an absolute indicator of poverty; it seems to be linked to economic growth during the recent period. Indeed in 1997, 12.9 percent of households faced at least four difficulties out of nine in this field. They were 9.7 percent in 2001. The most important decrease occurred between 1997 and 1998. During the next years, this proportion fell slightly or remained stable.

In the case of "late payments," the fall was also important, but remains difficult to explain because low-income households who need time over the deadline for paying the bills are taken into account as well as households with higher incomes facing temporary financial problems. The proportion of households facing such difficulties reached 6.5 percent in 2001 against 8.1 percent four years earlier. The most important decline occurred once again between 1997 and 1998. In fact, this evolution especially concerned rent payment and maintenance charges; for other charges like telephone, gas, or electricity the indicator was more stable.

Concerning the area of "comfort and quality of housing," 12 percent of households declared facing three difficulties or more. This indicator has not changed very much (-0.4) over the 1997-2001 period, probably because moving or making renovations to get a higher level of comfort involves expenses, far above what poor people can pay.

Between 1997 and 2001, the indicator of financial difficulties shows no correlation to the business cycle. On the contrary, the indicator on financial difficulties increased slightly between 1997 and 2001. The proportion of households facing at least three or more difficulties increased between 1997 and 2001, from 11.4 to 12.5 percent. In fact, this evolution is significant only between 1997 and 1998. A detailed analysis based on each item apparently shows contradictory evolutions. The most subjective question about income ("it's difficult; we need to get into debt to make ends meet") shows a negative evolution: 16.1 percent of households agreed with this formulation to describe their situation in 2001, against 18.4 in 1997. On the contrary, a higher number of households declared that their income could hardly cover their expenditures (17 percent against 10.3 percent). Concerning debts, the proportion of households whose reimbursement is higher than one-third of their income decreased (3.5 percent against 5.1 percent), but at the same time, a higher number of households declared having a regular bank overdraft (7.8 percent against 7.1 percent), and no savings (36.7 percent against 25 percent). Since these changes do not concern only poor households (according to the monetary approach), it may indicate real financial difficulties or a recovery in consumption. Previous studies showed that an increase in incomes yields an increase in the needs with an elasticity estimated on French data close to 0.8 (Gardes and Loisy, 1998). The evolution of "budget constraint" perceived by households may reflect this phenomenon.

In short, this analysis shows that the effect of economic growth on poverty depends on the choice of the poverty indicator. Relative poverty rate, as calculated in France, did not seem to be related to economic conditions in the 1980s. However, over the most recent period, changes of this indicator probably look more correlated to the business cycle. During times of high GDP growth, the income of poor households increases and the poverty gap diminishes, a feature that was particularly visible at the beginning of the 1990s. We also developed non-monetary indicators. These indicators involve several dimensions of poverty such as restrictions on consumption, which we found, in the recent period, relatively correlated to the business cycle. On the contrary, indicators of housing conditions have proved steady over time while the subjective indicator on households' financial conditions presented similarities with a relative monetary indicator.

We now explore the effect of the business cycle on one component of "administrative poverty," the number of RMI minimum income recipients.

The Effect of Business Cycle on Poverty: An Application to RMI

Background and Overview

Research on modeling aggregate RMI caseloads is a relatively recent addition to the welfare literature. The body of empirical research measuring the effects of the business cycle on RMI caseloads is therefore relatively limited. This stands in contrast to the large microeconomic literature that focuses mostly on the determinants of RMI participation, the living conditions of recipients and leavers, and on the evaluation of financial incentives to move to work. RMI caseloads studies address this issue in relating the labor market dynamics to caseloads using times series. The business cycle is captured by Employment and/or Unemployment variables. All papers agree that economic growth contributes to changes in recipiency in a causal sense although the magnitude and timing of the effect of the business cycle is not conclusive. All studies test the assumption of a "trickle effect" of the business cycle since the conventional wisdom is that RMI recipients are the more marginally attached to the labor market.

In France, four econometric models have been questioning the impact of the business cycle on RMI caseloads: Jacobzone's (1996), Jacquot's (2001), Afsa's (1997) and Cornilleau et al.'s (2000). Jacobzone (1996) related RMI caseloads to the business cycle using three different specifications. Based on flows data, the author estimated two equations. According to these equations the number of RMI entrants was explained by the number of unemployment claimants rejected by first, the Unemployment Insurance System and lastly by the Solidarity Unemployment System.[10] Both specifications were statistically robust, however, the second modeling stood out as the best specification since changes in new opening RMI cases were correlated by nearly one to changes in the number of Unemployed Claimants rejected by the Solidarity System. These two estimates explained inflows only of RMI caseloads, a third specification based on stocks data allowed to appreciate the whole dynamics of caseloads. Using time series over the 1990-1993 sample period, Jacobzone (1996) showed that changes in the number of RMI recipients depended on the changes in the number of uninsured[11] unemployed persons, with a lag of one and two periods (interpreted as the time requested to gather the necessary information when subscribing to the RMI program). This modeling emerged as the most appropriate one to assess the effects of the business cycle on the number of RMI beneficiaries while introducing the role of the Unemployment Insurance System,[12] reformed several times over the 1990-2001 period. The sample period 1990-1993 limits the interpretation of the results probably characterized by a surge in take up rates. Jacquot (2001) related RMI caseloads to the number of Unemployment Claimants.[13] Using Error Correction Models, he concluded that a 1 percent increase in unemployment led, in the long run, to a 0.7 percent rise of RMI caseloads. The model's specifications in Afsa (1997) differed mostly in the choice of long-term unemployment as the explanatory variable. Afsa (1997) found that a 1 percent change in long-term unemployment produced, three periods later, a 0.3 percent change in the number of RMI recipients. Finally, we modeled RMI caseloads (Cornilleau et al., 2000) using a structural equation reflecting the relationship between the labor market and RMI recipiency. Furthermore, this specification considers a threshold effect produced by changes in the maximum RMI benefit level as well as the impact of institutional changes concerning the Unemployment Insurance System.

Our Approach: A Model Based on a Structural Equation

A modeling reflecting the interactions between the business cycle and the labor market.

We developed a model[14] based on conventional macroeconomic interactions between Economic Growth, Employment and Unemployment. Furthermore, we make the assumption of a transition from Uninsured Unemployment to RMI recipiency, as shown by Audier et al. (1998). These relationships can be summarized as follows.

The relationship between Economic Growth, Employment, and Unemployment can be simplified by two identities: GDP growth equals the sum of Employment Growth and the Growth of productivity per capita (1). Change in Unemployment is negatively correlated with the change in Employment, in a proportion smaller than one since Labor Force Participation is pro-cyclical (2).

$$\text{Log (Y)} = \text{Log (L)} + \text{Log (Y/L)} \qquad \textbf{(identity 1)}$$
$$\Delta U = -\delta \, \Delta L \qquad \textbf{(identity 2)}$$

If we split Total Unemployment (U) into Uninsured (Uu) and Insured Unemployment (Ui) and say that p stands for the ratio of Insured Unemployment to Total Unemployment, a third identity can be set (3) which, combined with the above two identities, relates Economic Growth to Uninsured Unemployment.

$$\Delta U = \Delta U \, /(1\text{-}p) \qquad \textbf{(identity 3)}$$

Based on the above conventional economic relationships, our modeling results from a structural equation, we present thereafter.

Estimating the structural equation

First, we assume that RMI recipients (RMI) are those who are among a given population (P_r) *socially* at-risk and potentially eligible for RMI, not employed (Lr), and not insured by the Unemployment Insurance System (Uir). We have:

$$RMI = Pr - Lr - Uir \qquad (1)$$

Lr and Uir represent subgroups of Pr and therefore exhibit similar socio-demographic and economic characteristics. Under the assumptions[15] that the share (α) of total employment offered to potential RMI recipients is constant over time as well as the proportion (β) of insured unemployed potentially eligible for RMI, we obtain a relation (2) between the change in the number of RMI recipients and the change in the population of reference, Total Employment, Unemployment and Uninsured Unemployment (when replacing Total Insured Unemployment by the difference between Total Unemployment and Total Uninsured Unemployment:

$$\Delta RMI = \Delta\,Pr - \alpha\Delta L - \beta\Delta U + \beta\Delta Uu \qquad (2)$$

If we consider the existing relationship between Unemployment and Employment (3) and substitute terms, we finally obtain a relationship between the change in the number of RMI recipients and the change in the population of reference, Potential Labor force (P), Employment and Uninsured Unemployment (4).

$$\Delta U = \Delta P - \delta\,\Delta L \qquad (3)$$

where δ a parameter describing the flexion of Labor Force Participation

$$\Delta RMI = \Delta\,Pr - \beta\Delta P + (\beta\delta - \alpha)\,\Delta L + \beta\Delta Uu \qquad (4)$$

Lastly, we assume that the population of reference is growing at a regular rate (**è**) while affected by a random term produced by the change in the real maximum RMI benefit level (5):

$$\Delta\,Pr = \theta + \mu\,\Delta Benefit \qquad (5)$$

The relation (4) becomes:

$$\Delta RMI = \theta - \beta\Delta P + (\beta\delta - \alpha)\,\Delta L + \beta\Delta Uu + \mu\Delta Benefit \qquad (6)$$

Under the assumption that the Potential Labor Force's shift is constant over time, which transforms the first term of the relation **(θ - βΔP)** into a constant term, we estimate the relation (6).

According to this modeling, the incidence of the business cycle on caseloads is filtered by the labor market dynamics. Since RMI allowance is a means-tested benefit targeted on those of working age (above 25 years except those with children), we could test for the above relationship considering the population of RMI recipients as a whole. Differentiating the incidence of the business cycle on caseloads by age groups was moreover impossible because of the lack of quarterly data.

We therefore estimate[16] the relation (6) with the Ordinary Least Square method using quarterly data over the 1990-2001 sample period (see table 10.4). The dependent variable is the national administrative number of RMI recipients in metropolitan areas except those covered by the Farmers' Social Protection System (MSA). Explanatory variables consist of Total Non-Farm Payrolls in the private sector, Total Uninsured Unemployment[17] and the real maximum benefit level for a single person with no dependent children (this family type of recipients represents a stable 60 percent share of the total [CNAF (2001)]. Two dummies are introduced to control for a threshold effect produced in Q4 1998 by an exceptional bonus given to all recipients (Dum_A) and for the labor force's shift from 1995 onwards (Dum_B). All variables are seasonally adjusted. The estimate is done in first difference for the quarterly number of recipients are non-stationary in levels but stationary in first differences. Dynamics in the model is also introduced in the form of lagged business cycle variables (a lag of one period for Uninsured Unemployment).

We obtain the parameters described in table 10.4. This equation reflects a quarterly change in the number of RMI recipients negatively related to the quarterly change in employment, positively related to the quarterly change in uninsured unemployment with a one-period lag, and positively related to the quarterly change in the real maximum benefit with a lag of one period. Finally, over the 1995-2001 period, the shift of the labor force contributes to increasing the number of RMI recipients by 9,000 each quarter.

Table 10.4
Factors Related to Quarterly Change in RMI Recipients

	Uninsured Unemployment	Employment	Real maximum benefit level (-1)	Constant term	Dum_A	Dum_B	R2	DW
	(-1)							
Coefficients	0.175	-0.079	234.21	16168.22	15941.6	-6997.34	**0.86**	**1.8**
Student statistics	(7.87)	(-4.48)	(2.85)	(11.23)	(2.86)	(-3.1)		

Source: DREES.

Evaluating the Effect of the Business Cycle on the
Number of Recipients: A Global Approach

Using elasticities. We estimated this equation over the Q11990 and Q32001 period, which can be split into three different economic periods. The early 1990s have been characterized by weakening economic growth that materialized into recession in 1993. Between 1994 and 1997, economic conditions improved slightly with GDP up by 1.7 percent yoy on average. Over 1998-2000, economic growth rekindled its late-1980s level with GDP up by 3.2 percent yoy on average. Simultaneously, in the early 1990s, the deterioration of economic conditions led to a decline in non-farm payrolls (see figure 10.7) and to a surge in total unemployment. Between 1994 and 1997, non-farm payrolls increased slightly again and unemployment kept rising. The labor market situation clearly improved over the 1998-2001 period with unemployment down by 3 percent yoy on average compared to a 3 percent increase over the 1994-1997 period; employment went up by 2.6 percent yoy compared o 0.6 percent between 1994 and 1997. Finally, the year 2000 was characterized by an historical 530,000 increase in non-farm payrolls (+3.1 percent) and a 9.5 percent decline of total unemployment. Between 1990 and 2001, the number of RMI recipients grew nearly threefold and accounted in 2001 for 2 percent of the total French population compared to less than 1 percent in 1990. However, for the first time since the implementation of the program in 1988, caseloads decreased by 5.2 percent and 2.2 percent in 2000 and 2001, respectively.

Over this past decade, the relationship between the business cycle, employment and unemployment strengthened as economic growth became more job productive. In the 1990s, the level of economic growth required to create employment reached 1.3 percent on average compared to 2.3 percent in the 1980s (Lerais, 2001); Blanchard et al. (1998) estimated that the elasticity of employment to GDP had increased to the value of 1. This structural change might have distorted the incidence of the business cycle on RMI caseloads, a fact we cannot, however, assess since the program has existed from 1988 only.

Calculated over the 1990-2001 period, we find that a 1 percent increase in employment leads, in the long run, to a 1.8 percent decline in the total number of RMI recipients. In other words, a 100,000 increase in employment reduces the number of RMI beneficiaries by 12,500 and the number of RMI recipients stabilizes when (all else unchanged) non-farm payrolls increase by 350,000 (+ 2.3 percent yoy).

We now employ a second approach based on the contributions of the labor market to the changes in the number of recipients in order to assess the effect of the business cycle on RMI recipiency.

A decomposition of the effects over the 1992-2001 period. Over the 1992-2001 period, the effects of the business cycle on caseloads, reflected by the

Figure 10.7
Non-Farm Payrolls and Unemployment (in thousands)

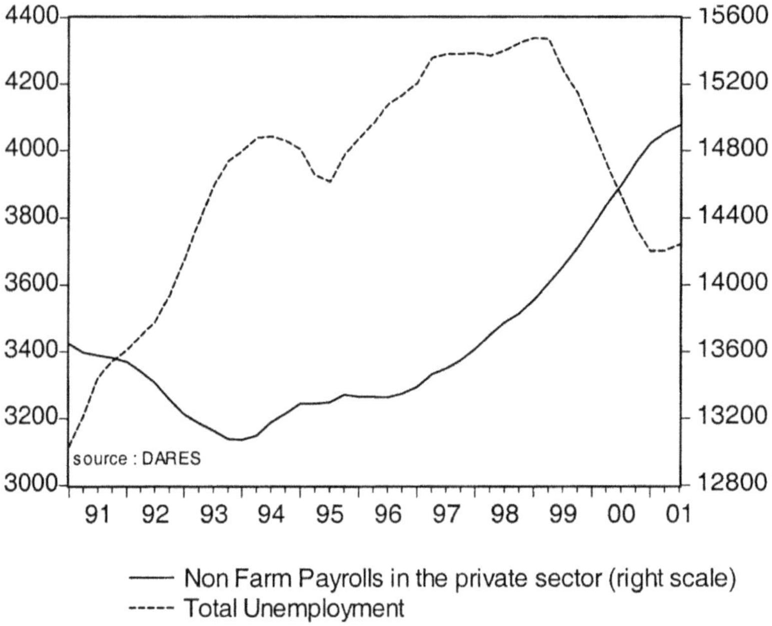

——— Non Farm Payrolls in the private sector (right scale)
----- Total Unemployment

contributions of the labor market dynamics to the change in the number of recipients, have been unequal over time. Four sub-periods can be accordingly defined (see figure 10.8): in 1992 and 1993, the contributions of the labor market dynamics were important and positive at a time when the situation of the labor market was characterized by declining Non-Farm Payrolls; between 1994 and 1997, the weak but recovering labor market had hardly any impact on caseloads. From 1998 onwards, employment and unemployment contributions became increasingly large and negative as economic growth accelerated and turned highly job productive: though negative, these contributions were not important enough in 1998 and 1999 to offset the effects of the other contributive factors as opposed to 2000 and 2001 when they translated into a net negative impact on caseloads, down, respectively, by 5.2 percent and 2.2 percent.

In more detail, the contributions of unemployment and employment to the change in the number of RMI recipients were positive in 1992 and 1993 and estimated at 31,500 and 44,000 (see figure 10.9), which explained on average one-third of the change in caseloads (see figure 10.8). Over the 1992-1993 period, the other explanatory factors, such as the shift in the labor force and the change in the ratio of insured unemployment to total unemployment and the rise in the real maximum benefit level had complementary and mostly positive effects on the total number of RMI recipients.

Figure 10.8
Average Contributions (In %) of the Change in the Number of RMI Recipients:
The Role of Employment and Unemployment

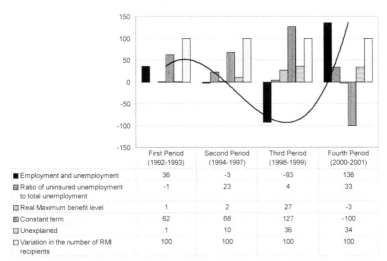

	First Period (1992-1993)	Second Period (1994-1997)	Third Period (1998-1999)	Fourth Period (2000-2001)
■ Employment and unemployment	36	-3	-93	136
▨ Ratio of uninsured unemployment to total unemployment	-1	23	4	33
☐ Real Maximum benefit level	1	2	27	-3
▥ Constant term	62	68	127	-100
▤ Unexplained	1	10	36	34
☐ Variation in the number of RMI recipients	100	100	100	100

From 1994 to 1997, the labor market hardly had any impact on caseloads and contributed on average to explain less than 5 percent of the change in RMI enrollment. The year 1998 stands out as a breakpoint from which the dynamics of labor market dynamics increasingly influenced the number of RMI recipients. While large and negative in 1998 and 1999, its contributions, estimated at 93 percent on average, helped to contain the rise in caseloads but did not offset the positive contributions of the other factors such as the shift in labor force and the change in real maximum benefit. Only in 2000 and 2001 did they translate into a net negative effect. Over these last two years, the labor market dynamics contributed to explain 136 percent of the change in the number of RMI recipients. According to our modeling, employment and unemployment reduced the number of recipients by 72,000 and 27,700 in 2000 and 2001, respectively, compared to a decline in the number of recipients of 52,500 and 21,000, respectively.

Conclusion and remaining questions. In short, preliminary evidence suggests that RMI caseloads do react to the business cycle. Our modeling sets up that a 1 percent increase in Non-Farm Payrolls reduces the number of recipients by 1.8 percent. The contributions of the labor market to the changes in recipiency highlight further the incidence of economic growth on caseloads: between 1992 and 1993 and 1998 and 2001, employment and unemployment strongly contributed to the changes in the number of recipients.

Figure 10.9
Contributions to the Change in the Number of RMI Recipients:
The Role of Employment and Unemployment

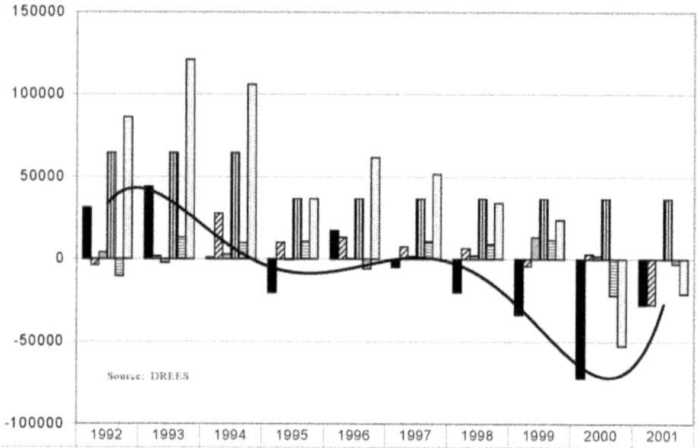

	1992	1993	1994	1995	1996	1997	1998	1999	2000	2001
■ Employment and unemployment	31500	44000	1100	-20200	17300	-4800	-20100	-33600	-72000	-27700
▨ Ratio of uninsured unemployment to total unemployment	-3600	1600	27700	10000	13200	7500	6500	-4300	3000	-27500
▫ Real Maximum benefit level	4000	-2200	2800	-500	300	1600	2100	13300	1800	200
▥ Constant term	64500	64500	64500	36700	36700	36700	36700	36700	36700	36700
□ Unexplained	-10400	13000	9900	10700	-5800	10600	9000	11600	-22000	-2700
□ Variation in the number of RMI recipients	86000	120900	106000	36700	61700	51600	34200	23700	-52500	-21000

Source: DREES

When compared to the elasticity of employment to GDP growth, RMI caseloads therefore look sensitive to economic growth. However, these results can be interpreted differently when compared with those of AFDC caseloads studies. According to major U.S. studies (see table 10.5), the long-term elasticity of the number of AFDC/TANF caseloads to unemployment rates, once controlled for the effects of welfare reforms, ranges from 4 to 6 compard to an estimated 2.5 in the case of French RMI. Although these two minimum income programs differ in various ways, these differences in caseload reactivity to economic growth remain striking since RMI is mostly attributed to single persons with no dependent children and TANF to single mothers, facing more employment barriers.

French minimum income recipients benefit less from economic growth than U.S. AFDC/TANF recipients. While French economic growth is, relatively to the United States, characterized by higher productivity gains and lower demand for low qualified jobs (Lerais, 2001), additive factors might explain the least sensibility of French caseloads to the business cycle. Microeconomic research (Rioux, 2001; Amira, and Canceil, 1999) based upon surveys on RMI recipients and leavers showed that their job characteristics are peculiar compared to the work situation of U.S./TANF recipients and leavers: a large proportion work part time and/or have government assisted jobs and mainly in the public sector. According to Loprest (1999) and HHS (1999), 85 percent of TANF leavers work in the private sector whereas the majority of recipients have a non-subsidized job.

Table 10.5
Sensitivity in Percent of AFDC/TANF Caseloads to a
Permanent 1 Percent Decline in Unemployment Rate

Studies	Period of Estimation	Current Year	Year one	Year two	Cumulated effect over three years
CEA 97	1976-1996	0,77	-4,97	na	-4,02
			-1,4	-1,7	-3,8
Figlio & Ziliak 99	1976-1996	na	na	na	-5,9 (4 years)
Bartik & Eberts 99	1984-1996	na	na	na	-6,49 (4 years)
Wallace & Blank 99	1980-1996	-1,5	-2,2	-2,3	-6
	1980-1998	na	na	na	-4 (2 years)
Moffit 99	1977-1995	-0,031	-4,33	na	-4,36 (2 years)
	1977-1995 (CPS)	0,512	-4,67	na	-4,16 (2 years)
	1981-1995	0,745	-4,5	na	-3,75 (2 years)
	1987-1995	-0,031	-2,22	na	-2,25 (2 years)
CEA 99	1976-1998	0,36	-1,5	-4,27	-5,41

Statistically significant at 5%
Source: Bell 2001

In this chapter, we considered that the business cycle was fully captured by total employment in the private sector. However, non-cyclical part-time jobs and counter-cyclical subsidized jobs should also impact caseloads. Our future research will consist of examining their respective role in order to better depict the effects of the labor market dynamics on caseloads.

Notes

1.   In his 1955 article, Kuznets investigated the relationship between income per capita and inequality in a cross-section of countries; he found his famous inverted-U pattern shape, that is, inequality first increased, and then decreased, as per capita income increased. The driving force was assumed to be structural change in a dual economy, in which labor shifted from a traditional sector to a more productive sector. Deriving from this view, from the 1950s to the 1970s, analytical emphasis was on the probable tradeoffs between growth and income distribution. This conclusion was reinforced by Kaldor's well-known growth model, in which capitalists have a higher marginal propensity to save than workers, which implies that inequalities are a factor of growth.

2.   In fact, this negative relationship is illustrated by debatable mechanisms: higher initial inequality is supposed to increase public expenditure, because it prompts a demand for re-distributive tax-policies, and induces political instability that undermines growth. It is not clear how a society that generates inequality could, at the same time, produce an underclass with enough political power upon a government to foster re-distributive policies (see Cramer, 2000).

3.   For a low degree of conflict, the relationship between the level of inequalities and future growth has an inverted-U shape, which means that there is less growth for low and high degree of inequalities; for a high degree of conflict in the society, the relationship has a U-shape, which means that there is less growth for intermediary levels of inequalities.

4.   The study covers eighty countries spanning a forty-year period. The authors used a version of the Deininger and Squire (1998) data set augmented by Lundberg and Squire (1999).

5.   We do not assess here these determinants, since we focus on the growth direct effect on poverty.

6.   Testing the Kuznets hypothesis—according to which inequalities tend to increase during the early stage of development and then decrease later on—authors assume

that transposed into their framework this hypothesis suggests that the coefficient for the income of the poor is less than 1 at low income stages, and more than 1 at higher income stages. They test this coefficient for rich and poor countries and find a coefficient of, respectively, 1.07 and 1.06 statistically indistinguishable. There is no apparent tendency for growth to be biased against poor-income households at early stages of economic development. Are economic crises particularly hard on the poor? Splitting the sample between negative growth periods and positive growth periods, The authors find an estimated relationship between income of the poor and mean income of 1.08 during crisis episodes and 1.09 for period of normal growth. Dividing the same sample into high growth (superior to the median growth) and low growth (lower than the median), the authors also find quite similar coefficients.

7. The consequence is a break between the two periods; this does not allow us to compare the evolution of income between 1994 and 1997. The level of median income measured in the 1997 survey is 27 percent higher than in 1994 in constant terms. This is due to changes in income measurements and does not reflect the actual evolution of income in France during this period.

8. On a longer period (1977-1994), an equation (based on Dollar and Kraay, 2000) estimating the link between poor households' income and the median income of the whole population indicates an elasticity of 1.1. But this result, obtained with OLS estimation is certainly biased by a problem of endogeneity. Unfortunately, we do not have enough variables in the survey that could be used as instruments.

9. This result is obtained by a simple regression of poverty rate or poverty gap on the economic growth between 1985 and 2000.

10. The Unemployment Insurance System mostly covers unemployed persons meeting the Work History Requirement whereas the Unemployment Solidarity System provides a safety-net for those rejected by the Insurance System basically because of long unemployment spells. By the end of 2001, nearly one unemployed person out of two was not covered by any system.

11. By neither the Insurance nor the Solidarity System.

12. The Unemployment Insurance and Solidarity System incurred major reforms in 1993, 1997, and in 2000.

13. Unemployed claimants refer here to those immediately available, having worked 78 hours at most during the past month and looking for long-term job contract based on full-time activity. According to the French unemployment typology, these unemployed persons represent the "first category" of total unemployment claimants.

14. Cornilleau et al., 2000.

15. $\Delta L_r = \alpha \Delta L$ and $\Delta UI_r = \beta \Delta UI$

16. Based on seasonal adjusted data available in February 2002. All 2000 and 2001 data were provisional at the date of writing.

17. Uninsured Unemployment are all categories considered in the typology of French Employment (i.e., categories 1-3 and 6-8, plus those exempt from job search).

References

Afsa, C. (1997). "RMI, chômage et activité." Solidarité Santé. No. 1-1997.

Aghion, P., Caroli, E., & Garcia-Penalosa, C. (1999). "Inequality and Economic Growth: The Perspective of the New Growth Theories." *Journal of Economic Literature* XXXVII, 4 (December).

Alesina, A., & Rodrik, D. (1994). "Distributive Politics and Economic Growth." *Quarterly Journal of Economics* 109: 2.

Amira, S., & Canceil, G. (1999). "Perte d'emploi et passage par le RMI." Premières Informations et Premières Synthèses, DARES, No. 25.1 (June).

Audier, F., Dang, A., & Outin, J. L. (1998). "Le RMI comme mode particulier d'indemnisation du chômage." METIS, CNRS, Rapport de recherche pour la DARES. June.

Banerjee, A., & Duflo, E. (2000). "Inequality and Growth: What Can the Data Say?" Working Paper, NBER. June.

Barro, R. (1999). "Inequality, Growth and Investment." Working Paper 7038, NBER. March.

Bell, S. (2001). "Why are Welfare Caseloads Falling?" Discussion Papers, No. 01-02. The Urban Institute. March.

Benabou, R. (1996). "Inequality and Growth." *NBER Macroeconomics Annual*, 11.

Bigsten, A, Levin, J, (2000). "Growth, Income Distribution and Poverty: A Review." Working Paper No. 32, Department of Economics, Göteborg University.

Blanchard, O., & Fitoussi, J. P. (1998). "Croissance et Chômage" in "Croissance et Chômage." Rapport du Conseil d'Analyse économique, 9-38.

Blank, R. (1997). "What Causes Public Assistance Caseloads to Grow?" Working Paper 6343, National Bureau of Economic Research. December.

Blank, R., & Schoeni, R. (2000). "What Has Welfare Reform Accomplished? Impacts on Welfare Participation, Employment, Income, Poverty, and Family Structure." Working Paper 7627, NBER. March.

Charpail, C., & Zilberman, S. (2002). "Regard sur trois mesures d'aide à l'emploi: les bénéficiaires s'expriment." Premières Informations et Premières Synthèses, DARES, No. 05.2. January.

CNAF. (2001). "Revenu Minimum d'Insertion au 30 juin 2001." Recherche, Prévisions et Statistiques.

Cornilleau, G., Demailly, D., Gilles, C., & Papin, J-P. (2000). "Les évolutions récentes du RMI: un effet perceptible de la conjoncture économique." Etudes et Résultats, DREES, No. 86. October.

Council of Economic Advisers. (1997). "Technical Report: Explaining the Decline in Welfare Receipt, 1993-1996." Washington, DC: Executive Office of the President. April.

Council of Economic Advisers. (1999). "Economic Expansion, Welfare Reform, and the Decline in Welfare Caseloads: An Update. Technical Report." Washington, DC: Executive Office of the President. September.

Cramer, C. (2000). "Inequality, Development and Economic Correctness." Working Paper series; No. 105. Department of Ecomomics, School of Oriental and African Studies, University of London.

Dagderiven, H., van der Hoeven, R., & Weeks, J. (2001). "Redistribution Matters: Growth for Poverty Reduction." Employment Paper 10. ILO.

Deininger, K., & Squire, L. (1998). "New Ways at Looking at Old Issues: Asset Inequality and Growth." *Journal of Development Economics*, 52, 2: 259-287

Dollar, D., & Kraay, A. (2000, March). "Growth is Good for the Poor." Working Paper. World Bank.

Dumartin, S., Gilles, C., Le Minez, S., & Loisy, C. (2002). "Conjoncture et évolution de la pauvreté: une approche pluridimensionnelle." In *Les Travaux de l'Observatoire national de la pauvreté et de l'exclusion sociale 2001-2002*. Paris: La Documentation Française.

Figlio, D., & Ziliak, J. (1998). "Welfare Reform, the Business Cycle, and the Decline in AFDC Caseloads." Mimeo. University of Florida. October.

Figlio, D., & Ziliak, J. (1999). "Welfare Reform, the Business Cycle, and the Decline in AFDC Caseloads." In *Economic Conditions and Welfare Reform*, edited by Sheldon H. Danziger. Kalamazoo, MI: W. E. Upjohn Institute for Employment Research.

Fleurbaey, M., Hagneré, C., Martinez, M., & Trannoy, A. (1999). "Les minima sociaux en France: entre compensation et responsabilité." *Economie et Prévision*, No. 138-139.

Forbes, K. (2000). "A Reassessment of the Relationship Between Inequality and Growth." *American Economic Review* 90, 4.

Gardes, F., & Loisy, C. (1998). "La pauvreté selon les ménages: une évaluation subjective et indexée sur leur revenu." INSEE, *Economie et Statistique*, No. 308-309-310.

Gilles, C. (2001). "La réforme de l'aide sociale aux Etats-Unis." Document de travail, Série Etudes, DREES, No. 17 (July).

Greene, W. H. (1997). *Econometric Analysis* (3rd ed.). Englewood Cliffs, NJ: Prentice-Hall, Inc.

Hourriez, J. M., & Olier, L. (1998). "Niveau de vie et taille du ménage: estimation d'une échelle d'équivalence." INSEE, *Economie et Statistique*, No. 308-309-310.

Jacobzone, S. (1996). "Les liens entre RMI et chômage, une mise en perspective." *Economie et Prévision*, No. 122.

Jacquot, A. (2001). Note 023/PREV, CNAF (2001).

Lal, D., & Myint, H. (1996). *The Political Economy of Poverty, Equity and Growth: A Comparative Study*. Oxford: Clarendon Press.

Lerais, F. (2001). "Une croissance plus riche en emplois." Premières Informations et Premières Synthèses, DARES, No. 07.1 (February).

L'Horty, Y., & Parent, A. (2000). "RMI et flexibilité sur le marché du travail." *Economie et Société* (March).

L'Horty, Y., & Parent, A. (1999). "La revalorisation du RMI." *Revue Economique* (May).

Loprest, P. (1999). "Families Who Left Welfare: Who are They and How are They Doing?" Wahington DC: Urban Institute.

Lundberg, M., & Squire, L. (1999). "The Simultaneous Evolution of Growth and Inequality." Manuscript. World Bank.

Meyer, B., and Rosenbaum, A. (2001). "Welfare, the Earned Income Tax Credit, and the Labour Supply of Single Mothers." *Quarterly Journal of Economics*, 16:33, 1063-1114.

Moffit, R. (1999). "The Effects of Pre-PRWORA Waivers on Welfare Caseloads and Female Earnings, and Labor Force Behavior, in *Economic Conditions and Welfare Programs,* ed. S. Danziger. Kalamazoo MI; W.E. Upjohn Institute for Employment Research.

Moffitt, R. (2002). "The Temporary Assistance for Needy Families Program." Working Paper 8749, NBER. February.

Nolan, B., & Wheelan, C. T. (1996). *Resources, Deprivation and the Measurement of Poverty*. Oxford: Clarendon Press.

Orshansky, M. (1965). "Counting the Poor, Another Look at the Poverty Profile." *Social Security Bulletin* 28 (January): 1.

Ravallion, M., & Chen, S. (1997). "What Can the Data Tell Us About Recent Changes in Distribution and Poverty?" *World Bank Research Observer.*

Rioux, L. (2001). "Recherche d'emploi et insertion professionnelle des allocataires du RMI." *Economie et Statistiques*, No. 346-347.

U. S. Department of Health and Human Services. (1999). TANF, Second Annual Report to Congress. Washington DC.: Government Printing Office

Part 5

Work-Oriented Reforms:
How Well Do They Work?

11

Leaving Welfare without Working:
How Do Mothers Do It?
And What Are the Implications?

Douglas J. Besharov

For nearly sixty years, it seemed to most analysts that welfare rolls in the United States could only grow. With the exception of a few short-lived declines, the rolls grew from 147,000 families in 1936 to about 5 million in 1994—from less than 1 percent of all American families with children to about 15 percent.[1] Then, starting in 1994, they began to fall. By June 2001, welfare rolls had fallen an amazing 59 percent from their historic high of 5.1 million families in March 1994.[2] That translates into about 9 million parents and children who are no longer on welfare.[3] (See figure 11.1.)

The declines were greater in some states than in others, and came earlier in some states than in others. But, by 2000, they had spread to almost all parts of the country, even to the big cities with the largest caseloads, the highest unemployment rates, and the hardest to serve populations.[4] It appears that it took longer for caseloads to fall in the big cities but, eventually, they fell almost as much as in the nation as a whole.

An Ignored Reality

A major, but little appreciated, aspect of the caseload decline is that many mothers seem to be leaving welfare without taking jobs. (Or, if they are working, it is only part time and they are not earning enough to be self-sufficient.)

The best source of data about families who have left welfare are surveys of former welfare recipients ("leaver studies") that have been conducted by various states and by the Urban Institute. Although all of these studies have some weaknesses, such as low response rates and insufficiently detailed information,

Figure 11.1
Welfare's Growth and Decline, 1960-2001

Millions of families

Source: Douglas J. Besharov, 2001.

the best studies tell roughly the same story: Between 60 and 70 percent of those who have left welfare were employed at the time they were surveyed (and 60 to 85 percent had been employed at some point since leaving). Of those who were working, about 60 to 80 percent seem to work full time, earning about $6 to $8 per hour (or about $800 to $1,000 per month). The remainder worked fewer hours and thus earned less money. (Many studies, however, exclude the 20 to 30 percent of leaver families who have returned to welfare, which tends to minimize the difficulty that some mothers face in finding and keeping a job.)[5]

Broader measures of employment are consistent with this high level of nonwork among leavers. For example, between March 1994 and March 2000, the number of employed single mothers with children under age eighteen increased by 1.34 million (from 5.712 million to 7.052 million).[6] During the same period, welfare caseloads (comprised mainly of single mothers) fell by 2.81 million (from 5.098 million to 2.288 million). Even if the entire 1.34 million increase in the number of single mothers working in this period represented those who were previously on welfare (or who would have gone on welfare during that time), an unlikely possibility, this would still amount to less than half of the caseload decline. (Of course, it is theoretically possible that many non-welfare mothers left the labor force, thus making room for all leaver mothers, but there is no indication of such an exodus.)

Some of the mothers who have left welfare, of course, may not be reporting their employment. A series of interviews in four cities conducted by researchers Kathryn Edin and Laura Lein (1997) found that about 30 percent of low-income working mothers and about 50 percent of welfare mothers did not report the jobs held (and hence the money they were earning),[7] but there is no reason that the percentage of individuals not reporting work should have grown in recent years. If anything, the expansions in earnings disregards and the Earned Income Tax Credit (EITC) should have encouraged more low-income mothers to report their employment.

Based on the various studies reported in this paper, a very rough estimate is that about 40 to 50 percent of the mothers who have left welfare (and have stayed off) are working regularly (that is, working at least almost full time for a substantial period of time). Depending on the measure, most of them seem to be doing better financially than when they were on welfare. Another 10 to 20 percent or so are working part time and are probably only making ends meet with support from other government programs and from family and friends (or from both). About 25 to 35 percent are relying only on these other sources of support, but they also seem to be doing at least as well as when they were on welfare. Finally, between 5 and 15 percent seem to be doing much less well–bouncing in and out of jobs, on and off welfare, and, perhaps, in and out of various living arrangements. (See figure 11.2.)

Figure 11.2
What are Welfare Leavers Doing—Roughly

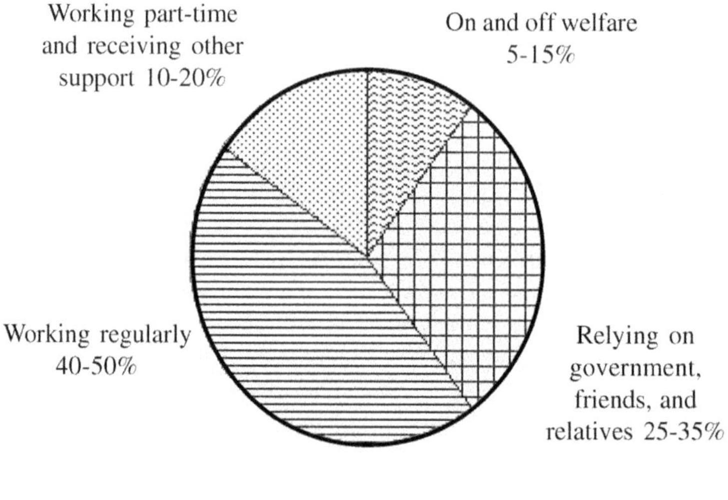

Working part-time and receiving other support 10-20%

On and off welfare 5-15%

Working regularly 40-50%

Relying on government, friends, and relatives 25-35%

Source: Author's estimates

The surprisingly large number of individuals leaving welfare without work—although calculated in most leaver studies—has been all but ignored by most commentators.[8] The only reference to this dynamic by a senior policymaker that we were able to find was a subordinate comment made by Donna Shalala when she was Secretary of Health and Human Services:

> Today, fewer than 4 percent of Americans are on welfare. What we don't know is precisely what is happening to all of these former welfare recipients. *We know that some have married or moved in with family or friends.* Others have left the rolls and are holding on to jobs that they were already going to—what is sometimes called the "smoke out effect." But what's important is that many are looking for work—and finding it.[9]

Even severe critics of welfare reform–who might be expected to see these mothers as being pushed off welfare–seem silent on the issue.[10] Yet this is key to a fulsome understanding of the dynamics of the caseload decline–and has profound implications for the economic and social conditions of low-income families.

Other Sources of Support

Some commentators have assumed that welfare leavers cannot survive without being employed, and so believe that since they are not employed they must be in dire straits. One group of researchers, for example, looking for the nonworking leavers in Wisconsin concluded that, since "these women had disappeared from the work and assistance rolls," the mothers must have migrated to other states.[11] But that cannot be right, because, nationally, there are over a million nonworking welfare leavers. They would all have to be on the move for that explanation to hold.

Work requirements and heightened levels of hassle in the process of going on welfare or staying on would be expected to cause mothers to leave welfare for work, even for relatively low-paying work. But why would mothers leave welfare without having jobs? And how could so many working leavers survive with such low earnings? The burdens placed on them hardly seem a sufficient reason to abandon the only means of support for themselves and their children. The plain fact is that they have other sources of support–both from other government programs (primarily food stamps, housing assistance, Supplemental Security Income[SSI], and Social Security) and friends, relatives, and boyfriends, with whom they are often living. And often, they have help from multiple sources. In a study of New Jersey leavers, researchers at Mathematica Policy Research, Inc., found considerable evidence of a wide variety of sources of support for nonworking leavers:

Clients who have left TANF (Temporary Assistance for Needy Families) and are not working are diverse. Some have conditions that have permitted them to switch to SSI; others are living with an employed spouse or have worked recently themselves. However, about half this group (12 percent of clients in our study) have none of these more substantial sources of financial support; they get by on very little income and face more hardships than other TANF leavers, relying heavily on help from friends and relatives to make ends meet.[12]

When faced with the newly established work and behavioral requirements, mothers who had other sources of support sufficient to permit them to forego welfare simply left welfare without looking for work. This would be nothing new. For example, in the Teenage Parent Demonstration, about 11 percent of the young mothers left welfare rather than comply with the program's requirements, explains Rebecca Maynard, "primarily because they had other means of support and so left welfare rather than participate."[13]

This is particularly the case in low-benefit states where it may simply no longer "pay" to be on welfare. In Alabama, for example, in 2001, the welfare benefit for a family of three was just $164 per month, compared to a food stamp allotment of $341.[14] (Moreover, the food stamp benefit comes with virtually no strings attached, whereas cash assistance can be accompanied by work and other behavioral requirements that further reduce its value.) So mothers in low-benefit states can leave welfare and not suffer a complete loss of income, especially if there are other adults in the household with an income. (The continued availability of Medicaid also encourages mothers to leave welfare without finding work, even if the family does not sign up for coverage until someone becomes ill.)

Their behavior makes economic sense. If one assumes that these mothers value their time at the minimum wage or above, then there is little incentive for them to engage in work activities for twenty to thirty hours per week to avoid being dropped from welfare, when the income loss can be as little as $20 to $50 per week.[15] The added income from complying with these requirements translates into an effective wage of fifty cents to two dollars per hour, which, for most, does not compensate for the lost free time (what economists call leisure time) that mothers can use, for example, to care for their children or take a job with unreported income.

These dynamics also explain the behavior of those mothers whom Larry Mead of New York University calls the "happily sanctioned." Such mothers accept less in welfare benefits rather than choose to work or meet other behavioral requirements, especially since the sanctions in higher-benefit states generally involve only a partial reduction in benefits. In about fourteen states—which include about half of the national welfare caseload—the sanction for non-compliance is only a partial reduction in benefits; that is, the family's grant is reduced by some percentage, usually representing the mother's share of the grant (about one-third of the welfare check). These mothers may not actually be happy, but since this reduction typically amounts to only one-sixth of their total benefit package (excluding Medicaid), one can see why they willingly make the trade-off.[16]

Even in states with high TANF benefits, though, it may not be worthwhile for a mother confronted with work first and other requirements to stay on welfare. It all depends on the amount of other government benefits she receives. For example, the average housing benefit for those who get one (about one-quarter of all welfare recipients) can easily exceed $500 per month[17] and the federal SSI benefit for an adult or child is $512 a month.[18] And, of course, she may receive help from a relative or friend, probably a boyfriend. All these sources of support are encapsulated in a case reported by Jason DeParle of the *New York Times*:

> Maggie Miller had eight children by six men, no diploma, no work history and no interest in the work program. She lost her check and moved in with her sister, Debbie, who is unmarried, pregnant and has seven children of her own. Now Debbie Miller, 37, supports the combined family with $324 in food stamps, $484 in Supplemental Security Income for a disabled daughter, and $744 in Social Security benefits for two sons whose father has died. Plus, she added, " I got a man–somebody's helping me with the kids."[19]

The big question, of course, is how common are cases like Maggie's and Debbie's? The evidence is that they are quite common.

Other Government Assistance Programs

Almost every study of welfare leavers finds that large numbers of leavers receive support from other government assistance programs, often a substantial amount. Significantly, nonworking leavers are appreciably more likely to receive such aid than are leavers with jobs, suggesting that such aid either made it easier for them to leave welfare or reflected underlying physical or emotional barriers to work. Here are some findings from the most reliable leaver studies:

- South Carolina: Nonworking leavers were almost twice as likely as working leavers to be receiving benefits from Social Security (13 percent vs. 6 percent) and SSI (20 percent vs. 8 percent).[20]
- Iowa: Nonworking leavers were more than twice as likely as working leavers to be receiving TANF, Social Security, Unemployment Insurance, General Assistance, SSI, and Emergency Assistance (56 percent vs. 22 percent).[21]
- New Mexico: Nonworking leavers were about three times as likely as working leavers to be receiving SSI or Social Security benefits (18 percent vs. 6 percent).[22]
- North Carolina: Nonworking leavers were more than twice as likely as working leavers to be receiving SSI or Social Security benefits (13 percent vs. 6 percent).[23]
- Washington, DC: Nonworking leavers were almost twice as likely as working leavers to receive some form of government assistance (TANF, food stamps, SSI, and WIC) in the previous month (72.7 percent vs. 38.3 percent).[24]

Richard Bavier, a policy analyst at the Office of Management and Budget, examined the income sources of welfare leavers in the month they exited using data from the 1996 SIPP panel.[25] Leavers reported a variety of income sources in the month of exit in addition to their own earnings, including: living with other household members who had income (62 percent), food stamps (44 percent), rental assistance (25 percent), child support (12 percent), general assistance (9 percent), SSI (14 percent), Social Security (9 percent), and a majority remained on Medicaid. He, too, found that nonworking leavers were much more likely to be receiving assistance from other government programs:

- food stamps (48 percent vs. 41 percent);
- general assistance (13 percent vs. 6 percent);
- SSI (22 percent vs. 6 percent);
- Social Security (15 percent vs. 6 percent);
- rental assistance (25 percent vs. 26 percent)–the one exception besides Medicaid;
- child support (9 percent vs. 15 percent)–presumably a sign that the working leavers were more likely to have been married; and
- a majority of both groups remained on Medicaid.

(These figures are for households, and so include government benefits to other adults and the children living with the mother. Interestingly, if the benefits to children are removed, the differences are more striking–suggesting that the mothers may be disabled and that is why they have not taken a job.)[26]

There is some evidence that participation in the Supplemental Security Income (SSI) program has increased as a consequence of welfare reform. SSI provides cash assistance to low-income individuals who are blind or have other disabilities (as well as to the low-income elderly).[27] Even before TANF, welfare families had an incentive to apply for SSI, because it generally offered higher benefits and imposed fewer requirements on recipients. For example, the federal SSI benefit standard for 2000 was $512 a month for an individual, compared to a $421 benefit for an entire family of three under TANF in the median state.[28] Moreover, SSI benefits are generally not counted in determining the eligibility of the remaining family members for welfare or TANF and, as a result, many families receive benefits from both programs at the same time.[29] Thus, researchers at Carnegie Mellon Census Research Data Center and the Heinz School of Public Policy find that the erosion of Aid to Families with Dependent Children (AFDC) benefits between 1975 to 1990 increased SSI participation:

Our results indicate that a 10% decrease in AFDC benefit levels is associated with roughly a 2.5% increase in SSI participation. While recent reforms that tighten the eligibility requirements for SSI might limit the extent to which low-income households can now substitute from one program into another, the presence of term-limits will clearly provide economics [*sic*] incentives for program participants to substitute out of AFDC into SSI where possible.[30]

However, before the passage of TANF, many mothers who might have qualified for SSI's disability payments simply did not apply, apparently because they either were unaware of their possible eligibility or because they did not want to go through the time-consuming disability determination process, which involves a medical examination and determination.

Whatever the past situation, TANF makes being on SSI rather than welfare even more attractive. Unlike TANF, SSI benefits are not time limited, and there are no work requirements. Thus, if the mother receives SSI for herself and the children receive TANF, the mother is exempt from TANF's various requirements. Moreover, as discussed below, the size of the SSI benefit is sometimes sufficient to allow a family to leave welfare (in order to avoid TANF's work and other requirements). Thus, if a mother obtains SSI benefits for herself, a child, or another family member, she may decide to leave TANF altogether.[31] Lucie Schmidt and Purvi Sevak of the Department of Economics at the University of Michigan elaborate:

> To illustrate the relative incentives, consider a single mother of one with no earnings in Maryland in 1996. As an AFDC recipient, she received a monthly benefit of $292. If she moved to SSI, she received a $470 monthly federal benefit. In addition, her child became an AFDC "child only case," and received $165 per month. As recipients of both programs were eligible for Medicaid, her family's health insurance was not affected by the move to SSI. The total monthly benefit she would have received under SSI was $343 higher than the benefit she received as an AFDC recipient. Alternatively, identification of her *child* as disabled for SSI purposes would have generated a similar financial gain.

> If the decision-making process is influenced solely by monetary benefits, there exists a clear incentive for an individual in this situation to switch to SSI. However, there are costs of participating as well. The application process for AFDC prior to welfare reform was relatively simple, and the requirements for benefits minimal. The application process for SSI includes the time-consuming disability determination process, which requires medical evaluation. Under the pre-welfare reform regime, for some individuals, the costs of participating in SSI likely outweighed the difference in benefit levels. However, as AFDC becomes increasingly restrictive, the individual calculus changes. The lack of time limits and work requirements in SSI shifts the relative costs of participating in the two programs, with SSI participation becoming relatively burdensome.[32]

Similarly, states have always had an incentive to shift cases from welfare (partially funded by the states under AFDC) to SSI (an open-ended entitlement funded primarily by the federal government), but that incentive increased with the creation of the TANF capped-block grant, which gives states a larger financial gain for shifting cases. Lynn Karoly and her colleagues at RAND summarize the research on the possibility that some individuals will move from TANF to SSI:

> Program shifting in the other direction–from TANF to SSI–is likely to be even more significant. Although we are unaware of any studies exploring this effect, earlier studies of welfare-SSI interactions imply a strong presumption that replacing AFDC with TANF induced some AFDC/TANF recipients to switch to SSI. Garrett and Glied (2000), Kublik (1998) and Brady, Seto, and Meyers (1998) find strong in-flows from AFDC to SSI following the ruling in *Sullivan v. Zebley*. Rupp and Stapleton (1995) find similar evidence with shrinkage of state general assistance programs. Schmidt and Sevak (2000) document a large movement from AFDC to SSI as a result of the state waivers that preceded the PRWORA [Personal Responsibility and Work Opportunity Reconciliation Act] legislation. Finally, post-PRWORA leaver studies consistently find that a significant fraction of TANF leavers are collecting SSI.[33]

Writing before the economic downturn began in 2001, they also caution: "Given the currently robust economy and the states' relative fiscal largesse, the motivation for cross-program shifting since PRWORA has been diminished. However, if the economy worsens or the size of the TANF block grants is reduced, states may face greater fiscal pressure to move as many recipients as possible from TANF to SSI."[34]

On the other hand, in some circumstances, restrictions on SSI eligibility in the 1996 welfare reform law also create incentives for SSI recipients who lose their benefits to seek assistance under TANF. According to Karoly and her colleagues: "[T]hose who lose SSI benefits may seek income support from TANF or other safety net programs (such as general relief or general assistance). To date, evidence of these program transitions is rather limited, although some case study evidence suggests that families of disabled children who lose benefits may turn to TANF for income support, while adult former SSI recipients may apply for GA."[35]

Sometimes the benefits from other government programs, especially if only food stamps, are not enough to make ends meet. But welfare leavers also get help from relatives, friends and boyfriends.

Relatives, Friends, and Boyfriends

There is a small amount of direct information about the financial assistance that relatives, friends, and boyfriends provide to welfare leavers. Here are some representative findings from various leaver studies:

- Iowa: Nonworking leavers reported being almost a third more than likely to receive income from other household members (46 percent vs. 35 percent).[36]
- New Mexico: Nonworking leavers were almost twice as likely as working leavers to be living rent free (19 percent vs. 9 percent). They were about twice as likely to receive financial assistance from friends and

family living with them (16 percent vs. 8 percent),[37] and about 50 percent more likely to receive help from family or friends not living with them (11 percent vs. 7 percent).[38]

- Milwaukee: A study conducted by the Hudson Institute and Mathematica Policy Research found that over two-thirds of all the mothers who left welfare received help (such as transportation assistance, a place to stay, or food) from family or friends. Nonworking leavers were about 15 percent more likely to be receiving such help (72 percent vs. 63 percent).[39]
- South Carolina: Nonworking leavers were more than twice as likely as working leavers to have another adult in the home who "helps to pay bills" (17 percent vs. 7 percent) or someone outside the home "helps to pay bills" (22 percent vs. 8 percent), and about 1.5 times as likely to get free housing from a parent or relative (15 percent vs. 10 percent).[40]

But, by far, the larger body of evidence is indirect, and involves the substantial amount of co-residency observed in the households of welfare leavers (as well as among welfare recipients generally).

- Connecticut: The Manpower Demonstration and Research Corporation's (MDRC) evaluation of Connecticut's Jobs First Program found that nonworking leavers were about twice as likely as either working leavers and those who remained on welfare to have other potential sources of support. For example, nearly 14 percent of nonworking leavers were married and living with a spouse, compared to 8 percent of working leavers and 3.5 percent of those who remained on welfare. Another 14 percent of nonworking welfare leavers lived rent-free with family and friends, compared to 5 percent of working leavers and 4 percent of those who remained on welfare.[41]
- Delaware: An ABT Associates evaluation of Delaware's A Better Chance Program (DABC) reported that a clear majority of nonworking leavers—58 percent–lived with another adult, compared to 49 percent of employed leavers. Specifically, nonworking leavers were nearly 63 percent more likely to be living with an unmarried partner and 40 percent more likely to be living with an adult other than their spouse or partner.
- North Carolina: Nonworking leavers were almost a third more likely to report that there was another adult living in the household than were working leavers (49.7 percent vs. 38.4 percent).[42]

Lastly, Bavier's review of the income sources of welfare leavers in the month they exited (using data from the 1996 SIPP panel) found that 69 percent of nonworking leavers lived with other household members who had income, while 56 percent of working leavers did so.[43]

A central question is the nature and extent of these co-residential arrangements–and whether their number has grown in the wake of welfare reform.

Increased Cohabitation (But Not Other Forms of Co-Residency)

When welfare reform was being debated in 1996, many experts predicted that mothers pushed off welfare would be driven to live with others ("co-residency")—either moving in with their parents (or other relatives), or moving in with a man ("cohabitation" with either a boyfriend or the father of one of their children), or "doubling up" with another adult (such as another low-income, single mother with children).[44]

There is little direct evidence about welfare leavers moving in with others when their benefits are terminated. In Florida, for example, as families began to lose welfare benefits due to the state's time limit, one-third of those who hit the time limit either moved or adopted a different living arrangement, such as adding another household member to help with the expenses.[45] Similarly, an Iowa study of how families coped after having their assistance terminated indicated that reliance on others for a place to stay increased by nearly one-third, from 24.9 percent before the sanction to 33 percent after benefits were terminated.[46] The researchers add, however, "While reliance on others for help with housing was a successful strategy for some clients, about 4 percent of clients in MPR's survey became homeless–that is, began living on the street and not in a shelter–since entry into a second LBP."[47]

But the richest data about living arrangements involve surveys of single mothers generally, not just welfare leavers. These studies tell a sufficiently consistent story to reach some broad conclusions:

Cohabitation generally has increased. Several studies have found an increase in the proportion of single mothers who are cohabiting. Bavier's analysis of CPS data finds that, between March 1997 and March 2001, the percentage of children under six living with a cohabiting unmarried mother rose nearly 28 percent, from 2.9 percent to 3.7 percent.[48] An indication that this was a real increase in cohabitation, rather than just a decline in other living arrangements, is that the absolute number of children in such arrangements climbed 22 percent, from about 637,000 to about 779,000.[49]

Similarly, Jencks, Swingle, and Winship found that, between 1994 and 2001, the only statistically and substantially significant change in the living arrangements of single mothers was a 46 percent increase in the share who reported having a non-relative (usually a boyfriend) in their own household (from 8.4 percent or 827,000 mothers to 12.3 percent or 1.15 million mothers).[50]

Urban Institute researchers found an even more rapid increase using data from the National Survey of American Families (NSAF): Between 1997 and 1999, the number of single mothers living independently dropped nearly 6 percent, from 6.3 million to 5.9 million, while the number cohabiting grew nearly 47 percent, from 1.5 million to 2.2 million.[51] Again, the change in absolute numbers suggests that this was a real increase, not just a decrease in other arrangements.

Cohabitation among low-income couples has also increased. Wendell Primus of the Center on Budget and Policy Priorities examined the living arrangements of lower-income children (generally about twice the poverty line) between 1995 and 2000 using data from the Census Bureau's Current Population Survey (CPS).[52] He found that the proportion of lower-income children living with a cohabiting mother increased 1.2 percentage points, from 4.8 percent to 6.0 percent. There were decided differences by race and ethnicity. The proportion of white lower-income children living with a cohabiting mother rose 27 percent (from 6.2 percent to 7.9 percent).[53] The proportion of African American lower-income children living with a cohabiting mother increased 61 percent (from 3.6 percent to 5.8 percent).[54] For Hispanics, there was no statistically significant change.[55]

Cohabitation among welfare recipients may have increased. There is only one study on the subject, and there are enough issues with the survey that no definitive conclusion can be reached. According to Sheila Zedlewski and Donald Alderson of the Urban Institute, using data from the National Survey of America's Families, the proportion of single parents on welfare living with a partner doubled between 1997 and 1999 (from 7 percent to 14 percent).[56] The authors speculate that some of this increase may be due to changes in TANF policies affecting two-parent families:

> It is not possible to assess from the NSAF data how much of this is due to changes in welfare rules and how much to changing societal norms. But the evidence suggests that at least some of the change is due to TANF. The proportion of low income mothers (below 200 percent of the federal poverty level) living with partners increased much less over the period (from 6 percent to 8 percent) than the increase in the proportion of TANF recipients living with partners.
>
> This change is consistent with the 1996 reforms. Most states, for example, have liberalized their TANF eligibility rules so that more two-parent families qualify for TANF benefits. AFDC required that the primary earner in a two-parent family be unemployed for at least 30 days, not have worked more than 100 hours per month, but have worked at least 6 of the last 13 months. Thirty-six states were using these rules in 1996, compared with only six states in 1999.[57]

On the other hand, according to Zedlewski and Alderson, using the NSAF, the proportion of single parents on welfare who were living "with other adults in [their] family" showed no real change, declining from 23 percent to 22 percent.[58]

No increases in single mothers living with parents or other relatives. A number of studies, using different data sources, have reached this conclusion. For example, Jencks and Swingle, using the Current Population Survey (CPS), found that the percentage of single mothers residing with adult relatives has remained stable since 1994, and so has the percentage living in a household headed by an adult non-relative.[59] Similarly, Acs and Nelson, using NSAF, found that the number of single mothers in other co-residential arrangements (living with parents or other adults who are neither parents or partners) barely changed, rising by less than 5 percent, from 2.3 million to 2.4 million.[60]

No increases in marriage. So far, there is a suggestion that there may have been increases in marriage, but the evidence is incomplete and mixed. An evaluation of the Florida Family Transition Program found no effects on marriage,[61] while an evaluation of Minnesota's Family Independence Program found, in ambiguous circumstances, a modest effect on marriage and family dissolution for some subgroups.[62]

A 1999 ABT evaluation of Delaware's A Better Chance experiment (ABC)–which enacted comprehensive revisions of welfare eligibility rules and implemented strict work requirements and financial incentives–offers modest evidence that welfare reform can lead to increases in marriage. After eighteen months of random assignment, women in the experimental group were 18 percent more likely than control group members to be living with a spouse, 9 percent compared to 7.6 percent. Even larger effects were found among some subgroups: women in the experimental group under age 25 were 70 percent more likely to be living with a spouse than women in the control group under age 25, 9.7 percent compared to 5.7 percent; and women in the experimental group who completed less than twelve years of school were almost 49 percent more likely to be living with a spouse than control group members with less than twelve years of education, 11.3 percent compared to 7.6 percent.[63]

Bavier's analysis, using the Current Population Survey (CPS), found that, while the share of children under six living with married parents increased slightly, from 68.8 percent in March 1997 to 70.8 percent in March 2001, the absolute number declined slightly over the period, from 15.1 million to 14.9 million[64]—suggesting that the effect may have had something to do with other factors, such as a relative decline in fertility among unmarried mothers.

When Primus used CPS data to determine the living arrangements of lower-income children between 1995 and 2000, he, too, found that the proportion of low-income children living with married parents rose by 2.2 percentage points, from 48.3 percent to 50.5 percent. But, again, this change could be the result of the decline in births to unwed mothers.[65]

Long-Standing Patterns of Co-Residency

These increases in cohabitation for low-income mothers involve mothers who may not have been on welfare, so they may not be large enough to account for all the welfare leavers who are either not working or not earning very much. Hence, it is important to remember that there is another way that mothers can leave welfare without working: They can fall back on *pre-existing* co-residency arrangements (together with other sources of support).

Based on a study by Rebecca London, using data from the Survey of Income and Program Participation, it appears that, in 1990, before the declines in welfare caseloads, at least 37 percent of all welfare mothers lived with other adults: 18 percent with their parents, 6 percent with a boyfriend, and 13 percent with others.[66]

Robert A. Moffitt, Robert Reville, and Anne E. Winkler provide a series of estimates based on their analysis of four data sets, each of which found that a significant number of welfare recipients were cohabiting. According to the Current Population Survey (CPS), in 1990, 9 percent of all welfare recipients were cohabiting, and among recipients under 30 years of age, with less than a high school education, and with children under eighteen, the rate was about 7 percent. Similarly, in the 1987, National Survey of Families and Households (NFSH), the overall cohabitation rate was about 9 percent, with the rate among those recipients who were under 30 years of age, with less than a high school education, and with children under 18 was even higher, at almost 14 percent. In the Panel Study of Income Dynamics (PSID), in 1987, the overall rate was about 9 percent and about 18 percent among those under 30 years of age, with less than a high school education, and with children under 18. The fourth data set, the National Longitudinal Survey of Youth (NLSY), did not report a cohabitation rate for all recipients. For those under 30 years of age, with less than a high school education, and with children under 18 in 1987, the rate was almost 24 percent.[67]

Finally, a new study designed to follow a birth cohort of nearly 5,000 children and their parents provides additional support for the position that living arrangements are an important part of welfare reform. In data collected from sixteen cities from April 1998 through November 2000, over half of all births to unwed mothers involved a cohabiting relationship and, in another third, the mother and father were romantically involved but living apart. Four-fifths of the mothers received financial support from the child's father. In addition, over half of the mothers receiving welfare also received financial help from relatives during the pregnancy.[68]

These figures may seem surprising, but for many years now, the welfare system has largely ignored household income in such co-residency arrangements. Depending on the situation, the income of the grandparents with whom a welfare mother was living would not be considered (for example, if the mother was an adult herself); and the man-in-the-house rule (which denied benefits to households with a cohabiting male) was abandoned years ago.

Under the old AFDC program, the income of stepparents (because, by marrying the child's parent they were accepting at least partial responsibility for the child) and the parents of minor parents was generally counted toward the income of an AFDC family, after allowing for three deductions: the first $90 of earned income; the amount of the state's "need standard" for the stepparent (or grandparent) and other dependents who were not in the AFDC unit; and the amount paid by the stepparent (or grandparent) to other legal dependents outside the home (e.g., for child support or alimony). This could result in the reduction of assistance or even ineligibility in some cases. A number of states received waivers to increase these income disregards, thus expanding eligibility and benefits for those with such living arrangements.

In the early years of AFDC, many states denied benefits to mothers who cohabited with a man, the so-called "man-in-the-house rule." But the income of cohabitors has essentially been ignored as a result of two anachronistic simplistic decisions made by the U.S. Supreme Court in the heyday of the welfare rights movement. In *King v. Smith* [1968], the Warren Court struck down Alabama's "substitute parent regulation" which had denied AFDC benefits to the children of mothers who permitted a man to live in the home for the purposes of cohabitation. Arguing that the once widely held notions of the "worthy" poor and "undeserving poor" had become outmoded, Warren claimed, "subsequent developments clearly establish that these state interests [in discouraging illicit sexual relations and illegitimacy] are not presently legitimate justifications for AFDC qualifications." After arguing for the unacceptability of Alabama's substitute-parent rule, in *Lewis v. Martin* [1970], the Supreme Court went even further in freeing the man in question from any financial responsibility, by striking down a California budgeting rule that included part of the cohabitor's income in the family being considered for AFDC. Based on the principle of "actual availability," the Court reasoned that welfare agencies could not attribute to the family, the income of any person not legally obligated to support the family.[69]

After these decisions, under AFDC, the income of the cohabitors was generally not counted, unless there was evidence of an explicit contribution from the man to the mother for the support of her family. (If the cohabiting male was the biological father of at least one of the mother's children, the family could only be considered for the AFDC Unemployed Parent program.) Similarly, if a single adult AFDC mother lived with her parents or other adults, their income was generally excluded as well.[70] Practice has apparently not changed under TANF.

The Financial Significance of Co-Residency

There is little large-scale, nationally representative data on the incomes of these "co-resident" households that include welfare leaver families. Census Bureau data about female-headed families in general, however, suggest the potential financial significance of co-residency.

Using the March 1999 Current Population Survey, Bavier calculates that, in 1998, the average income of all single-mother families was $20,682, counting just their own income. But 48 percent of female-headed families were living in someone else's household or had another adult in their household:

15 percent lived in a relative's household, 4 percent lived in the household of an unrelated adult (usually a boyfriend), and 29 percent shared their household with other adults (usually another relative or a boyfriend).[71]

Taking into account the total income in the households in which female-headed families reside provides a very different picture of their economic condition–and explains why it might be possible for mothers to leave welfare without taking a job. If one counts the income of the others in these mothers' households, the average household income of these women rises from $20,682 to $30,094, with large differences depending on the type of living arrangements:

- *All mothers living with others:* 29 percent of single mothers share their own home with other adults, including relatives or boyfriends. Considering the income of these other household members would raise average household income from $23,815 to $35,742.
- *Mothers living with relatives*: 15 percent of single mothers[72] live in their parents' home or that of another adult relative. Considering the income of these other household members would raise average household income from $11,267 to $44,534.
- *Mothers living with boyfriends*: 4 percent of single mothers live in their boyfriends' home or that of another unrelated adult. Considering the income of these other household members would raise average household income from $16,174 to $42,382.

Of course, having another person with income in the same household does not establish that there is any income sharing. As we saw, some leaver studies ask whether a leaver is receiving help from someone in the house. Other surveys ask the question the other way around, how many mothers in co-resident arrangements receive help?

For example, in their study of welfare reform in three states, Bruce Fuller and Sharon Lynn Kagan found that many single mothers with young children (who are were or had been on welfare) were living with others: 37 percent in Connecticut, 53 percent in Florida, and 62 percent in California.[73] About 25 percent to 40 percent lived with an employed co-resident.[74] Across the three study states, about half of the mothers indicated that they lived with another adult and that, in about half of such arrangements, the other adult provided economic support to the family. Of course, even in the absence of direct financial assistance, the mothers can benefit from the economies of shared living arrangements and other forms of support, such as babysitting. (The degree of economic support provided by other household members may be understated, if respondents are concerned that their responses may affect the amount of financial assistance they receive from various public programs.)[75]

By the way, there is a more positive way to view the exits from welfare of cohabiting mothers. With the strong economy of the 1990s and the growth in aid to the working poor, more cohabiting households would have *become* economically comfortable enough for the mother to leave welfare without working. This would be consistent with earlier patterns. Greg Duncan of Northwestern University and his colleagues used data from the PSID to determine why mothers left welfare between 1986 and 1991.[76] ("Leaving welfare" was defined as receiving welfare in one year but not in the next year.) They found that about one-half of welfare exits were for work (or a rise in earnings); about one-quarter were due to changes in marital status or living arrangements; about 5 percent occurred because there were no longer children under 18 living in the household; and the remainder were due to a variety of reasons, such as an increase in other transfer income or a change in the mother's state of residence. About one-third of the earnings-related exits involved an increase in the earnings of an adult *already* in the household other than the mother, thus demonstrating the importance of shared living arrangements.

This is also suggested by research on those dropped from welfare in Iowa. A 1998 survey of families conducted two to four months after their benefits had been terminated for a second time found that only one-third of sanctioned families reported a reduction in their household income (averaging $384 per month), despite the loss of their welfare check.[77] One-half of these families experienced an increase in household income (averaging $758 per month), nearly double their income before the sanction. The primary sources of this additional income were the former recipient's own earnings and an increase in the earnings of other household members—which is, as we have seen, an important alternate source of family support.

It is, however, extremely difficult to tell exactly how much of the income from non-family cohabitors actually goes to the benefit of the single mother and her children. In an effort to answer this question, Bauman used seven questions from SIPP which asked household heads if during the past year the household had trouble: (1) meeting expenses, (2) paying rent, (3) paying utility bills, (4) paying phone bills, (5) going to the doctor due to a lack of money, (6) going to the dentist due to a lack of money, and (7) eating "enough of the kinds of food we want."[78] By pooling the answers to these questions together, Bauman was able to create a "freedom from hardship index" which he used as the dependent variable in a regression model designed to determine if cohabitors' income contributed to relieving the material hardship of the household as compared to the contribution made by the head of household. Since so many factors affect the material hardship of a household, Bauman's model included as independent variables things such as total household income, income from other family members, number of household members, whether or not the cohabitant lived in the home part-year or for the full year, whether or not people in the household had insurance, and whether or not people in the household received food stamps.

Bauman found that the strongest factors in relieving household hardship were household income, the age of the householder, and whether or not the household had medical insurance for the entire year.[79] The income of cohabitors, however, was not a significant factor in reducing household hardship, although cohabitors who lived in the home year round contributed more than those who lived in the home for only part of the year. At the same time, the model did not show that cohabitors contributed less than other household members (such as housemates, where applicable) only that cohabitors contributed less than the household head. These results led Bauman to speculate that the more the cohabiting relationship approached that of a married-couple family, the more the cohabitor contributed.

Bauman's findings point to the final caveat of this discussion of family versus household income of female-headed families. As Mayer and Jencks have discussed, income measurements by themselves are relatively poor indicators of material hardship. Using the same types of questions later incorporated into the 1992 SIPP panel that Bauman analyzed, Mayer and Jencks asked 1,400 Chicago-area households about their experience with material hardship in 1982-83 and an additional 950 households about their experience with material hardship in 1984-85. They found that family income explained only about 14 percent of the variance in the number of times a household experienced hardship.[80] These results led Mayer and Jencks to suggest that perhaps more attention should be paid directly to measuring material hardship rather than relying solely on income measurements to determine how poor people are faring.

In a separate analysis, Mayer and Jencks have also written that income levels may not be correlated with levels of expenditure. In an attempt to correct for this problem, Mayer and Jencks looked at data from the Consumer Expenditure Survey (CEX) and compared it to the CPS. They found that CPS data from the late 1980s showed that households in the bottom quintile had 30 percent of the income of households in the middle quintile. The CEX, however, showed that households in the bottom quintile spent 40 percent as much as households in the middle quintile. When they looked at levels of consumption, they found that households in the bottom quintile consumed almost 45 percent of what the middle quintile consumed.[81]

Differences between levels of income, expenditure, and consumption among low-income families are commonly explained by four factors. First, families may borrow money during times of need in order to compensate for a loss in income. At the same time, low-income families may also spend their savings, thus allowing them to expend and consume more than they receive in income. Second, differences in income, expenditure, and consumption may be the result of wide-scale under reporting of income on the part of all income groups, something that both Christopher Jencks and Kathryn Edin say is more likely among low-income families.[82] Third, low-income families may be able to increase their levels of expenditure and consumption by selling off their assets. Fourth, the consumer survey and the income survey treat non-responses and incomplete responses differently.

To these four factors, we would add another possibility. The female-headed families may be consuming some of the income from other household members.

Implications

There are many explanations for the changing living arrangements described in this chapter. But certainly welfare reform is one of them. The failure of both sides of the ideological divide to acknowledge this reality is a two-edged sword: It threatens to undo past progress because it credits the wrong policies, and it makes it more difficult to assess any resultant hardship on welfare mothers (and their children) because it misunderstands the options available to them.

A myriad of factual and policy questions surround co-residency issues. The following seem to be among the most fundamental if we are to understand how welfare policy should take co-residency into account.

How voluntary are these arrangements? Assuming that the measured increases in cohabitation are real (and do not represent a greater willingness of respondents to acknowledge living together), why are the couples deciding to live together? According to Christopher Jencks and Joseph Swingle of Harvard University: "When single mothers cannot make ends meet on their own, they usually try to move in with relatives. Thus if welfare reform had left single mothers worse off, we would expect to see more of them to be doubled up."[83] There is another side to this equation, however. If welfare reform lessened the marriage penalty associated with being on welfare, say by reducing the value of welfare through a work requirement, then we would likewise see an increase in cohabitation, if not marriage.[84]

The large numbers of mothers cohabiting *while on welfare* suggests that the decision to cohabit involves more than simply needing a place to stay after leaving welfare. But that is supposition. More information, even rigorous ethnographic work, is needed to shed light on the origins, conditions, and terminations of this relationship.

Did these female-headed families really need welfare assistance? Before they left welfare, the mothers' own incomes were low enough to qualify for benefits and welfare agencies were not supposed to consider the incomes of those with whom the mothers lived. So, if the measure of need is formal welfare law, then the answer is apparently yes. However, as we have seen, there is at least some income sharing in such relationships, probably a great deal in some and less (or nothing) in others.

Surely, if only for reasons of horizontal equity, there is a need to at least reexamine the past policy of ignoring the incomes of those with whom welfare mothers live. For example, when a welfare mother is living with her middle-class mother, would imposing some expectation on the mother be so contrary to our sense of economic justice? What about work requirements? Why are they imposed on the mother if there is a man in the home? The problem, of course, would be to fashion rules that are not arbitrary, but that should not prevent the effort.

What is the impact of co-residency on children and mothers? Most observers seem to agree that cohabitation is not as good for children as is marriage,[85] while there is mixed opinion about whether it is at least better than having the mother and children on their own.[86] We do know that such relationships are more fragile. There is one study in the field on the subject,[87] but much more is needed to answer such questions as: How long do these arrangements last? How often do they lead to marriage? What is the nature of the relationship between the men and mothers? Do the men share income with the mother? Or do they get money from her? Do they help around the house? Are they abusive or exploitive? What is the impact on the children of having an unrelated man in the home? Do the men provide child care? Are they otherwise helpful? Are they abusive to the children ?

As for living with relatives, especially grandparents, most observers seem to assume that this is basically good for the mother and her children. Indeed, for teen parents, TANF prohibits states from spending TANF federal funds on assistance to an unmarried, minor, custodial parent unless the teen lives with a parent or in another adult-supervised living arrangement. Exceptions are allowed when a parent or other adult is not available or when such living arrangements could result in harm to the minor teen or her child. However, there is little rigorous evidence on the point and it surely deserves additional inquiry.

Conclusion

The importance of these various co-residency arrangements for the economic (and emotional) well-being of single-mother families is often underestimated, if not ignored. One reason is that they are embedded within other households and it can be difficult (as well as time-consuming) to parse out the patterns involved. Even more important as an obstacle is the unwillingness of either side of the ideological debate to follow the data to the conclusions they suggest. One thing is clear, though: Despite measurement imperfections and ambiguities, it is misleading to attempt to assess the well-being of families who have left welfare without considering the fundamental role of co-residency.

Notes

1.   Authors' calculations based on U.S. Department of Health and Human Services, Administration for Children and Families, "Temporary Assistance for Needy Families: 1936-2000," available from: http://www.acf.dhhs.gov/news/stats/3697.htm, accessed January 7, 2002.
2.   U.S. Department of Health and Human Services, Administration for Children and Families, unpublished data (March 1994) and "Temporary Assistance for Needy Families, Total Number of Families," available from: http://www.acf.dhhs.gov/news/stats/families.htm, accessed January 7, 2002.

3. U.S. Department of Health and Human Services, Administration for Children and Families, unpublished data (March 1994) and "Temporary Assistance for Needy Families, Total Number of Recipients," available from: http://www.acf.dhhs.gov/news/stats/recipients.htm, accessed January 7, 2002.

4. See, generally, Paul Leonard and Maureen Kennedy, *What Cities Need from Welfare Reform Reauthorizatio.* (Washington, DC: Brookings Institution Center on Urban and Metropolitan Policy, November 2001), 10-11, 17-18, available from: http://www.brookings.edu/es/urban/publications/leonkencitieswelfare.pdf, accessed January 23, 2002.

5. U.S. General Accounting Office, *Welfare Reform: Information on Former Recipient Status* (Washington, DC: GPO, April 1999); Sarah Brauner and Pamela Loprest, *Where Are They Now? What States' Studies of People Who Left Welfare Tell Us* (Washington, DC: The Urban Institute, May 1999); Pamela Loprest, *Families Who Left Welfare: Who Are They and How Are They Doing?* (Washington, DC: The Urban Institute, 1999); Pamela Loprest, *How Are Families That Left Welfare Doing? A Comparison of Early and Recent Welfare Leavers* (Washington, DC: The Urban Institute, April 2001), 3, available from: http://newfederalism.urban.org/pdf/anf_b36.pdf, accessed February 15, 2002, reporting that about 66 percent of single-parent former TANF recipient families in 1997 and 71 percent of single-parent former TANF recipient families in 1999 were "employed" at the time of the interview. (There was apparently no minimum amount of work required to answer in the affirmative.) See also Richard Bavier, "Welfare Reform Data from the Survey of Income and Program Participation," *Monthly Labor Review* (July 2001): 13-24.

6. Unpublished data from the Bureau of Labor Statistics.

7. Kathryn Edin and Laura Lein, *Making Ends Meet: How Single Mothers Survive Welfare and Low-Wage Work* (New York: Russell Sage Foundation, 1997), 150-151. The generalizability of these findings is not established, since the sample was not randomly selected. The mothers were recruited from various sources within the communities, and many of the mothers recommended friends who were also interviewed (a "snow-ball" sample). Nevertheless, although their sample is not representative of welfare mothers nationally, it provides important insights into the survival strategies of these mothers (often confirmed by more representative surveys).

8. A partial exception at least is Anu Rangarajan and Robert G. Wood, *Current and Former WFNJ Clients: How Are They Faring 30 Months Later?* (Princeton, NJ: Mathematica Policy Research, Inc., November 16, 2000), 95, stating: "Former WFNJ [Work First New Jersey] clients who have not worked recently and do not live with employed spouses have extremely low income. In fact, 23 percent reported having no income at all during the month prior to the survey. How do these clients support themselves on little or no income? A closer look at their living situations and sources of support reveals that these clients rely heavily on support from friends and relatives, many of whom share a household with the client." See also Robert A. Moffitt, *From Welfare to Work: What the Evidence Shows* (Washington, DC: The Brookings Institution, Policy Brief No. 13, January 2002), available from: http://www.brook.edu/wrb/publications/pb/pb13.pdf, accessed February 12, 2002; Richard Bavier, "Welfare Reform Data from the Survey of Income and Program Participation," *Monthly Labor Review* (July 2001): 13-24; and Pamela Loprest, *Families Who Left Welfare: Who Are They and How Are They Doing?* (Washington, DC: The Urban Institute, 1999), available from: http://newfederalism.urban.org/pdf/discussion99_02.pdf, accessed February 17, 2002.

9. Donna Shalala, remarks at the American Enterprise Institute Conference Welfare Reform: What Happens After Time Limits, Sanctions, and Diversion? February 6, 1998 (emphasis added).

10. Peter Edelman, "Reforming Welfare–Take Two," *The Nation*, February 4, 2002; and Barbara Ehrenreich and Frances Fox Piven, "Who's Utopian Now?" *The Nation*, February 4, 2002.

11. Sammis B. White and Lori A. Geddes, "Disappearing Wisconsin Welfare Recipients: Where Did They Go?" *Wisconsin Policy Research Institute Report* 14 (9) (December 2001): 1, *stating*: "The big question is what happened to the other 24,516 women (25 percent of the original 1990 cohort) who were not working or receiving aid in Wisconsin in 1998. These women had disappeared from these systems. The term 'disappeared' is ambiguous, as it must be in this situation. These women disappeared from the work and assistance rolls, the two most likely ways they can be supported. If these options are out, then the remaining ones, such as receipt of Social Security benefits, marriage or cohabitation, incarceration, and the like, are the options in the state. The other option is a move out of state. The move out is likely for a substantial portion of these women, especially those who left the welfare rolls and employment early in the decade. It seems less and less likely these women could survive without aid or work over the decade. This fact strongly suggests that many of these women left Wisconsin."

12. Anu Rangarajan and Robert G. Wood, *Current and Former WFNJ Clients: How Are They Faring 30 Months Later?* (Princeton, NJ: Mathematica Policy Research, Inc., November 16, 2000), xv.

13. Rebecca A. Maynard, "Paternalism, Teenage Pregnancy Prevention, and Teenage Parent Services," in *The New Paternalism: Supervisory Approaches to Poverty,* ed. Lawrence Mead (Washington, DC: Brookings Institution Press, 1997), 28.

14. Center for Law and Social Policy and Center on Budget and Policy Priorities, *Monthly Cash Assistance and Food Stamp Benefits For a Single-Parent Family of Three with No Earnings, 2001* (State Policy Documentation Project website, May 1999), available from: http://www.spdp.org/tanf/financial/maxben2001.pdf, accessed January 8, 2002.

15. The amount of income loss depends on whether the sanction involves a partial or complete reduction in assistance.

16. In the median state, the TANF benefit is $421, so a one-third reduction would be $139. However, in addition to TANF benefits, the family would receive $248 in food stamp benefits, raising its total to $669 before the sanction. Most families would also receive assistance from at least one other non-cash benefit program, such as Medicaid, the school lunch program, housing assistance, or other like program. Even excluding the value of Medicaid, the $139 sanction is conservatively estimated to be one-sixth of the benefit package. However, the reduction could be greater in those apparently few states that impose corresponding penalties on food stamp and Medicaid benefits, as allowed under the 1996 welfare law. [Vivian Gabor and Christopher Botsko, *State Food Stamp Policy Choices Under Welfare Reform: Findings of 1997 50-State Survey* (Alexandria, VA: U.S. Department of Agriculture, May 1998).]

17. In 2000, federal expenditures under the Section 8 housing choice voucher program averaged $6,948 per unit. See Vee Burke, *Cash and Non-cash Benefits for Persons with Limited Income: Eligibility Rules, Recipient and Expenditure Data, FY1998-FY2000* (Washington, DC: Congressional Research Service, November 19, 2001).

18. U.S. House of Representatives, Committee on Ways and Means, 2000 Green Book (Washington, DC: Committee on Ways and Means, October 6, 2000), 228.

19. Jason DeParle, "Welfare Reform Creates New Hardship in Mississippi," *New York Times*, 16 October 1997, available from: http://www_personal.umd.umich.edu/~mtwomey/newspapers/1016welf.html, accessed January 21, 2002.

20. South Carolina Department of Social Services, Office of Program Reform, Evaluation, and Research, *Comparison Between Working and Non-Working Clients Whose Cases Were Closed between January and March 1997* (Columbia: South Carolina Department of Social Services, March 1998), 7.

21. Jacqueline Kauff, Lisa Fowler, Thomas Fraker, and Julita Millner-Waddell, *Iowa Families That Left TANF: Why Did They Leave and How Are They Faring?* (Washington, DC: Mathematica Policy Research, Inc., February 2001), 70.

22. Philip Richardson, Greg Schoenfeld, Susan LaFever, Gary Larsh, Mark Tecco, and Kim Reniero, *New Mexico TANF Longitudinal Study: Results of the First Year of Follow-Up Surveys* (Washington, DC: MAXIMUS, April 14, 2000), V-5.

23. Philip Richardson, Kim Reniero, Susan LaFever, Gregg Schoenfeld, and Frances Jackson, *Evaluation of the North Carolina Work First Program: Study of Families Leaving Work First in Selected Counties* (Washington, DC: MAXIMUS, May 2000), IV-9.

24. Gregory Acs and Pamela Loprest, *The Status of TANF Leavers in the District of Columbia: Final Report* (Washington DC: The Urban Institute, January 3, 2001), 31.

25. Richard Bavier, "Welfare Reform Data from the Survey of Income and Program Participation," *Monthly Labor Review* (July 2001): 15. Bavier defines a leaver as someone with at least two months of AFDC/TANF receipt followed by at least two consecutive months without receipt of benefits.

26. Excluding children from the calculation, Bavier found that, in the exit month, nonworking leavers were more than eight times more likely to receive Supplemental Security Income (SSI) (16.1 percent vs. 1.7 percent), twenty-one times more likely to receive Social Security (10.6 percent vs. 0.5 percent), and 21 percent more likely to receive Medicaid (68.6 percent vs. 56.9 percent). [Richard Bavier, "Welfare Reform Data from the Survey of Income and Program Participation," *Monthly Labor Review* (July 2001): 15.]

27. The maximum income limit depends on the source of the income. For an individual receiving only Social Security, the maximum income limit was $532 per month ($789 per month for a couple) in 2000, but was $1,109 for an individual receiving only wage income ($1,623 for a couple). See U.S. House of Representatives, Committee on Ways and Means, *2000 Green Book* (Washington, DC: Committee on Ways and Means, October 6, 2000), 218.

28. U.S. House of Representatives, Committee on Ways and Means, *2000 Green Book* (Washington, DC: Committee on Ways and Means, October 6, 2000), 228 and 390.

29. See note 20 for an example.

30. Dan Black, Terra McKinnish, and Set Sanders, "Are AFDC and SSI Substitutes," September 13, 1998, p. 3, available from: http://www.heinz.cmu.edu/tmp/1998_20.pdf, accessed February 11, 2002.

31. See the text at note 28.

32. Lucie Schmidt and Purvi Sevak, "AFDC, SSI, and Welfare Reform Aggressiveness: Caseload Reductions vs. Caseload Shifting" (Ann Arbor: University of Michigan, Population Studies Center, May 15, 2000 [Draft]), 6, available from: http://www.psc.isr.umich.edu/pubs/papers/rr00_444.pdf, accessed February 17, 2002.

33. Lynn A. Karoly, Jacob Alex Klerman, "Effects of the 1996 Welfare Reform Changes on the SSI Program," in *The New World of Welfare*, edited by Ron Haskins and Rebecca Blank (Washington, DC: Brookings, 2001), 492.

34. Lynn A. Karoly, Jacob Alex Klerman, "Effects of the 1996 Welfare Reform Changes on the SSI Program," in *The New World of Welfare*, edited by Ron Haskins and Rebecca Blank (Washington, DC: Brookings, 2001), 493.

35. Lynn A. Karoly, Jacob Alex Klerman, "Effects of the 1996 Welfare Reform Changes on the SSI Program," in *The New World of Welfare*, edited by Ron Haskins and Rebecca Blank (Washington, DC: Brookings, 2001), 492.

36. Jacqueline Kauff, Lisa Fowler, Thomas Fraker, and Julita Millner-Waddell, *Iowa Families That Left TANF: Why Did They Leave and How Are They Faring?* (Washington, DC: Mathematica Policy Research, Inc., February 2001), 70.

37. Philip Richardson, Greg Schoenfeld, Susan LaFever, Gary Larsh, Mark Tecco and Kim Reniero, *New Mexico TANF Longitudinal Study: Results of the First Year of Follow-Up Surveys* (Washington, DC: MAXIMUS, April 14, 2000), V-5.

38. Philip Richardson, Greg Schoenfeld, Susan LaFever, Gary Larsh, Mark Tecco, and Kim Reniero, *New Mexico TANF Longitudinal Study: Results of the First Year of Follow-Up Surveys* (Washington, DC: MAXIMUS, April 14, 2000), V-5.

39. Rebecca Swartz, Jacqueline Kauff, Lucia Nixon, Tom Fraker, Jay Hein, and Susan Mitchell, *Converting to Wisconsin Works: Where Did Families Go When AFDC Ended in Milwaukee?* (Madison, WI: Hudson Institute and Mathematica Policy Research, 1999), 66.

40. South Carolina Department of Social Services, Office of Program Reform, Evaluation, and Research, *Comparison Between Working and Non-Working Clients Whose Cases Were Closed between January and March 1997* (Columbia: South Carolina Department of Social Services, March 1998), 7.

41. Laura Melton and Dan Bloom, *Connecticut's Jobs First Program: An Analysis of Welfare Leavers* (New York: Manpower Demonstration Research Corporation, December 2000), 17. Of the remaining nonworking welfare leavers, about 37 percent lived in public or subsidized housing, compared to about 31 percent of working leavers and about 51 percent of those who remained on welfare. About 40 percent rented homes alone or with family or friends where they made partial rent payments, compared to about 60 percent of working leavers and about 42 percent of those who remained on welfare.

42. Author's calculations from data supplied by MAXIMUS, prepared for North Carolina Department of Health and Human Services, *Evaluation of the North Carolina Work First Program: Study of Families Leaving Work First in Selected Counties* (Boston, MA: MAXIMUS, May 2000), ES-11, II-5, IV-11.

43. Richard Bavier, "Welfare Reform Data from the Survey of Income and Program Participation," *Monthly Labor Review* (July 2001): 15. Bavier defines a leaver as someone with at least two months of AFDC/TANF receipt followed by at least two consecutive months without receipt of benefits.

44. See, e.g., Gregory Acs and Pamela Loprest, *The Status of TANF Leavers in the District of Columbia: Final Report* (Washington DC: The Urban Institute, January 3, 2001), 28-29, stating: "Proponents of welfare reform argued that stricter welfare laws would promote stable two-parent families while critics of reform feared that, lacking resources, single mothers would be forced into unstable living arrangements or possibly to break up their families, sending their children to live with relatives or friends."

45. Dan Bloom, Mary Farrell, James Kemple, and Nandita Verma, *The Family Transition Program: Implementation and Three-Year Impacts of Florida's Initial Time-Limited Welfare Program* (New York: Manpower Demonstration Research Corporation, April 1999), 94.

46. Lucia Nixon, Jacqueline Kauff, and Jan Losby, *Second Assignments to Iowa's Limited Benefit Plan* (Washington, DC: Mathematica Policy Research, August 1999), C20.

47. Lucia Nixon, Jacqueline Kauff, and Jan Losby, *Second Assignments to Iowa's Limited Benefit Plan* (Washington, DC: Mathematica Policy Research, August 1999), 33.

48. Richard Bavier, *Recent Increases in the Share of Young Children Living with Married Mothers* (Washington, DC: Office of Management and Budget, December 21, 2001), table A-6.

49. Richard Bavier, *Recent Increases in the Share of Young Children Living with Married Mothers* (Washington, DC: Office of Management and Budget, December 21, 2001), table A-6. Absolute figures obtained from Richard Bavier on February 11, 2001.

50. Christopher Jencks, Joseph Swingle and Scott Winship, "Did Welfare Reform Alter Single Mothers' Income, Living Arrangements or Ability to Feed their Families?" prepared for the annual meeting of the Association of Public Policy and Management, Washington, DC, November 1-3, 2001.

51. Gregory Acs and Sandi Nelson, *"Honey I'm Home." Changes in Living Arrangements in the Late 1990s* (Washington, DC: The Urban Institute, June 2001), table 2, available from: http://newfederalism.urban.org/pdf/anf_b38.pdf, accessed January 16, 2002. Absolute figures obtained from Gregory Acs during telephone conversation on January 17, 2002.

52. Wendell Primus, "Child Living Arrangements by Race and Income: A Supplementary Analysis," paper presented at the Twenty-Third Annual APPAM Research Conference, *Public Policy Analysis and Public Policy: Making the Connection*, "Changing Incomes of Single-Mother Families Since Welfare Reform: What are the Implications for Policy?" November 1, 2001.

53. Wendell Primus, "Child Living Arrangements by Race and Income: A Supplementary Analysis," paper presented at the Twenty-Third Annual APPAM Research Conference, *Public Policy Analysis and Public Policy: Making the Connection*, "Changing Incomes of Single-Mother Families Since Welfare Reform: What are the Implications for Policy?" November 1, 2001, table 4.

54. Wendell Primus, "Child Living Arrangements by Race and Income: A Supplementary Analysis," paper presented at the Twenty-Third Annual APPAM Research Conference, *Public Policy Analysis and Public Policy: Making the Connection*, "Changing Incomes of Single-Mother Families Since Welfare Reform: What are the Implications for Policy?" November 1, 2001, table 5.

55. Wendell Primus, "Child Living Arrangements by Race and Income: A Supplementary Analysis," paper presented at the Twenty-Third Annual APPAM Research Conference, *Public Policy Analysis and Public Policy: Making the Connection*, "Changing Incomes of Single-Mother Families Since Welfare Reform: What are the Implications for Policy?" November 1, 2001, table 6.

56. Sheila R. Zedlewski and Donald W. Alderson, *Before and After Reform: How Have Families on Welfare Changed?* (Washington, DC: The Urban Institute, April 2001), 2, available from: http://newfederalism.urban.org/pdf/anf_b32.pdf, accessed February 15, 2002.

57. Sheila R. Zedlewski and Donald W. Alderson, *Before and After Reform: How Have Families on Welfare Changed?* (Washington, DC: The Urban Institute, April 2001), 2, available from: http://newfederalism.urban.org/pdf/anf_b32.pdf, accessed February 15, 2002.

58. Sheila R. Zedlewski and Donald W. Alderson, *Before and After Reform: How Have Families on Welfare Changed?* (Washington, DC: The Urban Institute, April 2001), 2, available from: http://newfederalism.urban.org/pdf/anf_b32.pdf, accessed February 15, 2002.

59. Christopher Jencks, Joseph Swingle and Scott Winship, "Did Welfare Reform Alter Single Mothers' Income, Living Arrangements or Ability to Feed their Families?" prepared for the annual meeting of the Association of Public Policy and Management, Washington, DC, November 13, 2001. Absolute figures calculated by author and Christopher E. Brown from data supplied by Joseph Swingle of Wellesley College, via e-mail correspondence, January 29, 2002.

60. Gregory Acs and Sandi Nelson, *"Honey I'm Home." Changes in Living Arrangements in the Late 1990s* (Washington, DC: The Urban Institute, June 2001), table 1, available from: http://newfederalism.urban.org/pdf/anf_b38.pdf, accessed January 16, 2002. Absolute figures obtained from Gregory Acs during telephone conversation on January 17, 2002.

61. Dan Bloom, James J. Kemple, Pamela Morris, Susan Scrivener, Nandita Verma, and Richard Hendra, *The Family Transition Program: Final Report on Florida's Initial Time-Limited Welfare Program* (New York: Manpower Demonstration Research Corporation, December 2000), 22.

62. Virginia Knox, Cynthia Miller, and Lisa A. Gennetian, *Reforming Welfare and Rewarding Work: A Summary of the Final Report on the Minnesota Family Independence Program* (New York: Manpower Demonstration Research Corporation, September 2000), 13 and 17.

63. David J. Fein, *Will Welfare Reform Influence Marriage and Fertility?: Early Evidence from the ABC Demonstration* (Cambridge, MA: ABT Associates, Inc., June 30, 1999), exhibit 2.

64. Richard Bavier, *Recent Increases in the Share of Young Children Living with Married Mothers* (Washington, DC: Office of Management and Budget, December 21, 2001), table A-6. Absolute figures obtained from Richard Bavier on February 11, 2001.

65. Wendell Primus, "Child Living Arrangements by Race and Income: A Supplementary Analysis," paper presented at the Twenty-Third Annual APPAM Research Conference, *Public Policy Analysis and Public Policy: Making the Connection*, "Changing Incomes of Single-Mother Families Since Welfare Reform: What are the Implications for Policy?" November 1, 2001.

66. Rebecca London, "The Interaction Between Single Mothers' Living Arrangements and Welfare Participation," *Journal of Policy Analysis and Management* 19, 1 (2000); and personal communication from Rebecca London, April 5, 2000.

67. Robert A. Moffitt, Robert Reville, and Anne E. Winkler, "Beyond Single Mothers: Cohabitation, Marriage, and the U.S. Welfare System," Institute for Research on Poverty Discussion Paper No. 1068-95, July 1995, table 1. The universe for the CPS includes all women eighteen to fifty-five who were family or non-family heads or spouses in one-family or two-family households. Cohabitors were defined as those women in the universe who live in the same two-family household as an unrelated adult male. AFDC recipiency is based on receipt by the woman, her spouse, or her male cohabitor. The universe for the NSFH included all respondent women ages nineteen to fifty-five only. Welfare recipiency includes Food Stamps and is based on receipt by the woman, her spouse, or her male cohabitor. The universe for the PSID includes all women eighteen to fifty-five who were household heads, spouses of heads, or cohabitors of heads (subfamily heads are excluded). AFDC recipiency is based on receipt by the woman, her spouse or her male cohabitor. The universe for the NLSY includes all women ages twenty-two to twenty-nine only. AFDC recipiency is based on receipt by the woman or her spouse.

68. Sara McLanahan, Irwin Garfinkel, Nancy E. Reichman, Julien Teitler, Marcia Carlson and Christina Norland Audigier, *The Fragile Families and Child Well-being Study*

Baseline Report (Princeton, NJ: The Center for Research on Child Well-being, August 2001), tables 2, 3, and 5, available from: http://crcw.princeton.edu/fragilefamilies/nationalreport.pdf, accessed February 19, 2002.

69. R. Shep Melnick, *Between the Lines* (Washington, DC: The Brookings Institution, 1994), 86-89. *King v. Smith* (1968), 392 U.S. at 334. 309. *Lewis v. Martin* (1970), 397 U.S. 552.

70. See generally Robert A. Moffitt, Robert Reville, and Anne E. Winkler, *State AFDC Rules Regarding the Treatment of Cohabitors: 1993* (Madison, WI: Institute for Research on Poverty, March 1995).

71. Unpublished tables prepared from the March 1999 Current Population Survey (CPS) provided to the author, from Richard Bavier, policy analyst, U.S. Office of Management and Budget, March 23, 2000.

72. Technically, in Census Bureau terminology, female-headed families.

73. Bruce Fuller and Sharon Lynn Kagan (Project co-directors), *Remember the Children: Mothers Balance Work and Child Care Under Welfare Reform* (Berkeley: University of California and Yale University, 2000), 55.

74. Bruce Fuller and Sharon Lynn Kagan (Project co-directors), *Remember the Children: Mothers Balance Work and Child Care Under Welfare Reform* (Berkeley: University of California and Yale University, 2000), 55.

75. Bruce Fuller and Sharon Lynn Kagan (Project co-directors), *Remember the Children: Mothers Balance Work and Child Care Under Welfare Reform* (Berkeley: University of California and Yale University, 2000), 57.

76. U.S. Department of Health and Human Services, Office of Assistant Secretary for Planning and Evaluation, *Indicators of Welfare Dependence: Annual Report to Congress* (Washington, DC: GPO, October 1998), table 8b.

77. Lucia Nixon, Jacqueline Kauff, and Jan Losby, *Second Assignments to Iowa's Limited Benefit Plan* (Washington, DC: Mathematica Policy Research, August 1999), C32.

78. Kurt Bauman, "Shifting Family Definitions: The Effect of Cohabitation and the Other Non-family Household Relationships on Measures of Poverty," Poverty Measurement Working Papers, U.S. Bureau of the Census (1997).

79. Kurt Bauman, "Shifting Family Definitions: The Effect of Cohabitation and the Other Non-family Household Relationships on Measures of Poverty," Poverty Measurement Working Papers, U.S. Bureau of the Census (1997), table 4.

80. Susan Mayer and Christopher Jencks, "Poverty and the Distribution of Material Hardship," *The Journal of Human Resources* 24, 1 (1989): 111.

81. Susan E. Mayer and Christopher Jencks, "Recent Trends in Economic Inequality in the United States: Income versus Expenditures versus Material Well-Being," 140-41.

82. Kathryn Edin and Christopher Jencks, "Reforming Welfare," in *Rethinking Social Policy*, edited by Christopher Jencks (Cambridge, MA: Harvard University Press, 1992), 204-35.

83. Christopher Jencks and Joseph Swingle, "Without a Net: Whom the Welfare Law Helps and Hurts," *The American Prospect* (January 3, 2000): 38.

84. Douglas Besharov and Timothy S. Sullivan, "Welfare Reform and Marriage," *The Public Interest*, No. 125 (Fall 1996): 81-94.

85. Wade Horn, "Comments," in *Family Well-Being After Welfare Reform*, edited by Douglas J. Besharov (College Park: The University of Maryland, 2002), pp. 5-16 to 5-27, available from: http://www.welfare_reform_academy.org/pubs/familywellbeing/ch5_manning.pdf, accessed February 19, 2002.

86. Sara McLanahan, Irwin Garfinkel, Nancy E. Reichman, Julien Teitler, Marcia Carlson and Christina Norland Audigier, *The Fragile Families and Child Well-Being Study Baseline Report* (Princeton, NJ: The Center for Research on Child Well-Being, August 2001), available from: http://crcw.princeton.edu/fragilefamilies/nationalreport.pdf, accessed February 19, 2002. See also "Fragile Families and Welfare Reform," Parts I and II, Irwin Garfinkel, Sara McLanahan, Marta Tienda, and Jeanne Brooks-Gunn (eds.), *Children and Youth Services Review* 23, Nos. 4, 5, 6, and 7 (2001).

87. Sara McLanahan, Irwin Garfinkel, Nancy E. Reichman, Julien Teitler, Marcia Carlson, and Christina Norland Audigier, *The Fragile Families and Child Well-being Study Baseline Report* (Princeton, NJ: The Center for Research on Child Well-being, August 2001), available from: http://crcw.princeton.edu/fragilefamilies/nationalreport.pdf, accessed February 19, 2002. See also "Fragile Families and Welfare Reform," Parts I and II, Irwin Garfinkel, Sara McLanahan, Marta Tienda, and Jeanne Brooks-Gunn (eds.), *Children and Youth Services Review* 23, Nos. 4, 5, 6, and 7 (2001).

12

The Static vs. Dynamic Inactivity Trap on the Labor Market: Revisiting the "Making Work Pay" Issue

Thierry Laurent and Yannick L'Horty

Introduction

Means-tested benefits are often disparaged for penalizing the return to the labor market. Mechanisms of guaranteed minimum income, of a purely differential nature, lead to marginal tax rates of 100 percent and can thus cancel out the monetary gains of returning to employment; targeted benefits, reserved for recipients of guaranteed income or the unemployed, magnify the phenomenon. Similarly, means-tested benefits, that depend on earnings brackets or that uniformly increase marginal tax rates when they are regressive with income, produce cut-off effects. When combined, all these devices seriously limit the interest of employment, creating inactivity traps and persistent unemployment.

This incentive or effectiveness problem is coupled with a problem of justice or equity. The way in which taxes and benefits are structured results in the fact that a nonworking person can receive the same income as a working person. If there are many concepts of justice, none seem to legitimize the outcome that work should bring in less than non-work.

Given these problems of incentive and justice, the catch sentence "*to make work pay*," widely circulated in publications by the OECD, progressively guides reforms in social benefits. Firstly, targeted benefits must be avoided, for example, those reserved for the unemployed or recipients of minimum income benefits. Secondly, the effect of cut-offs and regressivity on means-tested benefits must be limited. Finally, we recommend a supplement to earnings with benefits such as those provided by the EITC in the United States, the WFTC in the United Kingdom, or the *"Prime pour l'emploi"* in France. Beyond reforms, an improvement in the quality of jobs, working conditions, and the level of earnings could also contribute to more equity and effectiveness in the functioning of employment markets.

Nonetheless, criticism of the social systems and the resulting economic policy recommendations come from a very static approach to the rewards of returning to employment: an incentive to work problem is identified based on the simple comparison between the income in benefits and those of work. This type of static approach remains the one chosen, for example, in most applied studies in France on the rewards of returning to employment (Laroque and Salanié, 1999, 2000; Gurgand and Margolis, 2001; Bourguignon, 2001). The main limit of this so called "static approach" is that it does not allow consideration of the perspectives opened by the access to employment . If part-time or low-paid employment positions are a springboard to full-time employment and higher wages, this necessarily modifies the incentive to fill them and this also modifies the associated injustice. Literature on employment and earnings mobility (Stewart and Swaffield, 1999; Riddell and Jones, 1999) has not been sufficiently stirred by studies on the rewards of returning to employment.

The purpose of this chapter is to offer a larger perspective for measuring the benefits achievable by work, by also taking into account the inter-temporal nature of the calculus made by the unemployed and the fact that accepting employment today can modify future employment perspectives. In such a dynamic framework, where the mobility of workers between jobs is taken into consideration, we look at the effects of an inactivity trap on incentives and equity. We also examine the consequences on economic policy recommendations that result from this dynamic perspective.

We begin by looking at static and dynamic approaches on the rewards of accepting a job. This is followed with an empirical example of the differences between the two approaches. Next we consider the consequences for carrying out economic policy. The final section concludes with some implications of our analysis.

How Much Does Work Pay?

After a presentation of the static approach to the gains of employment, we introduce the dynamic approach, followed by a modeling of the two perspectives.

Static Analysis

Employment incentive is most often analysed within a classic microeconomic framework, in which labor supply is derived from consumer choice, in the context of a consumption/leisure trade-off where a budget increase implies both "income and substitution effect." In this model, the labor supply depends on the marginal disutility of work and the combined revenue associated with a transition between two states on the labor market: inactivity and employment, or part-time and full-time work, for example.

An individual who is offered work—going from non-employment to part-time or full-time employment, for example—compares what he/she will gain in refusing the offer with what he/she will gain in accepting. This comparison depends on the difference between earnings associated with each of the two situations, as well as the impact that the change in situation will have on the social benefits as a whole (means- or status-tested subsidies) and overall taxes. All of the costs associated with employment (childcare, commuting, meals taken outside the home, clothing, gains linked to access to company benefits, etc.) or inactivity (costs related to seeking employment, gains linked to the fulfillment of domestic work, etc.)[1] also come into play.

Therefore, if the difference between all net incomes associated with high and low employment activities is small, one can say that there is a problem of incentive to work given the marginal disutility and/or valuation of work. This situation, qualified as an *inactivity trap*, also raises a problem of equity.

The main limit of this approach is that it is inscribed within a static framework, where the problem of an incentive to work is restricted to a comparison of the immediate gains associated with work and non-work, whereas consumption/leisure choices are, by nature, inter-temporal.

Dynamic Analysis

The dynamic approach includes all the elements of a static approach and adds new ones, by adopting an inter-temporal framework. Immediate gains in income and perspectives for future improvements (accumulation of human capital, increased probability of access to a "better" job, increased rights to retirement benefits, etc.) are all taken into consideration. A low immediate monetary gain can therefore be compensated by favorable perspectives; symmetrically, a high immediate gain can, of course, be compensated by unfavorable perspectives.

The new elements under consideration are, first of all:

1. The probabilities of obtaining a better job in the future, are conditioned by the decisions made by the individuals during the present period.
2. The agent's preference for the present, that is, the discount rate he/she uses in his/her arbitrage.

Therefore, one needs to consider all the possible transitions on the labor market associated with a decision made in the current period. For this we use the matrix of probabilities of transitions between different situations on the labor market (full time, part time, unemployment, inactivity, etc.). The payment associated with the strategy "*I accept the job*" is thus evaluated by calculating the discounted expected value of all the present and future gains implied by the application of this strategy; the discount rate used for the computation indicates how the individual weighs immediate gains and future gains.

It is then a matter of identifying the ultimate effects of dequalification linked to having passed through unemployment, or, symmetrically, the accumulation of human capital linked to the transitions *via* employment (gains in "employability").

These new elements can modify the strategic choices of the individuals from those described in a purely static framework and lessen or reinforce the problems of incentive with regard to work and equity. In particular, *work can pay, even if it does not pay immediately and an inactivity trap situation does not have to be damaging in terms of incentive to employment.*

This is the case if accepting the job improves future wages perspectives and if the discount rate is moderate; it is also the case if job tenure increases the worker's human capital—and thereby ulterior employability—and/or if non-work deteriorates that of the unemployed or inactive individual. In these situations, work does not pay immediately, but it pays off in the end: an individual can therefore accept a job that pays nothing in the short term (even incurring cost), because this job increases the probability of transitions to one or more better jobs in the future, that is, the probability to get back on the "good" road.

The problem of justice or equity must also be reconsidered. To determine if an individual who accepted a job is the victim of an "injustice,"[2] relatively to another one who refused the same job, it is important to compare the *discounted flow of real incomes* associated with these two decisions, and not only the immediate incomes they bring about. If there is no dynamic trap, an individual accepting work for an immediate income inferior to that obtained when remaining unemployed, gains more, *in terms of expected real incomes*, than an individual who chooses not to work: therefore, there is no inequity.[3]

Modeling

The static approach requires building an income vector that corresponds with the net gains of each state on the labor market, ranking from the most to the least favorable situation.

$$W = (w_1, w_2, ..., w_N).$$

The net gain of an agent who does not work (w_N) is equal to the replacement income, or basic income, increased by the marginal utility of leisure and all other elements of income associated with non-employment, whether monetary or not. The net gain of the "worst" job offered to this agent (w_{N-1})—for example a part-time job paying minimum wage—includes the corresponding wage minus the marginal disutility of work, the valuation of the status and all other income elements associated with this job.

A static inactivity trap will exist insofar as:

$$\textit{Static trap: } w_N > w_{N-1}$$

The incentive of an individual to accept a part-time or full-time job, will thus be high when:

1. The net wage associated with the job is high;
2. The replacement incomes are low (basic or minimum income, unemployment benefits, social programs, etc.);
3. The level of social programs' benefits are not too regressive with earnings; and
4. The marginal disutility of work is low and/or the valuation of the fact of working is high.

A dynamic approach takes three additional elements into account. The first one is the matrix of transitions[4] P that gives, for each period, the probabilities of shifting from one of the N possible states on the labor market to any other states. The second is the discount rate—or rate of preference for the present—$r > 0$, which defines the discount factor $\delta = 1/(1+r) \in [0,1]$. Finally, the strategies of the agents who can accept all types of jobs, or states, on the labor market (strategy A) or refuse certain states (strategy R) will be compared. For an "A-strategy agent" who chooses to accept all types of jobs, the expected income for period $t+k$, according to the initial state, is given by $P^k.W$; in the case of a "R-strategy agent," who always refuses the worst jobs, expected income is no longer calculated with P but with another matrix P^* whose second to last column is made up of zeros.[5]

The individual's objective is to maximize the sum of discounted expected incomes:

$$\left(\sum_{k=0}^{\infty} \delta^k \bar{P}^k \right).W = (\text{Id} - \delta \bar{P})^{-1}.W$$

If the sum above is higher in P^* than P, that is to say in refusing the bad jobs, then strategy R is preferred to A; this indicates a dynamic trap, and eventually implies higher unemployment because the asymptotic probability of being unemployed is greater in P^* than P.

$$\textit{Dynamic trap: } \sum_{n=0}^{\infty} \delta^n \sum_{k=1}^{N} \left(P_{ik}^n - \bar{P}_{ik}^n \right) W_{k_{<0}}$$

This dynamic approach stresses that the additional following conditions must be satisfied to take a job:

5. The rate of preference for the present of the agent is low;
6. The probabilities for transitions to better jobs are high;

7. The dequalification process associated with unemployment situations is strong, that is, the probabilities for transition to better jobs strongly deteriorate with the duration of unemployment[6];

8. The number of years of work before retirement is high[7]; and

9. The agent's risk aversion is low.[8]

The more conditions (1) to (4) are satisfied, the weaker the static trap, and the more immediately employment pays. The more the conditions (1) to (9) are satisfied, the weaker the dynamic trap, and the stronger are incentives to work. These remarks highlight the following points:

- Static and dynamic traps can coexist;
- The weaker the implications of the static trap, the weaker the occurrence of a dynamic trap;
- There can be a static trap without any dynamic trap, if conditions (1) to (4) are such that a job does not pay immediately, but that the conditions (5) to (9) are "strongly" satisfied and do more than counterbalance the influence of (1)-(4): for example, a low discount rate associated with strong probabilities of transitions to better jobs, can counterbalance the fact that employment does not pay in the short term and encourage an agent to accept such a job; and
- There can be a dynamic trap without a static trap if conditions (1) to (4) are such that a job pays immediately, but that conditions (5) to (9) are "strongly" unsatisfied and do more than counterbalance the influence of (1)-(4).

In Laurent et al. (2000), we formally demonstrate that if the transition matrix respects certain favorable conditions of monotonicity (when bad jobs reinforce the chances of getting good jobs[9]), the existence of a static trap is a necessary condition, though not sufficient for a dynamic trap. In other words, there is a real problem of an incentive to work when the monetary gains (earnings) provided by a return to work are low, even though low earnings are not always associated with an incentive problem. In the general case, where the matrix of transitions does not necessarily respect such monotonicity conditions, the existence of a static trap is neither necessary nor sufficient for the existence of a dynamic trap: an incentive to work problem can then arise even if net short-run gains associated with employment are high. The dequalification process associated with unemployment duration and, symmetrically, the human capital accumulation associated with employment tenure reinforce, in all cases, the incentive to work (cf. Laurent et al., 2001).

Example

To illustrate these mechanisms, the dynamic path of the expected income of an agent can be calculated according to different job acceptance strategies

(A or R). Here, we consider a matrix of transitions providing the probabilities, in France, of going from one given labor market situation—unemployment, less than 15 hours/week part-time job, 16 to 29 hours/week part-time job, more than 30 hours/week job—to any other situation.[10]

According to these French probabilities, an unemployed individual has a better chance of obtaining a full-time job than any worker that already has a

Table 12.1
Probabilities of Transitions on the Labor Market

Situation in T in $T+1$	Job > 30h	15h < Part-time Job <30h	Part-time Job <15h	Unemployment
Job > 30 h	0,66	0,35	0,25	0,41
15h < Part-time Job <30h	0,12	0,36	0,28	0,06
Part-time Job <15h	0,06	0,1	0,3	0,03
Inactivity/Unemployment	0,15	0,18	0,17	0,49

Source: Employment Survey, INSEE, 1995 and 1996. Field: Men and women. For the actively employed, private sector wage earners except apprentices, government assisted workers and students.

part-time job. Obviously, such a situation dramatically increases the incentive (for an unemployed individual) to refuse part-time work that do not pay immediately; however, one will show that, despite the static trap, it is always in the interest of an individual to accept part-time work as long as his discount rate is not too high.

Each situation on the labor market can be associated with its corresponding income, as shown in the table 12.2 (the amounts listed are quite realistic, but given only for the purpose of illustration). Given the differential character of the guaranteed minimum income (the RMI, in France), an individual working less than 15 hours gets *in fine* the same income as an individual without employment, that is, the full amount of the minimum income support.[11]

Table 12.2
Income Vector

Employment > 30h	838 €
15h < Part-time <30h	595 €
Part-time <15h	381 €
Inactivity/Unemployment	381 €

Source: Employment Survey, INSEE, and authors computations.

Figure 12.1 shows expected income paths according to two different job acceptance strategies. The square symbols curve corresponds to the acceptance of all kind of jobs, that is, whatever the working time: strategy *A*; an individual of this type thus accepts a job even if it does not pay in the short-term (for example, he/she accepts a part-time job of less than 15 hours/week, even though his/her gains are not immediately higher than the amount of guaranteed minimum income). The diamond symbols curve corresponds to the acceptance of a job only if it pays immediately—work more than 30 hours— and to the refusal of other kind of jobs:[12] strategy *R*; the round symbols curve corresponds to the former strategy in adding a phenomenon of dequalification, which decreases the probability of transition to employment by 20 percent per year, from the second consecutive year of unemployment.

The fact that an unemployed individual has a higher probability of finding a full-time job than one already working part time, results, one year after the decision, in a lower expectation of revenue with strategy *A* than with strategy *R*, while the immediate gains associated with each of the two strategies are identical (381€).

Thus, an unemployed individual receiving the full minimum income support, has no interest in accepting a part-time job, if he/she takes into account only the short-term gains: there is a strong static trap effect. Despite this static trap, the interplay of transitions on the labor market is such that strategy *A* begins to pay after three years. It does so more quickly if the dequalification linked to a long stay in unemployment is introduced.

Figure 12.1
Expected Incomes According to Different Strategies of Employment Acceptance

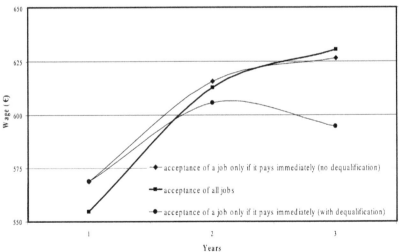

The notion of an inactivity trap must be handled carefully: *the identification of a trap in a static framework has no reason to be associated with the same diagnosis in a dynamic framework.* A second example (cf. appendix), shows that the same result held even if accepting a part-time job immediately implies a net income loss: in an inter-temporal perspective, it can be in one's interest to accept a job that not only does not pay in the short term, but moreover causes a loss of income.

The 1998 INSEE survey on minimum income recipients (RMI) provides some elements to confirm this analysis. First of all, nearly a third of beneficiaries of the minimum income support who return to work claim to have no financial gain (12.1 percent claim to be losing, 20.4 percent claim they are not gaining anything). Secondly, although the beneficiaries of the minimum income support generally claim that they are looking for a minimum wage full-time job, a majority have accepted a part-time job: among the 26 percent of beneficiaries of the minimum income support in December 1996 who held employment in January 1998, nearly two-thirds have a part-time job (in 90 percent of cases this part-time job is involuntary, and people would strictly prefer to work more). Finally, 28.1 percent of those who did receive the guaranteed minimum revenue and now have a job, qualify it as "a first step towards a real job" (32.9 percent claim it is "a job while waiting for something better" and 39 percent claim that it is a "real job"). In sum, beneficiaries of the minimum income support frequently accept—even when it is not a requirement stipulated in their insertion contract—a part-time job that does not immediately pay, which may even infer a cost, because it opens up perspectives for improvements in the future.

How to Make Work Pay?

Several economic policy recommendations are often put forward in order to "make work pay." It is first a matter of improving the quality of jobs, working conditions, and the level of net earnings. Next, the architecture of social benefits must be reformed in three directions: limiting recourse to targeted benefits reserved to the unemployed or beneficiaries of the minimum income support; limiting the resource-based cut-off effects and regressivity of benefits; finally, complementing work income with benefits such as the EITC in the United States, the WFTC in the United Kingdom, or the *Prime pour l'emploi* in France.

These recommendations are all inspired by a purely static approach. They only cover the income determinants and do not take into consideration the inter-temporal nature of the incentives, neither the possibilities of transition on the employment market; in short, they suggest that the income vector must be modified, but not the matrix of transitions.

As these reforms are costly and public decisionmakers must make, here and elsewhere, the best choices, it is important to discuss the effects of the different reforms in a dynamic framework.

The Inadequacy of Traditional Policies

The policies affecting only the income of those who have a job and those who do not, are, in any case, inadequate. Of course, they are on the right track, since static traps can create the preliminary conditions for the existence of real incentive problems, but one must remember that static traps are not always a necessary condition and never a sufficient condition for the existence of incentive to work problems. Income policies should therefore be considered only as a favorable element of large sets of possible measures.

Overall, policies that strive to improve transitions between jobs, in the sense of greater and ascending professional mobility, are beneficial. Favorable business conditions, for example, play a favorable role by increasing the incentive to work. When growth is strong, the probabilities of transitions, from bad jobs to good ones, are higher, which increases the expectation of gains for the unemployed and favors the choice of the A- strategy (as opposed to the R-strategy); macroeconomic growth supporting oriented policies find here an unexpected justification: in a dynamic framework they make work pay more and, thus, have incentive virtues.

The so-called "active policies on the labor market" also find new foundations; such policies always contribute to improve the human capital of workers, whether they are training policies geared towards those who already have a job or actions to provide new skills to those who lack them. In a static approach, these policies have no effect on incentive or equity; in our dynamic approach, the active policies also become profitable. By improving the chances of access to better jobs, the training strategies make work pay more. [13]

Temporary Aid Better Than Permanent

A dynamic perspective also allows us to compare the respective advantages of permanent vs. temporary mechanisms of income support to be discussed upon a return to employment. The permanent mechanisms correspond to the devices inspired by the negative taxes that are reserved for all those who have employment (EITC, WFTC, *Prime pour l'emploi*…) Temporary mechanisms deal with the possibility of keeping both part of the minimum income support and earnings from activity (for example, the case of the French earning disregards mechanism attached to the RMI allowance—that allows 100 percent of the two types of income to be cumulative for two quarters after returning to work and 50 percent during the three following quarters).

A static approach does not allow these two types of mechanisms to be distinguished from each other. In France, where the two types of mechanisms coexist, applied studies inspired by the static approach nonetheless ignore the existence of the temporary mechanisms (Laroque and Salanié, 1999, 2000; Gurgand and Margolis, 2001; Bourguignon, 2001).

To analyze the two types of mechanisms in a dynamic framework, let us assume there is a static trap, linked to the social benefits schedule design, and that we are looking for the best way to curb it: permanent vs. temporary aid. Two cases must be distinguished depending on whether there is or is not a financial incentive problem.

The first case corresponds with weak possibilities of ascending mobility on the labor market: in this case, the fact of occupying a part-time low paying job does not improve the chances of access to a full-time higher wage job, and the best strategy to access good employment is then to remain unemployed (*R*). In such a context, setting up a policy of temporary or permanent support for low income, may prove inadequate; indeed, it does not solve the incentive to work problem—which results from the weak possibilities of transitions and not from low income work—and by simply increasing the income of a low paid job, it has at best no effect on incentive. At worst, it can drive some unemployed people to accept bad jobs that lead nowhere, and those who already hold them, to keep them.

In the second case, there is a static trap but not a dynamic one and, therefore, no incentive problem; a job is attractive given the probabilities for transitions characterizing the labor market (which results in an increase in the discounted value of expected incomes when one has a part-time job) and the risk of dequalification linked to extended periods of unemployment. In this framework, three categories of individuals can be identified for whom returning to employment raises a problem:

1. "rational"[14] agents, characterized by a high discount rate: the lack of earnings in the short term is not compensated by the discounted future gains.
2. "irrational" or myopic individuals, who simply do not see the future gains associated with a return to employment decision and only perceive immediate gains.
3. "rational" individuals, characterized by a low discount rate, who know perfectly well that it is in their own interest to accept all kinds of job, but cannot make the temporary investment it involves:[15] it is just financially impossible for them to manage the immediate loss of revenues associated with returning to employment part time.

For individuals in the first category (1), a temporary financial aid is enough to make employment attractive, because given their high discount rate, they do not value gains set too far in the future. A permanent support would only add a weak incentive to return to employment for a much higher cost.

For individuals in the second category (2), the same reasoning applies: because they do not value gains situated too far in the future at all, a temporary aid is just as effective as a permanent one but far less expensive.

Finally, for individuals in the third category (3), the most important is to give them the possibility of making the *investment* they wish to: a temporary subsidy solves this problem.

One sees that *temporary support for the return to employment finds strong justifications*: in reducing the immediate costs associated with the return to activity, such a device, in fact, shifts the individuals from the three preceding categories, from non-employment to employment. For these individuals, a temporary credit is enough to drive them to make the choice to accept part-time jobs; this choice can then lead them, *via* the interplay of transitions on the labor market, to being trapped…in full-time employment.

One of the main advantage of a temporary financial aid to move to work, compared to a permanent one, is that *it targets the individuals belonging to "problematic" categories in terms of incentive to work:* such a device does not modify the long-run behavior of other agents who, in any case, always prefer employment to unemployment, even when it does not pay immediately.[16]

Conclusion

Theoretical and applied studies on financial incentives to go to work are generally limited to immediate gains associated with the return to employment or to the increase in work history, without taking into account the transitions of individuals on the labor market. In doing so, their conclusions remain partial. Through the interplay of transitions on the labor market, a job that does not pay immediately can pay later. Conversely, a job that pays immediately, can eventually lead to no improvement in earnings. An inactivity trap, clearly identified in a static framework, can therefore have no effect on agents' decisions when the latter are made in an inter-temporal perspective, in a world where job tenure opens new possibilities for access to better jobs.

The size of disincentive to work created by the tax system and social programs should not, therefore, be exaggerated. Of course, it does not justify the existence of an income area characterized by very high marginal tax rates, but leads to a deeper understanding of the economic effects of these "static" traps; in particular, situations of voluntary unemployment are probably less frequent in reality than often suggested by static analysis. Taking a look at the facts, it is usual to observe that unemployed or inactive individuals accept employment that does not pay immediately, or which may even cost them given the social programs of which they could take advantage. The expansion of part-time work in many countries, and especially in France, could not be explained by taking into account only the immediate gains. The beneficiaries of the minimum income support indeed have the financial incentive to go to work, even if on a longer term: if they are unemployed, most of the time, it is because they cannot find a job and not because they do not want to.

These remarks might have consequences in terms of economic policy. Setting up a permanent mechanism allowing support for low income responds to two objectives: the incentive to work problems and the fight against inactivity traps, on the one hand, and the reduction of inequalities in income among active workers on the other.

From a financial incentive to work point of view, one sees that permanent aid is not necessarily more efficient for a given budget than a temporary credit;

the problem of inactivity traps, when they are analyzed in a dynamic perspective, does not necessarily plead in favor of permanent aid for returning to employment, temporary mechanisms being adequate to bridge the traps of inactivity.

Concerning the treatment of inequalities, however, a permanent subsidy is a priori, more efficient, because it acts on the stock of employed people, whereas the temporary mechanisms act only on the flows of unemployed people. Arguments on redistribution would thus be more relevant than financial incentive arguments in order to justify reforms in social programs.

Appendix

The exercise is the same as the one in section 3, but now the men's matrix of transition is used; to accentuate the "trap" effect, we suppose here that due to the local services associated with receiving full rate guaranteed minimum revenue and the regressiveness of housing benefits with revenues from activity, an unemployed individual receiving the full rate guaranteed minimum revenue has *in fine* a revene higher (457€) than that of a worker with a salary for less than 15 hours (381€). This new configuration accentuates, if we use static reasoning, the trap effect and, consequently, lowers the incentive for returning to work.

Probabilities of Transitions on the Employment Market

Situation in T in $T+1$	Job > 30h	15h < Part-time Job <30h	Part-time Job <15h	Unemployment
Job > 30h	0,67	0,49	0,25	0,44
15h < Part-time Job <30h	0,11	0,24	0,33	0,05
Part-time Job <15h	0	0,05	0,19	0,02
Inactivity/Unemployment	0,22	0,21	0,23	0,51

Source: Employment Survey, INSEE, 1995 and 1996. Field: Men and women. For the actively employed, private sector wage earners except apprentices, government assisted workers and students.

Revenues Associated with Different Employment Situations (€)

Employment > 30h	838
15h < Part-time <30h	595
Part-time <15h	381
Inactivity/Unemployment	457

Given these new parameters, figure 12.1, presented in the text, becomes:

Figure 12.2
Expected Incomes According to Different Strategies
of Employment Acceptance (for a man)

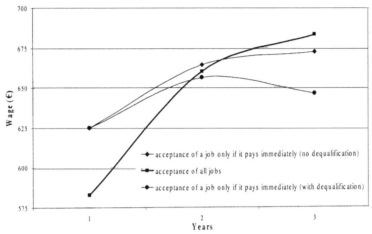

Like before, work does not "pay" in the short term but "pays" in the long term; the conclusions remain unmodified: a "static trap" in a dynamic framework does not necessarily imply the existence of incentive to work problems.

Notes

1. Nonmonetary factors are also likely to come into play, such as social status or the subjective valorization of a professional activity. Although not easy to measure, these factors can play an important role.
2. In the sense that he/she will not gain more by working than the individual who has refused work and decided to remain unemployed.
3. At least ex ante; ex post the actual trajectory on the employment market of an individual who has accepted employment may result in a situation *in fine* in which he/she will earn less than if he/she had initially refused employment, despite the lack of a dynamic trap.
4. This matrix is subjective and respects the properties of Markov's homogeneous chains in discrete time to finished number of states.
5. What interests us here is the refusal of the state $N-1$. If the N state is preferred when coming from N, we can show that it will be preferred when coming from any other state.
6. If non-employment is associated with a process of dequalification, the acceptance of a bad job can be a way to avoid it. The "investment" made by an unemployed who accepts employment that is not immediately remunerated can be interpreted as an investment in human capital that allows him/her to limit loss in employability, avoiding recurrent deterioration of probabilities of transition to better employment which generally occurs with long-term unemployment.

7. The older, and thus closer to retirement age an individual is, the more he/she has incentive to stay in non-employment, the return on investment being associated with choice A being insufficient to incite him/her to take a job; young people are more likely to make the "investment" of accepting a bad job.

8. The aversion relative to the risk of agents, i.e., the concaveness of the utilitarian function of payments, also plays a role: the more an individual is risk-averse, the more it is in his/her interest to adopt strategy R securing certain payment, replacement revenues, rather than strategy A associated with uncertain payment (whose real value expectancy can be stronger). To simplify here, we neglect the influence of aversion relative to risk by supposing that the utilitarian function of payments is linear.

9. A sufficient condition is that $\sum\limits_{j-1}^{P} P_{ij}$ decrease with i for all P. Under that condition, the following property is satisfied: $\forall n, \forall i \varepsilon [1..N], \forall p \varepsilon [1..N], \sum\limits_{j=1}^{P} P_{ij}^{n} - P_{ij}^{'n} \geq 0$

10. For example, a wage earner working part-time less than 15 hours, has a 30 percent chance of being in the same situation the following year, a 17 percent chance of being unemployed and a 25 percent chance of having obtained employment of over 30 hours. His/her probability of having "improved" his/her situation is 0.28+0.25=0.53.

11. Here, we are considering the case of a single. The role played by the family arrangement is thus not taken into account.

12. This amounts to saying that the valuation of one hour of leisure for an individual is basically 3€ which does not seem excessive. In such a case, working 22.5 hours for 595€ is, in the end, equivalent to not working and receiving 381€ (taking into account the costs initiated by employment: meals, transportation, etc.).

13. Only provided that access to the training expedient not be conditional to unemployed status. If not occupying a job in itself had little effect on the qualification of individuals and that an effective training expedient were reserved solely for the unemployed, the strategy of refusing employment would become more compensatory, all other factors being equal.

14. We mean those who correctly perceive the entire trajectory involved, on the employment market, by the decision of current employment.

15. This type of situation does not appear in a framework where all financial markets are perfect.

16. The temporary bonus is a bargain for the latter, but this effect will be even more considerable with a permanent bonus for returning to employment.

References

Bourguignon, F. (2001). "Revenu minimum et redistribution optimale des revenus: fondements théoriques." *Economie et Statistique*, No. 346-347.

CSERC. (1997). "Minima sociaux. Entre protection et insertion."éd. La Documentation Française.

Gurgand, M., & Margolis, D. (2001). "RMI et revenus du travail: une évaluation des gains financiers à l'emploi." *Economie et Statistique*, No. 346-347.

Laroque, G., & Salanié, B. (1999). "Prélèvements et transfert sociaux: une analyse descriptive des incitations financières au travail." *Economie et Statistique*, No. 328.

Laroque, G., & Salanié, B. (2000). "Une décomposition du non emploi en France." *Economie et Statistique*, No. 331.

Laurent, T., L'Horty, Y., Maillé, P., & Ouvrard, J-F. (2000). "Incitations et transitions sur le marché du travail: une analyse des stratégies d'acceptation et de refus d'emploi." *Document de travail du centre d'Etude des Politiques Economiques et de l'Emploi.* EPEE, Université d'Evry. October.

Laurent, T., L'Horty, Y., Maillé, P., & Ouvrard, J-F. (2001). "Incitations et transitions sur le marché du travail: le rôle de la déqualification." *Document de travail du centre d'Etude des Politiques Economiques et de l'Emploi*. EPEE, Université d'Evry. November.

Riddell, W. C., & Jones, R. G. (1999). "The Measurement of Unemployment: An Empirical Approach." *Econometrica* 67: 147-161.

Stewart, M. B., & Swaffield, J.-K. (1999). "Low Pay Dynamics and Transitions Probabilities." *Economica* 66: 23-42.

Contributors

Douglas J. Besharov is the Joseph J. and Violet Jacobs Scholar in Social Welfare Studies at the American Enterprise Institute, professor at the University of Maryland's School of Public Affairs and director of the Welfare Reform Academy.

Gary Burtless is John C. and Nancy D. Whitehead Chair in Economic Studies at the Brookings Institution in Washington, DC.

Sheldon H. Danziger is Henry J. Meyer Collegiate Professor of Social Work and Public Policy and director of the Center on Poverty Risk and Mental Health at the University of Michigan.

Michel Dollé is general inspector of INSEE and general secretary of the French Council for Employment, Income and Social Cohesion (CERC).

Madior Fall is economist at INSEE and researcher at the INRA.

Neil Gilbert is Chernin Professor of Social Welfare at the University of California—Berkeley, School of Social Welfare, and co-director of the Center for Child and Youth Policy.

Christel Gilles is economist at the Economic and Forecasting Division (DREES) of the French Ministry of Social Affairs.

Jean-Michel Hourriez is administrator of INSEE, head of the Division "Income and Wealth of Households," at INSEE.

Thierry Laurent is professor of economics at the University of Evry.

Yannick L'Horty is professor of economics at the University of Evry.

Christian Loisy is administrator of INSEE, head of bureau at the Economic and Forecasting Division (DREES) of the French Ministry of Social Affairs.

Jordan Matsudaira is a doctoral student in economics and public policy at the University of Michigan.

Sylvie Morel is professor of economics at the University of Laval, Québec, Canada.

Antoine Parent is associate professor of economics at the University of Paris 8, associated researcher at MATISSE-University of Paris I Sorbonne, and research program manager at the Research Division (DREES-MiRe) of the French Ministry of Social Affairs.

Alan Weil is director in charge of the project "Assessing the New Federalism" at the Urban Institute, Washington, DC.

Index

Acknowledgments

This volume has grown out of a mission to the United States in October 2000 conducted under the auspices of the Research Division of the French Ministry of Social Affairs (MiRe—DREES). The purpose of this mission was to learn about the 1996 U.S. Welfare Reform and the U.S. Social Security System. The research team met with experts from federal, state, and county administrations, with policy analysts and economists from prominent think tanks and with faculty from the University of Wisconsin and the University of California, Berkeley. The meetings with U.S. scholars included Neil Gilbert, Janet Yellen, Alan Auerbach, David Levine, Michael Wiseman, Karl Sholtz, Robert Haveman, Gary Burtless, Wendell Primus, Alan Weil, and Robert Lerman.

The quality of the information gathered during this mission and the receptiveness of U.S. scholars to share knowledge that was related to the French experiences with income support policy stimulated interest in further exchange and collaboration. Following up on this interest, Antoine Parent and Neil Gilbert invited a group of French and U.S. policy analysts and economists to prepare papers on several topics related to welfare and work for a workshop on the comparative assessment of welfare reforms, which was held at the University of California, Berkeley, in February 2002. After presentation of their findings and a robust exchange of ideas and perspectives on the French and U.S. systems, the workshop participants had an opportunity to reflect upon the deliberations and to prepare the final version of their analyses for publication in this volume. During the three-day gathering at the University of California, Berkeley, Michael Austin, Erica Baum, Jill Duerr Berrick, Mary Ann Mason, James Midgley, and William Runyan joined the formal and informal discussions. We should like to thank all the people who contributed their time and good counsel at the various stages of this project.

We are grateful to the Center for Child and Youth Policy at the University of California, Berkeley, the French Ministry of Social Affairs, and the International Social Security Association (ISSA), which jointly sponsored the workshop and this book. A special thanks is owed to Lorretta Morales at UC Berkeley for her diligent work in helping to prepare the chapters for publication.

We particularly acknowledge the encouragement and advice of Mireille Elbaum, director of the Research Division of the French Ministry of Social Affairs (DREES), Pierre Strobel, Head of Research at MiRe, Gerard Cornilleau, head of Economics and Forecasting division (DREES), and Dalmer Hoskins, secretary general of the ISSA. Finally, we thank Hubert Martin, social counselor at the French Embassy in Washington, for having organized all the meetings with administrators and U.S. scholars.

Although we benefited from the wisdom and insights of many people from diverse institutional arenas, the views expressed in this book are those of the authors and should not be construed as representing the official position of any sponsoring institution.

Introduction

Welfare Reform: A Comparative Assessment of the French and U.S. Experiences examines theoretical perspectives and empirical evidence on the relationships among welfare reforms, poverty, inequality, and economic growth in France and the United States. Through a comparative analysis of these cases, we attempt to identify the kinds of welfare reforms that are reasonably effective and efficient in lifting welfare recipients out of poverty under the constraint of a given level of economic growth.

In addressing theoretical questions and empirical findings, the lines of study in this volume incorporate various analytic methods including: descriptive economics (Burtless, Fall, and Hourriez), institutionalist (Morel) and normative approaches (Dollé), social policy (Gilbert, Besharov), microeconomics (Laurent, L'Horty), and finally macroeconomics and econometrics using panel data (Danziger, Matsudaira) and time series analysis (Gilles, Loisy, Parent). These analyses generally focus on the dynamics of the French and American welfare systems as they have unfolded over the past ten years. In the United States, the welfare system underwent a major reform in 1996, which emphasized the principle of Workfare. In France, a law against Social Exclusion was adopted in 1998, after which there was a growing debate on the efficiency of the insertion contract linked to receipt of the Revenu Minimum d'Insertion (RMI) allowance. The comparison of welfare dynamics in France and the United States principally involves two income support programs: Temporary Assistance for Needy Families (TANF), illustrative of welfare reform in the U.S. and the Revenu Minimun d'Insertion (RMI), the major means-tested benefit as measured by the number of its beneficiaries; the RMI is the only income support program in France representing a significant counterpart to the scheme of public allowances.

If the American efforts to reduce poverty are centered on income, the French efforts to reduce poverty are incorporated into measures designed to address the wider problem of social exclusion. This distinction probably reflects the fact that the French society is more sensitive to inequality than the U.S. society. Dealing with social exclusion may affect the nature of anti-poverty policies. However, this volume's comparative analysis of welfare states and their dynamics suggests that it is oversimplified to contrapose the American "Make Work Pay Strategy" against the French approach based on insertion. Indeed, to some extent, one can identify a convergence in the details of the implementation of welfare policy between the two countries, particularly in regard to the introduction of work incentive strategies. The evidence in this volume of a move toward convergence between the U.S. and the French welfare policies may help to modify conventional wisdom regarding the degree of opposition between these systems. Moreover, as welfare policies are advancing in the same direction, we believe that each country has increasing opportunities to learn about the consequences of social reforms from each other's experiences.

Work-oriented policies in France and the U.S. allow for a comparative evaluation on several related dimensions. This book is organized around five of these policy dimensions. Part 1 examines poverty and work in the U.S. and how the concept of the "working poor" applies to France. Part 2 analyzes the development and structure of the welfare systems in each country. Part 3 reviews the major evaluations of welfare reforms in the U.S. and their implications. Part 4 explores the relationship between economic growth and poverty in France and the U.S. Finally, part 5 addresses the question of the effectiveness of work-oriented measures in each country.

In the opening chapter, Gary Burtless examines the relationship among long-term trends in family composition, labor market institutions, and social policy, and their impact on poverty among children and the U.S. working-age population. He underlines the relationship between the shift in composition of households and the prevalence of poverty in the U.S. The rise of single parent families combined with the very unequal distribution of wages in the U.S. contribute substantially to high rates of poverty. These characteristics appear to be somewhat unique to the U.S. when compared to evidence from other industrialized countries. Burtless points out that a dramatic reduction in wage inequality and/or a sharp reversal in the family composition trends are required to substantially reduce poverty in the U.S. Madior Fall and Jean-Michel Hourriez apply the U.S. Bureau of Labor Statistics definition of the "working poor" to the case of France in order to make a comparative assessment of how this concept is measured on the two sides of the Atlantic. The authors identify four major groups of the working poor in France. Excluding the group of "long-term unemployed" they found no significant differences in the structure of the working poor populations in France and the U.S. However, when restricting the analysis to poor wage earners and following the approach of Klein and Rones (1989), Fall and Hourriez show that factors related to poverty in France largely differ from those identified in the U.S.

In Part 2, Neil Gilbert begins by analyzing the development of welfare policy in the U.S. He shows how client requirements and professional roles in public assistance programs were transformed as welfare policy moved in four distinct phases from income maintenance to workfare. Gilbert suggests that a normative shift in the employment expectations of mothers with young children helped pave the way to welfare reform. Michel Dollé assesses the architecture of income support policies in France. He first examines means-tested benefits (minima sociaux) and their position within the social transfer system in France. In order to conduct a meaningful comparative analysis with the U.S., Dollé suggests that one has to take into account accessibility to the social security system and to public services. Adopting a normative approach, he examines income support policies in France (including employment premium) in light of the minimum wage, poverty, labor market participation, and underemployment. Sylvie Morel examines both countries from a comparative institutionalist perspective, analyzing the transformations of the welfare systems in the U.S. and in France with regard to their workfare and insertion components—as two distinctive models of reciprocity. These two distinctive models showed some convergence in the mid-1990s. During that time, the U.S. came to emphasize expanding participation in work-oriented programs and helping families with the most severe barriers to employment; in France growing concerns about work incentives and "poverty traps" became evident and the RMI stimulated labor force attachment for social assistance recipients. Morel highlights how efforts to strengthen the reciprocal relationship between welfare recipients and the state has lessened the distance between the workfare and the insertion models, particularly with the emphasis put on the notion of responsibility and the widespread practice of contracting.

Turning to the evaluation of welfare reform in Part 3, Alan Weil reports a set of major findings on the outcome of the U.S. reforms based on the results of one of the most comprehensive efforts to date—the Urban Institute's project "Assessing New Federalism." Specifically, these findings show that more people on welfare are working than in the past, most former recipients who have left welfare are working but for low wages, states are doing more to support work but the work support system does not often meet the needs of workers, deep hardship has increased and the effects on children remain unclear. Jordan Matsudaira and Sheldon Danziger focus on the devolution of the welfare reform, examining the extent to which state policies make a difference in the implementation and the results of reform. They find a wide variation in the impact of welfare reforms on welfare participation rates, employment, earnings, and income across the states. Trying to explain these differences, Matsudaira and Danziger rank state policies according to their degree of sanctions, benefit generosity, and time limit requirements. Analyzing the results, however, they find no systematic relationship between state policies and outcomes. Christel Gilles and Antoine Parent raise several basic issues about the design of U.S. welfare reform in regard to the fundamental implications of time limits and the implicit risk of polarization. They analyze the limits of the U.S. approach to evaluating targeted programs, which among other things dampens interest and debate about other policy options that might pose more efficient solutions to the problem of poverty. In addition, they question the extent to which evaluations of welfare reform help to explain the economic behavior of recipients. Finally, Gilles and Parent explore the lessons that might be drawn for French policymakers from the experiences of welfare reform and evaluation in the U.S.

Part 4 delves into the relationship between economic growth and poverty. Christel Gilles and Antoine Parent survey the literature on the differential impact of the U.S. business cycle and welfare reforms at a national level on caseloads, employment, and poverty rates of single mothers. They note that the research reported in this literature does not provide a clear-cut answer to the question of the relative contributions of economic growth and policy reforms to changes in welfare participation, employment, and income of single mothers. Nevertheless, they call attention to the finding that the business cycle had a substantial effect on the level of caseloads. In that respect, empirical evidence suggests a high sensitivity to changes in economic conditions in the U.S.

Assessing the experience in France, Christel Gilles, Christian Loisy, and Antoine Parent measure the impact of economic growth on poverty as operationally defined by conventional poverty indicators and by an administrative indicator based on the number of RMI recipients. Their results show considerable differences depending on the poverty indicator employed. Finally, they examine some reasons for the striking differences in the degree to which caseloads are affected by economic growth in the U.S. and France.

Part 5 addresses the outcomes of policies designed to move clients from welfare to work in the U.S. and France. Douglas Besharov's data reveal that many American women have left the welfare rolls but do not work full time. He shows that a large percentage of these people live in households with other adults and that the size of these household incomes to some extent may explain how a significant number of women manage to leave welfare without working. This raises an issue of how welfare policy should treat the household income for the large number of welfare mothers cohabitating with boyfriends and relatives. Finally, Thierry Laurent and Yannick L'Horty offer a dynamic evaluation of various strategies to make work pay, as they apply to French welfare beneficiaries. Comparing the implications of temporary cash assistance to permanent public aid in promoting the objective of "moving" recipients to a stable job, they suggest that temporary measures, such as the RMI earnings disregard mechanism for a specified period, may be just as efficient and less costly than permanent measures such as income tax credits for low wage earners.

This volume offers insights into the trends in welfare reforms over the past ten years in the U.S. and in France and identifies the role played by economic conditions in the changes of the welfare systems as well as in the outcomes of these reforms. Finally, this volume highlights the weight placed on various criteria in the sociopolitical context of France and the U.S. For example, the central criteria employed for the evaluation of welfare policy in France differ from those of the U.S. and influence the evaluation of welfare reforms in these countries. In France, there is a long tradition of employment policy as compared to anti-poverty policy in the

U.S. French social policy focuses on the promotion of insertion through work: here the quality of employment is one of the major criteria applied in the evaluation of outcomes; in the U.S., priority is given to anti-poverty strategies and the absolute poverty rate stands as one of the main evaluative indicators. However, we think that the comparisons drawn in this volume are fundamentally beneficial. They not only stimulate thinking about social policies outside of the sociocultural box of participating countries, but also promote mutual learning based on the French and U.S. experiences in grappling with new designs for welfare, which aim to insure a decent level of social protection without undermining efforts to work and be independent.

Neil Gilbert
Antoine Parent

Part 1

Poverty and Work in the
United States and France

1

Social Policy for the Working Poor: U.S. Reform in a Cross-National Perspective*

Gary Burtless

Introduction

Europe and the United States face a number of common social problems. One of the most challenging is assuring that working-age families do not fall into severe hardship and achieving this in a way that does not undermine workers' incentives to care for themselves. Differences in popular attitudes and labor market institutions mean that common problems are reflected in different ways on the two sides of the Atlantic. Both Europe and the United States appear to face shrinking overall demand for workers with below-average skills. This problem is suggested by high overall unemployment in Europe and declining relative wages among the least skilled in the United States. The steep fall in the absolute and relative wages of unskilled American workers has slowed and possibly reversed in the past five years, as U.S. joblessness has reached a thirty-year low. However, both the real and the relative earnings of unskilled workers remain far below their level twenty years ago.

*This chapter was prepared for a workshop on "Welfare Reform: A Comparative Assessment of French and U.S. Experiences," sponsored by the Center for Child and Youth Policy, French Ministry of Social Affairs (DREES–MiRe), and the International Social Security Association, Berkeley, California, 21-23 February 2002. I gratefully acknowledge the research assistance of Molly Fifer. The views expressed in this chapter are solely those of the author and do not represent the views of the Brookings Institution, DREES–MiRe, the Center for Child and Youth Policy, or the International Social Security Association.

Low wages and long spells of joblessness can push affected workers and their children into poverty. Sinking wages can force increased numbers of marginal workers below the poverty line, even if they work on a full-time schedule. Disappearing employment opportunities can also depress family incomes. Young and middle-aged workers who are intermittently employed in temporary jobs or who are unable to find any employment at all can fall into poverty unless the state or their extended family provides an income cushion for the jobless worker to fall back on. Joblessness and intermittent employment are forms of marginalization that have become prevalent in Europe, especially among young workers who have not yet become established in the job market.

This chapter examines the relationship between trends in family composition, labor market institutions, social policy, and their impact on poverty among children and the working-age population. I discuss the relationship between social developments in the United States and those in Europe, especially with respect to developments that have changed the composition of households and hurt the employment prospects available to young and other unskilled workers. I also examine public policies established to address the problem of working-age poverty, including new policies to reduce the problem of long-term public dependency. Some of these policies in the United States are designed to push able-bodied adults into the work force by making joblessness less appealing, even though declining market wages have made employment less attractive. Others are designed to boost family incomes or child well-being without imposing any extra burdens on employers who give jobs to low-skill breadwinners.

The plan of the chapter is as follows. The first section examines the impact of household compositional shifts on the prevalence of poverty in the United States. The next section analyzes the effects of labor market structure and labor market trends on poverty among children and in the working-age population. The third section considers the impact of public tax and transfer policies on the level and distribution of hardship. In each of the first three sections, the effects of U.S. trends and policies are evaluated in light of evidence from other industrialized countries, especially France and the United Kingdom. Many of the social and economic trends that have contributed to rising child poverty in the United States are evident to some degree in other industrial countries. But no other rich country suffers from such a high rate of hardship among children. The comparison of the United States with leading countries in Europe sheds light on the distinctive features of U.S. social and political life that contribute to high rates of poverty among American children and their parents. The next section examines recent reforms in U.S. social assistance policy and considers their impact on poverty and employment patterns in the affected population. The chapter concludes with a brief summary.

Shifts in Family Composition

U.S. assistance policy for the working-age population is aimed at reducing severe financial, nutritional, and medical deprivation among children and physically and mentally handicapped adults. Working-age adults who are neither disabled nor caretakers of dependent children do not receive substantial support under the system. Benefit levels under the current system are not generous. They are far too low to eliminate poverty among the main target populations—indigent children and disabled adults.

The focus of this chapter is on the system that aids working-age families containing children. In comparison with assistance systems in other rich countries, the American system places exceptional reliance on family self-support and breadwinner earnings to remove children from poverty. This approach to poverty alleviation has not been conspicuously successful in holding down indigence among children (see figure 1.1). Under the nation's official poverty measure, slightly more than 16 percent of children under age 18 were classified as poor in 2000, a slightly larger percentage than was poor in the early 1970s and a greater prevalence of poverty than was found in other age groups. The official standard for measuring U.S. poverty has important defects (Burtless

Figure 1.1
Percentage of U.S. Children Who Are Poor under Official and Alternative Poverty Thresholds, 1960-2000

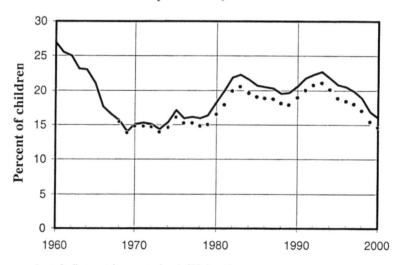

Annual adjustment in poverty threshold is based on --

● ● ● CPI-U-XI   ——— CPI-U

Source: U.S. Census Bureau.

and Siegel, forthcoming). Many experts are harshly critical of the U.S. poverty thresholds and the present method used to calculate who is poor. Most informed observers would agree, however, that child poverty is a more serious problem in the United States than it is in other industrialized countries, regardless of the exact method used to calculate poverty.

The high prevalence of child poverty is the result of three distinctive features of the American environment. An exceptionally large percentage of U.S. children live with only one rather than both of their parents. One-parent families find it more difficult than two-parent families to earn high wages, because it is hard for a single parent to combine child rearing with long hours on a job. In addition, many youngsters, even in families containing two parents, are maintained by a working parent who has few job skills. A sizeable percentage of low-skill U.S. parents earn wages below the poverty threshold, even if they work year-round on a full-time schedule. In comparison with other industrialized countries, the United States has a very unequal distribution of wages, increasing the percentage of low-skill parents who earn extremely low annual incomes. Finally, as just noted, government programs in the United States offer parsimonious transfers to working-age families with low incomes. Virtually all countries in northern Europe provide more generous benefits to working and non-working adults who support child dependents.

A child in a single-parent family faces an elevated risk of being poor. In March 2001 about 52 million U.S. children under age 18 were members of married-couple families. Just 8 percent of these children were members of families with an income below the official poverty thresholds. In the same month, 15.4 million youngsters were being raised in families headed by a

Figure 1.2
Distribution of Related Children under Age 18, by Family Type, March 2001

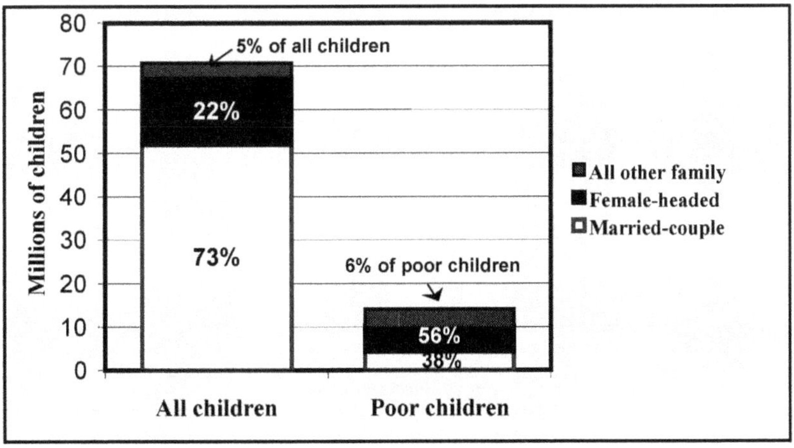

woman without a spouse in the home. Almost 40 percent of these children were members of families with incomes below the poverty line. Figure 1.2 shows the distribution of American children across three main types of families. Slightly less than three-quarters of children live in families maintained by a married couple. More than one-fifth are members of families maintained by a woman who does not live with a spouse. Five percent of youngsters are members of all other types of families, including families maintained by a man who does not live with a spouse.

The living arrangements of poor children are strikingly different from those of children in general. Well over half of poor children are members of families maintained by women who do not live with a marriage partner. Fewer than four poor children in ten live in married-couple families. Empirical research also suggests that poor children in married-couple families suffer less severe financial hardship and are likely to escape poverty more easily than poor youngsters in lone-parent families.

Figure 1.3 shows the combined effects of a family head's age and marital status on the family's poverty status. All of the families included in the tabulations contain at least one related child under age 18. Among married-couple families, just 6 percent are poor. The poverty rate among single-mother families is more than five times higher, or 33 percent. The impact of a parent's age on his or her capacity to earn money is straightforward. Older parents command higher wages in the labor market and so are more likely to earn enough money to keep their families from falling into poverty. The effect of a family head's age on the risk of being poor is striking. More than half of all 18-24

Figure 1.3
Poverty Rate of Families with Children, by Type of Family
and Age of Family Head, 2000

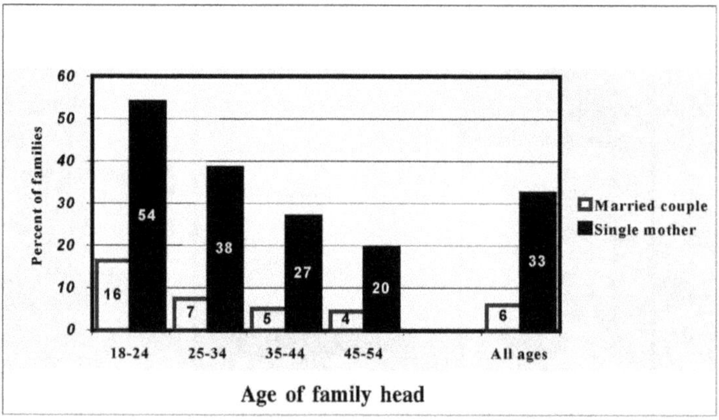

Source: U.S. Census Bureau.

year-old female heads are poor, whereas only one in five female heads between the ages of 45 and 54 is poor. Although age also has a sizeable effect on the poverty status of married-couple families, the prevalence of poverty among two-parent families is much lower at every age than it is among single-mother families. Note, for example, that the prevalence of poverty among 45-54 year-old single female heads is greater than it is among 18-24 year-old married couples. Single mothers who are near the peak of their work careers face a higher risk of being poor than married-couple parents who have just entered the work force.

Single-parent families are not all created equal. Some one-parent families form as the result of an out-of-wedlock birth to a mother who has never been married. Others are created as the result of a divorce or separation, which removes one parent from the household. In a small number of cases, a parent dies. Figure 1.4 shows the distribution of marital status among the custodial parents of children who received benefits under Aid to Families with Dependent Children (AFDC) in 1996. Children who collect benefits under AFDC and its successor program, Temporary Assistance for Needy Families (TANF), are among the most severely disadvantaged in the United States. Most AFDC recipients in 1996 were members of families headed by a never-married parent (almost always a mother). One-quarter of children were cared for by a parent who was separated or divorced, while a tiny number were in the care of a widowed parent. A small percentage of AFDC children were members of families containing two married parents. These families were eligible to receive benefits if one of the married parents was unable to provide support to the family as a result of incapacity or prolonged unemployment. Clearly, however,

Figure 1.4
Marital Status of Parents of AFDC Children, 1996*

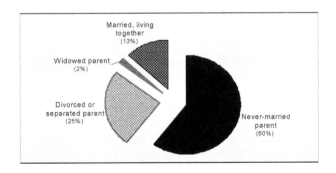

*Percent of all children receiving AFDC who live with parent.
Source: Committee on Ways and Means, *2000 Green Book.*

two-parent families do not constitute a large fraction of the families receiving support from the nation's main cash assistance program for children. The overwhelming majority of children receiving cash public aid are cared for by never-married, separated, or divorced mothers.

The prevalence of poverty among single-mother families is high. In light of this fact, the shift in American living arrangements toward single-parent households and away from two-parent families has noticeably increased the fraction of youngsters at risk of becoming poor. Figure 1.5 shows the long-term trend in living arrangements of U.S. children. In 1960, just 8 percent of children were reared in mother-only families; 88 percent were members of married-couple families. By 2000, 22 percent of children were members of mother-only families; the percentage of children in two-parent families had fallen to 69 percent.[1] Because the risk of being poor is five times higher for children in one-parent families than for children in married-couple families, the shift in family composition might account for as much as a quarter of the U.S. child poverty rate in 2000.

Figure 1.5
Living Arrangements of U.S. Children, 1960-2000

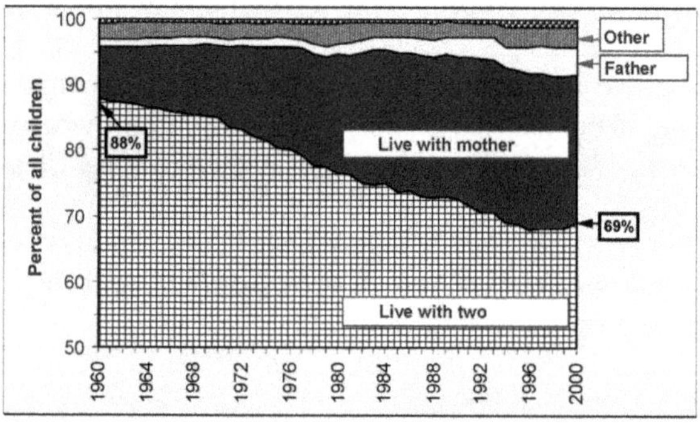

Source: U.S. Census Bureau.

The growth in single-parent families is not unique to the United States, of course. Other industrialized countries have experienced a similar trend as divorce and separation have become more common and births outside of marriage have accounted for a larger proportion of births. Table 1.1 shows living arrangements of children under age 16 in three rich countries, France, the United Kingdom, and the United States. Bruno Jeandidier and Etienne Albiser (2001) performed the tabulations using comparable micro-census files for the years 1993 or 1994. The estimates for France and the United Kingdom and one set of estimates for the United States are taken directly from Jeandidier and Albiser (2001). These tabulations suggest that children in one-parent families constitute 9 percent of all French children, 21 percent of British children, and 28 percent of U.S. children under age 15. In all three countries, most children reared in one-parent families are in families that are maintained by separated, divorced, or never-married mothers.

Table 1.1
Living Arrangements of Children under Age 16 in France,
the United Kingdom, and the United States, 1993-1994

Percent of all children age 15 and younger

Family type / Marital status	France (1994)	United Kingdom (1993)	United States (1994a)	United States (1994b)
Two-parent family	91	79	72	76
Married parents	81	75	72	72
Cohabiting partners	10	4	N.A.	4
One-parent family	9	21	28	24
Mother-only family	8	19	24	21
Father-only family	1	2	4	3

/a/ Jeandidier and Albiser (2001), Tables A2-1 and A2-2.
/b/ Author's estimates based on Jeandidier and Albiser (2001) and U.S. Census Bureau tabulations.
N.A. Not available.
Source: Authors' estimates and Jeandidier and Albiser (2001), Tables A2-1 and A2-2.

The published tabulations imply that parents in two-parent families have a distinctive marriage pattern in the United States. All U.S. children in two-parent families are reported to reside with married parents, whereas a modest percentage of French and British youngsters in two-parent families live with two unmarried parents. This seems inconsistent with U.S. Census Bureau analysis of unmarried-couple families containing children. According to Census Bureau estimates, households with unmarried, unrelated adults of the opposite sex which contain related children represent about 5 percent of the number of married-couple households with related children. It is possible that some of these households were misclassified to indicate that only a single parent was present, whereas in fact the family contained two unmarried parents. The column labeled 1994b represents my attempt to adjust the Jeandidier and Albiser (2001) estimates to reflect the presence of unmarried couple families in the United States. Even with this adjustment, however, the United States has the smallest proportion of children in two-parent families and the largest fraction in single-parent families. The gap between the United States and France is especially striking.[2] The proportion of American children in one-parent families exceeds the proportion of French children in such families by 15 percent to 19 percent.

Not surprisingly, France has the lowest child poverty rate of the three countries considered in Table 1.1, while the United States has the highest rate. Figure 1.6 shows the overall poverty rate and child poverty rate in France, the United Kingdom, and the United States during the mid-1990s. The calculations were performed using the Luxembourg Income Study (LIS), which contains micro-census data files for twenty-five nations (Smeeding, Burtless, and Rainwater, 2002). The definition does not correspond to the official U.S. poverty definition. We have defined the poverty threshold in each country as one-half of the median household-size-adjusted income in the country. Members of households with disposable cash and near-cash incomes below this threshold are counted as poor.[3]

Figure 1.6
Total and Child Poverty Rates in France, the United Kingdom,
and the United States (mid-1990s)

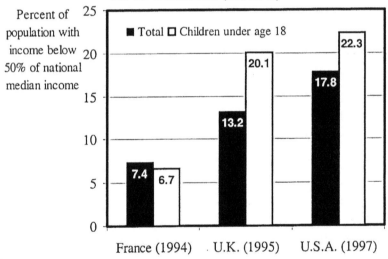

Source: Smeeding, Rainwater, and Burtless (2002).

Child poverty is substantially higher than overall poverty in both the United States and the United Kingdom; the child poverty rate is slightly lower than the overall poverty rate in France. The gap between the U.S. and French child poverty rates is particularly striking. Compared with a French child under the age of 18, an American child faces three times the risk of being poor. In part, the difference can be explained by differences in the living arrangements of French and American children, because children in one-parent families face a higher risk of poverty in both countries than children in two-parent families. But even with a generous estimate of the impact of family composition differences, the child poverty gap between the two countries would remain large.

Poverty and the Job Market

Most children in industrialized countries are reared in families headed by a working-age adult. In the absence of government transfers, the children in these families will be poor if an adult caretaker does not earn enough to comfortably support a family containing children. One reason that child poverty rates in the United States are so high is that many American parents do not have enough skills to hold jobs that remove their families from poverty. The very unequal distribution of wages in the United States means that a large fraction of these unskilled parents will be at risk of earning poverty-level wages.

Adults who receive public assistance (or who are at high risk of receiving aid) typically suffer the most severe disadvantage in the job market. Most adult assistance recipients are women who have limited schooling and very low scores on standardized aptitude and achievement tests. Even if these women were not responsible for the care of children, they would face serious problems finding and keeping well-paid jobs. Child care responsibilities make their employment problems even more formidable.

The weak labor market preparation of most assistance recipients, especially those who are most dependent on welfare, is obvious from simple tabulations of their work experience, educational attainment, and standardized test scores. Among women in their mid-20s who steadily collected AFDC in the 1980s and 1990s, fewer than half had completed high school. Less than one out of eight had received any schooling beyond high school. More than 70 percent of the most dependent 25-year-olds obtained a score on a standardized test that placed them in the bottom quarter of all test-takers in their age group.

The employment prospects of American women with poor educational credentials have never been bright, even in tight labor markets. In 1979, a woman who had not completed high school could expect to earn about $8.60 per hour (see figure 1.7). Many single mothers could not earn a wage this high, because child care responsibilities often prevented them from working full time, forcing them to accept part-time jobs, where wages are lower. Since the late 1970s, the job prospects of poorly educated women have worsened. Between 1979 and 1989, for example, the average hourly wage received by female high school dropouts fell 11 percent. Between 1989 and 1999, wages earned by women who failed to complete high school fell another 3 percent (see bottom panel of figure 1.7). The hourly wages of men without a high school diploma have fallen even more dramatically, and the earnings of men who have not received any education beyond high school have also shrunk. Even if the

Figure 1.7
Wage Trends

Average Hourly Earnings by Educational Attainment and Sex, 1973-1999

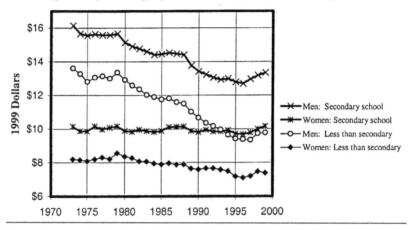

Source: Economic Policy Institute tabulations of BLS hourly earnings data.

Average Hourly Earnings by Educational Attainment and Sex, 1973-1999

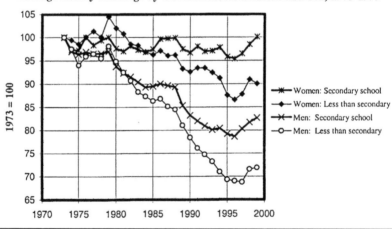

Source: Economic Policy Institute tabulations of BLS hourly earnings data.

proportion of children in one-parent families had remained unchanged, these trends in the market wages of Americans with limited education would have pushed many more parents and their children into poverty.

One way to assess the job prospects of the most severely disadvantaged parents is to examine the job qualifications and actual work experience of adults who collect public assistance under the AFDC and TANF programs. The

U.S. Department of Health and Human Services (HHS) periodically publishes information about the characteristics, including the work behavior of AFDC and TANF recipients using data obtained from its surveys of state assistance programs. Data from these surveys suggest that most recipients face daunting challenges to finding and keeping well-paid jobs. Table 1.2 presents information from the Department's surveys from 1979 to 1999. The first four rows in the table show the age distribution of children collecting AFDC and TANF.

Table 1.2
Characteristics of the AFDC/TANF Caseload, 1979-1999
Percent of persons or families

	Year			
	1979	1986	1994	1999
Ages of children				
Under 3	18.9	21.9	23.8	19.8
3 to 5	17.5	21.1	22.1	19.0
6 to 11	33.0	32.4	31.7	36.3
12 and over	29.8	25.3	22.2	24.9
Number of adults in family /a/				
None	14.9	9.6	17.3	29.1
One	78.9	81.2	74.4	66.3
Two or more	14.9	9.6	17.3	4.6
Education of mother or other adult				
8th grade or less /b/	18.2	11.9	7.4	17.5
1-3 years of secondary school /c/		39.8	35.5	32.6 31.5
4 years of secondary school /d/	36.0	42.9	44.6	51.1
Some college	5.2	8.4	14.3	N.A.
College graduate	0.8	1.2	0.9	N.A.
Mother's employment status				
Full-time job /e/	8.7	1.6	3.3	27.6
Part-time job /e/	5.4	4.2	4.6	
Families with reported earnings	12.8	7.5	8.9	25.2

Notes:
N.A. Not available.
/a/ Adults included in family unit that is receiving assistance payments. Data are for 1988 rather than 1986.
/b/ Ninth grade or less in 1999.
/c/ Two or three years of secondary school in 1999.
/d/ At least four years of secondary school in 1999.
/e/ No data in 1999 on percentage of employment that is full- or part-time. The 1999 estimate refers to the percentage of all assisted adults (rather than mothers) who are employed.
Source: U.S. House of Representatives, Committee on Ways and Means, *1996 Green Book*, pp. 473-74, and *2000 Green Book*, Table 7-27; and U.S. DHHS, Administration for Children and Families, *Characteristics and Financial Circumstances of TANF Recipients, FY 1999*.

About 40 percent of the families receiving TANF have children younger than age 6, and 20 percent have a child under age 3. Single parents, whether married or unmarried, who rear very young children ordinarily find it much harder to work than do women who are childless or whose children are 6 years old or older.

The educational attainment of assistance recipients is abysmally low. The HHS survey shows that nearly half of TANF adult recipients had failed to complete high school in 1999. In comparison, only 12 percent of all 25-44 year-old Americans had not completed high school by that year. In 1994, just 1 percent of AFDC mothers had graduated from college. In that same year, nearly 25 percent of all 25-44 year-old adults had obtained a college degree. Part of the discrepancy in educational attainment can be explained by the youth of many adult public aid recipients. About 6 percent of adult recipients are under age 20, and 40 percent are between 20 and 29. Even so, the percentage of AFDC and TANF mothers with some college education is far below the college completion rate of the population at large.

Education has a powerful effect on Americans' capacity to earn wages high enough to escape poverty. Figure 1.8 shows the relation between educational attainment and adult women's poverty status in 2000. To make the tabulations meaningful, I have restricted the sample to women in narrow age groups, those who are between 25 and 34 years old and those who are between 35 and 54 years old. Women in these age groups have substantially completed their schooling, so few of them are pushed into poverty as a result of combining

Figure 1.8

Poverty Rates among Adult women, by Age and Educational Attainment, 2000

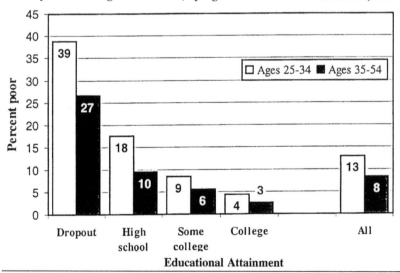

Source: U.S. Census Bureau.

schooling with job holding. The impact of schooling attainment on poverty status is enormous. Almost 40 percent of 25-34 year-old high school dropouts are poor compared with just 4 percent of 25-34 year-old women who have a four-year college degree and 9 percent of women who have obtained a two-year college degree. Among women between the ages of 35 and 54 the impact of schooling attainment is nearly as large. The percentage of high school dropouts who are poor is nine times the percentage of college graduates who are poor.

The gap in poverty rates between highly educated and poorly educated women is only partly the result of differences in the potential wage incomes of the two groups. Highly educated women have fewer children and are more likely to be married and living with a spouse when they are raising children. Both differences will tend to reduce the percentage of highly educated women who have family incomes below the poverty line. In addition, highly educated women are likely to marry men who have similar educational attainment and thus are likely to earn high wages, too. But even among single mothers who are raising children alone, those who have better educational credentials are more likely to earn incomes above the poverty threshold than women who have limited schooling.

Even taking into account their low educational attainment, American adults who receive cash public assistance have unusually meager job-market skills. One source of information about the job qualifications of welfare recipients is the National Longitudinal Survey of Youth (NLSY). The NLSY is an annual survey of young people who were first interviewed in 1979, when respondents were between 14 and 22 years old. Each year, the survey collects information on educational attainment, employment, and reliance on welfare. About a year after they entered the sample, most respondents completed a cognitive test known as the Armed Forces Qualification Test (or AFQT), which is used to determine which applicants are eligible to enlist in the U.S. military. The composite AFQT score is considered a reliable indicator of test takers' general problem-solving ability.

Information about young women's educational attainment and aptitude scores derived from the annual NLSY survey confirms that women collecting public assistance had serious educational deficiencies in the 1980s. Table 1.3 shows the educational attainments and aptitude scores of three groups of women, defined by their use of AFDC in the twelve months before they were interviewed at age 25. The least dependent group of 25-year-olds, comprising 92 percent of the sample, received no AFDC during those twelve months. The moderately dependent group, comprising 3 percent of the sample, received benefits during at least one but less than twelve months of the previous year. The most dependent 5 percent received benefits in all twelve months. Whereas only 14 percent of the women who did not rely on AFDC had failed to complete high school by age 25, among those who were most dependent on AFDC the comparable figure was 52 percent. AFDC recipients also performed very poorly on the standardized ability test. In the most dependent category, 72 percent of the women obtained a score on the AFQT placing them in the bottom quarter of all test takers. Only 12 percent placed in the top half of test takers. Women who are moderately dependent on AFDC achieved better test scores, but their performance on the test was well below the national norm. Only 16 percent obtained a score placing them in the top half of test takers.

Table 1.3
Educational Attainment and Ability Scores of 25-Year-Old Women,
by AFDC Status (Mid-1980s)

Percent

	Number of months received AFDC			All
	12	1 - 11	None	Women
Educational attainment by age 24				
Less than 4 years high school	52	44	14	17
4 years high school	35	48	40	39
1-3 years college	12	8	24	23
4 or more years college	0	0	22	21
Total	100	100	100	100
Composite score on AFQT				
Bottom quartile	72	52	22	26
2nd quartile	17	33	26	25
3rd quartile	9	14	26	25
Top quartile	3	2	25	24
Total	100	100	100	100

Source: Author's tabulations of National Longitudinal Survey of Youth (1979-1991).

A more recent examination of the basic skills of assistance recipients was performed by analysts at the Public Policy Institute of California (Johnson and Tafoya, 1999). Researchers obtained income, demographic, and test-score data for 26,000 adult Americans who participated in the 1992 National Adult Literacy Survey (NALS). They classified respondents into two main groups, adults who received and who did not receive cash public assistance. Among respondents who received public aid, the researchers also identified adults who were most dependent on public aid, defined to include all aid recipients who failed to work at all during the previous twelve months. Table 1.4 shows the distribution of basic skill scores obtained by the different groups of respondents. Fifty-seven percent of assistance recipients obtained low or very low scores on the NALS compared with just 42 percent of adults who did not receive any public aid. The contrast between aid recipients and non-recipients who hold a full-time job is even more significant. Less than one-third of non-recipients who hold a full-time job received a low or very low test score. More depressing still are the basic skill scores obtained by public assistance recipients who do not work. One-half of these respondents obtained a very low score and one-third received a low score. Just 17 percent of these respondents received a moderate or above-average score on the NALS test. In contrast, 70 percent of full-time workers among the non-recipients of public aid received a moderate or high score on the test of basic skills. Low ability indicated by poor performance on standardized tests greatly restricts the kinds of jobs that adults can expect to obtain. Compared with many northwestern European countries, although not with the United Kingdom, the United States has a somewhat elevated proportion of adults who perform poorly on basic skill tests, such as the NALS (OECD 2001: 57). However, the difference in basic skill distributions is far too small to account for the much higher poverty rates among American children and working-age adults.

One encouraging trend in table 1.2 is the recent surge in employment among adults who collect cash assistance payments. Whereas just 8 percent or 9 percent of AFDC families reported receiving any wage earnings in 1986-1994, almost one-quarter of adult recipients reported wage earnings in 1999. This

Table 1.4
Distribution of Basic Skill Test Scores Among U.S. Adults,
by Receipt of Public Assistance (1992)

Percent

Public assistance and work status	Percent of test-takers in skill category				Total
	Very low	Low	Moderate	High or very high	
Adults who do not receive public aid	17	27	36	20	100
Full-time workers who do not receive aid	10	20	39	31	100
Adults who receive public aid	24	33	32	11	100
Non-workers who receive public aid	50	33	15	2	100

Note: Sample consists of 26,091 adults who participated in the National Adult Literacy Survey in 1992. The sample was restricted to 16-55 year-old adults who were not enrolled in high school. Respondents who said they received AFDC, public assistance, or public welfare in the previous 12 months were classified as public aid recipients.
Source: Johnson and Tafoya, *The Basic Skills of Welfare Recipients* (1999), p. 27.

increase was mainly spurred by work-oriented public assistance reforms (see below), but it is partly the result of the changing character of adults who are enrolled in cash public assistance. Tough new policies require adults to work or participate in work-oriented projects, and these requirements have pushed many adults off the cash public assistance rolls. A smaller percentage of public assistance families includes an adult member in the family unit that receives assistance. A higher fraction of cases includes only children in the family covered by the assistance payment. The percentage of cash assistance families receiving benefits only for children increased from 10 percent in 1988 and 17 percent in 1994 to 29 percent of assisted families in 1999. Many of the excluded adults are not working and hence are not complying with the tough work requirements of the reformed system. As a penalty for noncompliance, many adults have been removed from the assisted family unit.

Although there is no definitive study of the labor market experience of single mothers after they enter the cash public assistance rolls, most studies show that a substantial minority of assisted mothers can only become employed after very lengthy periods of intensive job search, even when they are enrolled in special training or job placement programs. Friedlander and Burtless (1995) examined the long-term effects of four welfare-to-work experiments conducted during the 1980s. In the fifth year after women were enrolled in these experiments, the employment rate averaged 38 percent among women who had been enrolled in the experimental welfare-to-work programs and 36 percent among women who had been enrolled in the control group.[4] Among women enrolled in a six-county welfare-to-work experiment in California, only 40 percent held jobs at any time during the third year after they were enrolled in the work-oriented program. Among women in the control group, who were not eligible for special employment services, only 34 percent held a job sometime during the third year after the experiment began (Riccio et al., 1994). Employment rates were even more dismal in Alameda and Los Angeles counties, where enrollment in experimental work and training programs was offered mainly to women who had collected cash public assistance steadily for several years. The findings from these experiments suggest that extraordinary efforts are needed to boost the employment rates of single mothers who collect public assistance. For purposes of comparison, about 70 percent of American women who had children under age 18 were employed in March 2000.

Although low-skill working-age Americans with child dependents have low employment rates when compared with other American adults, their jobholding rates do not seem low when compared with those of unskilled workers in the rest of the industrialized world. Tabulations of OECD labor force data suggest that the United States has an above-average percentage of working-age adults in employment (see figure 1.9). Part of the U.S. employment advantage is due to comparatively high rates of job-holding among people who are between 55 and 64 years old, few of whom are responsible for rearing children.

The United States also has a higher employment rate among people between 15 and 24 than most EU member countries, including France. Among adults in families containing children, however, France may be more successful than the United States in ensuring that at least one adult in the family is employed.

Figure 1.9
Employment-to-Population Ratio in France, U.K., and U.S.,
by Age Group, 1996

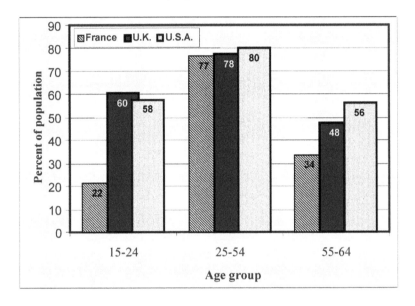

Source: Salverda et al. (2001), p.95.

Figure 1.10 shows non-employment rates among working-age families in France, the United Kingdom, and the United States in 1996. Among all working-age families, including both those with and those without children under 18, the United States has by far the lowest rate of non-employment. Among one-parent and two-parent families containing children, however, the French and American non-employment rates are essentially identical, and they are substantially below non-employment rates in the United Kingdom. Because a larger percentage of American children are members of one-parent families, however, the overall rate of joblessness among families containing children was higher in the United States than France. America's large advantage in achieving high employment rates in 1996 was concentrated among adult households that did not include dependent children under 18.

As noted above, the distribution of earnings among working adults is less equal in the United States than it is in other industrialized countries, especially

Figure 1.10
Rate of Non-Employment among Working-Age Families, 1996

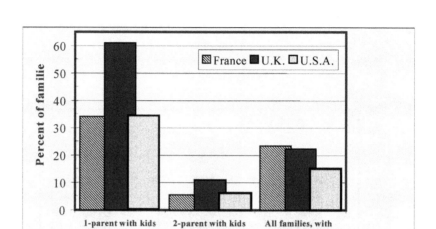

Source: OECD Social Indicators (2001), p.43.

countries such as France, Germany, and the Scandinavian countries, which have strong national labor unions and powerful institutions that tend to boost the wages of the lowest paid. Not surprisingly, a larger percentage of U.S. employment consists of jobs that offer very low wages. The wide inequality of wages is counterbalanced to some extent by the wider availability of jobs in the United States. Wiemer Salverda and his colleagues at the European Low-Wage Employment Network have tried to summarize the combined effects of these two offsetting factors (Salverda et al., 2001). Some of the results of their tabulations are displayed in table 1.5, which shows the distribution of employment and of earned income in France, the United Kingdom, and the United States in 1996. The top panel in the table shows the employment-to-population rate and the distribution of earnings among 15-64 year-old residents of the three countries, separately by gender. French employment rates are substantially below those in the other two countries, while the U.S. rates are somewhat higher than those in the United Kingdom.

The three columns to the right show the percentages of 15-64 year-olds who earn low, average, and high wages. "Low" wages are defined as those that are less than two-thirds of the median wage; "high" wages are more than 50 percent above the median wage; and wages in between those two thresholds are classified as "average" wages. French wages are the most equal, and American wages are the least equal. Not surprisingly, France has the smallest per-

Table 1.5
Employment-Population Rates and Prevalence of Low and
High Earnings by Gender and Age Groups in France,
the United Kingdom, and the United States, 1996

Percent

	Percent of age/gender group employed	Percent of adult population in earnings category		
		Earn < 2/3 x Median wage	Earn near Median wage	Earn > 1.5 x Median wage
Men ages 15-64				
France	*66*	*4*	**49**	*14*
U.K.	75	11	*40*	24
U.S.A.	**81**	**16**	38	**27**
Women ages 15-64				
France	*51*	*6*	**38**	*8*
U.K.	62	21	*31*	11
U.S.A.	**67**	**21**	34	**13**
Both sexes ages 15-24				
France	*22*	*9*	*13*	*0*
U.K.	**60**	34	**25**	1
U.S.A.	58	**36**	20	**2**
Both sexes ages 25-54				
France	*77*	*7*	**61**	*9*
U.K.	78	13	43	22
U.S.A.	**80**	**14**	42	**24**
Both sexes ages 55-64				
France	*34*	*2*	*23*	*9*
U.K.	48	9	24	15
U.S.A.	**56**	**14**	**26**	**16**

Note: Figures in **bold** indicate that the designated number is the highest for the category among the three countries that are compared. Figures in *italics* indicate that the designated number is smallest in the category.
Source: Salverda et al. (2001), pp. 90 and 95

centage of adults working in jobs that pay less than two-thirds of the median wage, while the United States has the largest percentage of low-pay workers. Just 4 percent of French males hold jobs that pay less than two-thirds of the French median wage. In comparison, 16 percent of American males are employed in jobs that pay less than two-thirds of the U.S. median wage. France has the highest proportion of people who work in jobs where their earnings are close to the median wage, while the United States has the smallest percentage of adults who fall into that category.

The United States has one important advantage over France and Britain, however. It has the highest percentage of adults who are employed in high wage jobs. The combined percentage of Americans in average- and high-pay jobs is greater than the combined percentage of French adults who hold average- and high-wage jobs. To be sure, a larger percentage of American than of French adults hold jobs that pay less than two-thirds of the median wage. However, a much smaller percentage of American adults are jobless. The gap between the prevalence in low-pay jobs between the United States and France is smaller than the gap between the United States and France in the percentage of jobless adults. One interpretation of this comparison is that many adults who are jobless in France would hold low-pay jobs in the United States; many adults who are employed in low-pay jobs in the United States would be jobless in France.

The lower panel of table 1.5 shows the employment-to-population ratio and the prevalence of low, average, and high wages in three different age groups. One striking feature of this tabulation is the three-country comparison of employment and earnings distributions among 25-54 year-old people. The employment gap among the three countries is very small. The U.S.-France employment difference is just 3 percent in the 25-54 year-old population. In this age group, there are fewer people who are jobless or who earn low wages in France than there are in the United States. Twenty percent of Americans are without jobs, and 14 percent hold jobs that pay less than two-thirds of the median U.S. wage. Twenty-three percent of French adults in this age range are jobless, but just 7 percent work in jobs that pay less than two-thirds of the median wage. Because most parents are between 25 and 54, the equitable distribution of average-wage employment among this age group is important in assuring that most children are kept out of poverty.

Differences in fertility patterns among the three countries also represent an advantage for French youngsters. Fewer French births occur to very young women and a much greater fraction occurs among women age 25 and older than is the case in the United Kingdom and the United States (see figure 1.11). Compared with French women of the same age, American women between 15 and 19 are more than eight times as likely to give birth. Among women aged 20-24 years old, the U.S. birth rate is more than twice the rate in France and 40 percent above the rate in Britain. At ages above 24 the French birth rate is higher than that in either the United States or the United Kingdom. It is also likely that the fathers of French children are older than fathers in Britain or the United States. Since older parents can earn higher wages than parents between 16 and 24, this is likely to be a major advantage for maintaining a low child poverty rate.

Figure 1.11
Age-Specific Fertility Rates in France, the United Kingdom,
and the United States, 1997-2000

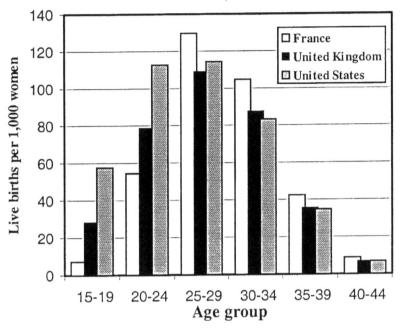

Source: U.S. Census Bureau, International Data Base.

Different birth patterns in the three countries can also account for the fact that higher employment rates in the United States and the United Kingdom do not translate into lower child poverty rates. The tabulations in table 1.5 imply that the biggest employment advantage in the United States compared with France occurs among 15-24 year-olds. However, the fertility statistics of the two countries suggest that many fewer French 15-24 year-olds are parents who support dependent children. The low French employment rate in this age group is thus unlikely to cause much hardship for most families that have dependent children. A very high proportion of French men and women between ages 25 and 54 hold jobs that pay average or above-average wages. If French joblessness is concentrated among secondary family earners and among family heads who do not support children, the low adult employment rate in France may not lead to widespread hardship among families containing children. In contrast, the high joblessness and wide prevalence of low-pay jobs among 15-24 year-olds in Britain and the United States can contribute substantially to high child poverty if many of the jobless and low-pay young adults are the parents of dependent children.

The Impact of Public Policy

All industrial countries redistribute income through government programs to benefit low-income children and adults in working-age families. Countries differ significantly in the amount they redistribute and the conditions under which they make such transfers available. The United States redistributes a smaller fraction of national income through income redistribution programs than other industrialized countries. In this respect, it is particularly parsimonious in the transfers it provides to working-age families. Table 1.6 shows poverty rates and public transfers as a percentage of national income in fifteen

Table 1.6
Poverty Rates and Public Redistribution in Fifteen Industrialized Countries, 1990s Percent

				Percent of GDP spent on:	
	Poverty rate (% of population)			Total	Non-aged Country
Year	All persons		Children	Transfers /a/	Transfers /a/
Sweden	1995	6.5	2.6	22.0	13.8
Norway	1995	6.9	3.9	15.9	10.1
Finland	1995	5.0	4.1	23.3	15.3
Belgium	1992	5.5	4.4	19.3	12.1
Denmark	1992	7.1	4.8	18.9	12.4
Austria	1992	6.7	5.9	18.6	8.9
France	1994	7.4	6.7	21.0	10.7
Netherlands	1994	7.9	7.9	21.0	14.1
Germany	1994	7.5	10.6	18.4	8.4
Spain	1990	10.4	12.8	14.1	6.8
Australia	1994	6.7	15.0	9.3	6.2
Canada	1994	11.4	15.3	12.5	8.0
Italy	1995	13.9	18.9	18.0	7.0
U.K.	1995	13.2	20.1	16.0	9.4
U.S.A.	1997	17.8	22.3	9.2	3.7

Note: Persons are classified as poor if their household-size-adjusted disposable cash and near cash income is less than 50 percent of median national income.
/a/ "Transfers" include cash and non-cash social expenditures. This excludes spending on health, education, and social services, but includes outlays on all forms of cash benefits and near-cash housing subsidies, active labor market program income subsidies, and other contingent cash and other near-cash benefits. "Non-aged transfers" include only those accruing to households with a head under age 65.
Source: OECD (2001) and Smeeding, Rainwater, and Burtless (2002).

OECD countries that provide micro-census data to the Luxembourg Income Study. In this table as in figure 1.6, a person is classified as poor if he or she is a member of a household with a household-size-adjusted income below 50 percent of national median income. Countries are ranked by the rate of child poverty, with the low-poverty-rate countries at the top of the table. The Scandinavian countries have the lowest child poverty rates, while the United Kingdom and the United States have the highest. France ranks somewhere in the middle of the fifteen countries, with a higher child poverty rate than Scandinavia but a lower rate than the other large EU-member countries.

The two right-hand columns in table 1.6 show OECD estimates of each country's spending on cash and near-cash social transfers, measured as a percentage of national GDP. One column shows total transfer spending, including outlays on pensions for the aged, while the second column contains estimates of the transfer spending that is focused on the non-aged population, including unemployment insurance and social assistance payments, food stamps, and housing subsidies. Obviously, the second category of transfers is more relevant in determining the well-being of children. There is a strong negative correlation between a nation's child poverty rate and the percentage of its national income that is transferred to the non-aged population. This correlation is highlighted in figure 1.12, which displays a scatter plot of child poverty rates and social spending levels in the fifteen OECD countries. Of course,

Figure 1.12
Relation between Child Poverty Rate and Public Spending on Transfers to the Non-Aged Population, 1990s

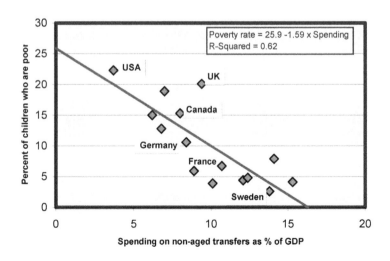

a strong inverse correlation between two variables does not confirm the existence of a causal link between the two.

Researchers working with the Luxembourg Income Study data set have attempted to measure directly the impact of taxes and state-provided transfer benefits on the poverty status of children and adults in OECD countries. One approach is to calculate poverty rates using the before-tax market incomes received by households and then calculate poverty rates using households' after-tax and after-transfer incomes. The first poverty calculation shows what percentage of a nation's population would be poor if it received only the investment and employment income (including employer-sponsored pensions) provided by the market. The second calculation shows the poverty rate as it is commonly measured. The difference between the two estimates of poverty offers an estimate of the direct impact of state taxes and transfers on household well-being, ignoring the possible effects of taxes and transfers on households' market incomes.

Figure 1.13 shows these two sets of calculations for three classes of people in France, the United Kingdom, and the United States. The dark bars in the chart represent poverty rates calculated with households' before-tax and before-transfer incomes. They show the poverty rates that would result in the absence of public taxes and transfers. The light bars indicate poverty rates after taxes and transfers are included in the calculations. In the top panel, I reproduce results obtained by Jeandidier and Albiser (2001), who tabulated poverty rates among French, British, and American children under age 16. France has the lowest before-transfer poverty rate (19 percent), and its state transfer programs do the most effective job of reducing poverty below the level that would be produced by market incomes alone. The United States has the second highest market poverty rate but the highest rate after taxes and transfers are included in the calculations. A plausible inference is that U.S. redistribution is less effective in reducing poverty than state transfer programs in either France or Britain. However, the United States also spends much less money on transfers for the non-aged population than either France or Britain (see table 1.6). Transfers to the non-aged population consume less than 4 percent of U.S. national income, less than half the percentage spent by the United Kingdom and about one-third the percentage spent by France.

The lower two panels in figure 1.13 show the before-tax and transfer and post-tax and transfer poverty rates of two kinds of families that contain children under age 18. The middle panel shows poverty rates among married-couple families, and the bottom panel shows rates among single-mother families. These calculations were performed with LIS income data by Karen Christopher (2001). Her tabulations cover the same years analyzed by Jeandidier and Albiser (2001). Not surprisingly, her findings mirror those of the earlier analysts. French tax and transfer policy is most effective in reducing child poverty, while U.S. policy is least effective. The effectiveness of French

Figure 1.13
Poverty Rates among Children before and after Taxes
and Transfers in Three countries, 1993-1994

Percentage of children under age 16 in poverty

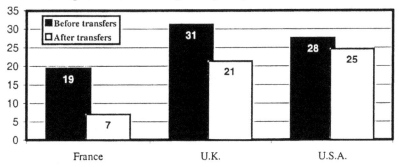

Source: Jeandidier and Albiser (2001).

Percentage of married families with children in poverty

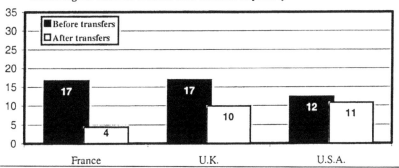

Source: Christopher (2001).

Percentage of single mothers with children in poverty

Source: Christopher (2001).

policy is visible both for one- and two-parent families, and the ineffectiveness of U.S. policy is equally apparent for both kinds of families.

Christopher's (2001) calculations of poverty rates in single-mother and married-couple families are interesting quite apart from the light they shed on policy effectiveness. One striking feature of the tabulations is the low level of market poverty rates in married-couple families in all three countries, though especially in the United States. In contrast, the pre-transfer poverty rates of single-mother families differ widely in the three countries. Single mothers in both France and the United States have high employment rates. Christopher (2001) estimates that 69 percent of single mothers are employed in France and 66 percent are employed in the United States, although a higher fraction of American than French single mothers work in a full-time job. In contrast, just 45 percent of British single mothers are employed, and only about one-third work on a full-time basis (Christopher, 2001, table 3). The pre-transfer poverty rate of U.K. single mothers is high because so many of them fail to work. Pre-transfer poverty is high among American single mothers because so many of them earn low wages even when they do work. In part, the low wages of these mothers are the result of very low labor market skills, as we have seen, but they are also due to the unequal distribution of U.S. wages, which leaves many workers with low annual incomes even if they work year-round on a full-time schedule. French single mothers have relatively high employment rates, and they benefit from France's narrower wage distribution. If an adult finds work in France, the job is likely to pay enough to bring her family up to the poverty threshold. Finally, as demonstrated in figure 1.13, French redistribution policy is much more likely to bring a poor family up to the poverty line than is the case in Britain or the United States.

U.S. Policy Reform

American voters and policymakers did not stand still in the face of increased child poverty and growing wage inequality in the 1980s and early 1990s. The direction of redistribution policy for children and working-adults shifted noticeably after 1985. The steep decline in hourly wages of low-skill workers worsened the problem of child poverty in a highly visible way. The wage trends illustrated in figure 1.7 caused earnings to fall steeply among less-skilled workers, especially high school dropouts under age 30. Measured in inflation-adjusted dollars, the wages earned by 25-year-old high school dropouts fell more than a quarter after 1979. Few American workers can support children on wages of $6 or $7 an hour.

Policymakers responded to this development by reforming tax policy toward low-income families and broadening eligibility for some publicly financed health benefits. The Tax Reform Act of 1986 removed millions of low-income Americans from the income tax rolls and boosted the tax rebates low-income workers receive under the Earned Income Tax Credit (EITC). This tax credit was further liberalized by legislation passed in 1990 and 1993, which significantly increased the size of credits paid to low-income breadwinners and their children. Spending on the credit increased eleven-fold in the decade after 1986, reaching $25 billion by 1996. Since the credit is payable to breadwinners even if they owe no federal income taxes, it has boosted the incomes of millions of families with extremely low incomes. The burden of federal payroll and income taxes once pushed millions of people into poverty. The generosity of the EITC now means that millions are lifted out of poverty by the federal tax system.[5]

The EITC is a distinctive American innovation in policy for the working poor, one that other rich countries may eventually adopt in a modified form. While most cash assistance for the poor is provided to people who do not work, the EITC is provided only to low-income people who *do* work. In 2001, the credit provided about $4,000 per year in refundable income tax credits to a breadwinner with two or more dependents. For a person working full-time in a minimum wage job, the EITC can increase the worker's net earnings by nearly 40 percent. The increased generosity of the credit has offset all of the

Figure 1.14
AFDC/TANF Benefit Payments and Refunded
Portion of Earned Income Credit, 1970-1999

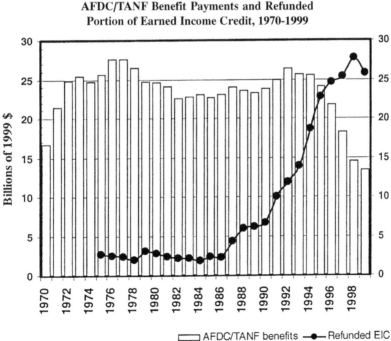

Source: U.S. DHHS and Committee on Ways and Means, 2000 *Green Book.*

reduction in real hourly wages that low-wage workers with dependent children have suffered over the past two decades.

The idea behind the credit is to boost work incentives by increasing the incomes available to low-income breadwinners, particularly those who have children.[6] Instead of shrinking as a recipient's earnings grow, the credit rises, at least up to a limit. At low earnings levels the credit increases by $0.34 or $0.40—depending on whether the worker has one or more than one dependent child—for each extra dollar earned by the breadwinner. Parents who have no wages are not eligible to receive the credit, so the credit provides a big incentive for unemployed parents to find work. Imitating the federal government's EITC program, sixteen state governments have now created state-earned income tax credits. Eleven states provide refundable credits, that is, credits that are payable to a family even if it does not owe any state income taxes.

Figure 1.15
Children Receiving AFDC/TANF as a Percent of All Children
and of Children in Poor Families, 1962-1999

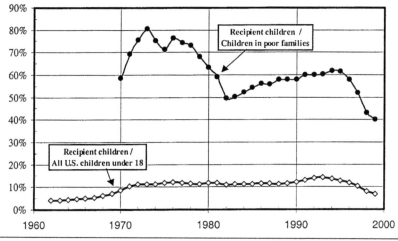

Source: U.S. Census Bureau and DHHS.

The growing generosity of the EITC has offset much of the impact of declining real wages for workers who have child dependents and hold poorly paid jobs. Over the past two decades, the American minimum wage has declined in relation to average production-worker wages. In comparison with the average hourly wage earned by production workers, the federal minimum wage fell one-fifth between 1980 and 2000. The purchasing power of the minimum wage fell by a similar percentage (see figure 1.16). Workers who earn the minimum wage and work on a full-time basis ordinarily qualify for the maximum EITC credit, however. The top line in figure 1.16 shows the trend in real hourly earnings for a worker who earns the minimum wage and claims the maximum EITC credit. It also subtracts from the worker's wage the tax payment for social insurance contributions. (The impact of state EITC programs is ignored.) Note that the after-tax wage is substantially higher than the worker's before-tax wage starting in 1987. By the late 1990s, the after-tax income of a minimum-wage worker, including EITC credit, was equal to the previous peak earnings that had been attained in the late 1970s. From the point of view of the worker, a minimum-wage job was no less attractive at the end of the 1990s than it was at the end of the 1970s. From the point of view of employers, the cost of paying a minimum-wage worker was considerably lower in the late 1990s, because the federally financed EITC provided about one-third of the worker's net earnings. The employer was responsible for paying only two-thirds of the net wage. The declining cost of offering minimum-wage jobs has probably increased the number of such jobs and increased the proportion of low-wage employment in the U.S. economy. Most labor economists who have closely examined the Earned Income Tax Credit conclude that it has contributed to a sizable increase in job holding among unmarried mothers.

State legislatures and Congress have also tried to increase the attractiveness of work by boosting child care subsidies available to working welfare

Figure 1.16
Purchasing Power of U.S. Minimum Wage, Including Payroll Tax Withholdings and EIC, 1950-2001

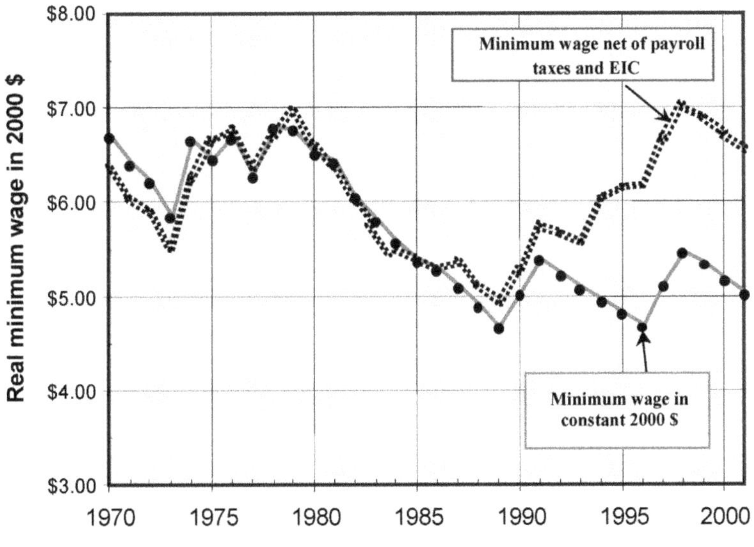

Note: Wage earner is assumed to have two child dependents.
Source: Author's calculations.

recipients, former recipients, and other low-income single parents. Although child care remains a big hurdle for many single parents who are seeking work, the increase in child care subsidies has reduced the hurdle a bit.

Beginning in the late 1980s, Congress also liberalized eligibility requirements for Medicaid, the primary public health insurance program for low-income Americans. Medicaid now offers benefits to a much broader population of low-income children with working parents. Until the late 1980s, publicly subsidized health insurance was usually restricted to cash public assistance recipients. Working-age families containing children were ordinarily eligible for health protection only if the families were actually collecting means-tested cash assistance (AFDC or Supplemental Security Income). Children usually lost their eligibility for free health insurance when the family left public assistance because a parent became employed. The Medicaid liberalization of the late 1980s and early 1990s expanded eligibility to large numbers of children whose parents had modest earnings and were not currently collecting public assistance.

A large number of states have established programs to provide subsidized health insurance to members of working-poor families, including the adult breadwinners in such families. In 1997, Congress passed legislation offering states generous federal subsidies to establish or enlarge health insurance programs for working poor and near-poor families containing children. Between 1998 and 2002, the federal government provided over $20 billion in matching subsidies for these new, state-sponsored Children's Health Insurance Programs (CHIP).

As policy has been reformed to expand tax credits and health benefits for the working poor, state and federal lawmakers have slashed the cash assistance available to the *non*working poor. General assistance, which provides cash aid to childless adults, has been scaled back in most states and eliminated in a few. AFDC was abolished in 1996 and replaced with the TANF program. The new federal program has forced all states to adopt aggressive policies to curtail cash benefits to poor parents who are capable of working. The head of each family on welfare is required to work within two years after assistance payments begin. Work-hour requirements are stringent, and states face increasingly harsh federal penalties if they fail to meet them. The law stipulates that the great majority of families may receive benefits for no longer than five years, and permits states to impose even shorter time limits. Eight states have done so.

Along with the strong economy, the new welfare law—and the new state welfare policies that preceded it—helped produce an unprecedented drop in the nation's child welfare rolls. Since reaching a peak in 1994, the number of families collecting public assistance for children has dropped more than 2.8 million or 56 percent. No drop this large has occurred in the past forty years. The recent trend in the public assistance rolls is somewhat less impressive if the number of children collecting assistance is compared with the number of children in poverty. Figure 1.15 shows the trend in child welfare caseloads measured in relation to both the number of American children (lower line) and the number who are members of families with incomes below the official U.S. poverty line. The steep fall in the caseload that occurred after 1995 is similar to an earlier drop that occurred between 1978 and 1982. The earlier decline was much less visible because the number of families collecting cash public assistance remained relatively stable. However, the number of poor children in the United States soared in the early 1980s, both because single-mother families were becoming more common and because job prospects for young, unskilled workers were deteriorating. In these circumstances, the stability of the public assistance rolls masked a very sharp drop in the fraction of needy children who received aid.

The drop in public assistance caseloads in the late 1990s took place under very different circumstances. Job prospects for unskilled workers were improving, after two decades of steep deterioration. The national unemployment rate was falling toward a thirty-year low. Cash aid payments from public assistance were being curtailed, but cash earnings supplements under the EITC program had replaced much of the lost benefits under AFDC and TANF (see figure 1.14).

Aside from allowing the minimum wage to fall, U.S. legislators have not changed other features of labor market regulation or social insurance law to make it less expensive for employers to hire the less skilled or unemployed. Bear in mind, however, that the American social insurance system imposes light tax burdens on employers (OECD, 1994: 243). Unlike labor law in continental Europe, U.S. law does not require that employers provide workers with costly fringe benefits in addition to a minimum wage. Nor does U.S. regulation obligate employers to provide workers with much employment security (Nicoletti, Scarpetta, and Boyland, 2000).

The comparatively small burden imposed by U.S. law helps explain the willingness of American employers to add to their payrolls when demand is rising. (Lenient employment protection also helps account for the rapid growth in U.S. joblessness when product demand shrinks.) In comparison with labor markets in which minimum wages and social insurance contributions are higher, employment protection is stronger, and mandated employer-provided benefits are more expensive, the American labor market provides more attractive incentives for employers to hire the unemployed. The success of the U.S. economy in generating jobs and maintaining high employment rates is due in some measure to these characteristics of the labor market. However, U.S. lawmakers have not consciously changed minimum wage laws, insurance contribution rates, employment protection, or regulations regarding employee fringe benefits in order to achieve a lower unemployment rate. Their main policy aim has been to change the work incentives facing unemployed and less skilled workers while maintaining the hiring incentives available to employers.

Conclusion

On the whole, U.S. social policy has become much less generous to the nonworking (but working age) poor, while it has become much more generous to the working poor. For many low-wage breadwinners with children, the increased generosity of the EITC, expansions in Medicaid, new state-financed health insurance plans, and enlarged day care subsidies have more than offset the loss of potential earnings due to shrinking hourly wages. The official U.S. poverty statistics do not fully reflect this fact because they fail to account for most of the improvements in benefits.[7] On the other hand, official poverty statistics fully reflect the drop in cash benefit payments that has been caused by cutbacks in the nation's main cash assistance programs.

The recent policy changes are having real economic effects in addition to offsetting the drop in wages. Poor breadwinners with children have been induced to enter the work force—and stay there. This can be seen in figure 1.17, which shows the changing work patterns of mothers rearing children under age 18. One line in the figure shows the trend in employment among married mothers currently living with their spouses; the other shows the trend among mothers who are separated from their spouses or divorced or who have never been married. Married mothers who live with their spouses saw a steady increase in employment over most of the past two decades. In contrast, divorced, separated, and never-married mothers saw little trend in their employment rates for most of the period up through 1994.

The relative trend in the two groups changed abruptly after 1994. Soon after EITC subsidies were liberalized and state public assistance programs were curtailed, employment rates among unmarried mothers began to soar, increasing fifteen percentage points (or one-quarter) between 1994 and 2000. This increase does not reflect a surge in employment among *all* mothers, since mothers living with their spouses have experienced only small gains in employment in recent years. The lower panel in figure 1.17 focuses on employment trends among the most disadvantaged single mothers, namely, mothers who have never been married. As noted earlier, these mothers are the most likely to participate in public assistance programs, so they are the ones who have been most directly affected by reform of U.S. public assistance programs. Employment gains among this group have been even more impressive than those among single mothers in general. Between 1994 and 2000, the employment-population rate of never-married mothers rose twenty percentage points (or 43 percent). Average weeks worked over the course of a year increased more than one-third, contributing to a 45 percent gain in real annual earnings. The entry of divorced, separated, and never-married mothers and other disadvantaged new workers has contributed to the downward pressure on wages of the least skilled. In effect, public subsidies to the working poor and cutbacks in welfare benefits to the nonworking poor have helped keep employer costs low and have encouraged U.S. companies to create millions of poorly paid jobs.

More generous public programs have improved the circumstances of many low-income American workers—if they can find and keep jobs. But the new social policies have not been so generous that poor, working-age Americans

Figure 1.17
Employment-Population Ratio of Married, Unmarried,
and Never-Married Mothers, 1978-2000

Employment / population ratio (%)

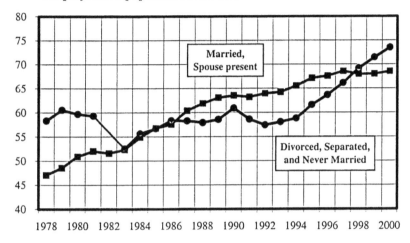

Employment / population ratio (%)

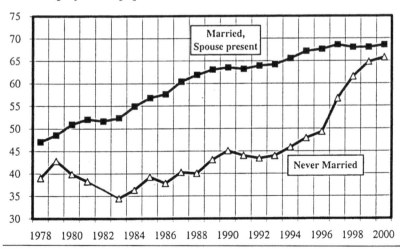

Note: Mothers included in tabulations are at least 16 years old and live with their own children under age 18. Widows are excluded from the tabulations.
Source: Author's tabulations of unpublished U.S. Bureau of Labor Statistics data.

have shared proportionately in recent U.S. prosperity. Compared with other industrial countries, the United States continues to experience very high rates of poverty, particularly among working-age families and families that contain children (see figure 1.6). One reason is that the U.S. policy mix offers Americans much less assurance that they will enjoy comfortable or even minimal incomes should they become and remain unemployed.

A different set of policies, such as those adopted in Continental Europe, can obviously produce different results. Some differences, such as low child poverty rates and high hourly wages, make Continental Europe a more congenial place to live for low-wage workers and the long-term unemployed. But some side effects of European policies, particularly high joblessness and heavy taxpayer burdens, are not especially attractive. It is not obvious that American voters, even those on the political left, would welcome the alternative outcomes or approve the policies needed to achieve them. Few U.S. voters favor giving undisguised cash transfers to people who are old enough and healthy enough to work. Yet the policies that help support wages and incomes in France and the rest of Europe include several that provide steady and generous transfers to able-bodied people who do not work.

In contrast with policies in Continental Europe, the U.S. mix of harsh and open-handed policies toward the working-age poor has spurred high employment, rapid job creation, and the expansion of a large and flourishing low-wage sector. While the combination is broadly consistent with popular American attitudes toward work and self-reliance, it would be much tougher to sell these policies in other rich countries. Any credible assessment of the effects of employment-oriented supply-side policies must take into account their impact on the distribution of living standards. While Americans may tolerate or even approve the distributional consequences of work-based social assistance policies, voters in other countries find them much less acceptable. The U.S. experience suggests, however, that large doses of work-based policy can boost the employment rates of the hard-to-employ.

Notes

1. The small difference between figures 1.2 and 1.5 is explained by a difference in child populations. Tabulations in figure 1.2 refer to "related children." Those in figure 1.5 refer to all children under 18.
2. The difference between France and the United States has a peculiar effect on measured poverty in the two countries. The U.S. Census Bureau calculates poverty using *family* size and *family* income, where a "family" is defined to include people who live in the same household and are related by blood, marriage, or adoption. Unrelated persons of the opposite sex who share a residence and live in a marriage-like relationship are almost never classified as a family under this definition, even if they are raising children together. This means that their incomes and families are not combined to calculate a poverty threshold or total family income. For this reason, one or another family unit in the household is much more likely to be found to have income below the U.S. poverty threshold than would be the case if the entire house-

hold were classified as a single family (as would be the case if the two adults were married rather than living in a marriage-like relationship). This distinction between the treatment of married and unmarried couples disappears when cross-national poverty rates are measured in the Luxembourg Income Study (LIS). Most researchers using cross-national micro-census data sets provided by LIS use *household* size and *household* income to determine poverty status. Thus, unmarried partners are assumed to share income and to enjoy jointly the economies of scale in consumption that come from sharing living quarters.

3. Income and payroll tax payments are subtracted and near-cash benefits, such as food stamps, are added to gross money income to determine disposable income. Limitations in national data sources prevented us from including health insurance and implicit or explicit housing subsidies in the measure of disposable income. To determine equivalent income per person (that is, income adjusted for household size), we divide household income by the square root of the number of household members. Under this assumption, as household size increases by a factor of four, the household would need twice as much disposable income to achieve the same equivalent income per person. The official U.S. poverty measure does not subtract tax payments or add the Earned Income Tax Credit (EITC) in the calculation of disposable income, nor does it include near-cash payments, such as food stamps, in the definition of family income. In addition, the official U.S. poverty thresholds are equal to roughly 40 percent of median U.S. income, substantially less than the 50 percent-of-median-income threshold used to calculate poverty rates in the LIS member countries.

4. The control group consisted of randomly selected AFDC recipients who were not enrolled in the experimental work and training program. See Friedlander and Burtless (1995), p. 88.

5. As recently as 1983, about 1.7 million persons in families containing children were pushed into poverty by the burden of federal income and payroll taxes. By 1996 about 2.2 million people in such families were lifted above the poverty line by the federal tax system. U.S. Department of Health and Human Services, *Indicators of Welfare Dependence, Annual Report to Congress* (Washington, DC: U.S. DHHS, October 1998), pp. III-17.

6. Single workers without dependent children are eligible for a much smaller credit, one whose maximum value is less than $500 per year.

7. The standard poverty measure is based on families' pretax cash incomes. It therefore ignores income received from the EITC and improvements in family circumstances that occur because of better health insurance and more generous reimbursement of child care expenses.

References

Burtless, G., & Siegel, S. (forthcoming). "Medical Spending, Health Insurance, and Measurement of American Poverty." In *Race, Poverty and Domestic Policy*, edited by C. Michael Henry. New Haven, CT: Yale University Press.

Christopher, K. (2001). "Welfare State Regimes and Mothers' Poverty." LIS Working Paper No. 286. Luxembourg: Luxembourg Income Study.

Friedlander, D., & Burtless, G. (1995). *Five Years After: The Long-Term Effects of Welfare-to-Work Programs*. New York: Russell Sage.

Jeandidier, B., & Albiser, E. (2001). "To What Extent Do Family Policy and Social Assistance Transfers Equitably Reduce the Intensity of Child Poverty? A Comparison Between the US, France, Great Britain and Luxembourg." LIS Working Paper No. 255. Luxembourg: Luxembourg Income Study.

Johnson, H. J., & Tafoya, S. M. (1999). *The Basic Skills of Welfare Recipients: Implications for Welfare Reform.* San Francisco: Public Policy Institute of California.

Nicoletti, G., Scarpetta, S., & Boyland, O. (2000). "Summary Indicators of Product Market Regulation with and Extension to Employment Protection Legislation." Economics Department Working Paper No. 226. Paris: OECD.

Organisation of Economic Co-operation and Development. (1994). *The OECD Jobs Study: Evidence and Explanations—Part II: The Adjustment Potential of the Labour Market.* Paris: OECD.

Organisation of Economic Co-operation and Development. (2001). *Society at a Glance: OECD Social Indicators.* Paris: OECD.

Riccio, J., Friedlander, D., & Freedman, S. (1994). *GAIN: Benefits, Costs, and Three-Year Impacts of a Welfare-to-Work Program.* New York: Manpower Demonstration Research Corporation.

Salverda, W., Nolan, B., Maitre, B., & Mühlau, P. (2001). *Benchmarking Low-Wage and High-Wage Employment in Europe and the United States: A Study of New European Datasets and National Data for France, Germany, the Netherlands, the United Kingdom and the United States.* Amsterdam: Instituut voor Arbeids Studies.

Smeeding, T. M., Rainwater, L., & Burtless, G. (2002). "United States Poverty in a Cross-National Context." In *Understanding Poverty*, edited by Sheldon H. Danziger and Robert H. Haveman, 162-189. Cambridge, MA: Harvard University Press.

U.S. Department of Health and Human Services. (1998). *Indicators of Welfare Dependence, Annual Report to Congress.* Washington, DC: U.S. Department of Health and Human Services.

U.S. Department of Health and Human Services, Administration for Children and Families. (2000). *Characteristics and Financial Circumstances of TANF Recipients, FY 1999.* Washington, DC: U.S. Department of Health and Human Services.

U.S. House of Representatives, Committee on Ways and Means. (1996). *1996 Green Book.* Washington, DC: U.S. Government Printing Office.

U.S. House of Representatives, Committee on Ways and Means. (2000). *2000 Green Book.* Washington, DC: U.S. Government Printing Office.

2

Applying the U.S. Bureau of Labor Statistics Concept of the "Working Poor" to France*

Madior Fall and Jean-Michel Hourriez

Introduction

The relationship between labor market status and poverty is an important issue when studying Welfare in developed countries. Historically, the issue of having a job and being poor was first raised in the United States in the 1960s. In 1989, the *Bureau of Labor Statistics* (BLS) defined an operational concept of the working poor (Klein and Rones, 1989): "as persons who have devoted at least half the year to labor market efforts, being either employed or in search of a job during that period, but who still lived in poor families." Following that pioneer analysis, many studies focused on the relation between labor market and poverty: Goings (1999) in the United States, and Lagarenne and Legendre (2000), Concialdi and Ponthieux (2000), and Hourriez (2001) in France.

Following these approaches, the purpose of this chapter is, first, to apply the BLS definition of the working poor to the French case and to compare the obtained results with U.S. statistics on the working poor. Second, when applying Klein and Rones' (1989) decomposition of poverty risks of employed persons, we identify the effects of low earnings, part-time work, and unemployment on poverty and compare them to U.S. findings.

In order to define the concept of "working poor," one first has to define poverty and second to identify the working people among the poor. Monetary poverty is measured at the household level with annual disposable income. Regarding the definition of the poverty threshold, European countries, including France, have retained a relative approach (see box 2.1): being poor

---

*We gratefully acknowledge the assistance of Nadine Legendre. The views expressed in this chapter are solely those of the authors.

means having income well below the normal standard of living of the country. This standard is defined as a fraction of the median standard of living: INSEE set this threshold at 50 percent and EUROSTAT at 60 percent. In 1997, 7.4 percent of French people were under the 50 percent median threshold, and 13.9 percent under the 60 percent median threshold. In the United States, the official poverty threshold is an absolute one, defined in 1964 according to food needs (see box 2.1). An absolute threshold is supposed to reflect fundamental needs and is therefore set below a relative poverty threshold. Indeed, the American absolute poverty threshold would be equivalent to 36 percent of the U.S. median income. In 1997, 13.3 percent of American families lived under the official poverty line (see box 2.2). The American threshold appears to be much lower than the French threshold. But this comparison is not relevant: it is probably easier to make ends meet with a very low monetary income in the United States (where some special benefits are in-kind) than in France (where almost all benefits are included in monetary income).

Considering that the definition of poverty is conventional, considering also the difficulty of international comparisons of poverty, we will restrict our analysis to the structure of the poor population and deliberately omit a comparison of poverty rates between France and the United States.

Identifying the working poor is a difficult exercise for at least two reasons: first, employment status is an individual characteristic whereas poverty is defined at a household or family level (see box 2.2). Second, the employment status is an instantaneous notion whereas the measure of poverty refers to an annual basis. In the United States, the operational concept adopted by the BLS defines the working poor as those living in a poor family and who have participated in the labor force (either in being employed or searching for a job) for at least twenty-seven weeks (Klein and Rones, 1989).

This six months' cutoff in the BLS definition of working poor emerges as a compromise between a restrictive definition (person who had worked during the whole year of reference) and an extensive definition (person who had worked once a year or more). Indeed, depending on the definition retained of working poor, the number of working poor could be twice as high in the United States.

Poor Population in France and in the U.S.

The poor population is composed of working poor (BLS definition) and of persons out of the labor force.

The poor populations in France and in the United States are mainly composed of persons out of the labor force: 64.3 percent in France and 79 percent in the U.S., in 1997. The percentage of those belonging to the labor force is respectively 35.7 percent in France and 21 percent in the U.S., in 1997 (see table 2.1). Thus, applying the BLS definition, we find that poor people are more often working poor in France than in the United States. One difference between the two countries is that the United States counts many poor children. If we restrict our field to poor adults, we always find the same result: the share of working poor is higher in France (45.4 percent) than in the United States (32.8 percent).

However, the structure of the population belonging to the labor force differs significantly between France and the United States: the unemployment group (people who never had a job during the reference year) is almost nonexistent in the United States (2.2 percent) whereas in France it represents 14 percent of poor adults. This results from higher long-term unemployment in France (4.8 percent of total labor force) than in the United States (0.6 percent).[1] A symmetric result is that inactive non-retired adults are more numerous in the United States (52.4 percent of poor adults) than in France (43.4 percent of poor adults). Some people without jobs for a long period of time are probably classified as long-term unemployed in France while they had been classified as inactive in the United States.

Table 2.1
Share of Poor Population in France and the U.S. in 1997
(Numbers in thousands)

	France			U.S.		
	Number	Share	Share of adults (%)	Number	Share	Share of adults (%)
		(%)	(%)	(%)	(%)	
27 weeks or more in the Labor Force	**1,695**	**35.7**	**45.4**	**7,453**	**21.0**	**32.9**
Person who had a job	1,173	24.7	31.4	6,944	19.5	30.6
Person who had no job (unemployed)	522	11.0	14.0	509	1.4	2.2
Out of the Labor Force or less than 27 weeks work	**3,053**	**64.3**	**54.6**	**28,121**	**79.0**	**67.2**
Children less than 17 years old	1,013	21.3		12,846	36.1	
Inactive adults from 17 to 64 years old	1,621	34.1	43.4	11,899	33.4	52.4
Persons 65 years and older	419	8.8	11.2	3,376	9.5	14.9
All poor	**4,748**	**100.0**	**100.0**	**35,574**	**100.0**	**100.0**

Field: all age persons (including self-sufficient students as head of household).

Sources: Income tax survey 1997, INSEE-DGI; Bureau of Labor Statistics, Current Population Survey.

Working Poor in France

Applying the BLS definition of working poor to the French income tax survey in 1997, 1.695 million persons attached to the labor force belonged to a household whose income stood below the French poverty threshold: they represented 6.5 percent of the labor force. Four groups can be identified of similar importance (see table 2.2) as described below:

1. 315,000 self-employed (SE group). This group contains small farmers, craftsmen, and shopkeepers.
2. 453,000 are "full-year" workers (W group), defined by no unemployment period during the period of reference. This W group embodies full-time and involuntary part-time workers.
3. 404,000 are workers having experienced unemployment spell(s) during the year of reference. For that group (WU), there are two factors for poverty consisting in short period of unemployment and low monthly income.
4. The last identified group, called the "all year" unemployed[2] (U), concerns 522,000 persons.

Table 2.2
Groups of Working Poor in France in 1997

	Labor population (Numbers in thousands)	Threshold 0.5*median of income		Threshold 0.6*median of income	
		Poor workers (Numbers in thousands)	Poverty rate (%)	Poor workers (Numbers in thousands)	Poverty rate (%)
27 weeks (6 months) or more in the labor force	25,964	1,695	6.5	3,024	11.6
. W Group (full year worker)	17,915	453	2.5	998	5.6
. WU Group (work and unemployment)	3,501	404	11.6	1,735	21
W+WU (All wage earners)	21,416	857	4	481	8.1
. SE Group (self employed)	2,494	315	12.6	481	19.3
All workers who had a job	23,911	1,173	4.9	2,216	9.3
. U Group (full year unemployment)	2,054	522	25.4	808	39.4

Source: Income tax survey 1997, INSEE-DGI.

When comparing the results for these four different groups, we find that the poverty rate is correlated to the unemployment status (employed, short-term, or long-term unemployed). For a threshold set at half the median of income, the lowest poverty rate observed is 2.5 percent for the full year working group (see table 2.2), compared to 11.6 percent among workers with unemployment spell(s) (WU) and 25.4 percent among full year unemployed (U). The poor self-employed present a particular case: they have a rather high poverty rate (12.6 percent) but they also take profit from a higher wealth not taken into account in the measurement of poverty.

If we restrict the analysis to the first three groups (i.e., excluding the U group) among the four groups of persons attached to the labor force, in order to keep only people who actually worked during the reference year, the number of working poor reaches only 1.173 million in 1997 (see table 2.2). With this new definition, we find that the working poor in each country represent around

30 percent of poor adults: 31.4 percent in France and 30.6 percent in the United States (see table 2.1).[3]

In sum, the percentage of working poor found in each country and the related comparative exercise appear to be highly sensitive to the field retained. We now assess the influences affecting the probability to be working poor in France, when restricting the analysis of the working poor to poor wage earners who had a job (Groups W and WU), excluding self-employed.

Three Labor Market Factors of Annual Low Earnings: Part-Time Work, Unemployment, and Low Wage Rate

Klein and Rones (1989) identified three labor market problems—unemployment, part-time jobs, and low earnings—which can be responsible for workers' poverty. In this section, we test Klein and Rones' findings in the case of France.

To that end, we restrict our analysis to poor wage earners consisting of two groups: the full-year workers (W group) and the workers with unemployment spell(s) (WU group). We then distribute these two groups according to the three labor market problems and their family status in order to identify any possible relations between family status and labor market problems.

Among all wage earners (W + WU), 20 percent (see table 2.3)[4] are concerned with only one of the three labor market problems, 8.5 percent combined only two problems, and, finally, 6 percent cumulate all three labor market difficulties. In other words, one-third of all wage earners are concerned with at least one labor market problem in France. Looking at each labor market factor, we find that 22 percent (table 2.3) of all wage earners have been on part time at least once during the reference year, 21 percent have been low paid[5] at least once during the reference year, and finally 17 percent have been at least once unemployed during the reference year.

Table 2.3 also allows us to achieve a gender analysis. When the partner is working, women are more likely than men to present one, two or three labor market problems except when unemployment is the only factor.

We essentially observe that the poverty rate is positively correlated to the number of labor market factors: poverty rate stands at 1.3 percent among wage earners presenting no factor, between 2.9 percent and 8.6 percent for those exhibiting one of the three factors, between 10.7 percent and 13.9 percent for those showing two of the three factors. Finally, the poverty rate reaches 15.7 percent among those cumulating the three factors.

When examining the most contributive factor to poverty, we find that unemployment is the major contribution to poverty followed by low earnings and part-time work. This contrasts with the U.S. situation where according to the BLS (Goings, 1999) low hourly wages are the prevailing factor of poverty.

It must be noted that part-time work does not automatically create poverty when it is the only factor. Part-time work increases the poverty risk when combined with low earnings and/or unemployment.

Table 2.3

**Share (in % of total) of Wage Earners According to
Three Explicative Factors of Low Annual Earnings:
Low Hourly Earning, Part-time, and Unemployment in France**

	Group	All population (in thousands)	Share of the all population by family status (in %)				Number of poor wage earners (in thousands)	Poverty rate (in %)
			Female with a partner with a job	Male with a partner with a job	Youngsters living with their parents	Other family situations		
Without factor:								
Full-time job in all year and with earnings rate more than the threshold (1)	W	13,307	22	34	5	39	173	1.3
One factor:								
- Part-time work (2)	W	1,696	64	6	5	25	49	2.9
- Low earnings rate (1)	W	1,262	37	14	17	33	66	5.2
- Periods of unemployment (or inactivity)	WU	1,261	17	23	26	35	108	8.6
Two factors:								
- low earnings rate (1) and unemployment	WU	630	23	13	37	26	67	10.7
- Part-time work (2) and low earnings rate	WU	1,397	46	5	19	29	158	11.3
- Part-time work (2) and unemployment	WU	385	41	9	19	32	53	13.9
Three factors:								
Low earnings rate (1), part-time work (2) and unemployment	WU	1,262	31	5	37	26	198	15.7
All wage workers (W and WU groups)		21,200	29	26	11	35	872	4.1

Notes: (1) For low earnings threshold: see box 2.3.
(2) Part-time work or low weekly time work duration.
(3) For example, among the whole population, we identify 1,696,000 wage earners exhibiting only one labor market problem, part- time work. Among this population, 64 percent are female with a working partner, 6 percent are male with a working partner, 5 percent are youngsters living with their parents, and finally 25 percent are presenting other family situations. Among those 1,696,000 part-time workers, 49,000 are poor which makes a 2.9 percent poverty rate among this group (part-time wage earners). Field: wage earners occupied more than six months, who work at least one month (W and WU groups).
Source: Income tax survey 1997, INSEE-DGI.

If low earnings do not appear as the main factor of poverty risk in France (as opposed to the U.S.) it comes from the relatively high legal minimum wage and from the existence of social security benefits (family allowances, housing benefits) which limit the impact of low hourly wage on poverty. The fraction of the working poor who dropout of poverty by receiving social benefits (see table 2. 4, column 3) is high for all kinds of labor status (65 percent for full-time workers, 49 percent for part-time workers). In France, the level of social benefits implies that no big difference exists concerning the average disposable income between the low earnings groups (see table 2.4, column 6).

Table 2.4
The Impact of Social and Family Benefits on the Income of the Low Earnings Wage Earners and Unemployed Workers in France in 1997

Monthly income per unit consumption in Euro

	Low earnings persons (1)						
	Proportion of people with low earnings (in %) (a)	Poverty rate (b)	Proportion of workers dropping out poverty by social benefits (in %) [(a)-(b)]/(a)	Average declared income (c)	Average social benefit amount (less income tax) (d)	Average disposable income (c)+(d)	Part of social benefits on disposable income (in %) (d)/[(c)+(d)]
12 months employed (W group)							
Full time work	6.0%	2.2%	65%	389	221	610	36%
Part-time work	18.1%	9.2%	49%	358	191	549	34%
Employed with unemployed period (WU group)							
Full time work	19.1%	9.4%	51%	328	221	549	41%
Part-time work	30.2%	15.3%	49%	297	236	534	45%
12 months unemployed (U group)	43.9%	25.4%	42%	252	267	518	52%

Field: 27 weeks work without self-employment (W, WU and U groups).
Source: Income tax survey 1997, INSEE-DGI.
(1) A household is called "low earnings" when its earnings (activity income before tax and benefits) per unit consumption are below the poverty threshold (see box 2.1).

Finally, the family structure, or more precisely the number of children, does not affect the poverty rate for the three identified groups W, WU, and U (table 2.5). This illustrates the efficiency of the French family allowance system. Family allowances are provided in France for children under 20 years old and from the second child only. The poverty rate among families who have one or more children aged 19 years at most appears to be hardly sensitive to the number of children, except for the third group (those unemployed during the year of reference, U). Indeed, for this group, family allowances do not compensate for the loss of earning gains.

Table 2.5
Proportion of Declared Low Earnings (1) and the Poverty
Rate of Wage Earners or Unemployed with less than 19
Years Old Children or 19 to 24 Years Old Children in France

(in %)

	Employed all year (W group)		Employed and unemployed (WU group)		Unemployed all year (U group)	
	Proportion of low earnings	Poverty rate	Proportion of low earnings	Poverty rate	Proportion of low earnings	Poverty rate
No child	3	2	19	12	39	24
1 child:						
Less than 19 years old	4	2	25	11	41	21
From 19 to 24 years old	2	2	16	11	30	28
2 children:						
Both have less than 19 years old	7	2	31	13	51	24
One of them have 19 to 24 years old	4	4	20	14	35	28
3 children or more:						
3 are less than 19 years old	22	2	54	12	74	34
At least one child aged 19 to 24 years old	23	10	38	23	78	52

Field: Wage earners or unemployed, who work more than 6 months (W, WU, and U groups) and who live alone or are isolated parent or who live with a partner.

Source: Income tax survey 1997, INSEE-DGI.
(1) A household is called "low earnings" when its earnings (activity income before tax and benefits) per unit consumption are below the poverty threshold (see box 2.1).

Conclusion

In this chapter, we applied the U.S. Bureau of Labor Statistics (BLS) definition of working poor to France and found accordingly 1.7 million poor persons in the labor force in France versus 7 million in the United States in 1997. In excluding the unemployment group, which is very important in France, we also restricted the analysis to three groups of working poor: the self-employed, the full year workers, and those evolving between work and unemployment. We then compared the share of these three groups among poor adults in the two countries that appeared similar. Regarding poverty risks of the working population, large differences between the United States and France emerge. In France, three factors affect the poverty risk with a decreasing intensity: unemployment, low wage, and part-time work. In the United States, low earnings are the major contributor to poverty.

In order to better understand the relation between low earnings, part-time work, and unemployment with poverty we must introduce the dynamic of each labor market. To get more relevant comparisons, the use of panel data in both countries seems very useful. These panels would be necessary to build a theoretical framework to analyze the dropping out due to poverty, to avoid the fictitious dropping out due to measurement errors in panel data.

Box 2.1
Poverty Measurement: Absolute or Relative?

The "absolute" approach takes as a given a minimal basket of goods to be consumed in order to survive. The concepts of minimum living wage (defined as the minimal level of consumption for survival) are based on eating needs, as defined by nutritionists as per sex and age: they also can explicitly include needs considered as basic (accommodation, clothing). This concept used by researchers is different from the official minima income concepts, as *minimum vieillesse* (minimum income for elderly people), and RMI (minimum income for integration). To a larger extent, the minimum social income concepts include goods considered "normal" and "obvious" by most members of society.

The "relative" approaches are the ones adopted in France by INSEE and also by the European Community and assume that whenever incomes are unequal there are cases of relative poverty. The bottom of the distribution defines poor even if the lowest income in society is high enough to obtain the minimal consumption basket.

The "absolute" approaches suffer from the normative nature of the basket definition that is more and more embarrassing since only food consumption is taken into account (and even on that point agents differ). They are considered inadequate for developed societies by most of the European analysts.

According to the threshold definition (half of the median of the income distribution for France), the countries with less income inequality would have a relative lowest monetary poverty rate. That is why for our comparison between France and the United States, we prefer to adopt the official definition of poverty for the United States and for France a cutoff of the median of the income distribution (0.5). It can be noticed that the threshold defined in terms of half of the median income per consumption unit is covered by the legal minima. The SMIC (minimum wage) when it is considered the income of one individual is over the poverty threshold. But if one considers a two-children family, the SMIC made up with family benefits remains very much under the poverty threshold. The same two-children family receiving two SMIC will drop out of poverty. The RMI is lower than the poverty threshold, but to the opposite the *minimum vieillesse*[6] level is above. Consequently, the *minimum vieillesse* directly affects the relative poverty of the elderly.

Box 2.2
Statistical Unit in Poverty Measurement

A big difference between the United States and France involves the unit of analysis. In France, the basic statistical unit is the household (the group of persons living in the same dwelling with or without family link), with a head who is chosen according to criteria of age, sex, and activity. The survey covers what one calls "ordinary households." Consequently, the population living in a residence outside of the metropolitan area and people living in collective households or in apartments or the homeless population are excluded from analysis. The U.S. basic unit is the family and there is a great debate around the most appropriate unit: the family, the household, or some other grouping. This debate becomes more and more important because of the rapid growth of cohabiting couples in the United States (Casper, Lynne, and Bryson, 1998). There are some recommendations to treat these kinds of unmarried couples like other families in poverty measurement (Citro and Michael, 1995).

Box 2.3
Technical Definitions

Household income: In France, the choice is annual household monetary income, since it corresponds to the conventional notion of income and it is captured directly by statistical surveys. It is the sum of cash income received by all household members over twelve months, after social security contributions have been deducted.[7] This includes income from work and investments, along with social benefits, such as retirement pensions, unemployment benefits, child benefits, housing benefits...

Low earnings:

- For individual wages, the low earnings threshold is given by two-thirds of the annual median of wage of the full-time workers. The labor force survey is the usual data source for the calculation of this threshold. In 1997, the monthly low earnings threshold was 10 percent higher than the monthly minimum legal wage (SMIC), which was 817.76 euros per month in 1997.
- For tables 2.4 and 2.5 people in "low earnings" households are defined as such: in these two tables we compute the total earnings of all members of the household, then divide this total activity income by the number of consumption units of the household, and finally compare these earnings per unit consumption with the poverty threshold.

Unemployed: "Unemployed persons are those who looked for work while not employed or those who were on layoff from a job and expecting recall" (*BLS: Report 947*).

French poverty threshold: It is defined as 50 percent of the median income per consumption unit (OECD scale).

Notes

1. Authors' computation.
2. All people in the labor force more than six months who had no job during the reference year: in fact, they are either long-term unemployed, or unemployed with inactivity spell(s).
3. Authors' computation for France and Goings (1999) for the United States. In the European Ceommunity, we find also figures near 30 percent for other countries (Hourriez, 2001).
4. Computations of the authors from table 2.3.
5. The low wage threshold is defined in a relative manner. The threshold is given by 2/3 of the annual median of wage of full-time workers. In 1997, this threshold was equivalent to 1.1 times the legal minimum wage (SMIC, see box 2.1).
6. The social minima implicitly use equivalence scales: for instance, concerning the *minimum vieillesse* if we consider a couple, the second recipient receives 80 percent of the benefits allowed to the first. When considering the RMI the second person of the household receives 50 percent of the amount received by the first one, and the third one receives only 30 percent of this amount.
7. Personal income tax and other direct taxes should be deducted in order to obtain the after-tax disposable income. However, the nature of the data available led us to prefer pre-tax income in this study.

References

Breuil, P., Ponthieux, S., & Zoyem, J. P. "Les actifs pauvres: trajectoires sur le marché du travail et caractéristiques familiales." à paraître dans *Economie et Statistique*, INSEE.

Burtless, G. (2002). "Social Policy for the Working Poor: U.S. Reform in a Cross-National Perspective." Workshop on "Welfare Reform: A Comparative Assessment of French and U.S. Experiences." Berkeley, California, 21-23 February 2002.

Casper, L. M., & Bryson, K. (1998). "Household and Family Characteristics." U.S. Census Bureau, Current Population Reports, Population Characteristics, P20-515. Washington, DC: U.S. Government Printing Office.

Citro, C. F., & Michaels, R. T. (Eds.). (1995). *Measuring Poverty: A New Approach.* Washington, DC: National Academy Press.

Concialdi, P., & Ponthieux, S. (2000). "Salariés à bas salaires et travailleurs pauvres: une comparaison France—Etats-Unis," *Premières synthèses, DARES,* No. 2000.01—No. 02.1 ou *IRES, Revue de l'IRES,* IRES, No. 33-2000/2.

Goings, G. (1999). "A Profile of the Working Poor, 1997." U.S. Department of Labor, Bureau of Labor Statistics, report No. 936.

Hourriez, J. M. (2001). "Avoir un emploi et être pauvre. Bas salaires, sous-emploi et chômage, quels liens avec la pauvreté ?" *France Portrait Social 2001*, INSEE.

Klein, B. W. & Rones, A. L. (1989). "A Profile of the Working Poor." *Monthly Labor Review* (October).

Lagarenne, C., & Legendre, N. (2000). "Les travailleurs pauvres en France: Facteurs individuels et familiaux." *Economie et Statistique*, INSEE, No. 335.

Part 2

Development and Structure of Welfare Policies

3

Welfare Policy in the United States: The Road from Income Maintenance to Workfare

Neil Gilbert

Introduction

The course of welfare reform in the United States is notable in that it cuts a clear path, step by step, from income maintenance to work-oriented programs. Public welfare for families with dependent children was initiated, as part of the New Deal, under Title IV of the Social Security Act of 1935. Originally entitled Aid to Dependent Children (ADC), it was designed as what used to be called an *income maintenance* program (today income maintenance is seen as a "passive" policy in contrast to "active" work-oriented policy).[1] Since 1935 the name of this program has changed, first to Aid to Families with Dependent Children (AFDC) in 1961 and then to Temporary Assistance for Needy Families (TANF) in 1996. As the name changed, so did the program emphasis and its orientation to work. To provide a context for the U.S. experience, I will examine some benchmark reforms that convey a sense of how the conversion from income maintenance to work-oriented policy occurred and what was tried along the way.

The journey begins with ADC, which was designed to provide financial support to needy deserving widows and their children. The ADC grants, $18 for the first child and $12 for each additional child, were based on the amount for each child received by families of servicemen who lost their lives in World War I. In 1935, the New Deal planners expected the ADC program to wither away as widows became eligible for survivors insurance and were absorbed into the newly formed social security system. History, of course, proved this

For Product Safety Concerns and Information please contact our EU
representative GPSR@taylorandfrancis.com
Taylor & Francis Verlag GmbH, Kaufingerstraße 24, 80331 München, Germany

www.ingramcontent.com/pod-product-compliance
Ingram Content Group UK Ltd.
Pitfield, Milton Keynes, MK11 3LW, UK
UKHW010752250425
457613UK00046B/446